INTERNATIONAL POLITICS SINCE WORLD WAR II

INTERNATIONAL POLITICS SINCE WORLD WAR II

A SHORT HISTORY

CHARLES L. ROBERTSON

M.E. Sharpe
Armonk, New York
London, England

International Politics Since 1945: A Short History was published in
two previous editions (1966, 1975) by John Wiley & Sons.

Library of Congress Cataloging-in-Publication Data

Robertson, Charles L.
International Politics Since World War II: A Short History /
by Charles L. Robertson.—3rd. ed.
p. cm.
Includes bibliographical references and index.
ISBN 0-7656-0026-9 (c : alk. paper).—ISBN 0-7656-0027-7 (p : alk. paper)
1. World politics—1945– .
D843.R623   1997
909.82′5—dc21
96-46431

Printed in the United States of America

The paper used in this publication meets the minimum requirements of
American National Standard for Information Sciences—
Permanence of Paper for Printed Library Materials,
ANSI Z 39.48-1984.

BM (c)   10   9   8   7   6   5   4   3   2   1
BM (p)   10   9   8   7   6   5   4   3   2   1

Contents

*New Course: "Containment"; The Truman Doctrine; The
Marshall Plan; The North Atlantic Treaty Organization* • **The
Soviet Bloc: Coordination and Conflict** • *Titoism in Yugosla-
via* • **The Far East Front Stage** • *Communism in China and
War in Korea: China Enters the War: The Risk of World War
III* • **The Impact of Korea and Western Rearmament** • *The
Creation of West Germany; Japan* • **The Impact of Nuclear
Weapons and the Failure of International Control** • **Ameri-
can Frustration and the Election of Eisenhower** • **The
United Nations in a Divided World** • **Conclusion**

The Soviet Bloc • *Change in the Soviet Union; Geneva, 1955;
Instability in the Soviet Bloc; The Brezhnev Doctrine; The
Break with China* • **Strains in the Western Coalition** •
*European Unity; The Common Market; De Gaulle and the
Challenge to Supranationalism; England and Europe; America
and Europe: The Economic Front; America and Europe: Secu-
rity Policies* • **Conclusion**

The Troubled Road to Peace in Asia • *The First Vietnam
War; Taiwan and the Southeast Asia Treaty Organization* • **The
Middle East** • *The Creation of Israel; The Rise of Nasser; The
Soviet Union Enters the Middle East; The Suez War of 1956;
The Promise and the Illusion of Arab Unity; Iran: The First
Crisis* • **Bandung, 1955: Emergence of the "Third World"** •
Unrest and Independence in Africa • **The Third World
Captures the United Nations** • **Guatemala and Things to
Come** • **Conclusion**

From Eisenhower to Kennedy • *The Missile Gap; The End of
the First Détente* • **Kennedy, Castro, Khrushchev, and the
Future** • *Castro's Cuba; John F. Kennedy; The Bay of Pigs
and the Alliance for Progress; The Berlin Wall; The Cuban
Missile Crisis; The Beginning of Arms Control and the Soviet
Buildup; Dominican Interlude* • **Vietnam** • *Laos and Cambo-*

dia; *The Second Vietnam War; The American Commitment; The Nixon Strategy; The End in Vietnam* • **The Great Realignment: Communist China and the United States** • *War in the Subcontinent; The Soviet Navy's New Worldwide Role; China in Turmoil; The Proletarian Revolution and Chinese Foreign Policy; Nixon Visits Mao* • **Détente** • **Conclusion**

Africa After Independence • *The Spread of Conflict; Regionalism in Africa* • **Asian Turmoil** • *Sukarno's Indonesia and a New World Order; Japan's Reemergence in Southeast Asia* • **The Middle East: More Wars** • *The Palestine Liberation Organization and the Third Round, 1967; Anwar Sadat and the Fourth Round, 1973; Colonel Qaddafi* • **Struggle in Latin America** • **Conclusion**

PART III. GLOBAL POLITICS

High Politics and Low Politics • *The End of Bretton Woods; The Rise and Impact of OPEC; The New International Economic Order; Iran, 1979* • **New Economic Players: The EEC, Japan, and the NICs** • *Enlarging the EEC; Japan Inc. and the NICs* • **The United States in Retreat?** • *Carter and the Reorientation of American Foreign Policy; Revolution in Iran; Central America in Upheaval; Carter and the Russian Invasion of Afghanistan* • **Brezhnev: Détente, Soviet Expansion, and Soviet Decay** • *Disarmament and Arms Control; The End of Arms Control; Brezhnev's Global Foreign Policy; Socialist Economies in Difficulty* • **The Global Agenda** • *The Role of International Organizations* • **Conclusion**

PART IV. THE END OF THE COLD WAR

The Soviet Union Changes Course • *Glasnost and Perestroika; The Fatal Blow: Afghanistan; The Breakup of the Soviet Empire; The End of Comecon and the Warsaw Pact* •

Drugs • *Development; The North American Free Trade Agreement; The Caribbean; Haiti; Drugs* • **Conclusion**

General Works • International Organizations • World War II
and Its Aftermath • Military and Security Affairs • Economic,
Social, and Environmental Affairs • The United States • The
USSR, Successor States, and Eastern Europe • Europe, Western
European Countries, the European Union, and the Atlantic Alliance • Asia and Asian Countries • The Middle East • Africa and
African Countries • The Americas • The Post–Cold War World

List of Maps and Tables

Maps

Figures

Preface

World leaders have recently celebrated the fiftieth anniversary of the end of World War II—not without pain and soul-searching. So much has happened since then, so much that was unimaginable at the time, when so many hopes were pinned on a new world that would emerge from the wreckage of the old. This book is a summary and a synthesis of the broad sweep of international history of these fifty years, chronicling successes as well as failures. It is intended primarily as supplementary reading for students of international politics or world history, but it may also be of interest to other people who have lived through these times. It tries to describe as objectively as possible both the great changes across the half century since the end of the war and many of the specific events that brought about the changes. It tries, in other words, to see what happened as we got from there to here, and why it happened.

To do all this in a single volume requires extreme compression and selectivity. Controversy abounds over the events of the period, and readers will inevitably disagree with both what has been selected and how it has been interpreted. An early version of this book was published thirty years ago, and people or events that seemed of capital importance then have simply disappeared from this version. The second edition appeared twenty years ago, shortly after President Richard M. Nixon engineered détente with Leonid Brezhnev's Soviet Union. Since that time, the whole interpretation of the accords and what they meant has shifted radically. This time, the book appears seven years after the euphoria that greeted the fall of the Berlin Wall and the "liberation" of Eastern Europe; those seven years have dashed many hopes and expectations, yet much that is positive has happened. The outcomes of these and many other events remain uncertain—"only time will tell," but different people will interpret what it tells quite differently. Many peoples, events, and places that were of supreme importance to the people directly involved are hardly mentioned in this book. I have had to select on the basis of what I think is important to the global system as a whole. I can only say that I have tried to be fair, and to base what I say on reliable, multiple sources.

One word about the concept of international politics: to me, international politics has become all-encompassing in a way that it was rarely thought to be in the past, when the actions of governments toward each other constituted its prime focus. "Sovereign" and "independent" states, with their own bureaucracies, armies, laws, and currencies, still interact through the traditional means of diplomacy, war, trade, and intervention. They conflict, compete, and cooperate in pursuit of their aims. But, to a much greater extent than in the past, demographic change and interdependence have put the traditional state system into question. Environmental context needs to be kept in mind. International trade, financial flows, and economic developments are often crucial. Grand strategy becomes subservient to exchange rates. International institutions as varied as oil markets or the office of the secretary-general of the United Nations are all a part of the picture. A "realist" analysis based on a global system of sovereign, independent states interacting with each other on balance-of-power terms still tells us much about how international politics works within this new context, but what goes on within states also has much to do with how their policymakers see the world and how they devise their policies. They have to act on the basis of uncertain and incomplete information, often making errors, and in the face of numerous constraints. Interactions at nongovernmental levels as well as the working of the thousands of governmental and nongovernmental international organizations affect the system. I have tried, very briefly, to show how and why this more complex world has come into existence.

Finally, since this book is based on secondary sources, memoirs, journals, and collections of documents, and is intended primarily as an overview, I have not provided an elaborate scholarly apparatus. Readers wanting references may use the Selected Bibliography to guide them to the sources I have used. It should be said, however, that the opening up of the Soviet Union and the writings of Russians and others since the era of glasnost have done much to resolve numerous issues that gave rise to polemics in the West in the past. No one can ignore these: they have invalidated works that might well have been cited in earlier editions.

INTERNATIONAL POLITICS SINCE WORLD WAR II

Introduction:
Fifty Years of Change

It is no less true for being trite to say that we live in a rapidly shrinking world. In the last half century, modern technologies have allowed the flow of goods, people, capital, and especially information to increase at a dizzying pace. People are inevitably forced to screen out much of this information, to select and reject what is important and what is unimportant to them. This book tries to provide a summary of global events of the last fifty years against a background of major trends, in an effort to make some sense of the events, to provide a framework that will help in that necessary screening process.

A perspective of fifty years enables us to discern trends that are often unclear at the time events unfold; what is quite remarkable is how people living through the times fail to foresee what the trends are and where they may lead. The most obvious recent case is that of the failure of "experts" of almost every stripe to discern the tendencies leading to collapse not only of the Soviet empire but of the Soviet Union itself. Innumerable other cases can be cited—though none perhaps as important. It is for this reason that as our story of the last fifty years of global politics unfolds, we must avoid the temptation of using hindsight to establish how foolishly people acted. Instead, we must try to see the world through the eyes of the actor—the statesman or stateswoman or the policymaker—who acts on the basis of uncertain and incomplete information, and whose acts may change the very nature of the situation as he or she has defined it in order to act.

A brief review of the most significant trends of the period since World War II should include the following:

1. These fifty years have seen world population grow at such an unprecedented rate as to appear to burst the globe's seams; the two billion of 1939 is the five billion of today, and will be the eight billion of twenty years from

now. Most growth is occurring and will occur in what has been called for years the "Third World." (The "First World" included the mainly Western, capitalist powers, the "Second World" the socialist powers under the leadership of the Soviet Union.) The rate of increase has slowed, but the "momentum effect" of previous rapid growth and a resulting young population mean that unprecedented rates of growth will be with us for decades to come.

2. New technologies have developed at an increasing rate in the fields of communications and computers. They have allowed vast flows of information, goods, short- and long-term capital, and people, integrating the world economy in such a way as to virtually destroy any state's capacity to run its own economy within its own borders. Local communities are undermined by developments across the world, and governments grapple with how to deal with this, looking to global and regional institutions or seeking to isolate themselves from far-off changes. At the same time, weapons technologies have become more and more sophisticated; the threat of disaster from nuclear war between the superpowers—the Soviet Union and the United States—has decreased just as the capacity of smaller states to acquire sophisticated weaponry has increased.

3. The European states that contained one-fifth of the world's people only 300 years ago and that still dominated the world system at the outset of World War II in 1939 no longer do so. The attempt to create a united Europe to compensate for this has been a major development of the last half of the century. The uniting of Europe has advanced only by fits and starts, with issues of breadth as against depth coming to fore in recent years. Nevertheless, Europe still remains one of the great centers of world politics.

4. At the same time, the breakup of the European empires that still embraced most of the globe in 1939 means that the Europe-centered world system has become a dispersed global one. More than a hundred new states have come into being in the last fifty years. Yet European ideas and institutions still pervade the global system. If many states give only lip service to the notions of democracy and human rights that developed within the context of the Western state system, and many challenge the particularities of Western democracy and notions of human rights, many more states adhere to these ideals than ever before.

5. During these years, the United States emerged from a long history of attempted isolation to become the dominant world power and the reluctant head of a coalition locked in a "Cold War" with the Soviet Union. The Soviet Union, itself the greatest continental power as a result of World War II, grew into a world power in the 1970s, able and willing to project its influence into the far reaches of the globe, and with a leadership that still predicted the emergence of a global socialist system under the Soviet

Union's leadership. For a great many years it was possible to speak of a "bipolar world" or "bipolarism"—a world system dominated by the presence of the two superpowers.

6. The later stages of the period, however, witnessed both a decline of American hegemony and the almost incredible and largely unforeseen collapse of Soviet power and influence and finally of the Soviet Union itself. The dream of a triumphant world socialism came to an abrupt end. What had appeared to be a vast increase in Soviet influence—in Southeast Asia, in Africa, and in Latin America—in fact helped to bankrupt the Soviet Union. In the meantime, a reconstructed Europe with a vastly *diminished* world role nevertheless exhibited a dynamism no one foresaw at the beginning of the postwar period, and Japan and other East Asian countries developed their own formulas to become economic rivals to the West. Four hundred years ago the Atlantic replaced the Mediterranean as the main axis of world trade. The Pacific basin now looms as large in international trade as the Atlantic. Power and influence in the global system are distributed in a far more complex pattern than ever previously, and the uncertain relationship of economic influence to military power has complicated political analysis even more. One thing is clear: the old view that a large empire meant increased resources and power no longer holds true in any guise.

7. Under the umbrella of a nuclear standoff the United States and the Soviet Union maintained a precarious peace for forty-five years after World War II. In the last five years they have dismantled their nuclear weapons and their giant armies at a remarkable pace. At the same time, the area that bounded the northern Atlantic Ocean—the cradle of previous world wars— became in the post–World War II era an area of peace, where no major state was prepared to use arms against another. On the other hand, despite a United Nations system created to maintain international peace and provide mechanisms for peaceful change, a hundred localized but often intense wars have been fought in other areas of the world since the end of World War II, even while UN "peacekeeping" has grown. In a period when modernity— either in liberal-democratic or in Marxist-Leninist guise—was supposed to supplant such things as nationalism, ethnic assertion, and religious fundamentalism, all have instead played an increasing role on the world scene, relying upon contemporary technologies of communication and destruction, and provoking numerous intractable conflicts. A consequent increase in the flow of refugees has taxed global institutions' capacities to deal with escalating numbers of distressed homeless and stateless persons.

8. In the meantime, the world has witnessed a period of economic growth unlike any in the past, demonstrating the globe's ability to sustain an incredible increase in population while feeding and clothing more people

better and better, as world food production increased beyond anyone's predictions. From 1950 to 1980, Third World countries, taken as a whole, grew faster than the industrialized countries—faster, in fact, than the industrialized countries had ever grown in the past—and faster than almost anyone had predicted they would. Two countertrends eroded the benefits: population expansion, unfortunately, kept Third World per capita growth only roughly equal to that of the developed countries, which meant that the income gap widened between rich and poor. Moreover, growth was highly uneven: large areas of the world—mainly in Africa south of the Sahara and in south Asia—remained mired in poverty, hunger, and conflict, just as other Third World states began to rival the developed countries in all the standard indicators of development. In some areas, notably in Africa, already low incomes shrank further.

9. Contentious worldwide environmental issues never before encountered have arisen—in the fields of pollution, resource availability or depletion, and climatic change—and these issues appear to call for global action at a time when global institutions still remain weak. Innumerable organizations and conferences have begun, but only begun, to cope with them at national, regional, and global levels.

10. International institutions, both global and regional, have grown in number, in response to many of these developments, but most have achieved neither the power nor the influence commensurate with the tasks assigned to them. At a time when many people have looked to these institutions as necessary concomitants to growing international issues and problems, people have also turned inward to seek identity in smaller communities.

The events reviewed in the balance of this book have contributed to, or unfolded against the background of, these trends. To many analysts they add up to a progressive undermining of the state system as it existed earlier in this century, and many have sought new paradigms to explain what is happening and to either replace or to supplement the older "realist" view of the global system. The brief account of global politics of the last fifty years in this book should provide the student with at least some basic information with which he or she can arrive at useful conclusions.

Part I

Introduction: The World that Emerged in 1945

1

The Collapse of the European System and the Shaping of a New World

When World War II came to an end in 1945 with the dropping of two atomic bombs on Japan, writers and journalists around the world were convinced that the world as we had known it was finished, that international politics must be reinvented, that some form of world government must come into being. (State legislatures throughout the United States passed resolutions in favor of world government!) Since the Charter of the United Nations organization, which had been born only a few months earlier in San Francisco, did not take into account nuclear weapons, the United Nations would have to serve as the nucleus of a much stronger world organization.

Much had changed in the previous half century. Under the impact of new weapons and mass politics, the *relatively* orderly, peaceful, and progressive European-dominated world of the nineteenth century had collapsed into the unanticipated and useless carnage of the Great War of 1914–18. The Great War, which later came to be called World War I, was followed by a weak attempt at reconstruction of the system in a new guise, under the League of Nations, and then an economic collapse into the Great Depression of the 1930s. Challenged by new ideologies—communism and fascism—Western democratic powers that had abandoned the League were unable to avoid a second and even more destructive global war. As the war neared its conclusion, planners again worked hard to create institutions that would provide some degree of order and justice. But they had to deal with intractable realities that falsified much of what they did.

This first chapter outlines briefly the nature of the state-centered, European-dominated, worldwide balance-of-power system that developed in previous centuries, within the framework of which the world still largely works. It relates the plunge into a thirty-year crisis that comprised World War I; the world depression; the rise of fascism and communism in all their guises; World War II; and a new, conscious effort to create a different and better world in the form of the United Nations system. The political realities that emerged from the war, however, led to an unanticipated global structure of power and hardened into what became known as the "Cold War," a feature that was to dominate the global system for the next forty years.

The Balance-of-Power System

We live in a world system that developed over the space of 400 years. It bequeathed to our own revolutionary times the sovereign, independent, territorial state as the main unit of politics, and balance-of-power politics as the main method of maintaining some degree of political order in a world-wide political system without any central political authority. The sovereign state has proved a hardy institution in the face of new challenges: weaponry that seemed to make the state unable to defend itself as it could in the past, the communications and computer revolution that has increased interdependence to an unprecedented degree, and the resultant creation of a web of transnational enterprises that have put sovereignty at bay. When the postwar years gave birth to over a hundred new nations, all these new nations sought to become "sovereign" and "independent" on the earlier European model.

Europe's rise to world dominance and its creation of the sovereign state system was certainly not foreordained. In the centuries after the sack of Rome by the barbarians in 476, as Europe either repulsed or absorbed its Norse and Muslim invaders, a process began that led this relatively small peninsula of the Eurasian continent to become the center of world power and the creator of a civilization that spread to the rest of the world, combining and recombining with other cultures, but leaving none of them unaffected.

What happened in Europe differed from what was happening in the rest of the world. Throughout human history, as population has pushed up against the limits of food production imposed by existing methods, communities have either reached an equilibrium in which high death rates and short life spans were the rule; or they have spread into new areas, often conquering and destroying existing peoples in the process, or they have created slave systems that supported a small elite—or else they have developed or adopted new technologies that increased productivity and enabled farmers to feed more people. European society developed a capacity to borrow from other cultures and to continue to innovate that set it apart from others. By the time the Peace of Westphalia of 1648 confirmed the existence of the modern state, 100 million of the world's 500 million people lived in Europe. Only China and India had greater populations. But only Europe had developed the basis for the continuing if uneven economic growth that provided the underpinnings for the climactic event that would come a century later—the industrial revolution.

In the meantime, the new states of Western Europe consolidated their power. For a state to be "sovereign" meant that it had complete control over persons within its defined territorial limits: only the state could command the loyalty of the individual and legitimately enforce that loyalty. Neither the Catholic Church, whose sway had extended over all Christendom, nor any noble could command the individual to disobey his or her state. If the state was "sovereign," it was also "independent": it could make its own foreign policy and be the sole judge of what was right and wrong vis-à-vis other states. While warfare within the territory of the state was minimized, warfare between states was a constant.

Nevertheless, without any central power over them, the new states developed a series of rules and institutions to enable them to coexist and to fulfill mutual interests: international law, formalized diplomacy, and a class of diplomats exempt from the jurisdiction of the country to which they were accredited. Perhaps most important, they came to rely upon balance-of-power diplomacy to maintain their independence. If one state threatened to become too powerful, others would seek territorial compensation to remain equal; would shift alliances to face it with a new, more powerful coalition; or would engage in an arms race to remain militarily as powerful. A state might seek to avoid war, but must be prepared to fight if its independence— its "vital interests"—were threatened. Small states had to accept it that larger states could decide their fates, but they designed strategies of playing off larger states one against another, allying with larger states, and presenting themselves as buffer states whose independence it was in the interest of larger states to observe. The result was a genuine system, in the sense that a general order was maintained, in which conflicts could be resolved peacefully, by the threat of force, or by its use. Coexistence of sovereign states came to be the general rule.

A number of underlying factors helped to maintain order in this decentralized system: states had only limited means to carry on warfare, they shared a common cultural heritage, and there existed a common ruling class with much intermarriage. Diplomats shared a sense that their task was to compromise and to accommodate so as to maintain peace—unless vital interests were threatened.

As modern commerce grew in the nineteenth century, reflecting the vastly increased productivities of industrializing economies, the new bourgeoisie—everywhere beginning to share political power with the older ruling classes—developed a relatively free, multilateral trading system based on greater specialization and exchange. Gold served as the common currency; London was the financial center; and men, money, and goods came to flow far more freely across national frontiers. Exaggerated claims developed that the increased links created by international trade would ensure perpetual peace. It did not happen that way, but the ideas had some merit: members of the new bourgeoisie frequently pressed governments to forgo strategic interests, confident that their counterparts in other countries would also renounce attempts to achieve military or political predominance; the trading state promised more than the military state. Nevertheless, war was always sanctioned in law and morality as a way of resolving conflict.

Much of the rest of the world came to be incorporated into the European system, mainly in a subordinate status as colonies or dependencies or merely minor players. Organizational and technological superiority—often interpreted as cultural superiority—came to play a part, as Europeans fanned out over the globe to absorb relatively less populated areas into their empires. Disease also played a key part in some areas: in the Americas, for example, nine-tenths of the native population fell before the scourge of smallpox brought by European explorers.

The causes of imperialism were many; no single overarching theory could explain it. Nevertheless, much of the pattern of imperialism can best be explained by the extension of the principle of territorial compensation for European balance-of-power purposes, rather than by any economic necessity: if one European power incorporated a new territory, others had to be compensated lest it become too powerful. More often, the threat that a territory might be taken by others led one to seize it. Local rivalries outside Europe often produced calls for help and for intervention of the more powerful European states. And there were cases in which access to markets or resources played a crucial part, or in which powerful personalities imposed their wills.

The Thirty Years' Crisis: 1914–45

World War I

Nineteenth-century stability was deceptive. The Great War, which broke out in 1914 and lasted until 1918, is perhaps the watershed between an older and a simpler world and our own times. Fundamentally different from what had gone before, this war appeared to demonstrate the inadequacy of balance-of-power politics under contemporary conditions.

If the industrial revolution produced increased welfare, it also produced modern weapons of mass destruction: rapid-fire artillery, machine guns, tanks, armored steamships, submarines, gas, and airplanes. Modern industrialized economies made it possible for states to carry on warfare with an intensity no one had ever imagined previously, over a longer span of time, and at greater distances. World War I was fought between the Central Powers on the one side—Imperial Germany, Austria-Hungary, and Turkey—and the Allies—initially France, England, Italy, and Russia, joined in 1917 by the United States—on the other. No one expected the war to last more than a few weeks, and no one was prepared at the outset to carry it on much longer. The carnage on the western front from 1914 to 1918 reflected first a failure of general staffs to realize and plan for the revolutionary implications of the new weapons, and then the effect of the weapons themselves and the capacities of industrialized economies to supply them despite the mobilization of manpower on a scale never seen before. Total, global war had come into being. The original issues that led to the war were largely lost sight of; the desire to make someone pay for the effects of the war became the new goal.

Modernized industrial economies thus changed the nature of warfare. Increased income also meant mass education and mass media, and the growth of these led to popular pressures on governments and their diplomats. Political theorists had long argued that such popular pressures, operating through democratic institutions, would reduce the incidence of war, since most people wanted peace and only the ruling classes benefited from war. They were wrong: popular pressures often limited the capacities of governments to compromise, and when, as in World War I, economic interdependence and the mobilization of whole peoples brought war home to the masses, it was they who denied their leaders the possibilities of a negotiated peace, demanding that governments extract reparations from the vanquished to compensate for the fantastic hardships total war had brought them. There would be no peace without victory.

The Great War had drastic effects on the international system and on society as a whole. The millions of dead and of horribly mutilated survivors made war seem absurd, totally unrelated to original aims. It unnerved what was left of optimistic nineteenth-century liberalism, just when it had to face new challenges from both the left and the right of the political spectrum. The great Czarist, Austro-Hungarian, Turkish, and German empires disappeared, and a series of weak and unstable successor states came into being in Eastern Europe, most of which—with the exception of Czechoslovakia—ultimately opted for some form of military dictatorship. In Russia, nascent liberal institutions fell before the victory of Communism. The new Union of Soviet Socialist Republics first declared its intention to destroy the whole international system and produce world revolution, and, when this failed retreated into isolation—although it continued to control and manipulate Communist Parties abroad in its own interest.

The presumed victors—Italy, France, and Britain—emerged greatly weakened. An unstable and dissatisfied Italy witnessed the disappearance of democracy when Benito Mussolini seized power in 1922 and established the first fascist dictatorship. France and England had depended greatly upon the resources of their empires in fighting the Central Powers, and within the empires this led to the stirring of a new nationalism—just when the colonial powers had a greater need for their support. But more, the Allies, now in debt to the United States, had had to depend upon American power to balance that of Germany. For a long time, few people realized quite how much this signified a change in the distribution of power; most people thought of the United States as another power, more or less equal to Great Britain and France, but unwilling, after the war, to play the game. It was a serious miscalculation that would have fatal consequences when the Germans and the Japanese launched their campaigns of conquest in the 1930s, underestimating American potential.

In the Far East, another of the World War I Allies, Japan, assumed a more prominent role. The first of the non-Western countries to adopt and adapt Western technologies within its own cultural context, Japan had already fought with and defeated China in 1895 and Russia in 1905. In 1919 it was deprived by other Allied Powers of some of the fruits of victory, but, like the United States, Japan would be a power on the world scene from that time forward. European predominance had begun to erode on all fronts.

The Interwar Years

The interwar years hastened the process. Burdened by a complicated war-debt and reparation structure, world trade recovered only precariously. Following the Wall Street crash of October 1929 and the crash of the great Kreditanstalt bank in Vienna a year later, credit and trade dried up. New protectionist policies took over, countries defaulted on their debts, and extremist parties took advantage of the growing depression. In Germany the Depression brought Adolf Hitler and his Nazi Party to power in 1933. Hitler destroyed the fragile Weimar Republic and created an absolute dictatorship, the Third Reich. In retrospect, we know that Hitler intended to establish German hegemony in Eurasia, to ultimately challenge and defeat the United States of America, and to create an empire that would last a thousand years.[1] In Japan the military, who had already seized Manchuria from China in 1931, took power within the framework of the Japanese constitutional monarchy; attacked China in 1937; and set out upon the creation of a new, vast, and brutal empire, the Greater East Asia Co-Prosperity Sphere. By 1939, with America weak and the Soviet Union riddled by

Stalinist purges on the sidelines, the Depression-ridden Western democracies faced a challenge from the "Axis": Nazi Germany, fascist Italy, and militarist Japan. This challenge could be met only by war, a war these democracies were ill equipped and reluctant to fight.

The League of Nations System

These effects were hardly what the victors in World War I had intended. Faced with the collapse of their prewar world, they had deliberately tried to construct a whole new, more peaceful one. The Versailles Treaty of 1919, bringing an end to the war, incorporated within it the Covenant of the League of Nations. The League, in effect, represented a blueprint for a new world.

For the first time all states, large or small, would be permanently represented in one organization, the League Assembly, where they could constantly consult with one another and pass nonbinding resolutions on virtually any matter of international concern. They would represent, it was hoped, "world public opinion." The large states, with their special responsibility arising out of their power, would be in constant contact with one another in the Council of the League. No longer would a war break out while the Great Powers failed to meet, as had happened in 1914. The Council would be a standing organ, always prepared to mediate or conciliate disputes. Most important, it could ultimately invoke the principle of "collective security," the keystone of the new structure of peace, designed to replace balance-of-power policies, which tended to inspire arms races and alliances that were used, presumably, to "maintain the balance of power." Under collective security all states would be legally bound to take action against a state designated as an aggressor by a specified body, the Council. If the designated state did not desist from its aggressive behavior, a country so stigmatized could suffer from a rupture of all diplomatic communication or a trade blockade; in the extreme case, it could find itself under attack from the armed forces of the major members of the League. There would no longer be alliances or spheres of influence, since all members would have to be prepared to undertake such "sanctions" against *any* other member.

With a system of collective security in place, disarmament was supposed to become a real possibility, since countries would no longer have to maintain substantial armed forces against a potential foe. Finally, to eliminate colonial rivalries as a cause of Great Powers war, the League, rather than merely transferring the former colonies of the defeated Central Powers to the victors, put them under international supervision by a body called the

Permanent Mandates Commission. The peace conference also created the Permanent Court of International Justice as a final arbiter of judicial disputes between states.

The only trouble was that the whole structure simply did not work. Collective security proved a hollow promise. Countries were unwilling to take action against a distant state that seemed to threaten no vital interest of theirs. The aggressor of today might be the needed ally of tomorrow; perhaps a better course would be to let it have its way. In the face of domestic economic depression in the 1930s and the overwhelming recollection of the carnage of trench warfare, England and France were unwilling to risk war when challenged by Japan's seizure of Manchuria in 1931 and its attack on China in 1937, by Mussolini's attack on Ethiopia in 1936, by Hitler's remilitarization of the "permanently demilitarized" Rhineland in 1934, and by Hitler's annexation of a more or less compliant Austria in 1938.

England and France could not look to aid from the United States, the power that had tipped the balance in 1918 but had rejected League membership in 1920, then legislated itself into isolation in the 1930s, when it had only the nineteenth-largest army in the world. The Soviet Union under the blood-drenched dictatorship of Joseph Stalin hardly inspired confidence as a reliable ally either. Stalin's collectivization policies in the early 1930s and his purges of his opponents and of the officer corps of his army in the late 1930s led to the death of millions of Russian citizens and the creation of enormous labor camps. His attempt at a rapprochement with the Western powers to forge an anti-Axis front in the mid-1930s was looked upon with widespread and justifiable skepticism.

As a result, England and France followed a policy known as "appeasement," offering limited territorial gains to expansionist Nazi Germany, wooing it with the promise of favorable economic arrangements, and listening to Hitler's assurances that what he wanted was to rectify the unjust terms of peace fixed upon Germany by Versailles. The symbol of appeasement policy came to be "Munich," the site of the 1938 meeting at which France and England agreed to let Hitler have the German-populated area of Czechoslovakia known as the Sudetenland. Both had guaranteed Czechoslovak territorial integrity. Now, in return for the promise of no further territorial expansion by Hitler, for—as British Prime Minister Sir Neville Chamberlain put it—"peace in our time," they opted not to oppose him and forced the Czechs to give up their defensible borders.

Many have argued that the Western allies were unready to challenge Germany militarily at the time, but others consider the lack of such a challenge to be the most drastic diplomatic error of modern times. The shadow of Munich has hung over all contemporary diplomacy, symbolizing the mistaken appeasement of insatiable dictatorships. (In the years since World War II, face to face with a menacing Soviet Union or other regional expansionist states, statesmen have frequently invoked the error of Munich.) Hitler seized the rest of a now-indefensible Czechoslovakia six months later and prepared his campaign against Poland. The British and French, frantic for peace, had ignored the basic rules of balance-of-power politics: even at the risk of war, a state should never allow a potential opponent to become so powerful that it can risk war with a real probability of success.

It took little persuasion on Hitler's part to let Stalin see that Hitler could offer him territory in Eastern Europe that the Western powers could not, and in August 1939, an astounded world witnessed the signing of a nonaggression pact between the two bitter ideological enemies, Nazi Germany and Communist Russia. Hitler could now attack Poland with impunity, even though France and Britain had given it their guarantee. The two proceeded to declare war on Hitler, but geographical realities prevailed: they could take no real action to save Poland. Only Russia could have done so. Instead, under the terms of a secret protocol to its pact with Germany, it seized the eastern half of Poland (and reincorporated the independent Baltic states of Latvia, Lithuania, and Estonia). World War II had begun, the League system had failed, and the world had been plunged into darkness.

World War II

Most people fail to realize today that the Axis powers almost succeeded. The Nazi war machine rapidly subjugated virtually all Europe but Britain, where Churchill rallied his people against those who were tempted to agree to peace with a Hitler triumphant on the continent. Frustrated by his inability to defeat Britain, Hitler turned, as he had always intended to, against his erstwhile ally Stalin. Hoping for a prolonged period of continued cooperation, Stalin had gone on feeding the Nazi war machine until the last minute. The mighty German armies came close to defeating the Soviet Union. In the meantime, German troops advanced across North Africa, poised to take the Suez Canal and dominate the Middle East with its oil and its vital trade route between Europe and the Far East.

The Japanese, for their part, took advantage of the defeat of European powers to advance into Southeast Asia. Determined to end the American threat to their dominance in Asia, they attacked and destroyed most of the American fleet at Pearl Harbor on December 7, 1941, then overran the Philippines, Malaysia, and the Dutch East Indies. Their ships could now sail at will into the Indian Ocean to bombard ports on the Indian subcontinent, and they appeared poised to take the north of Australia. A successful attack upon Midway Island would open the way to the capture of Hawaii and control of the Pacific sea-lanes. Pro-Nazi South American leaders organized their armies on the German model; U.S. East Coast beaches were black with the oil from tankers sunk by German submarines that roamed Atlantic sea-lanes freely. The Axis seemed everywhere triumphant.

Then, in 1942 and 1943, the tide slowly began to turn. The overconfident Japanese suffered—by a hair's breadth—strategic defeat at Midway. Hawaii was saved. Revitalized American forces began their long journey north toward the Japanese islands. German Field Marshal Erwin Rommel's Afrika Korps was turned back at El Alamein by the British under Field Marshal Bernard Montgomery, and the Middle East was saved. In Russia winter, space (and a huge volume of American supplies) came to the aid of Soviet troops, who defeated enormous German forces at Stalingrad and Kursk, and began their long march into Europe. On D-Day, June 6, 1944, under the command of General Dwight D. Eisenhower, Allied forces successfully landed in France.

Another year and a half of bitter, bloody fighting and unmeasurable destruction would be required for the final defeat of Axis and Japanese power. On May 8, 1945, with Hitler dead in his bunker in the midst of a Soviet-occupied Berlin consisting mainly of miles of rubble, the German armies finally surrendered. In the Far East, events moved faster than anticipated. The Japanese military, who advocated a fanatical final resistance, were heartened by the tremendous casualties they inflicted on Americans who invaded the islands of Iwo Jima and Okinawa to the south of Japan, and by the numbers of ships sunk by their "kamikaze" suicide planes. Once captured, however, the islands provided bases for the aerial onslaught that finally began to cripple the Japanese war effort. Nevertheless, war correspondents in the area agreed that the war would last for another year.

While Japanese diplomats put out tentative peace feelers, Allied probes revealed that if these became known they would be disavowed by hard-liners in Japan who planned to inflict a crushing defeat on invading forces. To hasten events and avoid what could have been horrendous casualties in a landing on the home islands, the Americans dropped the first atomic bomb upon Hiroshima on August 5, 1945. Japanese leaders debated surrender, but hard-liners still held out until, on August 9, the Russians finally came into the Pacific war, launching an attack upon the presumably intact Kwantung Army in Manchuria the same day that a second atomic bomb was dropped on Nagasaki. Despite a last-minute attempt by an army clique to prevent the surrender, the Japanese Emperor recorded and broadcast an imperial declaration of surrender to his troops, who were still scattered throughout the Pacific, and World War II came to an end on August 14.

The Shape of the Postwar World

During the final stages of the war, statesmen tried to lay out the shape of the postwar world in terms that would be widely acceptable. Large-scale planning and diplomatic activity and the great wartime conferences, at Teheran in 1943, and at Yalta, San Francisco, and Potsdam in 1945, led to a series of important structures and organizations. The disposition of troops when the fighting stopped, however, proved even more significant, for despite all the diplomatic efforts, the lines of division for the next forty years between communist East and democratic West lay largely where the troops had stopped.

The United Nations System

Planners inevitably draw lessons from the immediate past as they look to the future. As the war drew to a close, Allied leaders were determined to prevent a recurrence of the thirty-year crisis and to rectify the weaknesses and failures of the League of Nations system. Under the leadership of the United States, they devised once again a new world order—this time, one that would provide both military and economic security, yet would be able to provide for necessary political change, as any political system must do. The organizations included the United Nations itself, whose Charter was signed at San Francisco in June 1945; three international economic organizations that came to constitute what was known as the "Bretton Woods system"—the International Bank for Reconstruction and Development (IBRD, also called the "World Bank" or simply, the "International Bank"), the International Monetary Fund (IMF), the International Trade Organization (which was never brought into being, but was superseded by the General Agreement on Tariffs and Trade [the GATT], which in turn was transformed, finally, on January 1, 1995, into the World Trade Organization [WTO], after previous failures to do so)—and a host of related organizations in the fields of labor, health, air transport, telecommunications, and so forth.

In the United Nations, the Security Council—a strengthened version of the League Council—was charged with the maintenance of international peace and security—that is, the preservation of order. It could use a variety of means for peaceful settlement, but was ultimately empowered to threaten the use of a revised collective security system, in which a qualified majority, including the five permanent members (the United States, the USSR, Britain, China, and France), would be able to vote sanctions. The Security Council was to have armed forces allocated to it; therefore, it—unlike the League—would have teeth. The League Council had required the unanimity of *all* members; in the new UN Council, only the five permanent members would have to agree. The founders hoped the five would be forced to reach a consensus through their desire to maintain a peaceful order. If not, the system would not work anyway.

The General Assembly, in which all states large or small were to be represented, could talk about virtually anything and could pass nonbinding resolutions, again presumably representing majority world opinion. The new Trusteeship Council was to take over from the old League Mandates system the supervision of former colonies as they moved to self-government. American planners, perhaps naively, hoped that most parts of the remaining empires—including the French, the British, the Dutch, and the Portuguese—would be put under the Trusteeship Council's international supervision. It was planned to be one of the major institutions to provide peaceful change in the world.

The myriad economic and social organizations were intended to provide the world with an open, liberal world trading system, and a stable international payments system, and to encourage the free flow of capital. All these had disappeared during the 1930s era of the Great Depression. Not only had this produced economic disaster, but it had also been a direct cause of the unstable political situation that had brought war. Global interdependence could bring prosperity and growth; as the Great Depression had shown, it could also spread economic disaster from one country to another. The new agencies, created to foster economic cooperation, were designed to encourage the former and prevent the latter. The economic underpinnings of a stable world political order would prevent a repetition of the events of 1914 and 1939. A brave new world would come into being.

Political Realities

The political context of this new world system was not yet clearly understood, although it appeared that Europe could hardly again be the center of the global political system. Germany and Italy lay shattered, and the cities of Germany were in ruins. France's new leader, General Charles de Gaulle, might aspire to grandeur and to reconstruction of the French empire along new lines, but the myth and the reality of French power were destroyed in May 1940, when Nazi Germany overran France in six weeks. French power could never be restored. In Europe, only Britain appeared to have emerged capable of carrying out worldwide responsibilities, but appearances were deceptive: Winston Churchill might rumble, "I have not become the King's First Minister in order to preside over the liquidation of the British Empire," but Britain's industrial plant was worn and damaged, and her radical shift

THE COLLAPSE OF THE EUROPEAN SYSTEM *21*

from world creditor to world debtor destroyed much of her capacity for influence. The United Kingdom could ill afford expenses incurred overseas in support of her still far-flung responsibilities. Churchill and his successors felt there would be no security in Europe if they could not persuade the United States—with all its power—to stand with them.

Stalin's Russia was another matter. No other country had suffered such casualties, no other more damage. But the Soviet Union emerged with enormous prestige as a result of her victory over the mighty Wehrmacht; the Red Army occupied all of Eastern Europe and much of Central Europe, ensuring participation in German and Austrian occupation; the Allies had legitimized Russian retention of the territorial gains from the Hitler-Stalin pact; and Stalin had regained Czarist rights and territories in the Far East, lost after World War I. His belated entry into the Asian battle had, in addition, given him control over North Korea as well as cession of several northern Japanese islands (still a bone of contention fifty years later). All around Russia, in the "rim lands" of the great Eurasian continent, chaos and weakness prevailed. Despite horrendous losses, the Soviet Union had emerged as a military giant.

Nowhere was chaos and weakness more evident than in Asia. Japanese power was crushed, but it was hard to see what could replace it. The U.S. attempt to present Chiang Kai-shek's Republic of China as the East Asian great power appeared dubious. Torn by years of war, and with Mao Zedong's Communists firmly ensconced in the north, Chiang's Nationalist government hardly seemed capable of decisive action. In South Asia and Southeast Asia the prospects for European countries' retention of their colonial positions looked equally poor. Iran, like Korea, was occupied by Russia in the north and by England and the United States in the south. In all these areas, traditional power structures were crumbling or gone; where American power had flowed in, it seemed generally ready to pull out, and no one knew what might follow. Japan, on the other hand, now occupied by GIs, lay firmly under American control.

Success of the Normandy landings in 1944 meant that Western armies in Western Europe ensured the reestablishment of democratic regimes throughout the areas they occupied. Moreover, the Western powers' presence meant they could block a number of Stalin's demands—meaningful Russian participation in the occupation of Italy, control of the great German industrial area of the Ruhr, and trusteeship over the former Italian colony of Libya—which, in conjunction with joint Russian-Turkish control of the Black Sea straits into the Mediterranean, would have immediately made Russia a Mediterranean power. In other words, success of the Normandy landings meant that Russia was kept out of Western Europe and the Mediterranean.

Map 1. **Soviet Gains in World War II**

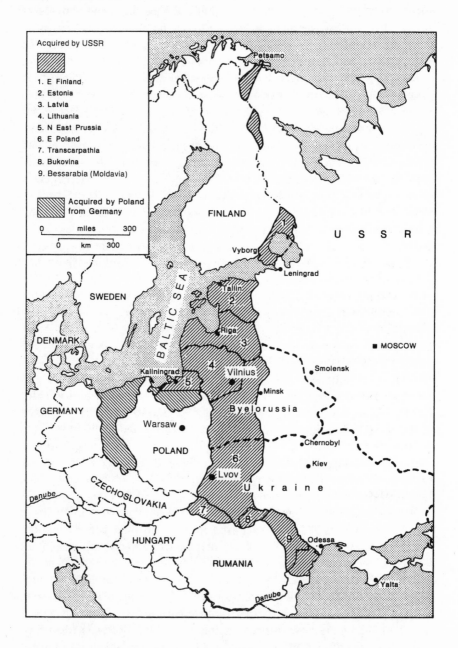

Source: Andrew Boyd, *Atlas of World Affairs* (London: Routledge, 1991).

Stalin, in the long run, proved ruthless about translating military control over areas around the Soviet Union into political control. The Western allies, on the other hand, were divided. Churchill accepted Stalin's desire for a sphere of influence in Eastern Europe, but wanted to persuade Stalin both to limit its extent and to allow friendly "democratic" regimes in the area.

The big question was what the United States would do with its newfound global position, whether it would retreat as it had done after World War I. Americans largely agreed with Secretary of State Cordell Hull that world interdependence and the horrors of modern warfare meant that spheres of interest and balance-of-power policies should be a thing of the past. A new, strengthened United Nations, drawing on the League of Nations, should replace them. For Hull, obtaining Russian commitment to joining the UN appeared to be one of his greatest diplomatic triumphs. (Now enormous effort would have to go into persuading the U.S. Senate not to reject membership, as it had done with respect to the League of Nations in 1920, with disastrous results.)

The Americans therefore disapproved both of European efforts to regain their empires (whose resources had been so important in enabling them to resist Axis pressures, and might prove important again in the future) and to block Communist influence in places like Greece and Italy. In April 1945 Churchill made clear to President Harry Truman's envoy Joseph Davies his despair at Western disarray and division. Strong Communist Parties existed everywhere in Europe, and if it was true, as Roosevelt had told him earlier, that the Americans were not prepared to keep troops in Europe for more than two years, there was a strong possibility that Stalin would use the opportunity to dominate all of Europe. Davies decried Churchill's fears, telling him that if this was how he felt, he should have sided with Hitler!

Still, leaders of other states wondered how the United States would act. Only North America and South America remained relatively untouched by the fighting. The United States had suffered neither bombardment nor occupation. Her industrial capacity, mobilized and expanded in support of twelve million men in the armed forces, could be far more easily reconverted than that of other countries. Her power and influence extended to Western Europe, North Africa, the Middle East, and East Asia; her troops occupied a sizable segment of Germany, Austria, Italy, as well as all of Japan and half of Korea. The United States had hosted the conferences that created the United Nations and most of the other new international agencies. If the United States had been able and willing to take the role its power permitted back in the 1920s and 1930s, both the Depression and World War II might have been prevented: Germany and Japan would certainly have hesitated more before launching their armies upon the path of conquest.

It was thus not only Americans who sought world leadership for the United States; many Americans in fact still opposed such a role. But people and leaders throughout much of the rest of the world drew their conclusions from the immediate past and therefore looked to the future with hope that the United States would now play the leading role in peacetime it had finally come to play during the war and in the creation of the UN system. Among other things, only the United States possessed that new and terrifying weapon, the atomic bomb.

The Attempt to Reconstruct the Old World

Making Peace

Most American planning for the postwar period concentrated on creation of the UN system, through which foreign policy could be channeled in the future and where world order and justice could be achieved. Occupation forces were to stay in Germany only as long as necessary (Roosevelt had thought for two years) and in Japan long enough to make certain the realization of occupation policies intended to destroy Japan's military potential. The main immediate foreign policy effort should go into negotiating peace treaties for former enemy states and providing relief to shattered countries as they began to rebuild their war-torn economies. Then, essentially, Americans could pick up their marbles and go home, to begin to consume all they had not consumed during the last four years of war production and strict rationing.

At Potsdam, Germany, in August 1945, the new American president, Harry Truman; the new British prime minister, Clement Atlee; and Joseph Stalin agreed to creation of the Council of Foreign Ministers, which was to speedily negotiate peace treaties with former enemies and present them to the United Nations for enactment.

> I assumed (wrote American Secretary of State James Byrnes) that at the end of hostilities an era of peace would be so deeply desired by those nations that had fought the war in unity that the inevitable differences of opinion could be resolved without serious difficulty.[2]

It did not work that way. The problem was that the British Labour Government and the Truman Administration rejected Russian policies in the occupied countries of East Europe as contrary to the Yalta Declaration on Liberated Europe signed by Roosevelt, Stalin, and Churchill in 1944, which had promised free elections in the area.

While the various Foreign Ministers meetings dragged on in acrimony through November 1946, events in other parts of the world helped to embitter the peace treaty debates: delayed departure of Russian troops from northern Iran and from Manchuria, Russian demands upon Turkey for territorial concessions, and civil war in Greece. Germany became an object of struggle by mid-1946, and Korea remained divided—occupied in the north by Russian troops and in the south by Americans, both ostensibly there merely to take the surrender of Japanese troops. In the meantime the Congress of the United States, preoccupied by domestic affairs, had made it clear that it would not consider reconstruction loans to Stalin's Russia, given the nature of Russian activities in Eastern Europe.

One interpretation of those activities was given in a speech at the dedication of a library in Fulton, Missouri, by Winston Churchill, now leader of the Conservative opposition in the British Parliament. "Nobody," he said,

> knows what Soviet Russia and its Communist international organization intends to do in the immediate future, or what are the limits, if any, to their expansive and proselytizing tendencies . . . from Stettin in the Baltic to Trieste in the Adriatic an Iron Curtain has descended across the continent.

He went on to say that in the face of the Soviet attempt to expand, the Western democracies must stand together to prevent a war that the Soviet Union did not want either. A considerable uproar in the press the next week showed that many Americans did not share Churchill's interpretation, and saw his speech as merely an attempt to embroil the United States in a British quarrel with Moscow. But the phrase "Iron Curtain" entered into current usage.

Stalin himself, a month earlier, gave a major speech that appeared to redefine World War II. It was not simply a war against fascist powers—an isolated and unique incident—but a part of a developing conflict between capitalist-imperialist powers. He thus linked the Western Allies and Nazi Germany as largely similar states who had fought each other in one phase of a conflict which would ultimately lead to the downfall of capitalism and the triumph of the Communist world.

Nevertheless, peace treaties with Italy, Romania, Hungary, Bulgaria, and Finland were finally signed in Paris on February 10, 1947, denuding Italy of its colonies; ceding a number of border areas in Eastern Europe to the Soviet Union (the one country that gained substantial territory as a result of the war) and placing Trieste, a city claimed by both Italy and Yugoslavia, under UN control. Finally, the Council of Foreign Ministers in New York called a meeting in Moscow for March 1947 to start work on the German and Austrian peace treaties. Unlike the other European countries with which peace treaties had been worked out, both countries were under four-power occupation: France, the United Kingdom, the United States, and the Soviet Union each administered a separate zone, with a four-power occupation of Berlin and Vienna.

In retrospect, the attempt at a peace treaty for Germany was doomed from the start. Germany, in short, remained divided simply because neither West nor East wanted to take the chance that a united Germany would come under the domination of the other.

Local necessity prodded occupying powers into reestablishing order and authority in order to allow restoration of production and distribution, simply to prevent mass starvation. The three Western zones were swollen by the influx of millions of immigrants: Eastern Europeans of German descent expelled from their homes (the "Volksdeutsch"), "displaced persons" unwilling to return to homes in Eastern Europe which were occupied by Soviet Russia or where there were now hostile national governments, and Germans expelled from the eastern area of Germany "occupied" by Poland. No grain was forthcoming from the Russian-occupied Eastern Zone, although the Russians insisted upon continued "reparations" deliveries from the West (agreed upon in principle though not in quantity earlier at Yalta, but contingent upon treating Germany as an economic unit). When the Western occupiers found themselves importing food to alleviate hunger, they decided to suspend reparations to the Russians in May 1946: they would be funneling in resources at one end and shipping them out at the other. The war-ravaged British and French economies couldn't afford it, and the Americans saw it as disguised aid to the Soviet Union that wouldn't solve the German problems.

Secretary of State James Byrnes tried to mollify Russian negotiators by offering a twenty-five-year demilitarization treaty for Germany, for which the United States would be the guarantor. It meant an American commitment to the continent of a kind never dreamed of before. Perhaps this would enable an agreement on implementing Potsdam. It did not work, and in July 1946 Byrnes offered to merge the American zone with any or all others. Two weeks later the British accepted, and "Bizonia" was created in January 1947, out of the American and the British zones—a move termed a "flagrant violation" of Potsdam by the Russians. In the meantime, both the Soviet Union and the United States changed their policies toward Germany, appealing to the Germans by pledging to rebuild their zones while denouncing the other for continuing to hold the Germans in subjection.

In the circumstances, the March–April 1947 Moscow Conference of the Council of Foreign Ministers and a later one in November, the purposes of which were to draft the peace treaties, did little but ratify the split, while rehearsing interminable arguments about all the matters at issue. Germany was to remain divided for the next forty-three years.

Creation of the Soviet Bloc

While Germany split, the rest of the process described by Winston Churchill in his Iron Curtain speech at Fulton, Missouri, speeded up: Eastern Europe witnessed the transformation of Russian military occupation into political domination through the creation and imposition of local Communist governments.

Western powers used the only means they had—diplomacy—to try to halt the development. During the war they had accepted that neighboring governments must be friendly to the Soviet Union, but at Yalta and elsewhere had tried to persuade Stalin that free governments would in the long run be friendlier. The fascism that had run rampant in Eastern Europe before the war was thoroughly discredited, and long-submerged democratic movements had finally been able to emerge. But the Western efforts were fruitless.

Some Western historians have tried to argue that American efforts to interfere in the Soviet sphere in Eastern Europe, coupled with withholding of American reconstruction aid to the Soviet Union and the threat of the atomic bomb, brought on the Cold War. The argument largely ignores the nature of Stalin's regime, the long record of repression as the only means to maintain power by Eastern regimes, and subsequent revelations about Stalin within the Soviet Union itself. Stalin certainly had no master plan to take over the Eastern European states, but he wanted no opposition parties unfriendly to the Soviet Union, and step by step he saw that all were eliminated.

Communist-dominated wartime resistance efforts in Yugoslavia and Albania meant that the two emerged from the war solidly in the Russian camp. The process varied in Hungary, Poland, Romania, and Bulgaria, but Communist control of the key ministries of the interior, information, and the economy ensured domination, despite widespread popular opposition. By 1948, often with open Russian intervention, Communist governments were firmly established throughout Eastern Europe and opposition parties had been destroyed.

Finland and Czechoslovakia could be used by those ready to excuse Russia to prove that the brutal tactics used in much of Eastern Europe were a local phenomenon, that Russians were being overzealous in their standards for "friendly" governments, or that "progressive" political movements were sweeping away old feudal structures and their representatives. Numerous Western commentators believed this, and so did many Communist voters in Western Europe. After all, the Russians left Finland largely to itself after the peace treaty signed in Paris in February 1947 ratified the transfer to Russia of certain strategic territories, and they withdrew their forces from Czechoslovakia in December 1945 after cession of the eastern tip of the country to Russia. Communist Party leaders in Prague shared in a coalition government with three other parties. Dr. Eduard Beneš retained his wartime exile position as president, and Communist Clement Gottwald became premier. Many in the West—and within Czechoslovakia—saw the country as a bridge between East and West, proving that coexistence was possible. In 1948, however, even this hope was confounded when the Communist Party seized power (see page 51).

In the meantime, in Western Europe, for the forty years after 1947, no Communist Party participated in any government.

The Far East

Far away on the other side of the globe, in Japan and Korea, as in Europe, military occupation also proved to be the decisive factor in determining subsequent political alignments. General Douglas MacArthur, named Supreme Commander for the Allied Powers—acting as much on his own as for the American government—resisted the efforts of all other wartime Allies to obtain a real voice in occupation policy. The Americans imposed a new, democratic constitution (widely known as the "MacArthur Constitution") that renounced the use of armed force in the conduct of foreign policy, but maintained Emperor Hirohito as symbol, while stripping him of any formal authority. Japan came to bear the imprint of occupation by a single—on the whole, sympathetic—power.

Korea was a different matter. A small country between three giant neighbors, it was long the subject of power rivalry between China, Russia, and Japan. In 1910 it was formally annexed by Japan. At the Cairo conference of 1943, Roosevelt, Churchill, and Chiang Kai-shek had pledged that Korea would become independent "in due course." Russian armies, entering the Pacific war only on August 8, 1945, took the surrender of Japanese forces in the north, while Americans occupied the south, with the thirty-eighth parallel—roughly across the center of Korea—arbitrarily and hastily chosen as the demarcation line. Attempts to create joint administrative organs and then a provisional Korean democratic government by the two occupying powers faltered. A Moscow-trained Korean, Kim Il Sung, First Secretary of the Communist Party, became the first premier of the Russian-installed Democratic People's Republic of Korea in the north in 1948, from where the Russians withdrew their troops in October. (Kim Il Sung, the longest-ruling head of state since World War II, finally died in 1994. As of this writing, his son and heir Kim Jong Il appears to have taken over his functions.)

The Truman Administration, having acquiesced in a hasty and massive demobilization of American armed forces, found itself in a weak and exposed position in the south. In November 1947 it therefore turned the issue of Korea over to the UN General Assembly, which, though it supervised elections in the south and certified their validity, was unable to do the same in the north or to bring about reunification. The United States, while supporting the government of the old nationalist leader Syngman Rhee in the south, withdrew American troops shortly after the Soviet Union announced withdrawal of their own. Korea, like Germany, was split in two, and it remains so fifty years later.

The Beginning of the Retreat from Empire

It took centuries for the independent, sovereign nation-states of Western Europe to emerge, and once they did so, they spread out to bring most of the world under their control. Only in the Americas, North and South, did parts of the colonial empires of these European states break away at the end of the eighteenth and the beginning of the nineteenth centuries. In 1945 some fifty-one states, primarily European and American, signed the UN Charter. Twenty-five years later, in one of the most extraordinary, profound, and rapid changes in world history, more than fifty new states, with a population of a billion, had emerged from colonial status.

World War II, in the main, merely hastened a process that had begun much earlier: Europe's hold on the rest of the world was already far weaker than it appeared. The underlying demographic trends—the rapid expansion of population in non-Western areas—and the weakening of Europe in World Wars I and II speeded up the emergence of new nation-states. The births of these nation-states were not easy: force played a part in almost all of them, and the resistance to hasty granting of independence by the colonial powers was based on a variety of considerations. In some cases, these considerations were strategic or economic, but in many, resistance was based on a sense that the areas now claiming the European-born attributes of statehood simply did not yet have them—would not hold together as sovereign states, could not be truly independent, would fall prey to domestic tyrannies, or would erupt into conflict with neighbors over borders and minorities, where the colonial powers had been able to maintain peace. To the often European-educated nationalist leaders fighting for independence, these were merely flimsy excuses.

30

Map 2. States Independent Since 1945

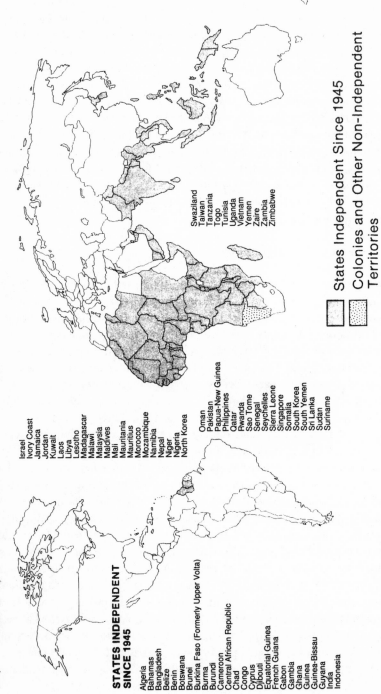

States Independent Since 1945

Israel
Ivory Coast
Jamaica
Jordan
Kuwait
Laos
Libya
Lesotho
Madagascar
Malawi
Malaysia
Maldives
Mali
Mauritania
Mauritius
Morocco
Mozambique
Namibia
Nepal
Niger
Nigeria
North Korea

Oman
Pakistan
Papua-New Guinea
Philippines
Qatar
Rwanda
Sao Tome
Senegal
Seychelles
Sierra Leone
Singapore
Somalia
South Korea
South Yemen
Sri Lanka
Sudan
Suriname

Swaziland
Taiwan
Tanzania
Togo
Tunisia
Uganda
Vietnam
Yemen
Zaire
Zambia
Zimbabwe

**STATES INDEPENDENT
SINCE 1945**

Algeria
Bahamas
Bangladesh
Belize
Benin
Botswana
Brunei
Burkina Faso (Formerly Upper Volta)
Burma
Burundi
Cameroon
Central African Republic
Chad
Congo
Cyprus
Djibouti
Equatorial Guinea
French Guiana
Gabon
Gambia
Ghana
Guinea
Guinea-Bissau
Guyana
India
Indonesia

☐ States Independent Since 1945

▫ Colonies and Other Non-Independent
Territories

Source: Joseph Weatherby, Jr., et al., *The Other World: Issues and Politics in the Third World* (New York: Macmillan, 1987).

Each of the colonial powers reacted somewhat differently to the emerging postwar situation. In the early years, only Britain and the United States moved rapidly to shed some of the remnants of empire; France and the Netherlands tried to transform their relationships to their empires; Portugal and Belgium simply held on.

The British Empire Dissolves

It is hard to realize now that at the turn of the century tiny England dominated a quarter of the land surface of the world, and a quarter of its people. The sun never really set on the British Empire. In 1931, self-governing "dominion" status was established for settler communities like Canada, Australia, and New Zealand, as well as South Africa. All of them declared war independently in 1939 (Ireland never did go to war against Nazi Germany), and participated as independent states in the formation of the United Nations. It seemed reasonable at the end of the war that other territories of the Empire would soon achieve the same status.

India—the "Jewel in the Crown"—was a special case. It was enormous and diverse, and during the war the Japanese appealed to Indian nationalists led by Mohandas K. Gandhi and Jawaharlal Nehru to resist the British. Muslim separatism developed under the leadership of Mohammed Ali Jinnah and the Muslim League, and all efforts both during and after the war to create a single state failed to bridge the gap between the largely secular but Hindu-dominated Congress Party of Nehru and Gandhi and the Muslim League. Consumed by domestic problems and the emerging Cold War, the British Labour government announced that the transfer of power would proceed by June 1948, whether to a unitary India or to two states.

Lord Mountbatten, charged with liquidating the British "Raj," could not reconcile Muslim fears of Hindu domination with Hindu desire for a secular state that would encompass all religions. The British Parliament passed the Indian Independence Bill in July, and on August 15, 1948, India and Pakistan became two separate, independent sovereign states. On the night of August 14, Prime Minister Nehru of India declared to the Constituent Assembly, "At the stroke of the midnight hour, when the world sleeps, India will awake to life and freedom." Unfortunately, it also awoke to an orgy of looting and violence, as Hindu attacked Muslim within the Indian boundaries, and Muslim attacked Hindu in Pakistan. Millions of refugees left their homes and streamed across boundaries, under attack all the way. Over twelve million people were finally resettled, but relations between the two countries could not help but be bad from the beginning, although both remained within the British Commonwealth of Nations.

Map 3. **The Partition of India**

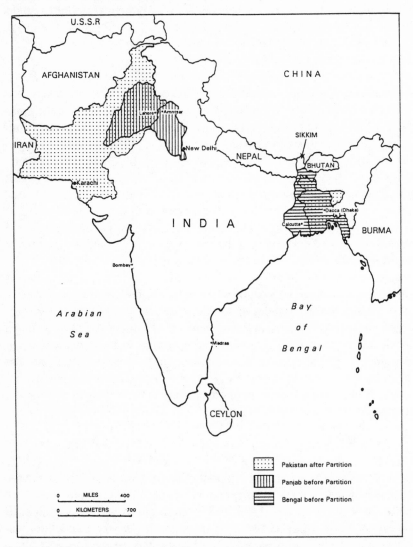

Source: Karl J. Schmidt, *An Atlas and Survey of South Asian History* (Armonk, NY: M.E. Sharpe, 1995).

Most of the hundreds of more or less autonomous princely states acceded to either India or Pakistan, thereby guaranteeing them unity. One large state, Hyderabad, was entirely within India, and was forced into submission by blockade and then invasion. But one of the largest and most important, Kashmir, remained at issue. Located on the borders of Afghanistan and

China, it contained the headwaters of the Indus River; its population was predominantly Muslim, but its maharajah—who had hoped to remain independent—was Hindu. Faced with invasion by Pakistan-backed irregular Muslim tribesmen, he acceded to India, and Indian troops were sent to help. Each country charged the other with aggression, and UN observers were sent to oversee a UN-sponsored cease-fire until a plebiscite to determine the future of Kashmir could be held. Such a plebiscite has never been held, and in the face of continued Pakistani opposition, India has integrated the three-fifths of Kashmir that it holds into India. Forty years later, despite attempts to settle matters, Kashmir remains an issue that has caused sporadic warfare, one that continues to trouble an India that faces an incipient independence movement. Pakistan was able to settle its share of Kashmiri borders with China, but India fought a border war with China in 1962 when China refused to compromise over the lines it claimed.

To the south, the island of Ceylon—renamed Sri Lanka under the new constitution of 1972—also achieved independence within the Commonwealth in early 1948. Although minority problems would erupt in the future, there were fewer issues in Sri Lanka than in countries like Burma and Malaya, where Japanese occupation complicated matters, creating nationalist leadership tainted by collaboration with the Japanese. Nevertheless, the British transferred power to an unstable Burmese government in early 1948. To the southeast, Malaya, with its large minorities, presented the British with numerous problems they were ready to resolve until a Communist insurrection erupted, in this case while the British were still running the country. As a result, independence was delayed for a decade until British forces defeated the Communists.

The United States and the Philippines

The United States entered the war in the Pacific committed to the eventual independence of its chief Pacific colonial possession, the Philippines, and its troops returned as liberators rather than to restore discredited colonialism. The United States carried out large-scale relief operations; independence came on July 4, 1946, and the new government of the war-battered country received emergency loans, tax refunds, and funds to satisfy war damage claims. The United States also extracted concessions: a privileged tariff position, certain special economic rights, and perhaps most important, ninety-nine-year leases on a number of military and naval bases. The United States was not going to get caught napping in the Pacific as it had five years earlier. At the time, Filipinos by and large approved of all the agreements, though eventually the bases were to become a focus of nationalist agitation.

The Belgians, the Portuguese, and the Dutch

For the Belgians and the Portuguese, whose large colonial holdings were in
Africa, there was no question of relinquishing their hold, and they faced no
organized opposition. Belgium, in fact, emerged from German occupation
with a trade surplus with the United States, thanks to sales of uranium ore to
the United States from the Belgian Congo. The Dutch, on the other hand,
were determined to return to the Dutch East Indies, where a very different
situation prevailed.

At the end of the war there were 200,000 Dutch interned in Indonesia,
and 200,000 Japanese troops to be repatriated. When Australian and English troops landed to take the surrender of Japanese troops and return
control of the islands to the Dutch, they faced nationalist resistance in many
areas. For four, long, confused years, sporadic fighting and truces between
the Dutch and nationalist forces marked the attempt to create a Dutch-con-
trolled federation. Eventually, under strong international pressure in the
United Nations, led by the United States, the Dutch granted unconditional
independence to the United States of Indonesia. In contrast to British and
French colonial administration and that of the United States in the Philippines, the Dutch had done little to prepare Indonesia for self-government,
and centrifugal tendencies would play a large part in the future.

The French Union

For France the French empire was a central matter. The empire had provided resources and manpower to counterbalance Germany's greater population and industry for both World Wars, it was in Algiers in 1943 that de
Gaulle created the embryonic French government that would become the
Fourth Republic, and it was from bases in Africa that French forces returned to France in 1944. Determined to maintain the empire for the future,
de Gaulle recreated it in the form of the "French Union," with a greater
measure of representation and the promise of technical aid from France.
But, by the end of World War II, French weakness had come to be understood throughout the empire, and much of the history of French politics in
the first postwar decades would revolve around the struggle to preserve the
French Union against native independence movements.

At the outset, in Africa south of the Sahara, there was little problem in
retaining control; in North Africa, in 1945, a brief nationalist revolt in
Algeria was easily put down. Far-off French Indochina, occupied during the
war by the Japanese, was a wholly different matter. In 1945, when British
and Chinese troops moved into French Indochina to take the surrender of

Japanese troops and to liberate the surviving French who had been interned under inhuman conditions, they found the Democratic Republic of Vietnam in existence, headed by and under the control of the founder of the Communist Party of Indochina, Ho Chi Minh, whom the Americans had helped, while his guerrilla forces had come to occupy substantial portions of the country. In March 1946, Ho and a French mission signed an accord creating Vietnam as a "free state" within the Indochinese Federation and the French Union. While further negotiations faltered, French troops returned in force, and the French government, underestimating the task, succumbed to the temptation to crush the Republic. By the end of 1946 France was once more at war. Handicapped by instability and economic weakness at home, however, the French never sent sufficient forces to Indochina, nor were they able to devise a political strategy that would find support among non-Communist Vietnamese, of whom there were many. (How very different the world might have been if the French had granted independence to Vietnam in those years.)

Two Middle East countries, Lebanon and Syria, formerly French mandates under the League of Nations system, became independent toward the end of the war and declared war on the Axis in order to attend the San Francisco conference. An effort by de Gaulle to retain control of their armed forces was blocked by the British, leaving a legacy of considerable bitterness.

The Americas

The Americas had a peculiar position in the Europe-dominated global system of prewar years. For the hundred years before World War II the United States claimed a preeminent position in the Americas on the basis of the Monroe Doctrine, a presidential declaration of 1823 to the effect that the United States would not allow European balance-of-power policies to extend to the Americas and would not countenance European interference in the independence of American nations. At the turn of the century, United States hegemony in the Caribbean was encouraged by the British who transferred to the United States the right to build the Panama Canal. It was a way of enlisting growing American power in such a way as to check German attempts to get a foothold in the area without the British having to do it, and the United States, having built the Panama Canal, intervened in Cuba, Mexico, and Haiti to keep order in the region.

Nevertheless, most countries of South America continued to have closer cultural, financial, and commercial relations with Europe than with the United States. Argentina, with its temperate climate, produced exports that competed with those of the United States. Its per capita income exceeded that of many European countries, and its capital city of Buenos Aires considered itself to be the Paris of South America, far more cosmopolitan than the rough cities of the bully to the north. Latins frequently manifested their distaste for U.S. pretensions and for U.S. intervention in the Caribbean; President Franklin D. Roosevelt tried to repair relations through what was called the "Good Neighbor" policy, a closer attention to Latin sensitivities and an acceptance of nonintervention as a general rule of inter-American affairs.

In the 1930s, however, the influence of various brands of European fascism was strong in Latin America, and Germany cultivated its many admirers. The Nazis organized the large German settlements and enhanced German primacy among the military: Latin armies tended to be modeled on the German army. The United States countered by working to produce "hemispheric solidarity" during the war in economic, diplomatic, cultural, and military fields, greatly expanding both its trade with and aid to Latin American states. As Italian Fascism and then Nazism lost their glow, most Latin states broke off relations and eventually declared war on the Axis. Argentina and Chile resisted, and the end of the war found Argentina with a populist, authoritarian, "fascist" government in power under General Juan Peron.

In early 1945 all the American states but Argentina signed the Act of Chapultepec in Mexico City, promising the creation of an inter-American security system. Belatedly, Argentina signed and declared war on the Axis in order to attend the San Francisco Conference on creation of the United Nations organization. At San Francisco the American states joined other smaller states in strengthening the capacities of the General Assembly and diluting the authority of the Great Powers, while also insisting that the Charter recognize and accept the authority of regional security systems. Despite failure to get rid of Peron in Argentina, American states meeting at Rio de Janeiro in 1947 and Bogota in 1948 finally created the regional system. The Organization of American States (OAS), as the new organization was called, had a permanent council at the ambassadorial level, a permanent secretariat, periodic meetings, and the trappings of a regional collective security system designed to settle quarrels among its members before they reached the level of the United Nations.

As a well-intentioned attempt to reconcile the overwhelming postwar economic and military power and influence of the United States with the desires of Latin states to be politically independent and legally sovereign, the system could not help but come under severe strain. The late 1940s saw the disappearance of Latin American war-born trade surpluses and the development of much resentment about the resources the United States was devoting to Western Europe. The issue of lagging development came to the fore, along with an increasingly voiced view that in some form or another exploitation by the north was a reason for "underdevelopment."

One important change had become apparent by this time: before World War II, in the 1920s and the 1930s, the United States was one great power presence among several in Latin America. In the postwar period, the United States was virtually the only outside power with which Latin American countries had much contact. Before World War I, only 12 percent of Latin American exports went to the United States; after World War II, almost 50 percent did. U.S. investors replaced Europeans, the United States became the principal weapons supplier, and in international organizations the Latin American states were usually found supporting U.S. positions. Yet, while the American presence grew, engendering much hostility toward the crass and materialistic colossus of the north, many Latins also resented the fact that the United States directed most of its foreign policy attention elsewhere.

Conclusion

"How new will the better world be?" asked historian Carl Becker in 1945.[3] His own answer was, in essence, "not so very new or different." A cataclysmic event like World War II might rearrange the structure of power, but the new international institutions would leave intact the state-centered balance-of-power system, with all its potential for conflict and violence as well as cooperation, and this despite the presence of the one wholly new factor, the atomic bomb.

After six long years of war, people all over the world began to return to their homes or to settle in new localities, tried to rebuild their lives and their houses, and attempted to return to some semblance of normalcy. Governments—perhaps more aware of the major changes and of the difficulties that lay ahead—largely followed suit, seeking to end the war by peace treaties and to rebuild a structure that would restore the normal lives their people sought.

The euphoria in the West and in Russia brought by liberation and victory dissipated quickly. With large parts of Europe in ruins, reconstruction would be slow in the best of all possible circumstances, and the circumstances were not of the best: the beginnings of the division in Europe and the deliberate destruction of transportation systems in the course of the war slowed the resumption of necessary trade. Their industries in ruins, European countries had little to export to the United States to permit them to buy the export surplus of food and essential raw materials that this country alone could generate. In the Russian sphere of influence, Stalin began to consolidate his wartime gains while using millions of prisoners of war to start rebuilding the thousands of shattered towns and villages the German invasion had left in its wake. In China, Nationalist President Chiang Kai-shek moved to regain control of all of battered China; the Communists maneuvered to block him, and the Americans tried to mediate. Japan, its overseas empire gone, lay in ruins. But the U.S. occupation would be a benevolent one. In the meantime, the United States demobilized most of its enormous wartime armed forces as rapidly as it could manage to do, while pursuing plans to put atomic weapons under secure international control and to make the United Nations into a workable global system.

France and Holland tried to rebuild their ties to their empires. Britain tried to divest itself of major parts of the British Empire by granting them the Commonwealth status it had already granted to other segments. But all three of these countries, along with Belgium and Portugal, sought to maintain the ties of empire and something of a global role.

Meanwhile, the UN organization, that new guarantor of international peace and security, began to set up shop in New York and in Geneva, Switzerland, where it took over the remnants of the defunct League of Nations. Its beginnings were not auspicious, for it depended very much on Great Power consensus, and that consensus—shaken by the struggle over the peace treaties with former enemies—was about to break down completely. Moreover, negotiations over creation of the UN and over the peace treaties tended to divert attention from the most crucial change of all in the global system: a soon-to-be-reconstructed Soviet Union, whose power extended deep into central Europe, and a giant United States, untouched by wartime destruction, had emerged from the war incomparably stronger than any other nation in the world.

Notes

1. See Andreas Hillgruber, *Germany and the Two World Wars* (trans. William C. Kirby) (Cambridge: Harvard University Press, 1981).
2. James F. Byrnes, *Speaking Frankly* (New York: Harper and Brothers, 1947), p. 71.
3. Carl Becker, *How New Will the Better World Be?* (New York: Knopf, 1945), p. 1.

Further Suggested Readings

On wartime diplomacy one classic remains essential: Herbert Feis, *Churchill, Roosevelt, Stalin: The War They Waged and the Peace They Sought* (Princeton: Princeton University Press, 1957). More recent sources include one that focuses on Stalin's policies:

Vojtech Mastny, *Russia's Road to the Cold War: Diplomacy, Warfare, and the Politics of Communism* (New York: Columbia University Press, 1979). Robert James Maddox, in *Weapons for Victory: The Hiroshima Decision Fifty Years Later* (Columbia, MO: University of Missouri Press, 1995), reviews the controversy over the dropping of the atomic bomb and comes down strongly on one side. His references, however, are a useful further guide. An English review of the peacemaking is John Wheeler-Bennett and Anthony Nicholls, *The Semblance of Peace: The Political Settlement After the Second World War* (New York: St. Martin's Press, 1972). An important early reaction to the new atomic weapon is Bernard Brodie (ed.), *The Absolute Weapon* (New York: Harcourt, 1946). For a short, informed view of the creation of the United Nations, see the first two chapters of Inis Claude, *Swords into Plowshares*, 4th ed. (New York: Random House, 1971).

Part II

The World of the 1950s and the 1960s:
A Bipolar Structure and a
Third World Challenge

2

The Development of the Bipolar World

The first attempts to reconstruct the pre–World War II world between 1945 and 1947 failed. The Americans and the Europeans found themselves in bitter disagreements with the Soviet Union on many fronts. In 1947, prompted by threatened European economic collapse and a new assessment of Stalin's aims, the United States reversed a century and a half of foreign policy to assume a series of new commitments abroad—economic, political, and military—under the general policy of "containment." These commitments included a military guarantee to the security of Western Europe that is still in force nearly fifty years later, and subsequently a similar guarantee to Japan. A series of events brought a new appraisal of the structure of world power: consolidation of Soviet control over Eastern Europe, the Communist coup in Czechoslovakia, the blockade of Berlin, the triumph of Mao Zedong in China, Communist Party assertiveness throughout the world, and Soviet explosion of its own atom bomb in late 1949. In Europe, by 1950, reconstruction with large-scale American aid had finally begun to bear fruit and European leaders had taken the first halting steps toward unity. A more or less stable world, divided into two great blocs, appeared to have developed.

The shock of the North Korean attack upon South Korea in mid-1950 was therefore great, strengthening as it did a new view of Soviet/Communist aggressiveness: leaders in both Europe and the United States believed that the Cold War had become hot. Reluctantly, five years after the end of World War II, Western governments undertook a hasty rearmament in the face of what appeared to be a massive new Soviet threat. Polls showed that many people in the West feared a new world war would take place.

The worst did not happen. If anything, the presence of nuclear weapons seemed to have produced caution. Americans, however, frustrated by the realities of a containment policy that promised little but its own costly continuation, in 1952 elected a president, Dwight D. Eisenhower, who

promised a more vigorous policy than containment but also a cut in government expenditures based on a slowing down of hasty rearmament, as well
as peace in Korea.

Amid all this, the United Nations—that new hope for humankind—
struggled to survive, becoming in large part simply another theatre for Cold
War politics, where majorities legitimized Western containment policies but
where, also, some global concerns began to be articulated.

Iran, Turkey, and Greece: The Bipolar Balance Precipitated

The Soviet Union was the only power to make substantial territorial gains in
the war. In the immediate postwar years, Stalin also sought territorial increase at the expense of Iran and Turkey, and a Mediterranean role at the
expense of Turkey.

When Hitler attacked the Soviet Union in 1941, the Allies forced the
pro-Nazi shah of Iran to abdicate in favor of his son in order to establish a
supply route to Russia. The only alternative route was around the north of
Scandinavia to Murmansk, and Nazi submarines seemed to hover in every
fjord, ready to emerge and attack. The new shah signed a treaty with the
Soviets, who occupied the north, and with the British, in the south, reaffirm-
ing Iranian independence and promising withdrawal within six months after
the war. American armed services subsequently created an enormous base
and supply line to the Soviet Union through Iran.

In the last months of 1945, the Soviet Union sponsored the creation of a
separatist regime in the Soviet-occupied region of Azerbaijan and another in
Kurdish territory, kept Iranian troops from entering the areas, and maintained its own forces in the region after the deadline for withdrawal. To the
anger and embarrassment of Moscow, the shah's government brought the
matter to the newly created United Nations. Britain and the United States
appealed to the Soviets, whose price for withdrawal was an oil concession
in the north, the admission of several Communists to the Iranian cabinet,
and withdrawal of the Iranian complaint from the Security Council agenda.
Iran accepted and the Soviet troops withdrew. When the Iranian army reentered Azerbaijan province in December 1946, the rebel regime collapsed.
The next year the Iranian parliament refused to ratify the Iranian-Soviet oil
agreement. Stalin had gained little from the crisis, but he created suspicion
and ill will. (World War II, we should note, marked the beginning of an
American involvement with the shah that ultimately led to creation of the
present anti-Western fundamentalist regime and its view of the United
States as the "Great Satan.")

Stalin also created ill will in relation to Turkey, a country that had maintained a precarious Allied-supported neutrality in World War II. In February 1945, to gain admittance to the UN Conference, Turkey finally declared war on Germany. A triumphant Stalin, however, saw the opportunity to achieve the age-old Russian goal of access to the high seas from a warm-water port. He demanded a share in postwar control over the Dardanelles and the Bosporus strait—the passageway from the Black Sea to the Mediterranean—and the installation of Soviet military bases, along with cession of border areas of Kars and Ardahan and a revision of the border with Bulgaria, now Communist-controlled. The move, coupled with Soviet demands for a trusteeship over the former Italian colony of Libya, in North Africa, would have made the Soviet Union a Mediterranean power.

All through 1946, Moscow kept up the diplomatic offensive against Turkey. In the meantime, political developments in neighboring Greece and in Western Europe affected the situation. Greece, a poor country to begin with, was further impoverished by a brutal Nazi occupation, polarized politically with a well-organized Communist-led political grouping on one side—with its own guerrilla forces created to fight the Germans during the occupation—and ineffectual and divided political groupings on the other. Greek government existed only because British forces had supported government troops when civil war broke out in early 1945. (Stalin had agreed with Churchill that Greek affairs would be Britain's special responsibility). The Communist-led guerrillas, regrouped in the north, received aid and sanctuary from across the borders, from Yugoslavia, Albania, and Bulgaria.

It was Britain that had backed up Turkey against Russian expansion in the nineteenth century. It found itself doing so again, while continuing to aid an ineffectual and none-too-popular Greek government—and also facing enormous demands elsewhere in the world. Britain's resources were strained to the limit. The end of the war seemed only to have multiplied problems.

What seemed obvious was that Stalin was trying to take full advantage of British weakness. The probability was that the United States, with an inexperienced President Truman and an isolationist Congress, would not respond. The Soviet Union, at little cost and risk, would achieve age-old Russian ambitions in areas to its south and in the Middle East.

The British situation, moreover, differed only in degree, not in kind, from that of the rest of Western Europe.

The Weakness of Postwar Western Europe

Before the war, Western Europe essentially exported manufactured goods while importing raw materials and foodstuffs. Investments overseas that generated a part of its income for imports were liquidated during the war. Its export capacity was destroyed by the war; so were livestock, transportation systems, and stocks of foodstuffs. As a result, hunger and deprivation affected everyone in the early postwar years: the effort at reconstruction failed because of the very shortages reconstruction was aimed at eliminating.

Only the Americas, untouched by warfare, had an export surplus capacity. But wartime rationing in the United States and production for the armed forces had resulted in an enormous pent-up peacetime demand, and the question other world leaders faced was whether the United States would use some of its peacetime productive capacity to help restore a stable world order, or would insist that it be used for domestic consumption. (There was little question of needing export markets, as some recent writers have argued—and as Stalin thought, counting upon an American need to make him peacetime loans.)

The United States responded with several billion dollars in relief aid in the immediate aftermath of liberation, to both East and West. To avoid burdening the postwar trading world with a debt structure similar to that of the 1920s, it virtually canceled Lend-Lease debts incurred during the war. It was both a farsighted and, in the context of the times, a generous gesture. (Only the Soviet Union's $11 billion debt remained unresolved as a consequence of the growing tensions. Finally, in 1972, the Nixon Administration negotiated a solution, only to have the Congress torpedo it. See page 156). But "relief" was limited and inadequate.

The particularities of the British situation led the Truman Administration to consider one major measure that foreshadowed the future: a loan of almost $4 billion to put Britain back on its feet. The loan was proposed in late 1945, but its passage was secured only after seven months of congressional debate, for Congress questioned the rationale behind it in a way that reveals that Americans were by no means certain of what America's postwar role should be. The administration viewed it as a loan that would enable Britain to continue to play a major role. Like other Western European countries, Britain had once been a giant creditor, but was now a major debtor. To pay its debts (primarily to Commonwealth countries that had funded its war effort), it needed to export more than it imported, yet it had little export capacity. Tight wartime rationing remained in effect to limit consumption. The loan, planners hoped, would help Britain reestablish its export capacity, make possible the elimination of import restrictions and currency controls (as the Bretton Woods system envisaged—and Bretton Woods was viewed as crucial to the postwar system), and enable the country to continue to support its commitments in the Middle East and in Asia.

The loan passed, though not by an overwhelming majority. The difficulty in securing its passage reveals two things. The first is why the administration never really considered a large-scale postwar loan to the Soviet Union. It was hard enough to get one for England, but no Congress would have passed a Soviet loan in the face of Soviet activities in Eastern Europe and the Middle East, particularly since administration advisers who knew Russia cautioned that such a loan would have no effect on Stalin's present hostile policies. The second is that Congress was far from convinced that the United States needed to commit resources to the global leadership role it was being asked to play.

The British loan and other piecemeal credits and the resources of the International Monetary Fund (IMF) and the International Bank for Reconstruction and Development (IBRD) were insufficient to cope with Europe's desperate and worsening economic situation. When the winter of 1947 struck, the stark realities became apparent. It was the worst winter in recent memory. Winter crops were lost. Canals froze, blizzards blocked railroads, and countries ran out of the coal that fueled industry and electrical utilities. States needed dollars for imports of necessities, and they had none. France, desperate for American grain and coal, nevertheless had to cut all dollar imports and institute two days a week without electricity. Britain banned all foreign travel and arbitrarily cut imports by 25 percent. It appeared the British government might well have to withdraw from Greece, Turkey, and the Middle East; withdraw from its occupation zone in Germany and Austria; hasten its departure from Asia; default on its debts; and institute even more rigid controls.

The full effect of the war, of the results of the attempt at German hegemony, were now revealed: the Europe that had so long dominated the world faced utter collapse, and no one was sure of what this would mean—particularly in the face of the Soviet Union's pressures on Turkey, as well as Communist Party and guerrilla activities elsewhere.

America's New Course: "Containment"

On February 21, 1947, two months after General George C. Marshall became secretary of state, the British ambassador delivered to the U.S. State Department a note which, in effect, declared Britain's inability to continue the stabilizing role it had played in the eastern Mediterranean area for the past century. It would be unable to meet the needs of the Greek government after March 31, and could no longer provide resources for the maintenance and reequipment of the Turkish army or aid to strengthen its economy. The ambassador further expressed the hope that the American government would "agree to bear the financial burden of which the major part has hitherto been borne by His Majesty's Government."

Suddenly, everything seemed to gel. At the end of the war in Europe, a dominant American view had been that the United States would have to mediate between Britain and the Soviet Union; Churchill's "Iron Curtain" speech in early 1946, suggesting an Anglo-American front, had been met with considerable hostility. After all, spheres of interest and balance-of-power politics had been supposed to disappear in the new UN era. In subsequent months, however, a long telegram had arrived in Washington from a then-obscure Soviet specialist in the United States' Moscow Embassy, George F. Kennan, analyzing Moscow's aims and tactics. Kennan had suggested that the internal dynamics of the Stalinist system dictated a constant probing for weak spots on the Soviet periphery, which should be met with firmness. Eventually, internal developments in the Soviet Union would lead it to desist. Impressed Washington personnel had circulated this telegram widely. It seemed to put into focus events not only in Europe but throughout the rest of the Eurasian periphery. The British note, coming hard on the heels of Kennan's telegram, appeared to corroborate all that he had said. The United States should step into the breach, should balance Soviet power. George Kennan came to be viewed as the author of the new, overall principle of American foreign policy, "containment."

The Truman Doctrine

The result was the Truman Doctrine, the first broad statement of containment. In a dramatic speech to a joint session of Congress, the president declared that it should be the duty of the United States "to support free peoples who are resisting attempted subjugation by armed minorities or by outside countries," and he asked for an appropriation of $400 million for aid to Greece and Turkey.

Ensuing debate revealed that congressmen still did not think in balance-of-power terms. The attack came from right and from left: this was another proposal to pull more British chestnuts out of the fire; it was sloganizing about "free peoples" and sustaining democracy, when neither Greece nor Turkey was very democratic; it represented a retrogression to the power politics that had characterized the European system; and the proposal would divide the world into two armed camps and bypass the United Nations, and would lead to intervention in Greek and Turkish affairs. In a real sense, all this was quite true. Administration spokesmen, however, invoked the shadow of Munich and appeasement in the 1930s: without U.S. aid, the whole Middle East might fall. After acrimonious debate, the Congress approved the program along with several other interim aid packages, but it served notice on the administration that a piecemeal approach was not enough. It needed a clearer statement of overall foreign policy. It never quite got that, but it soon got the next steps—the Marshall Plan and the North Atlantic Treaty.

Again, events hastened the onset of new policy. In Moscow, for reasons already discussed, the Foreign Ministers' meeting of March and April 1947 to draft German and Austrian peace treaties had broken up. Germany, for the foreseeable future, remained divided between east and west. And open Soviet intervention to destroy precarious Hungarian democracy began that spring and continued through the summer.

The Marshall Plan

Still, it came as a surprise when, on June 5, 1947, at Harvard commencement ceremonies, Secretary of State George C. Marshall delivered an address that launched the European Recovery Program, immortalized as the Marshall Plan, and called by Winston Churchill "the greatest act of creative statesmanship of modern time."

Marshall reviewed the imbalance between what European countries needed to import and the little they could earn through exports, described U.S. interest in seeing the gap filled—the alternative would be "economic, social, and political deterioration of a very grave character"—and then went on to add that the policy was "directed not against any country or doctrine but against hunger, poverty, desperation, and chaos." The speech appeared to allow for Soviet and Eastern European participation in the new venture, in which, if the European countries cooperated in developing a joint reconstruction plan, pooling their productive resources and needs, the United States would finance the gap.

European leaders reacted immediately. British Foreign Minister Ernie Bevin, who heard excerpts of the speech over the radio, said later, "I don't mind saying that as I listened, tears came to my eyes. For the first time I saw a ray of hope for Europe." Bevin and French Foreign Minister Georges Bidault invited Soviet Foreign Minister V.M. Molotov to Paris to consider how to respond to the American offer. They—like many Americans—still hoped the Russians and the East Europeans would participate. A joint economic plan could bridge the widening gap, demonstrate to Stalin the benefits of a cooperative relationship, and maintain vital prewar economic ties between Western European countries and those in the East, whose coal, grain, and petroleum the Westerners had long depended on. But Stalin refused.

The temptation to participate must have been great; Stalin's government had once acknowledged that American material aid during World War II was enormous and possibly crucial (though in later accounts it was always denigrated). But the possibilities must have been outweighed by negative features of the proposal: a joint venture would have involved revealing many aspects of the Soviet economy and might have weakened Moscow's hold over Eastern Europe; and success might well have weakened the appeal of Communist Parties in the West. In any event, the Soviet Union subsequently aimed its enormous propaganda apparatus against the Marshall Plan, created the Communist Information Bureau (Cominform) in Poland, blasted the plan as thoroughly exploitative, and scolded the Italian and French Communist Parties for not having seized power when they presumably could have done so. The breach now appeared to be complete: when a conference of European countries convened in Paris only two weeks later, at the invitation of the British and the French, to draft a reply to the Americans, the Eastern European countries—including Finland and Czechoslovakia—failed to appear. Their presence had been forbidden by Moscow.

The Communist coup in Czechoslovakia in February 1948 (see page 51), Communist-led strikes and riots in France designed to get the party back into the government from which it had been ousted earlier, and the prospects of a strong showing by the Italian Communist Party in forthcoming elections, all strengthened the administration's capacity to appeal to Congress, where intense battles took place over innumerable aspects of the proposal. Ultimately, in April 1948 the Congress authorized a four-year program of expenditures, called the European Recovery Program (ERP); created the European Cooperation Administration (ECA) under industrialist Paul Hoffman, to carry it out from the American side; and appropriated $6 billion for the first year.

Enabling legislation specified that the aim of the act was to encourage unification of Europe. Hoffman spelled this out:

> The long-range goal . . . was the effective integration of the economy of Western Europe—the building of a single market of 270 million consumers, in which quantitative restrictions on the movement of goods, monetary barriers to the flow of payments and eventually all tariffs should be permanently swept away.

The model was the powerful and wealthy United States of America. Only because it was a continental economy with no internal barriers to trade had it been able to mount a massive war effort, carry on a war in Europe and in the Pacific, and provide crucial aid to the Soviet Union. European leaders began to share Hoffman's view that creation of a similar European market was the key to European recovery, to an eventual regaining of European influence in the world.

Over the next forty years, Europeans would still be working at creating a genuine common market. But the ERP laid the groundwork of cooperation that led to creation of the European Economic Community (EEC) much later, reintroducing multilateral trade and payments. It also spurred an extraordinary recovery: by 1950, industrial production had increased by 50 percent over 1947 and exceeded the 1938 level by a quarter, while agricultural production surpassed the prewar average. The ERP helped to restore to Europeans a measure of confidence in their own future that encouraged planning and investment. When German reconstruction became widely accepted as essential to other European economies, it stimulated French master planner Jean Monnet to devise plans to integrate German industrial production into that of Europe, so that Europeans would no longer fear German industrial might as a base for military power. The ERP laid solid foundations for the future.

The North Atlantic Treaty Organization

The American commitment to Europe unfolded gradually. The year 1947 produced the Truman Doctrine, aid to Greece and Turkey, and the Marshall Plan, and 1948 produced the North Atlantic Treaty. The North Atlantic Treaty represented the reversal of a century and a half of American policy of what President Thomas Jefferson had called "no entangling alliances." The impetus came not from the United States, but from Europe, where public figures—especially British Foreign Minister Ernie Bevin—called for an American military guarantee to balance perceived Soviet power.

Two crucial events ensured American participation: the Czechoslovak coup of February 1948 and the Berlin blockade.

Czechoslovakia appeared to be more Western than the Eastern European countries, and Czechs as well as Westerners continued to see Czechoslovakia as a sort of bridge between East and West that might survive the Cold War. But under direct Soviet pressure in February 1948 a domestic political crisis that had festered for several months was turned into a Communist coup d'état. Foreign Minister Jan Masaryk, son of the founder of Czech democracy, who had hoped to keep Czechoslovakia independent by carefully cultivating good relations with the Soviet Union, was found dead in the courtyard of the Foreign Ministry. He had either committed suicide, as the official version had it, or been assassinated, as most Czechs believed.

Western powers were simply not prepared to take any action. For many old socialists in the West, however, and for many who had tried to find security excuses for the brutality of Soviet foreign policy, the Czech coup was a major turning point in their assessment of the Soviet Union and Stalin.

The "Berlin Blockade" also hardened Western opinion. Reconstruction of Western Europe required some measure of reconstruction of Germany. Creation of common governmental organs for the western zones of Germany, and a common zonal currency led Moscow to try to force the West to abandon the project. Soviet forces began to harass train and truck traffic in and out of Berlin in the spring of 1948, and cut off all land communication in late June. The American commandant, General Lucius D. Clay, arguing that the Soviets were trying to squeeze the Western powers out, declared that loss of the city would lead to the loss of a Western Europe that would lose its nerve.

Instead, under American leadership, the Western powers organized an amazing airlift to the besieged city, pressing every available airplane into the hazardous operation. The airlift allowed West Berliners to eke out an existence through the winter of 1948–49.

From the point of view of Moscow, the brutal blockade was a bad mistake. Rather than delaying the creation of the West German Republic, the blockade speeded it up; perhaps most important, it eased the Truman Administration's task in securing Senate approval of American commitment to Western European defense and reconstruction. On April 4, 1949, eleven countries signed the North Atlantic Pact, and two years later Greece and Turkey were admitted to membership.

It was a historic event for Western Europeans and for Americans. Twice in the twentieth century, France and England had almost succumbed to a German challenge. Each time the United States had stood on the sidelines for several years, and the Allies had managed to defeat the Germans only when American weight was thrown into the scales. Now they faced the power of the Soviet Union and Stalin; the United States would be with them from the start, and the Soviet Union's understanding of this would—they hoped—guarantee that it would not be tempted. Despite attacks by senators on the power of the president, as commander-in-chief, to move troops around, Truman and his successors satisfied the Europeans by keeping American divisions in Europe: the United States would automatically be in the line of fire. The American troops were a hostage given to the Europeans to guarantee there could be no American equivocation.

In subsequent months, Congress also approved the first military aid to Western Europe for strengthening European armies, and the new Allies created the unprecedented, elaborate peacetime North Atlantic Treaty Organization (NATO), with its Supreme Headquarters outside Paris, with its joint regional commands, and with its ability to coordinate military policies. In 1951 General Dwight D. Eisenhower was named the first Supreme Allied Commander, Europe.

Europe was thus the focus of the revolution in American foreign policy.

In Truman's inaugural address of January 1949, after his completely unexpected upset victory over Republican Thomas Dewey, the president also paid some attention to the rest of the world, declaring, as a fourth point of his program for the future, that the United States should embark on a "bold new program for making the benefits of [its] scientific advances and industrial progress available for the improvement and growth of underdeveloped areas." This was the halting beginning of what would become a permanent effort and commitment, parallel to that already begun by France and England in their colonial possessions and by the United Nations and the International Bank. A century or so earlier, there had been little differential in wealth between countries. The nineteenth and twentieth centuries had brought enormous increases in Western productivity and production, built on the developments of the previous several centuries, thus creating for the first time in human history rich and poor nations, side by side and visible to each other. Various analysts offered different explanations for the development, and different prescriptions for what should be done about it, but Truman's "Point Four Program," as it came to be called, was an acknowledgment that the wealthier nations had a duty toward the poorer ones.

The Soviet Bloc: Coordination and Conflict

While Western Europe and the United States thus strengthened their own ties and began to rebuild their economies jointly, the Soviet Union, in its very different way, created its own bloc, finding loyal, local Communists whom it could confirm in power over an often all-too-reluctant population. Stalin felt his way cautiously, exploring how far he could go and what actions on his part might provoke a Western response. Despite what many Westerners asserted, he had no "master plan." Even so, in a fairly short span of time, opposition parties in Eastern European countries were destroyed; leaders were imprisoned or exiled; and an iron control was exerted through party, bureaucracy, army, and secret police.

Stalin responded to the creation of the European Recovery Program with creation of the Cominform and the Council for Mutual Economic Assistance (CMEA, or Comecon). The Cominform provided a sort of cover for Soviet dictation to other parties, designed to make it appear that the socialist countries took decisions jointly. The Council for Mutual Economic Assistance had a checkered career. In Stalin's time, while the Cominform propagandized about America's exploitation of Western Europe through the Marshall Plan, CMEA imposed terms of trade so clearly exploitative that they helped lead to the Communist bloc explosions of the mid-1950s, and had to be renegotiated in order to maintain any unity. Subsequently, trying to coordinate production and trade within the Communist bloc on the basis of a "socialist division of labor" that would have largely reserved high technology and heavy industrial production to Russia, CMEA would run into increasingly nationalist resistance.

Finally, in the eyes of many Westerners, the Communist bloc expanded enormously in 1949, when the People's Republic of China was proclaimed by Mao Zedong in Peking (see below). Mao traveled to Moscow to sign the Treaty of Friendship, Alliance, and Mutual Assistance; to negotiate a $300 million loan; and to receive several concessions concerning Soviet rights in the Far East. (Mao also accepted joint stock companies in fields such as aviation and mineral and petroleum extraction, similar to those through which the Soviet Union dominated the economies of Eastern European countries.) At about the same time—in September 1949—the Soviet Union carried out its first atomic explosion. There was consternation in the West about what this would mean for the future, particularly in the light of Western strategies of containment and reliance upon the American atomic bomb as a counter to superior Soviet conventional armed forces.*

Titoism in Yugoslavia

While Moscow organized and strengthened its bloc, Stalin made Communist Parties outside its sphere jump through the hoops. French Communist leader Maurice Thorez declared publicly that if Russian troops moved west, he would greet them in France as liberators and with open arms; but his comrade Jacques Duclos confessed in later years that he cried with impotent rage when lectured at Cominform meetings about how he had missed the opportunity to seize power at the time of liberation. It was a time, after all, when Anglo-American armies were still in France and he had to obey Moscow's injunctions to cooperate so as not to break up wartime unity. In 1948, however, Josip Broz Tito, Communist leader of a war-torn Balkan state comprising sixteen million people of different nationalities, defied Stalin, hunted down Stalin supporters, and dared the Soviet Union to do its worst—and Stalin failed to overthrow him.

The break was not clearly understood at the time, since Tito clung to a hope of reconciliation. Tito's crime was an intolerable degree of indepen-

---

*Russian scientists revealed in 1993 that the bomb exploded in 1949 was a copy of the early American bomb, produced thanks in part to espionage. Two years later they exploded their own, more sophisticated bomb, twice as powerful and much lighter. Revelations that Communist Party members in the West had been recruited for espionage contributed to anti-Communist "hysteria," especially in the United States.

dence in domestic and foreign policy. Stalin appears to have miscalculated, thinking that an appeal to Yugoslavs and anathema from the other Cominform states would get rid of Tito and his cohort. Soviet leader Nikita Khrushchev later reported Stalin as having said, "I will shake my little finger—and there will be no more Tito." He therefore took no military action. Tito—stoutly maintaining his Communist purity—turned to the United States for support, and received both military and economic aid, thus demonstrating that anti-Communism was not the main force behind American foreign policy, but that, instead, balance-of-power considerations were of primary importance.

One result of the break was that numerous other Communist leaders in other East European states were ruthlessly hunted down and executed as "Titoists." Tito might profess his Communism, but, "objectively," Titoism strengthened the capitalists against the socialist bloc. Titoism, however, continued to attract people who wanted socialism without Soviet Russian domination. (Ironically, in the light of the breakup of Yugoslavia forty years later, many Third World leaders in the 1960s and the 1970s looked to Yugoslavia as a model, and its diplomats played an important role in forging Third World unity at the United Nations.)

A further consequence was the collapse of the Greek guerrilla movement, which could not operate without outside support.

The Far East Front Stage

In the immediate postwar years, American and Soviet attention tended to focus on Europe, since events there essentially shaped the new bipolar world. Crises erupted in the Middle East and in South Asia and Southeast Asia, but appeared—for the time—to be removed from the center of world conflict. (These will be recounted in chapter 4.) The Far East was different: The United States, essentially, had entered World War II over Japanese refusal to withdraw from China. In 1945 the United States found itself occupying Japan and half of Korea, with Soviet Russian troops in the north and in Manchuria. So it was that the continuation of conflict in China following the defeat of Japan was a matter of great concern.

Communism in China and War in Korea

The Communists in the north and the Nationalist government, while nominally allied in their fight against the Japanese invader, had spent much of their energy in maneuvering against each other for postwar advantage.

For a year, as the war drew to a close, the two parties negotiated formation of a coalition government. Each, however, wanted terms that would keep the other from taking it over, and the talks failed. The United States remained committed to supporting the Nationalists and to helping them to move into areas vacated by Japanese troops, but numerous American observers were convinced that the Communists might well win in any all-out struggle: years of fighting both civil war and war against the Japanese had sapped Nationalist capacity—and will—to carry out necessary reforms. As a result, in November 1945, President Truman dispatched General George C. Marshall as his personal representative to try to bring about unification and cessation of hostilities. General Marshall brought with him the distinction of having been chief of staff of the victorious American armies, as well as his immense personal prestige. All this availed him nothing: fourteen months later he announced the termination of his efforts and returned to the United States to become secretary of state. In July 1947, the Nationalists, having moved into the north in force, proclaimed the Communists outlaws—whereupon the initiative passed over to the better organized though much smaller Communist forces, which benefited from public resentment directed against the Nationalist government and its overextended, unruly, unpaid troops. Within two years, a gradual Nationalist retreat became a rout, and in the autumn of 1949 Chiang Kai-shek ferried as much of his army as he could to the island of Formosa (Taiwan), ninety miles from the mainland. Most people expected that his demoralized and ill-equipped forces on the island would soon suffer defeat at the hands of an invading— or a liberating—Communist army.

In the interim, Mao Zedong proclaimed the existence of the People's Republic of China, with its capital in the ancient imperial city of Peking. He also firmly aligned China with the Soviet bloc. His victory brought a dramatic change to Asia: the Communist bloc now bordered troubled areas like Burma and Indochina, extended as far as the poorly defined border with India, put the future of Formosa in doubt as Communist troops massed across from the island, and brought fear to Japan. Only six months later, on June 25, 1950, North Korean troops rolled across the frontier into South Korea in what the neutral United Nations Commission on Korea called "an act of aggression initiated without warning and without provocation in execution of a carefully prepared plan."

Recent sources show that Mao and Stalin supported it, although North Korean leader Kim Il Sung planned it. The impact of victory of the Chinese Communists in China a year earlier was an important factor. In the United States it brought reassessment of both American aims and American capacities in the Far East, as well as an orgy of blame that would color American politics until the time of President Richard Nixon, twenty years later. The

Truman Administration and the Democratic Party were tarred by Republican spokesmen as having "lost China," as having succumbed to pro-Communist influence in the State Department, and as having been "soft on Communism"—despite the revolution in American foreign policy toward Europe they had engineered. The administration had had few resources to use in influencing the situation in China; Congress had been niggardly, and *total* military appropriations in the years before Korea had been kept in the $11–$14 billion range.

So it was that Secretary of State Dean Acheson made a January 1950 speech defining the American defense perimeter as *excluding* both South Korea and Taiwan. In April 1950 Stalin urged the North Koreans on, expecting only a minimal response from the United States, since Acheson had declared that countries outside the perimeter would have to depend upon their own resources and upon the United Nations. In the event, the administration hurriedly changed its mind. Taking advantage of Soviet absence from the United Nations Security Council, it responded by immediately obtaining Security Council recommendations for aid to South Korea, for putting all military units under unified command with a UN flag, and for authorizing the United States to appoint a UN commander. Truman named General Douglas MacArthur Supreme Commander and authorized him to use American ground forces, to blockade the Korean coast, and to bomb targets in North Korea. Five years after the end of World War II, the United States was once more at war—though without calling it war. It was a "UN Police Action."

The decision to resist in Korea was not an easy one. The strongest argument in favor of action was simple: if the United States did not stand by South Korea, people in other areas would have no faith in American commitments. "Credibility" of American commitments had become the major issue. Republican charges that the Truman Administration had been "soft on Communism" undoubtedly played a part, although administration officials denied it.

While this flurry of activity took place in New York and Washington, the North Koreans swept down the peninsula, driving all before them. In short order they pushed the weak resisting forces, along with small British units rushed from Hong Kong, into a small pocket on the southeast tip of the Korean peninsula. American personnel were rushed to the Far East, and on September 15, 1950, General MacArthur effected an audacious and successful amphibious landing 150 miles to the north, on the west coast at Inchon, while simultaneously launching an attack from the perimeter in the south. Within days the whole situation changed radically. Enormous numbers of North Korean prisoners were taken and the rest pushed back toward

Map 4. **The Korean Conflict**

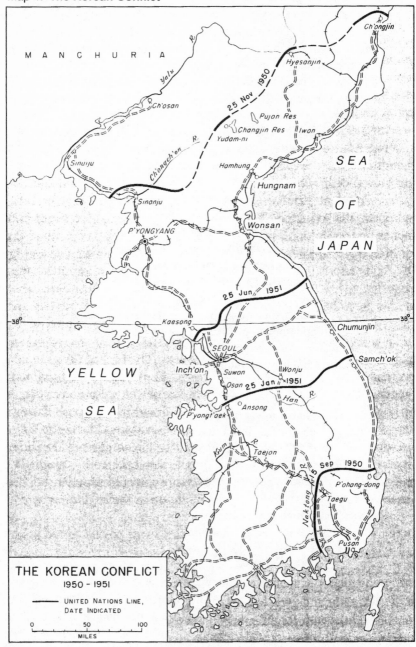

Source: Maurice Matloff, ed., *American Military History* (Washington, DC: Office of the Chief of Military History, United States Army, 1969).

the north. The war had entered a new phase. (In all, under UN auspices, forty-five countries contributed troops or supplies or transport. But nine-tenths of the non-Korean troops in action were American. It was less an example of collective security than one of balance-of-power politics with a fig leaf of UN legitimacy.)

Policy on China changed, too. The uneasy administration had been ready to let Formosa fall and to seek a means to establish diplomatic relations with an openly hostile but victorious People's Republic of China. It now reversed course: as Truman ordered American soldiers into Korea, he also ordered the American Seventh Fleet into the Formosa straits to protect the Chiang regime. To the president—if not to American allies—it all seemed part and parcel of a response to Communist aggression. To the Chinese, it was an open and aggressive interference in the Chinese civil war. In the face of the American action, the Chinese halted their buildup opposite Formosa and began to move troops north, near Korea.

Despite warnings presented in Chinese leaders' speeches and delivered through India's ambassador in Peking, MacArthur's troops pursued the retreating North Koreans across the thirty-eighth parallel—the dividing line between North Korea and South Korea—authorized to do so by the Truman Administration, and ultimately, if ambiguously, by the UN General Assembly. The General Assembly had reaffirmed its desire for a "unified, independent, democratic Korea" and recommended that steps be taken to "insure conditions of stability throughout Korea." UN forces under MacArthur's command were to stay just long enough to achieve these objectives. To transform the anticipated military success into political reality, the Assembly created the UN Commission for Unification and Rehabilitation of Korea. On October 15, 1950, President Truman flew to Wake Island in the Pacific to meet with MacArthur, who told him that there was little danger of Chinese intervention and that he would be free to transfer one division from Korea to the real trouble spot—Western Europe—by the end of January.

China Enters the War: The Risk of World War III

On November 24, 1950, MacArthur launched an offensive with the announced intention of ending the war and bringing back his Eighth Army to Japan by Christmas. Two days later an enormous Chinese force counterattacked, splitting MacArthur's forces and sending them back down the peninsula in a headlong, though orderly, retreat.

Mao had hesitated, although Stalin had promised him air cover (a promise on which he later reneged). But Stalin had urged Mao on in a telegram sent on October 7, telling him that if war between the blocs was inevitable "then let it be waged now," rather than later, when the Western bloc would have gathered strength. He believed the Communist bloc could win a "World War III."

MacArthur, rallying his exhausted troops, insisted that the new war called for expanded measures: the bombing of Chinese bases in Manchuria, a blockade of the China coast, and the use of Chiang Kai-shek's army on Formosa to attack the mainland. The Truman Administration and its allies wanted to keep the war limited, justifiably worried about where a more general war might lead, especially given Western vulnerability in Europe and the new factor of Soviet possession of the atomic bomb. UN troops rallied in the meantime and began to move slowly back northward, inflicting heavy casualties on the Chinese. But MacArthur sought to build public support through Congress for his ideas, and an exasperated Truman was forced to relieve him of his command and replace him with the able General Matthew B. Ridgway.

For a brief moment, General MacArthur basked in the limelight back in the United States, receiving a hero's welcome and addressing a joint session of Congress in an emotional speech. In the final analysis, however, Congress was unwilling to see the war extended, with all the domestic consequences this would entail and the foreign ones it might bring. Other participating states also counseled strongly against such a move. Ridgway began a grinding war of attrition to force the Chinese into negotiation, while the United States coerced the UN General Assembly into branding the Chinese Communists as aggressors. Countries like India, which had supported the initial UN action and provided an ambulance corps, now demurred: the United Nations had received ample warning of what would happen if it moved into the Communist sphere in the north, and U.S. action in the Taiwan straits was a clear interference in Chinese domestic affairs. Branding the Communists as aggressors would only make negotiations difficult.

Nevertheless, the military pressures brought the Chinese to the negotiating table. Armistice talks dragged on for two years while China used every propaganda device possible to discredit the United States and its allies; for the People's Republic of China, the United States was now *the* enemy.

July 1953 finally brought an armistice, as a result of military pressure, the economic impact of the war, Indian efforts at securing compromise, and—perhaps also—discreet threats of use of nuclear weapons and of a widening of the war by the newly elected Eisenhower Administration. Korea has remained divided ever since, and American troops have remained for over forty years to deter the North.

The Impact of Korea and Western Rearmament

Until 1950 the Cold War appeared to involve primarily a hardening of the blocs created by defeat of the Axis powers in World War II—unwelcome, to be deplored, but certainly a lesser evil than war. Even the coup in Czechoslovakia could be seen in these terms. China's firm alignment with the Communist bloc caused more of a shock, since it had not been within the Soviet sphere (and most Americans saw the matter in terms of an extension of Russian influence, though the reality was more ambiguous; the term "Sino-Soviet bloc" came into wide use in Washington). But the war in Korea changed everything: in the West it was widely viewed as portending an overall revolution in Communist strategy and tactics, a willingness to use force and to risk a major war. This view was buttressed by the intensification of warfare by Communist guerrillas in French Indochina, Malaysia, and a series of other uprisings in Asia that seemed to have been orchestrated by a Moscow-sponsored meeting of Asian Communist Parties at Calcutta in 1948.

Truman's State Department had already made a new assessment of the world situation and the American role in early 1950, in what became a famous (and to some a notorious) document, NSC 68 (National Security Council memorandum #68). The document portrayed an expansionist Soviet Union, ready to use force if necessary, likely to make a surprise nuclear attack unless faced with a strong retaliatory capacity. To deter the Soviets it would be necessary to face them with well-armed alliances on their periphery, able to hold them off until the United States could come to its allies' aid. It required therefore a sharp increase in American military appropriations, both for air-atomic striking power and for conventional forces, from the current $13–$14 billion a year to $35 billion. Nineteen hundred and fifty-four was the "danger year," when the Soviet military buildup would put the world at risk.

In the spring of 1950, however, the Truman Administration and a number of military men felt no such American spending increase was either politically or economically feasible. Korea resolved all doubts. In the United States, congressional appropriations for both the war and a broad overall increase in military strength soared, and economic aid to Western Europe was rapidly replaced by military aid for a North Atlantic Treaty Organization (NATO) buildup. In short order, NATO created its system of unified commands and a network of supply, communication, and airfield facilities scattered throughout Europe. By 1953, it could field a respectable number of well-armed divisions; in 1952, despite objections from some members, Greece and Turkey with their additional twenty divisions became members of NATO. (For a brief period, Communist Yugoslavia became virtually a member by entering through the back door: it joined Greece and Turkey in a Balkan defense pact just as they entered NATO; their commitment to Yugoslavia would therefore entail a NATO commitment. But the Balkan Pact died soon after, with the death of Stalin.)

In 1954, to make up for manpower shortages, NATO decided on deployment of "miniaturized" atomic weapons for battlefield use (so-called tactical nuclear weapons in the form of artillery shells, short-range missiles, and bombs that could be carried by fighter-attack planes). Even in limited war, the use of these weapons would cause tremendous devastation in Western Europe; but the Soviet Union also deployed such weapons, so the Western ones stayed, to bedevil relations in the future.

The Creation of West Germany

Another solution to the manpower issue was equally simple—or equally complicated: include German manpower in defense of the West. To Europeans who had suffered at the hands of the Wehrmacht only a few years earlier, the idea was hard to swallow when it was first floated in 1950. For four years the idea was sidetracked by a French idea for a European army—the European Defense Community (EDC)—in which small units including German contingents would be integrated, so that there would be no national armies. In the final analysis, after years of negotiation and agonizing, and strong pressure for ratification from Eisenhower's secretary of state, John Foster Dulles, it was the French who rejected the project in 1954. The Germans used other countries' need for German manpower to extract concessions, and the upshot in 1955 was, in addition to the creation of German armed forces, full sovereignty for West Germany. But Germany renounced the right to build atomic, chemical, and biological weapons, as well as such strategic weapons as missiles or long-range bombers. An organization called the "Western European Union," created for the Brussels Treaty Organization in 1948, was revived to monitor the arms limits clauses of the treaty. In May 1955, with NATO ratification secured, the occupation of West Germany ended, occupation troops became NATO troops, Allied High Commissioners became ambassadors, and the German Federal Republic came into existence.

A week later the eight states of Eastern Europe signed the Warsaw Treaty, creating their counterpart to NATO, with joint command headquarters in Moscow, where a drumbeat of propaganda against the Western moves had been kept up. Moscow denounced the treaties of friendship and alliance it had signed with Britain in 1942 and France in 1944, and announced that the Warsaw Pact was necessary because "West Germany is

being turned into a bridgehead for deployment of large aggressive forces."
(It is clear now—see page 74—that following Stalin's death in 1953 a
debate occurred in the Soviet Union about whether withdrawal of occupation forces and the creation of a neutral unified Germany could be envisaged. Western leaders feared it would mean a withdrawal of American
troops beyond the Atlantic, while Soviet troops would still be stationed
nearby, in Eastern Europe, and few ever wanted to explore the possibility.)

Japan

The Korean War also had a long-lasting effect on neighboring Japan. The
Japanese islands served as a staging area for the Americans in Korea, and
American expenditures and procurement helped move the country from a
period of postwar depression and slow, painful reconstruction into one of
rapid growth that made it an economic superpower thirty years later, despite—or perhaps because of—its loss of empire. The war also convinced
the Truman Administration to sign a peace treaty with Japan in September
1951, ending its occupied status; however, the treaty was accompanied by a
security agreement allowing America to retain bases in Japan in exchange
for a guarantee of American protection. It set Japan on the long road to
respectability in the international community. The Japanese even established diplomatic relations with the Soviet Union in 1956, in spite of territorial disagreements persisting to this day. At the same time they gained
admission to the United Nations.

In pursuit of the policy outlined in NSC 68, the United States also signed
mutual defense treaties with the Philippines and with New Zealand and
Australia, creating the Australia, New Zealand, and U.S. grouping
(ANZUS). The United States had been the one power able to shield the
latter two countries from Imperial Japan in World War II. China's accession
to the Soviet bloc, the Korean and Indochinese wars, and the instability of
the newly independent countries to the north all gave impetus to the move.

The Impact of Nuclear Weapons and the Failure of
International Control

When the first atomic explosion took place at Alamogordo, New Mexico,
on July 16, 1945, with the war still on, all those responsible for it felt awe at
what they had achieved. Robert Oppenheimer, one of the key players in
bomb development, thought of a line from the Hindu scripture, the
Bhagavad-Gita: "Now I am become Death, the destroyer of worlds." Another nuclear physicist, James Finney Baxter, declared that the bomb "had

blasted the web of history and, like the discovery of fire, severed the past from the present." The state system, in other words, was outmoded.

The first two atomic bombs, dropped upon Hiroshima and Nagasaki, brought a rapid end to the war. Scientists who worked on the atomic project did so with an urgency resulting from the feeling they were in a race with Germany. Once Germany was defeated, some agonized over use of the bomb against Japan, but Japanese determination to fight to the last man, evinced by the incredible casualties in the taking of the islands of Iwo Jima and Okinawa, convinced the Truman Administration that there was no question about using the bomb.* Another issue that arose at this time was what to do about nuclear weapons: they could not be disinvented, and the "secret" could not long be kept. Science ultimately knows no boundaries.

To many observers and participants, some form of international control seemed essential. Others, however, convinced that any authority accepted by the Soviets would mean that they could pervert it to their own uses, and sure that the American monopoly would be a long-lasting one, preferred trying to maintain the American monopoly. In November 1945, Canada, the United States, and the United Kingdom issued a formal declaration in favor of some form of internationalization. But in the face of events in Eastern Europe, the Anglo-Americans decided to keep control of the weapons until such time as a thoroughly trustworthy and competent international authority could be established. Lengthy negotiations, carried out against the background of the growing Cold War, bogged down and ultimately failed utterly.

The American "Baruch Plan" of June 1946 proposed to establish an "International Atomic Development Authority" to which would be entrusted "managerial control or ownership of all atomic energy activities potentially dangerous to world security" as well as the "power to control, inspect and license all other atomic activities." This authority would itself be "the world's leader in the field of atomic knowledge and development." To this radical proposal to separate atomic matters from national sovereignty, Moscow answered with a suggestion for immediate prohibition of the use, production, and accumulation of atomic weapons and for the de-

---

*Since Gar Alperovitz first published his pioneering work *Atomic Diplomacy: Hiroshima and Potsdam* (1965; revised eds. 1985, 1994), revisionists have argued that the bombs were dropped in order to bring pressure on Moscow. More plausible is the argument that the decision by the British and the Americans to work on the bomb together without including the Russians contributed to postwar difficulties. Yet it could not have been otherwise. Churchill had insisted upon a signed agreement with Roosevelt that secrecy would be preserved. One view of the tragedy is that the people of Hiroshima and Nagasaki suffered a sacrifice that virtually ensured that nuclear weapons would not be dropped again, since their suffering demonstrated to the world the nature of nuclear war.

struction of existing stockpiles within three months after the conventions had come into force. Each nation would enact domestic legislation to punish violators of the convention—which, in the light of the nature of Soviet society, was palpably ridiculous. All through 1946, attempts to negotiate on these matters proved fruitless.

The Soviets shifted to a worldwide propaganda campaign to "ban the bomb," in line with their UN plan, and then suggested international control by the Security Council (with its veto) after destruction of all weapons. General Assembly support for the Baruch Plan brought no progress, and it became doubtful that the American Congress itself would now support the international ownership and management set forth in the American project. By the time of the Soviet Union's explosion of its first bomb in 1949 and then the outbreak of the Korean War, disarmament was out of the question. The UN Atomic Energy Commission (AEC) was merged into the Disarmament Commission, which would consider both conventional and nuclear weapons at the same time, but not until the mid-1950s did the subject become one for truly serious discussion.

In the meantime, the United States and Western Europe came to rely—in theory, at least—on the American monopoly of the atomic bomb as a counterweight to presumed Soviet conventional superiority and to its capacity to use disruptive activities by Communist Parties abroad. By 1948, and particularly after the outbreak of the Korean War, the West began to seek security in rearmament rather than in disarmament.

In the early postwar years, the United States possessed few bombs and virtually no real means of delivery. Nevertheless, the idea of "deterrence" began to take shape: since a totalitarian society could prepare a surprise attack that democracies never could, the soundest strategy was to prepare to retaliate in massive fashion in such a way as to "deter" any such attack—or even a massive conventional attack. (In March 1949 Winston Churchill was to declare, "It is certain that Europe would have been communized and London under bombardment some time ago but for the deterrent of the atomic bomb in the hands of the United States." This is perhaps more of a comment on the temper of the times than on reality.) Even Soviet explosion of its own first weapon in 1949 failed to shake this view, since most analysts thought it would still take years for the USSR to develop an intercontinental capability. Nevertheless, this Soviet explosion spurred the Truman Administration on to hasten development of the "superbomb": the hydrogen, or fusion, bomb (H-bomb), which was potentially thousands of times more powerful than the atomic bomb.

When the Eisenhower Administration came into office in 1953, it faced the problem that it had condemned the previous administration's level of spending, but had also promised a more vigorous policy—along with no more limited, dragged-out wars like the Korean War. Its supposed solution was "massive retaliation," a policy of responding to small probes not by limited force but by direct attack upon those backing them. The United States, Secretary of State John Foster Dulles declared, would "retaliate instantly, and by means of our own choosing. We can now shape our military establishment to fit what is *our* policy, instead of having to try to be ready to meet the enemy's many choices." The only trouble was that this came at roughly the same time that the Soviet Union exploded its own H-bomb. (Soviet scientists have since said that espionage played no part in their accomplishment. Ironically, the father of the Soviet bomb was Andrei Sakharov, many years later a leading dissident who helped bring down the Communist system in the 1990s.) People asked whether the United States would in fact use massive retaliation in the event of a "new Korea" (another situation similar to the Korean War), once the Soviet Union could strike back with hydrogen weapons. The basic logic seemed to have been faulted by events as much as by anything else, and army generals fought hard for a policy that would strengthen resistance on the ground, on the basis that mutual possession of nuclear weapons made their actual use impossible.

The USSR had begun its own nuclear weapons program in 1943, followed by a missile program in 1947, well before the American missile program was begun. The aging Stalin discouraged discussion of the role of nuclear weapons, particularly since American superiority in the nuclear field might bring into question the inevitability of the triumph of socialism. Nuclear weapons, Stalin wrote in 1952, had not outmoded war. "To eliminate the inevitability of war, it is necessary to abolish imperialism." The issue surfaced in 1953, however, and played a role in the struggle to succeed Stalin. One of Stalin's successors, Georgi M. Malenkov, proceeded to declare that world war in the nuclear age would mean the "destruction of world civilization," echoing an Eisenhower statement of the year before—and the declaration was subsequently used against Malenkov by other Soviet leaders as fundamentally un-Marxist. Ultimately, in early 1960, Khrushchev, who reoriented Soviet military spending toward nuclear rocket forces and boasted of the Soviet Union's superiority to the United States in this domain, declared that world war had been made unlikely by a mutual retaliatory capacity. Nevertheless, if war should break out, the Soviet Union would be prepared for victory.

The failure of the early attempt at international control meant that the nuclear arms race was on in earnest. The American Strategic Air Command (SAC) developed a large bomber fleet and a long list of strategic targets in the Soviet Union that it would hit in one massive, retaliatory strike if the

Soviet Union were to attack. Nikita Khrushchev never built as great a bomber fleet, but moved ahead of the United States in developing intercontinental rockets. Even before he did so, by the mid-1950s, a thermonuclear standoff appeared to have developed, and Eisenhower and Khrushchev met in Geneva to ratify it informally (see chapter 3). But technological progress and fear of what the other side might develop fueled a continued arms race.

American Frustration and the Election of Eisenhower

Success in organizing the grand coalition against Stalin's Soviet Union nevertheless created frustration in the United States. The expense of rearmament and the grinding continuation of war in Korea underlined the view that containment led nowhere but to continued stalemate. From the right, the Truman Administration faced a two-pronged attack: one school argued that abandonment of traditional American hemispheric policies had brought only costs and obloquy. The country should return to a "fortress America" concept and bring American troops home. More influential was the charge that the administration had been "soft on Communism" and had "lost" China because of traitors and the proliferation of spies in government. A tougher foreign policy was needed, one that would help end the Soviet threat, bring victory, and liberate Eastern Europe. The few voices on the left who charged the administration with having exaggerated the Soviet threat and helped to produce the bipolar Cold War by so doing were too often weakened by their own proclivity for finding excuses for Stalin's horrendous regime and its policies.

The frustrations of being directly enmeshed in global balance-of-power politics for the first time in history—in seemingly endless fashion—played a large role in bringing to an end twenty years of Democratic rule in 1952. (Europeans, who were used to ongoing, endless attention to security policies in the face of potentially hostile strong neighbors, were bemused by the nature of the American debate.) Democratic standard bearer Adlai E. Stevenson of Illinois was swamped by General Dwight D. Eisenhower (and would be again in 1956). "Ike" was supported by the eastern liberal wing of the Republican Party, having triumphed over Robert Taft of Ohio who represented a more isolationist tendency. Eisenhower promised to cut government expenditures; strengthen the military; end the war in Korea and, perhaps most fatefully, go beyond containment to aid the liberation of the countries of Eastern Europe, which, he said, had been delivered over to the Communists by inept Democratic administrations. His secretary of state, John Foster Dulles, spelled out the peaceful liberation policy, citing Yugoslavia's successful defiance of Stalin as the model of what he had in mind. "Those who do not believe that it [liberation] can be accomplished by moral pressures, by the weight of propaganda, just do not know what they are talking about," he declared to a Senate committee.

Events quickly made it clear that the administration would actually restrain itself to a continuation of containment. Although Eisenhower "unleashed" Chiang Kai-shek, rescinding Truman's order to the Seventh Fleet to keep the Chinese leader from raiding the mainland, the move was made mainly for domestic effect. When East German workers rose against their Communist bosses in Berlin in June 1953, and when Hungarians overthrew their Communist regime (see chapter 3), three years later, the Eisenhower regime stood by helplessly while Soviet forces crushed the rebellions. (The American emphasis on liberation of Eastern Europe may well have prolonged the Cold War, feeding Soviet paranoia and preventing a general settlement. However, it is clear from the events of 1989—almost forty years later—that Eastern Europeans largely wanted such liberation.)

On the other side of the ledger, in July 1953 Eisenhower secured the armistice agreement in Korea. Nominally the armistice was to be the prelude to negotiations for unification, but nobody really believed it. No one would have believed, either, that until forty years later North Korea—the most heavily armed state in the world on a per capita basis—would still be under the domination of Kim Il Sung, while the impoverished and war-torn South Korea would have become one of the most prosperous of non-Western states.

The United Nations in a Divided World

In the midst of the emergence of a bipolar world, the UN system never operated as its original planners had hoped. Force and the threat of force in the hands of nation-states or of people that wanted to create new states continued to be used both to bring change and to maintain some degree of order. The Security Council could never be allocated that monopoly of force necessary to make collective security a reality, given the political differences and conflicts that characterized its members. The North Atlantic Treaty, while it was often referred to as "collective security," was in fact a return to balance-of-power policies that marked the end of the second attempt at creating collective security as an alternative to balance of power. Korea was in reality a war to maintain the balance, collectively legitimized by the General Assembly, and many members declared that they would not again be drawn into the position of supporting such an action. The Security Council and the General Assembly were the focus of world attention in those years primarily because they were useful arenas for the airing of differences, for propaganda, and for gaining legitimacy for national action by proving that other states supported a nation's position. For the UN's first decade it was the United States that could command almost automatic majorities, while the Soviet Union berated the organization generally. The thaw in policy after Stalin's death brought change: only three weeks later, Moscow accepted a new secretary-general, Swedish diplomat Dag Hammarskjold, and soon it joined several UN agencies the Soviets had previously boycotted. The breaking of the membership logjam in 1955, when sixteen states were admitted to the UN—four Soviet bloc; four Western; and eight diverse, uncommitted states—meant the end of the era of automatic U.S. majorities, as new members from Africa and elsewhere began to flood into the organization.

On the economic side, economic dislocations were much greater than foreseen when the new global economic agencies were planned. The liberal multilateral trade and payments envisaged by the Bretton Woods system of the International Monetary Fund, the International Bank, and the International Trade Organization (ITO) simply could not be established. The IMF saw widespread use of its escape clauses, the International Bank played a minor role in reconstruction, and the ITO failed to come into being, attacked from one side by free traders for the excessive protectionist concessions it made to state traders that simply planned how much and what they would export and import, and to developing states, and from the other side for being too oriented toward free trade. Yet the IMF and the IBRD continued to exist, and once reconstruction got under way in the late 1940s, the groundwork was laid for both of them to become central institutions in a system that by the late 1950s began to evolve toward what had been envisaged earlier. Fundamental to this evolution was the General Agreement on Tariffs and Trade (the GATT, as it came to be called.) The GATT was originally merely an interim agreement drawn up in 1947 by a preparatory conference for the creation of the ITO, binding nations to tariff concessions they would make to each other on a reciprocal basis. By the time the ITO died its quiet death in the U.S. Senate, the GATT had inaugurated a series of meetings at which signatory states could negotiate reciprocal tariff reductions. Like the IMF and the IBRD, the GATT became more and more important. By the mid-1950s, the international economy was launched upon an unprecedented and largely unforeseen expansion: in the decade between 1948 and 1958, when full currency convertibility was restored to European currencies, international trade came close to doubling, world manufacturing increased by 60 percent, and the incomes of even the non–oil-exporting less developed countries (LDCs) grew at an unprecedented 3.8 percent per year. These were achievements that whetted appetites for more.

Conclusion

The brave new UN world envisaged at San Francisco and Bretton Woods largely disappeared during the first postwar decade. The first years brought an attempt to rebuild, with the new institutions supposedly guaranteeing some degree of order and justice; their failure was perhaps one of fundamental concept, and not just the product of the Cold War that developed between the Soviet Union and the West. It was certainly the Cold War and its myriad manifestations that dominated the period: the wrangling over peace treaties; the communization of Eastern Europe; crises over Iran, Greece, and Turkey; the Truman Doctrine; the Marshall Plan; reconstruction and integration of West Germany into Western Europe; the Berlin blockade; NATO, the failure to establish control of atomic energy and the start of the arms race; the triumph of the Communists in China; the Korean War and its international effects; the explosion of the first H-bombs; and the development of intercontinental bombers. The litany of major events carries us through the development of a bipolar, nuclear-armed world dominated by the Soviet Union and the United States and the creation of a legacy of suspicion that would haunt the world for the next forty years. To Stalin, the world was divided into the freedom-loving "socialist camp" and the war-threatening "imperialist camp"; to Americans, the division was between the totalitarian "Soviet bloc" and the "free world."

Allowing the North Koreans to invade South Korea was perhaps Stalin's greatest mistake: it led to hardened Western assumptions about Soviet aims, the wholesale rearmament of the West, the rhetoric of massive retaliation, and liberation. In 1950 large numbers of people were prepared to see "World War III" break out, and recent revelations from Soviet archives show their fear was justified: Stalin was willing to risk such a war, at the time of the Korean conflict. To others, the Cold War and bipolarism had become durable fixtures, facts of life with which the world would have to live. Bipolarism, however, was never very stable, as the course of the 1950s shows.

Further Suggested Readings

Literature on the onset of the Cold War is enormous. Useful and general are Herbert Feis, *From Trust to Terror: the Onset of the Cold War, 1945–1950* (New York: Norton, 1970); and two English views, first, Hugh Thomas, *Armed Truce: The Making of the Cold War* (London: Hamish Hamilton, 1986), and a second, highly influential book often ignored by recent scholarship, Barbara Ward, *The West at Bay* (New York: Norton, 1948). John Lewis Gaddis, *The United States and the Origins of the Cold War* (New York: Columbia University Press, 1972), incorporates "revisionist" views about U.S.

responsibility for the Cold War. On the Russian side, the brilliant Yugoslav Milovan Djilas gave a remarkable view of Stalin in his short *Conversations with Stalin* (New York: Harcourt, Brace and World, 1962). Adam Ulam, *The Rivals* (New York: Viking 1975), is one of a series of excellent, readable syntheses of Russo-U.S. relations, and David Holloway, *Stalin and the Bomb: The Soviet Union and Atomic Energy, 1939–1956* (New Haven: Yale University Press, 1994), uses the latest documentation on the Soviet Union.

3

Bipolarism Challenged—Within the Blocs

By the mid-1950s, several underlying changes surfaced. Despite Russian and Western rearmament and the decisive split in Europe, a number of developments brought a sense of relaxation. Settlements—however indecisive—of wars in Korea and Indochina; resolution of numerous Soviet conflicts with countries like Iran, Turkey, Greece, and Yugoslavia; an Austrian peace treaty; and tentative attempts to tone down Cold War rhetoric all played a part. Many, including Churchill during a brief return to power, argued that with mutual possession of hydrogen bombs a seemingly more stable military balance had been created, and contributed to these developments. The death of Stalin in 1953 promised an easing of tension. Churchill's call in 1953 for a summit conference similar to the conferences of World War II was answered only after his retirement, but the 1955 meeting of Eisenhower and Khrushchev in Geneva appeared to confirm Churchill's views.

If the first postwar decade brought about the growth of a bipolar world, it also saw that bipolar world begin to unravel within and fray about the edges. Under the impact of "de-Stalinization," the Soviet bloc developed numerous fissures, one of which turned into a chasm: Mao's China became embroiled in bitter conflict with Soviet leaders. The more consensual Western bloc also witnessed division, most notably between the United States and its allies over issues of decolonization and nuclear strategy. The return to power in France of the nationalist wartime Free French leader Charles de Gaulle in 1958 presaged further dissension.

Then, too, Western Europe began to exhibit an unexpected resiliency. What many had viewed as merely a temporary, unstable, and delicate economic spurt in the years after Korea proved to be far more durable. To Europeans bred on the economically disastrous twenty interwar years when in France, for example, net *dis*investment had actually taken place and the Great Depression was a fact of life, it was almost unbelievable that the figures for 1953, and then for 1954 and 1955, showed constant economic improvement on every front. Even in England, where successive governments had wrestled with an export-import imbalance in the face of heavy overseas commitments and the imperatives of reconstruction, these years produced a favorable trade balance, the final abandonment of wartime rationing and of many direct controls, and the maintenance of full employment with containment of inflation.

The European movement faltered, but Europe was alive, and 1958 would see a giant step forward in the form of creation of the European Economic Community. In the Far East, the defeated Japan of 1945, deprived of its empire, burdened by an enormous ingathering of its people, having painfully rebuilt among the devastation wrought by American bombing, began to show a similar spurt of growth. Westerners now take for granted that all segments of society may have modern comforts—indoor plumbing, automobiles, and central heating—an assumption that was a new development in the 1950s.

Dwight D. Eisenhower assumed the presidency of the United States in 1953 with a strong desire to slow the developing arms race and to establish a more stable relationship with the Soviet Union. Despite peace in Korea, his meetings with Khrushchev, and eight years of domestic growth and prosperity, Eisenhower nevertheless left office a disappointed man: by the end of the 1960s, the arms race would again pick up momentum; "détente" with the Soviet Union in the mid-1950s had been but fleeting.

The Soviet Bloc

Change in the Soviet Union

Soviet Russia grew enormously in industrial strength and world power under the virtually unchallenged dictatorship of Josef Stalin. In the 1920s and the 1930s Stalin carried out policies and purges that would cost millions upon millions of Russian lives; in later years the almost oriental potentate ruled in an atmosphere of mystery, terror, and seclusion. Yet he was the object of sycophantic adulation, fostered by an enormous propaganda machine.

Only the devices of historical rewriting and repetitious propaganda kept his mistakes from becoming evident. The Nazi-Soviet pact had almost cost the Soviet Union its independence; obtuse insistence on the imminent failure of American capitalism after the war had led to a bold policy—including Stalin's encouragement of the attack on South Korea—that had brought on an American reorientation to containment with its concomitant commitments abroad, including the rebuilding and the rearming of Western Europe. The attempt to penetrate Western Europe, Turkey, Greece, and North Africa had failed, and Yugoslavia had slipped out of Soviet grasp. Stalin had underestimated the new Chinese leaders, and his relations with them were not satisfactory: Mao was independent and demanding, and Stalin was penurious.

He had, however, successfully consolidated the Soviet system throughout Eastern Europe (supervising in the last years a ruthless purge in which tens of thousands of Communists perished or were imprisoned so that there could be no new Tito). He could congratulate himself that, by making the USSR a nuclear power, he had weathered a dangerous period in which the United States, with its monopoly of nuclear weapons, might have attempted to coerce the Soviet Union by threatening their use (but never did so).

Somewhat more flexible in his last years, he opened the way to negotiations in Korea. At the 1952 Nineteenth Party Congress, an opening was made toward nationalist leaders of new states, heretofore stigmatized as "bourgeois lackeys of imperialism." On the European front, in an effort to halt the rearming of West Germany, Stalin hinted in early 1952 that he might be willing to abandon the Communist government of East Germany in the interest of a unified and neutralized Germany. The Western powers saw in this primarily an effort to forestall the necessary strengthening of NATO in the face of Russian superiority.

Internally the regime was enmeshed in a bizarre and labyrinthine plot that foreshadowed a new, large-scale purge similar to those of the late 1930s. Already, in 1951, Jewish officers in the army and security services had been purged. In late 1952, just as a series of Czech Jews were executed for a supposed plot against Czech party leadership, a group of primarily Jewish doctors were charged with plans to eliminate Kremlin leadership. No one knew who might be implicated in the plot, and a vague dread seems to have gripped official Moscow. In the midst of this came the news of Stalin's death from a cerebral hemorrhage—and reprieve for all those who might have been attacked.

The ensuing struggle for leadership greatly affected both Soviet domestic and foreign policy. For a brief period the old Kremlin leaders who had been threatened by Stalin's last moves hung together in a form of collective leadership, courting public favor by a large-scale liberalization and an enormous release of citizens from Stalin's infamous camps—the "Gulag Archipelago" as dissident writer Aleksandr Solzhenitsyn was to call these camps in his famous book. In July 1953, however, the head of the secret police, Lavrenti P. Beria, was arrested and executed, presumably for having tried to consolidate his own personal power. In 1955 Prime Minister Georgi Malenkov, associated with a new economic course that emphasized consumer production, fell by the wayside, to be exiled to a minor job. Within three years, Nikita Khrushchev, the great policy improviser, emerged as the head of the Soviet Union, having eliminated all further rivals.

In foreign policy terms, the maneuvering for legitimacy meant a greater willingness to court Western Europe. When West Germany regained its sovereignty and joined NATO in the summer of 1955, Khrushchev nevertheless invited West German Chancellor Konrad Adenauer to visit Moscow and established diplomatic relations with the new state.

Then, in short order, Khrushchev abandoned conditions that had long stalled an Austrian peace accord. Events moved rapidly, and the wartime allies signed a treaty returning sovereignty to Austria under conditions of permanent neutrality on July 27, 1955. All occupation troops were withdrawn by September, and, in a remarkable change in the heart of Europe, Austria became free and independent.

New leadership in the USSR also meant relief for China from pressure to continue the Korean War as well as economic concessions to Mao, who had begun to emerge as more of an equal partner: Khrushchev abandoned Russia's last special rights in China, including the joint stock companies created in 1950 and the old Russian naval base of Port Arthur. The Kremlin leaders returned the Porkkala naval base to Finland (whose president, as of 1956, was Urho Kekkonen, secretly a Soviet KGB agent), resumed diplomatic relations with Israel and Greece, formally abandoned the postwar claims Stalin had made on Turkey, settled financial and border affairs with Iran, and began to negotiate a series of new trade treaties.

Clearly, although the course could be reversed, this was no longer the brutal Soviet Union of Stalin. His successors felt more secure, and able to influence rather than threaten their neighbors. While some in the West saw the moves as merely tactical, others—like Churchill and Eisenhower—hoped for a more stable and more open relationship. In retrospect, many observers wondered whether there had not been a lost opportunity for an overall settlement between East and West. The withdrawal of Russian troops from even a small part of Austria, in central Europe, seemed particularly significant.

Geneva, 1955

In fact, and despite the views of some of his advisers, Eisenhower did make an effort at a settlement. By the time the Big Four foreign ministers met to sign the peace treaty with Austria in May 1955, Eisenhower—who had wanted "deeds not words" to show Moscow's good faith before he would meet with Khrushchev—thought he had them, and accepted European appeals for a summit meeting.

The summit occurred in the old League of Nations building in Geneva from July 18 to July 23, 1955. It was very different from the intimate conversations Churchill envisaged when he called for it in 1953. The Americans, who still saw the Cold War in terms of good and evil, were hardly in a mood to sit down and compromise, as statesmen had done in the great nineteenth-century conferences; the shadow of appeasement at Munich was still too strong. Recent Soviet flexibility had not been over essentials.

The participants met in a glare of publicity, anyway, so it was bound to be mostly an exercise in propaganda—on the surface, at least. The fiction of the Big Four (that is, including France and England) was maintained, but Eisenhower and Khrushchev as leaders of the two superpowers shared the limelight. What each party wanted to do was demonstrate to the world his peaceful intentions; what also appeared to take place was a tacit agreement that in the thermonuclear age, neither side could afford the risk of a major war.

Thus, in a dramatic speech in which Eisenhower turned to the Soviet leaders and declared, in front of all the world's media, "the United States will never take part in an aggressive war," he also advanced a startling proposal to the effect that each major power should supply the other with complete blueprints of its military establishment and permit the other to make aerial photoreconnaissance missions over its national territory.

To Eisenhower's disappointment, Khrushchev turned this proposal down cold. Four years later, when the Soviet Union shot down an American U-2 spy plane, secretly doing exactly what Eisenhower's "Open Skies" proposal had suggested should be done openly and by permission, Khrushchev charged Eisenhower with the most heinous behavior and proceeded to torpedo a summit conference. Yet, in one of those ironies of history, the successful achievement of arms control proposals a decade later rested upon the acceptance by both parties of open satellite surveillance of each other's territories. In that sense, the Open Skies proposal that many mocked as simply propaganda was really simply ahead of its time.

The supposed tacit acceptance of the idea that neither side could afford a nuclear war also had its ambiguities: for the next decade or more, both sides continued to build and brandish nuclear arsenals as though they might be used. Khrushchev may himself have believed that—and was certainly under pressure to act as if—Russian missile superiority in the late 1950s meant the balance of world power had shifted in Russian favor. He argued openly in 1961 that nuclear war was not winnable, and yet the threat of nuclear weapons played a real role in the Cuban missile crisis of 1962. It was then, rather than earlier, that both sides began to act as if nuclear war must be avoided at all costs. (Like a phoenix rising from the ashes, the issue of preparing to "win" a nuclear war arose again in the 1970s when both multiple missile warheads and missile accuracy increased.)

The relaxation of relations had its own ambiguities, too. Khrushchev appeared unable to avoid exploiting Western weakness to use any situation to embarrass or weaken the West. If the danger of capitalist use of nuclear weapons had receded, then the opportunity to make use of and profit from the uneasy stalemate must be seized. Russian propaganda increased, and Nikolai Bulganin and Nikita Khrushchev began something entirely new for Russian foreign policy: a peripatetic diplomacy that took them to Yugoslavia to mend fences with Marshal Tito, and to India, Afghanistan, and Burma. There they could capitalize on the views of Third World leaders that continued American military spending, bases abroad, and all the new alliances threatened the "peaceful coexistence" so recently established at Geneva. Khrushchev and Bulganin sided openly and emphatically with India and Afghanistan in their quarrels with pro-Western Pakistan. For the first time in Soviet foreign policy, the USSR offered economic and technical aid and long-term barter agreements that would avoid the recent fluctuations in world prices for raw materials.

American Secretary of State John Foster Dulles had recently called the proclaimed neutralism of newly independent states toward the two blocs "immoral." The choice in the world, after all, was between good and evil, freedom and communism. This was a characteristic and unfortunate statement, and Prime Minister Jawaharlal Nehru of India and other Third World leaders reacted angrily. Whatever anticolonial statements Dulles might make, it was the West that had been colonialist, that was reluctant to give up empire, and that gave it up only under pressure. The Russians were supportive of the new states, neutral or not, and their attitude contrasted favorably with that of Dulles, whose views therefore helped confirm the new leaders in their growing neutralism.

One thing was clear: the resolving of a number of conflicts, the relaxation of tensions, and "peaceful coexistence" did not mean to Khrushchev that the struggle between capitalism and communism would be muted. The non-Western world offered new opportunities and its leaders could look to Soviet support against the West.

Instability in the Soviet Bloc

There were, as it turned out, great dangers in the maneuvers taken by Stalin's successors. Georgi Malenkov's bid for popularity, the "New Course" in economic policy, led a repressed population in Eastern Europe to clamor for some of the same. The stage was set for upheaval in the Communist bloc. Its first manifestation—the East German workers' revolt—occurred in mid-June 1953, shortly after Stalin's death. Khrushchev's willingness to take the risk of a rapprochement with Tito brought the next ones.

In May 1955, Khrushchev and Bulganin made a pilgrimage to Bucharest to try to woo Tito back into the fold with a simple and blatantly hypocritical message: the whole orchestrated program of vilification, attempted subversion, and economic and diplomatic ostracism of Yugoslavia on the part of Communist bloc members was the responsibility of Lavrenti Beria, the executed head of Stalin's secret police. Khrushchev apologized abjectly: the accusations against Tito "were fabricated by the enemies of the people, detestable agents of imperialism who by deceptive methods pushed their way into the ranks of our party." This apology may have been transparent, but Tito accepted it for what it was—a repudiation of the campaign against him—and the two leaders signed a number of trade, debt, and communication agreements. To cement the rapprochement, Khrushchev dissolved the Cominform. But Tito reassured the West, promised to abide by restrictions on strategic trade with the socialist bloc, and received Dulles cordially in November.

It turned out that Khrushchev had opened a Pandora's box. All through the socialist bloc there were rulers who had ruthlessly purged and executed other bloc leaders for "Titoism." Repudiation of the campaign against Tito obviously put their legitimacy into question. Tito himself pressed home the point, charging Communist leaders who had followed Stalin's lead with lacking "the Communist courage to admit their errors. . . . These men have their hands soaked in blood, have staged trials, given false information, sentenced innocent people to death."

Worse yet, if Tito, who had followed his own socialist path, were readmitted into the good graces of the bloc, could not other countries also follow their own paths to socialism?

At home Khrushchev was busy consolidating his position with domestic reforms, granting amnesty to political prisoners, reestablishing legality in the place of arbitrary police action, allowing greater freedom in the arts, and filling local party positions with his own men. Then, at the Twentieth Party Congress in February 1956, he made one of the most important speeches in history: he attacked Stalin in the most violent terms, outdoing Western anti-Communists in describing dictatorship by terror; injustice on an unbelievable scale; and unjustified executions of hundreds of thousands of innocent people, many of whom, though dead, were being "rehabilitated." The only reason Stalin's associates failed to stop him, Khrushchev explained, was that they lived in fear themselves.

The fault, he declared, lay not in the system, but in the "cult of the individual," now replaced by "collective leadership."

The speech changed Soviet history: it may have been inevitable that such an analysis would have to be made, but there is a direct line from the Twentieth Party Congress speech to the collapse of the Soviet Union in 1992. The problem was that it was impossible to make Stalin the scapegoat for every horror: current leadership was too involved. The system itself came into question. Many of those now in power had helped imprison or execute those accused of anti-Stalin activities, now declared innocent and wrongly condemned. The "secret" speech was bound to leak beyond the confines of the Party Congress.

In Poland the fires it lit were successfully damped down. Wladyslaw Gomulka, imprisoned six years earlier for Titoism, was released to popular acclaim: he appeared to stand for national communism and radical reform, and was quickly restored to the Party Central Committee. Two days later, on October 23, 1956, demonstration turned to rebellion in Hungary, where Khrushchev's acceptance of leadership change in Poland aroused the Hungarians. Demonstrations began with demands for reappointment of Imre Nagy, the man who had been most closely associated with the New Course but then had been dismissed at the time Malenkov was dismissed in Russia. Security police fired on the crowd, but the army sided with the demonstrators against the secret police, and Nagy was named prime minister. Political prisoners were freed, young people calling for Western aid took to the streets, Soviet troops entered the fray, and confusion reigned: under popular pressure the whole Communist state and party apparatus simply collapsed. Nagy formed a multiparty government, and Poland and Yugoslavia sent messages of friendship and support.

Khrushchev promised withdrawal of Soviet troops, thereby forestalling any action by the UN Security Council in session in New York. Then Nagy learned that new Soviet forces were, in fact, rolling across the frontier.

In response, Nagy's government announced withdrawal from the Warsaw Pact, proclaimed Hungarian neutrality, and asked the United Nations to guarantee it. The Soviets agreed to open negotiations for withdrawal of their troops, but this was only a ruse: when they met at the headquarters of the Soviet forces, the Hungarian negotiators were arrested. The Russian army was ordered to crush the regime. Hungarians of every stripe fought the Russians while appealing to the West for help that never came. The battle was, of course, hopeless, and eventually 200,000 Hungarians fled their country. Nagy took refuge in the Yugoslav embassy, where he was issued a safe conduct to leave by the Soviets, who then promptly seized and subsequently executed him. Janos Kadar, made head of government by the Russians earlier so that he could appeal for the Russian troops and give them the requisite fig leaf of legality, took over the job of reconciling the Hungarians to geopolitical reality. He would stay on the job for thirty-two years.

The Brezhnev Doctrine

It was clear now that the Soviet Union would use force to maintain the unity of the Soviet bloc, and that the United States, as leader of the West, would not interfere. To buttress the unity imposed by force, Khrushchev renegotiated the exploitative economic relationships with Eastern European countries imposed by Stalin in the years after World War II. For the next ten years, people accepted enforced bloc unity as a fact of life. Then, in another crucial year in world history, 1968, Khrushchev's successor, Leonid Brezhnev, once again dispatched the Soviet army to crush resistance. This time Soviet troops were sent to Czechoslovakia, where a new government had tried to produce "Communism with a human face," keeping within acceptable limits—the so-called "Prague Spring." Soviet policy was spelled out clearly, in what came to be known as the "Brezhnev Doctrine":

> When internal and external forces that are hostile to socialism try to turn the development of some socialist country towards the restoration of a capitalist regime, when socialism in that country and the socialist community as a whole are threatened, it becomes not only a problem of the people concerned, but a common problem and concern of all socialists.

In other words, Moscow would prevent it. And for twenty long years, until 1989, Soviet leaders adhered to the doctrine, keeping Eastern Europe under Soviet domination. But long before this the total break between China and the Soviet Union had come to complicate relations both within and without the bloc.

The Break with China

In the 1950s Khrushchev blew fresh air through the stale doctrines and practices of Stalinism, establishing in foreign affairs several long-lasting themes for Soviet policy: with the shift in world power based in part on the development of the hydrogen bomb, war between capitalist and socialist states was no longer inevitable. "Peaceful coexistence" of systems had become necessary although nothing would stop the triumphant onward sweep of Communism: "Your grandchildren will live under communism," Khrushchev told Americans when he visited the United States in 1959. "We will bury you." There were also different pathways to socialism, although only some were acceptable. Ultimately, Communist society must be achieved by satisfying the material needs of the people. But Khrushchev, in pursuing these themes, alternately cajoled and threatened, blustered and bluffed, violently vilifying those who opposed him and frequently confusing Westerners as to his aims—and getting himself into severe difficulties as a consequence.

In November 1957, leaders of Communist Parties from throughout the world gathered in Moscow as the Soviet Union celebrated the fortieth anniversary of the revolution, and Khrushchev used the occasion to try to resolve the problem of differences within the bloc once and for all by proclaiming Russian Party primacy. Mao Zedong had provided necessary support during the Polish and Hungarian troubles. He came to Moscow sobered by his experience with intellectual liberalization in China, when he had said, "let a hundred flowers bloom, let diverse schools of thought contend," and the resulting revelation of intellectual opposition had led to a hasty and severe repression. As a result, he was willing to see a strong line laid down for all parties, especially on bloc unity. The error of rapprochement with Tito was rectified: the Yugoslav leader was once more condemned for his many errors and for refusing to acknowledge the primacy of the Soviet Union.

Only two years later, however, any semblance of unity in the world Communist movement proclaimed in Moscow in November 1957 was destroyed when Chinese-Soviet differences exploded into conflict.

Mao was determined to transform Chinese society and turn China into a powerful, modern state, its borders rounded out and clearly defined, self-reliant, dedicated to egalitarian principles. A series of aid agreements negotiated with Stalin's successors helped Mao begin building a modern industrial base. By the late 1950s, 50 percent of Chinese trade was with the Soviet Union. The Korean War enabled Mao to hasten the processes of mobilization and transformation, but its costs were heavy. Despite the peace agreements of 1953–54, the archenemy—the United States—still ringed China with bases and alliances. It provided aid to South Vietnam, and blocked China from its legitimate seat in the United Nations.

Yet the United States was the very nation toward which Khrushchev now meant to follow a conciliatory policy of peaceful coexistence in which Russian material superiority would assure its ultimate victory. Khrushchev initiated serious disarmament discussions with the United States that included a proposal for a nuclear test ban, just when the Chinese had begun to build their own bomb. In 1959 he toured the United States in a circuslike atmosphere (arriving two days after a well-timed Russian space vehicle had hit the moon); sat down for heart-to-heart talks with President Eisenhower at the latter's retreat at Camp David (giving rise to the phrase "the spirit of Camp David"); and allowed an expansion of cultural exchanges. A young Texan, Van Cliburn, won the Tchaikovsky Competition to great acclaim in Moscow, while the spectacular dancers of the Moiseyev Dance Company enraptured American audiences. Mao, bent on new radical policies, was not amused.

Americans were therefore surprised when Khrushchev, at the end of the decade, provoked a series of crises over the status of Berlin, over an American surveillance overflight of the Soviet Union, and over the United Nations. Western leaders did not know that conflict between Khrushchev and the Chinese was about to come into the open at a June 1960 meeting of Communist Parties in Bucharest. Khrushchev, screaming that the Chinese Communists were mad adventurists who wanted to start a nuclear war, attacked them for splitting the world Communist movement and for their opposition to his efforts at peaceful settlement of disputes. In the summer of 1960, somewhat more quietly, Khrushchev withdrew all Russian technicians in China and ceased all aid to Chinese nuclear development. During the next year, Russian exports of machinery to China dropped by 80 percent. Mao, trying to maintain revolutionary spontaneity and egalitarianism, now attacked Khrushchev for revisionism, the very issue on which the Chinese had supported him in 1957. Mao knew that Khrushchev was trying to establish links to Mao's own, internal opposition, and Khrushchev knew that Mao was doing the same thing.

In other words, despite Khrushchev's ebullient boasting, nuclear bluffing, cajoling, and threats, by 1960 he was again in deep trouble, both at home and abroad: at home, where the military and other bureaucracies resented his policies, and abroad, where he faced a major and historic split within the Communist world. The split widened further at the time that Khrushchev provoked the Cuban missile crisis of 1962 (see page 134), and widened still further a few years after his deposition in 1964, when the Soviet Union and China fought a number of border skirmishes that came close to exploding into open war. In the meantime, the two countries competed for influence among the emerging Third World nations and over their relations with North Vietnam when that tiny Communist country came into conflict with the United States. Brezhnev's attempt to get a formal condemnation of China at the Moscow-sponsored world conference of Communist Parties in June 1969 failed. This failure was further evidence that any world Communist movement that once existed under Russian leadership was long gone.

Long before this, the Chinese-Russian split had affected relations within the bloc. As the conflict with Mao began to develop, Khrushchev was forced to seek support among Communist leaders, and this gave them a measure of leverage over the Russians. Romania, first under Gheorgiu-Dej and then under Nicolae Ceausescu, while following a relatively rigid Stalinist policy at home, became more and more independent in the realm of economic affairs and foreign policy, reorienting trade away from the Soviet Union, refusing a large degree of economic integration into the bloc that would have required it to forgo certain industries, remaining neutral in the Russian-Chinese conflict, maintaining friendly relations with Israel against bloc policy, and abandoning compulsory Russian language training in Romanian schools.

Maintaining some degree of cohesion among countries whose governments presumably shared Marxist-Leninist ideology proved to be a continuing, ongoing, and, in the long run, unsuccessful affair. There is little doubt, however, that the split with China had pushed Khrushchev into the forceful stance of his last few years: it was necessary to prove he was still leader of an expanding socialist world. What was remarkable and unfortunate was that too many Americans in the 1960s still thought in terms of a world Communist movement, with fateful consequences in Vietnam (see page 140).

Strains in the Western Coalition

In contrast to the situation in the Soviet-dominated Eastern bloc, where revolt against Moscow became endemic in the 1950s and the 1960s, the Western bloc was not held together by any threat of U.S. force. The Americans played a very different role: popularly elected governments demanded an American economic, political, and military commitment, while differing over specific policies and over the nature of the Soviet "threat." But while Western Europe as a whole considered an "Atlantic" relationship absolutely necessary, as the years wore on, Western Europe also developed its own—though often confusing—political and economic identity.

European Unity

No one surveying the ruins of Europe in 1945 would have predicted the renaissance so soon to take place. If the invasion of Hungary in 1956 symbolizes the failure of the Soviet Union to create a socialist commonwealth, so the 1958 Treaty of Rome that created the European Economic Community (EEC) most certainly symbolizes the rebirth of a prosperous, democratic, and self-confident Europe after forty years of war, depression, and social and political chaos.

The early postwar years did not inspire much hope. Europeans struggled almost helplessly with a virtually endless series of intertwined problems that enmeshed them: painfully slow attempts at reconstruction, clashes over occupation policy in Germany, the dreadful winter of 1947, fear of the Soviet Union and of a rebuilt and resurgent Germany, conflicts over empires, omnipresent inflationary pressures, black markets, unwillingness to accept that Europe might be permanently divided, and the strength of local Communist Parties.

European recovery and European unity were closely intertwined. Representatives of Belgium, the Netherlands, and Luxembourg took one early step in London, in 1944, where they signed a convention creating a customs union called Benelux, which eventually would merge into the Common Market. In September 1946 at Zurich University, former Prime Minister Winston Churchill called for a "kind of United States of Europe," sparking a widespread European movement. It culminated in 1949 in the founding of the Council of Europe, in Strasbourg, France. The Council of Europe and the accompanying Committee of Ministers were essentially cooperative rather than supranational organs, reflecting the reluctance of all the governments concerned to surrender any of their powers. The council's basic purpose was to suggest ways of effecting European integration; in fact, it found itself debating activities taking place outside its limited purview and within a host of new European organizations.

Some of these organizations were directly stimulated by the Marshall Plan: the European Payments Union, which restored multilateral payments and thus made possible the resumption of multilateral trade, and the Organization for European Economic Cooperation (OEEC), which allocated Marshall Plan aid (and later became the Organization for Economic Cooperation and Development, or OECD, which is still in existence). Others were a product of fear of Russian military power: the Brussels Treaty Organization, with its governing Western European Union (WEU), which was soon superseded by NATO.

The Marshall Plan also stimulated the real precursor to the Common Market—the European Coal and Steel Community (ECSC). The French wanted to keep Germany permanently weak, but by 1949, European reconstruction appeared to require an increase in the level of German industrial production. To sweeten the pill, the French visionary of a united Europe, Jean Monnet, and French Foreign Minister Maurice Schuman devised the Schuman Plan, to pool all European coal and steel production under an international authority. Because it would place French, Italian, and Benelux iron and steel production under international control, it would also make international control acceptable to the Germans. At the same time, it would forever bar Germany from having an independent industrial base for new German armed forces.

As a French adaptation to the new unforeseen pattern of world politics, the Schuman Plan was a stroke of genius. But on June 13, 1950, the British Labour Party stated it could not participate: "European peoples do not want a supranational authority to impose agreements." The European movement was now split. On the security level it comprised the Atlantic Community; on the political level it included Western Europe as a whole. But on the economic level, although cooperation among all the Western countries was guaranteed through the OEEC and EPU, the little Europe of the Six began to emerge.

The Common Market

A series of events in the mid-1950s gave a new impetus to European unity under French leadership: defeat of France in Indochina, West German independence and entry into NATO, the spectacle of Khrushchev and Eisenhower seeming to divide up the world at Geneva in 1955, and the humiliation inflicted upon Britain and France by the United States at the time of the Suez War of 1956 (see page 106–108). Together, these events strengthened the sense that Europe must unite as much to protect itself against the vagaries of the powerful United States as for any other reason. The two must be able to deal with each other as equals. Within the space of eighteen months, Europe-minded negotiators produced two treaties and signed them in Rome on March 25, 1957, creating the European Economic Community (EEC) and the European Atomic Energy Community (Euratom). It was a remarkable feat.

On the other hand, British Prime Minister Harold Macmillan, Anthony Eden's successor, declined to participate in the negotiations, pleading Commonwealth ties and Atlantic commitments, and instead sought primarily to bolster what had come to be called the United Kingdom's "special relationship" with the United States, since it seemed obvious to him that without American support nothing could be accomplished.

The EEC, or Common Market, was intended to be a customs union: an association of states in which trade barriers among them would be eliminated and a common tariff to the outside world established around them. It would create a huge internal market. Some—Monnet included—hoped that the internal logic of this so-called functionalist approach would also force countries to harmonize their tax systems, fiscal policies, social security systems, corporate laws, and so on. Limited cooperation with respect to certain governmental functions, in other words, would provide the need for broader intergovernmental agencies, and would eventually lead to strength-ened centralized political institutions. Despite various crises, within ten years internal tariffs disappeared completely and the common external ones came into effect. In 1967 the various organs of the EEC, the ECSC, and Euratom were fused into a common body, the Council of Ministers, with its Commis-sion appointed by member governments, its Parliament, and its Court of Justice. The broadened structure was known as the European Community (EC), and in 1994 it became the European Union (EU). (The twenty-one-member Council of Europe retained its own parliamentary institutions.)

Europe was already booming in 1958 when the Common Market got under way. Workers were for the first time really beginning to share in prosperity—taking paid vacations, buying cars, and moving into decent housing. All this made it easier to negotiate the merging of European econ-omies. Yet, at that very time, France was also mired in a new war in Algeria that would bring radical change to the French political system.

De Gaulle and the Challenge to Supranationalism

Algerian revolt against French domination began in 1954. The French Army resorted to brutal methods to counter the guerrilla warfare, and publicity at home began to beget vocal domestic opposition to the war and its conduct. On the other hand, a million French Algerians insisted that Algeria remain French; the discovery of oil and gas deposits in the desert that might make France less reliant upon the Middle East added to the urgency. But the government wavered. As a result, officers seized power in Algeria. Under threat of paratroop attack from Algeria upon Paris, the government gave in and named the army's choice as prime minister: Charles de Gaulle, wartime leader of the Free French, the man most re-sponsible for reestablishing a united non-Communist France after the war—but also the man who had retired in disgust at the resumption of partisan politics in the Fourth Republic.

To retain a measure of legality, de Gaulle insisted that he be voted in by the National Assembly, and that it award him emergency powers to rule by decree. This done, he produced a new constitution that greatly strengthened the presidency and curtailed the Assembly's powers. Approved by a vote of 4 to 1 in a national referendum, the Constitution established the Fifth Re-public, and de Gaulle became its first president. (De Gaulle is a constant reminder that while international influence may be partly dependent on raw power, it depends on much else. France was by now only a medium power, but de Gaulle's astute use of his limited resources and his personal prestige made him a towering figure on the world scene.)

De Gaulle's success and failures colored much of the development of the Common Market. In his first years in office, he succeeded—in the face of brutal opposition by the army that had put him into power—in disengaging France from Algeria. Ultimately the vast majority of the million French Algerians moved to mainland France. Liberated from the agony of Algeria, French energies could be turned to other tasks, and de Gaulle took more and more command in the international field. The French economy entered a boom period, and a favorable balance of payments led to substantial gold and dollar reserves. The end of the Algerian affair enabled France to reknit its ties with Third World countries. The general appeared, therefore, to be in an almost unassailable position of strength when he diluted the supranational features of the Common Market in 1965 by simply boycotting its institutions for six months. His aim was to reduce the independence of the Common Market Commission, which had taken to making too many proposals on its own, and to resist the forthcoming transition to the third stage of EEC development, when the Council of Ministers could begin to make decisions on certain policies by a qualified majority vote. In 1966 the six EEC countries agreed to a compromise that would slow EEC development for a full twenty years, well into the 1980s: in cases of "vital national interests," states could forgo acceding to the Council of Ministers' decisions. In fact, de Gaulle had touched a deep chord of feeling: to many groups throughout Europe the EEC now stood for a kind of technological modernization through complex regulatory activities by bureaucrats in Brussels, unswayed by local or national feelings and differences. Nevertheless, the progress toward unity did not come to a full stop: harmonization measures continued slowly, and, perhaps more important, over the years the Six doubled in number.

England and Europe

The key to this enlargement was Great Britain's continually diminishing position in world affairs. If, in 1957, Conservative Prime Minister Harold Macmillan rejected membership in the nascent Common Market, it was because he still envisioned a wider, more independent role for Britain in tandem with the United States. Nevertheless, England and other European countries would obviously be affected by creation of the EEC, and were worried about possible EEC protectionism. Led by England, seven "outer" countries, therefore created the European Free Trade Association (EFTA). The EFTA would eliminate tariffs between its members—Britain, Austria, Denmark, Norway, Portugal, Sweden, and Switzerland—but each would maintain its own tariff toward other countries. Most important, the original

Map 5. **EEC and EFTA**

Source: Andrew Boyd, *Atlas of World Affairs* (London: Routledge, 1991).

intent was to negotiate an agreement with the EEC making the EEC one more (larger) member of EFTA. To EEC members this looked like trying to have the advantages of EEC membership—free access to the market—without the obligations. When de Gaulle became president of the Fifth Republic, to most people's relief, he accepted the EEC. But he vetoed the arrangement suggested by EFTA, with the result that it came into existence as an association of the outer seven, without membership of the inner six.

In the ensuing years, intra-EEC trade soared, and so did growth rates. While Britain's Commonwealth trade partners depended heavily on their trade with the United Kingdom, they took a shrinking percentage of its exports. Swallowing his pride, Macmillan applied for British membership in the Common Market, and sought to appease Commonwealth and domestic opposition.

He could have saved his breath: with superbly contemptuous disregard for the views of other EEC members, de Gaulle announced to the press on January 14, 1963, that he would veto British membership. The British and the Americans, he explained, were insular. They were not continental countries, and consequently they had a different culture and outlook. England would be an American stalking-horse within the EEC.

The ultimate aim of de Gaulle's diplomacy was breathtaking: a sweeping change in global politics that would result in a Europe independent of the United States, made up of cooperating sovereign states stretching from the Atlantic to the Urals—that is, including Eastern Europe and western Russia. It would mean the end of the two "hegemonies" of the USSR and the United States, an end to outmoded bipolarism, a truly independent Europe. Within a few days, de Gaulle persuaded the reluctant West German government to sign a treaty of friendship and cooperation that showed how European matters should be settled: not by technicians and bureaucrats and interest groups at EEC headquarters in Brussels, but by the political heads of sovereign states who would consult with each other at the political level.

De Gaulle blocked British entry again in 1967. Not until 1971, after a weakening of the French financial position and de Gaulle's withdrawal from the French political scene, did British membership become possible. Negotiations took until 1973, when Britain, Ireland, and Denmark all joined. Norway signed an agreement to join, but it was repudiated in a referendum by Norwegians who objected to its terms. Still, Norway and the remaining EFTA members were able to negotiate a free trade agreement with the EEC in manufactured goods; Commonwealth countries were given the option of association or free trade agreements; and by 1973, over 100 less developed countries had preferential tariff access to the market. Despite continued national resistance, Europe seemed to be once more on its way. It would expand further in the 1980s and the 1990s.

America and Europe: The Economic Front

For America the unsteady rise of a democratic, wealthy, and more or less united Europe meant an extraordinary success for a basic American foreign policy. It also inevitably created problems.

The revolutionary American commitment to Europe in the late 1940s was largely at European demand; even Charles de Gaulle asked for an American military guarantee of Europe in 1948. But American leadership was frequently resented by many Europeans who saw America as inexperienced, erratic, and unstable, and others who saw it as reactionary. But democratically elected governments wanted and needed both the American presence and American dollars. In the period of the Marshall Plan and NATO, American aid and expenditures by the American military helped provide the dollars Europeans could use for imports; as the 1950s wore on, European sales to America increased, and so did the flow of American tourists to Europe, also ready to spread their dollars. By 1959 the American balance of payments on current account began to show a deficit, as America spent and spread more dollars abroad than it earned through exports. The so-called dollar gap of the early postwar years—the gap between the dollars Europeans wanted to spend buying from the United States and what they could earn selling to it—had now reversed.

The deficit helped finance world trade increases: the dollar surplus provided a necessary increase in foreign reserves, since virtually all countries were willing to use gold-backed dollars as their reserves. The dollar had definitively replaced the pound as the main international currency, and most payments between countries were made in dollars.

In the 1960s, though, the whole informal system came into question. As the Common Market grew, American companies began to buy crucial European industries, particularly in the field of electronics. The relatively high external EEC tariffs stimulated American and other foreign industries to increase their productive capacity *inside* tariff barriers. By 1966, for the first time, American investments in Europe exceeded those of Europe in the United States. Europeans concluded that the dollar as international reserve currency was what made it possible for Americans to invest so heavily in Europe: as long as foreign banks were willing to hold onto surplus dollars, Americans could recklessly continue to spend more abroad than they earned, buying up crucial industries. President de Gaulle, always ready to demonstrate that influence was not a result of military capacity, mounted an attack on the dollar: referring to "Europe, the mother of modern civilization" and "America, her daughter," he attacked the "privileged" position of the dollar, and suggested it was time for the international system to return to the gold standard, which had been abandoned in the interwar period. With this, worried that others would get there before them, banks and businesses in other countries began to cash in their dollars for American gold, reserves of which proceeded to decline dramatically.

On August 15, 1971, as the drain continued, President Richard M. Nixon announced that the United States would no longer pay out gold at the previous fixed price to central banks holding American dollars. For the first time in the postwar period that *Time* magazine publisher Henry Luce had called the "American century," incredulous Americans were stranded abroad as they found that people didn't want to take their dollars in exchange for local currencies. The "almighty dollar" was no more, reflecting the rise of economic competitors to the United States.

Following several intermediate steps, negotiated with great difficulty, currencies began to "float" in value against each other, in the now familiar way, reflecting relative demands for each of them. The Bretton Woods system of relatively stable exchange rates under international supervision sponsored by the United States had come to an end; it had been established as a reaction to the disastrous currency manipulations and trade restrictions of the Great Depression of the 1930s, but it was destroyed by states following different internal fiscal and monetary policies—in particular, because Lyndon Johnson's America had tried to finance the Vietnam War by borrowing, and because fixed exchange rates could not accommodate the resulting American inflationary pressures.

The dollar, however, despite all efforts to devise a different international currency, remained for the time being the chief global medium of exchange.

The need for enormously expanded international reserves in the form of dollar holdings was a result of the equally enormous expansion of international trade in the 1950s and 1960s. The administration of John F. Kennedy began to worry that the united Europe which America had helped to bring into being might have an externally restrictive trade policy, and it therefore sponsored a new round of tariff reduction talks under the auspices of the GATT that lasted from 1964 to 1967 and became known as the "Kennedy Round." These talks were, on the whole, highly successful in diminishing trade barriers: as the London *Economist* put it, they "demolished the follies of the 'thirties."

America and Europe: Security Policies

In the 1950s American troops in West Germany under NATO command served as a guarantee to the Europeans that if the Russians contemplated an attack on Western Europe, they would also be attacking America, which would have to respond—and planned a nuclear response in order to deter the Russians. As long as the Soviet Union could not deliver nuclear weapons directly upon the United States, there was some logic in the position. In 1954 the Russians flew intercontinental bombers over Moscow during the May Day parade, bringing the concept into more doubt than already existed. In October 1957 the Soviet Union launched both the world's first artificial satellite or "sputnik," forerunner of thousands of others that would serve dozens of purposes, and the world's first intercontinental ballistic missile (ICBM), forerunner of thousands of others whose purposes would be considerably less clear. The impact of the first sputnik was soon heightened when a hurried and much-publicized American first effort at a satellite launch failed in front of television cameras and then, in November, the Russians launched another sputnik carrying the first living being, a dog, into space. American successes followed later, but the Russians launched larger payloads, and Khrushchev boasted widely of Russian space and missile superiority.

Could Europeans still depend on NATO as a tripwire to provoke an American nuclear response to deter Soviet forces from a conventional attack when, for the first time, the USSR would be able to retaliate with nuclear-tipped rockets directly upon the United States? Dulles's successor, Secretary of State Christian Herter told a congressional committee, "I can't conceive of the President involving us in an all-out nuclear war unless the facts showed clearly that we are in danger of devastation ourselves. . . ." The British, who had exploded their own first thermonuclear device in May 1957, drew their own conclusions. Duncan Sandys, the defense minister, told Parliament:

> We think it is just as well to make certain that an appreciable element of nuclear power shall, in all circumstances, remain on this side of the Atlantic, so that no one shall be tempted to think that a major attack could be made against Western Europe without the risk of nuclear retaliation.

The French military reacted similarly, but each country took a different path to maintaining a nuclear deterrent: the financially strapped English accepted American aid, while the French worked on their own. British programs were therefore at the mercy of American decisions, ultimately confirming de Gaulle's view that Britain's excessive reliance upon the Americans destroyed its national independence, and provoking his veto of British membership in the Common Market.

As though to underline decline, the Labour government that came to power in 1964 proceeded with a general cutback of British forces. It abandoned what was left of British commitments "east of Suez"—that is, in Singapore, in Malaysia, in the Persian Gulf, and in the eastern Mediterranean—and cut the size of the British Army of the Rhine, in Germany. The withdrawal from east of Suez raised serious questions about stability in the areas from which the British presence disappeared: it was no coincidence that both Russian and American naval activity soon increased in the whole Indian Ocean area, while Iran under the shah sought to establish itself as the preeminent Persian Gulf power.

In the meantime, the French followed their own path. General de Gaulle had frequently and elegantly articulated his own view of politics. Regimes might come and go—monarchic, republican, fascist, Communist—but the nation remained, with its interests defined by the context of the world without. As that context changed, so should policy: an alliance like NATO might be required for a while, and discarded when no longer necessary. France could not match the power of the United States or the Soviet Union; de Gaulle often spoke of the "two hegemonies." But they were not really in the same class. France needed the United States to stand up to the USSR; it needed its own power to stand up to the United States. The French people had to realize that France had a special role to play in the world, product of its long experience and the understanding its statesmen could bring to world affairs.

In line with this, de Gaulle, in September 1958, sent a memorandum to President Eisenhower and Prime Minister Macmillan, suggesting "that an organization comprising the United States, Great Britain and France should be created and function on a worldwide political and strategic level." They should, in other words, on a basis of equality, concert Western strategy worldwide. Eisenhower turned him down: France and Britain certainly had an interest in what happened throughout the world, but the United States was the one with the power, and to expect it to do only what the three could agree upon was too much. Consequently, and with his jaundiced view of England confirmed by subsequent events, de Gaulle turned to a partnership with Konrad Adenauer's West Germany. But he also oversaw the building of France's own, successful independent nuclear deterrent. Then in early 1966, to the consternation of his allies, he announced that all French armed forces were to be withdrawn from NATO commands and that all NATO units and commands would have to leave French soil by the spring of 1967—the immense communications, staff, and command complexes around Paris; the logistic network with its great supply bases; and some 26,000 U.S. troops and dependents, mainly attached to air defense and attack units. "France," wrote de Gaulle to President Johnson, "is determined to regain on her whole territory the full exercise of her sovereignty, at present diminished by the permanent presence of Allied military elements or by the use which is made of her air space."

The Americans, other allies, and even de Gaulle's domestic opponents protested strongly, but to no avail. In 1967 NATO headquarters was split up and transferred to Brussels, to Brunssum in the Netherlands, and to Stuttgart. The de Gaulle government insisted it was still a party to the North Atlantic Treaty, but would no longer participate in the elaborate organization devised at the time of the Korean War.

The year 1969 marked the twentieth anniversary of the signing of the North Atlantic Treaty. In the light of the French attitude, the determination of the British to diminish the size of the British Army of the Rhine, pressures within the United States to withdraw some of the expensively maintained American troops, general dissatisfaction with the organization, and increased distrust of the United States under the impact of the Vietnam War, many people thought that at the very least the French would withdraw. The one attempt to satisfy Europeans about the American deterrent had been creation of closer cooperation at the level of nuclear planning.

If any one event revitalized the organization, however, it was the sudden and brutal invasion of Czechoslovakia by the USSR and other Warsaw Pact nations on August 21, 1968, just twenty years after the Communist seizure of power in Prague. Testifying as it did to Russia's willingness to use what was now seen to be highly modernized conventional force, the invasion ensured the continuation of NATO and French adherence to the treaty. In subsequent years, French successor governments would cooperate more and more closely with the organization, and French units continued to be stationed in Germany. (In December 1995, as the NATO mission was being redefined following the collapse of any immediate Soviet threat, France finally rejoined NATO!)

Conclusion

The seeming bipolar stability exemplified by the meeting between Eisenhower and Khrushchev in Geneva in 1955 was deceptive. Khrushchev's repudiation of many of Stalin's harsh domestic policies and of his rigid foreign stance produced better times, but also provoked both revolt within the bloc leading to the invasion of Hungary, and ultimately the disastrous split with China. The world Communist movement was irrevocably divided. Khrushchev, in part to prove his continued Communist militancy, provoked several international crises—over Berlin, in the Middle East, and, finally, in Cuba.

In the meantime, spurred on by the humiliation inflicted upon them by American opposition to their venture at Suez, the French revitalized the movement toward European unity. The British, still seeking a global role as their worldwide power diminished, tried to find it by maintaining their World War II "special relationship" to the United States. As the new European Economic Community flourished, however, and as British resources proved inadequate for maintenance of a global role, the British sought and finally obtained EEC membership. In the meantime, and for a decade, the figure of Charles de Gaulle loomed large on the world scene as he eloquently articulated a different vision of world politics, in which the "two hegemonies" of the Soviet Union and the United States would be curbed by a rising, continental "Europe of nations," now with regained influence in the new "Third World." In pursuit of the vision, he forced NATO to leave French soil and withdrew from its structure. Although de Gaulle left the scene with the vision obscured by the Soviet invasion of Czechoslovakia, much of his legacy endured, for the world, in fact, was no longer simply dominated by the two superpowers.

Under Eisenhower the United States abandoned the attempt to substitute "liberation" for containment. In subsequent years, it also became evident that the preeminent American economic position in the world was eroding. Europe and Japan not only recovered from World War II, but began a surge of modernization that made them rivals to the United States, with uncertain results for the future structure of world power. The fruits of successful American postwar policy had begun to ripen. They were not all sweet.

Further Suggested Readings

On U.S.-Soviet relations during this period, see the work by Ulam, listed in chapter 2, and also Walter Z. Laqueur and Leopold Labedz, *Polycentrism: the New Factor in International Politics* (New York: Praeger, 1962). Alfred Grosser, *French Foreign Policy Under de Gaulle* (Boston: Little, Brown, 1967), is a contemporary account by a top French analyst. Desmond Dinan, *Ever Closer Union? An Introduction to the European Community* (Boulder, CO: Lynne Rienner Publishers, 1994), is a good basic book, while Emile Benoit, *Europe at Sixes and Sevens* (New York: Columbia University Press, 1961), gives the flavor of the time of the split. Alexander de Porte, *Europe Between the Superpowers*, 2d ed. (New Haven: Yale University Press, 1986), provides an account of the resurgence and limitations faced by Europe in the new global structure of power.

4

Bipolarism Challenged—
The Non-Western World

The *first* decade following World War II produced "bipolarism"—the division of the political world into two blocs, in which the two superpowers emerged, each armed with thermonuclear weapons. The next decade produced the *"Third* World," conscious of itself, organized as such at the United Nations, made up of states of enormous variety, but all claiming a common heritage—they were the products of colonialism—and most claiming, essentially, that they belonged to neither bloc. In the process of creating this Third World, the already independent states of Latin America and a smattering of others joined with the 100 new states that emerged from the breakup of the remaining colonial empires in those two postwar decades.

Inevitably, the emergence of this world posed issues for both the United States, the Soviet Union, and European countries that they had not previously encountered. The Soviet Union, freed from Stalinist dogma, courted the countries in various ways, a course that was fraught with dilemmas: if Soviet leaders established good relations with a government, they had to disavow the local Communist Party dedicated to overthrowing that government. Conversely, successive American administrations, fearing Russian successes, tended to see local developments in a global balance-of-power context, and reacted accordingly. The result was that although Americans thought of themselves as anti-colonialist and as friends of the newly independent states, the new states frequently saw Americans as interventionist and imperialist. Europeans sought to maintain old relationships in modified form, with mixed success.

The Troubled Road to Peace in Asia

From the beginning, the march to independence became complicated by Communist attempts to capture nationalist movements and pose as the major anti-imperialist force. So it was that Britain, having granted independence to India and Pakistan in 1947, and to Ceylon and Burma soon after, found itself engaged in antiguerrilla warfare in Malaysia, where the Communists were well entrenched in the large Chinese minority. (With Communist Parties up in arms in Malaysia, Indonesia, Burma, India, and Indochina, and Mao's armies triumphant in northern China, Western observers concluded that, in the wake of failure in Western Europe, the world Communist movement had switched to a new, Asian insurrectionary strategy: the uprisings followed upon a Russian-organized Calcutta meeting of Asian parties.) A determined effort under British leadership eventually crushed the Malaysian rebellion, and with the development of Malay-Chinese cooperation, the British were able to relinquish power to an independent Malaya on August 31, 1957. In 1965 Singapore seceded to become an independent and, eventually, a very wealthy republic.

Under strong international pressure brought to bear against the Netherlands in 1948–49, the Dutch transferred authority from the Netherlands to the United States of Indonesia in November 1949. The two would be joined in a union under the Dutch crown, in emulation of the British Commonwealth of Nations. Ahmed Sukarno—a long-time nationalist imprisoned by the Dutch but promoted by the Japanese—emerged as the preeminent if erratic political leader of the islands, dedicated to forming a stronger and more unitary state, eventually rejecting parliamentary government with opposition parties as an unsuitable form of government for Indonesia, and coming to rely more and more on the well-organized Communist Party of Indonesia, even though he had crushed a Communist rebellion earlier.

The First Vietnam War

Ho Chi Minh, in Indochina, was far more single-minded in the path he chose to create an independent, Communist Vietnam, once war with the French broke out in 1946.

For the first few years French governments failed to devote the forces necessary to crushing what they saw primarily as a minor guerrilla effort. Mao's victory in China in late 1949 changed everything: it meant that Ho Chi Minh's Vietminh forces could now find sanctuary across the border, over which flowed new aid from the Chinese Communists, and Ho's government received recognition from China and the Soviet Union. The French found groups with whom they were able to negotiate an independent status for Vietnam, Laos, and Cambodia within the French Union, and some thirty-five Western states recognized the three new governments. The outbreak of war in Korea in July 1950 made the French struggle look like part of a common, interdependent effort to contain communism in Asia. By 1952, the Truman Administration could announce that the effort there was "essential to the security of the free world, not only in the Far East but in the Middle East and Europe as well," and by fiscal year 1954, American aid under the new Eisenhower Administration covered almost four-fifths of the cost of the French effort.

The deteriorating French military situation worsened dramatically in March 1954, however, when the Vietminh besieged the isolated fortress of Dien Bien Phu, where some 10,000 French troops were supposed to smash any besieging force, but found themselves outmanned and outgunned, with no relief possible. Ho Chi Minh wanted a decisive military victory that would give him a political victory at a nine-power conference on the general situation in the Far East then in session in Geneva, Switzerland.

The 1954 Geneva Conference took place by Soviet request. The Western powers acceded to this request in order to test post-Stalinist leadership's willingness to compromise. A reluctant Dulles accepted the call for a conference because he still wanted the French to agree to German rearmament. To get them to do so, he consented to their wish for a general settlement in the Far East, dictated by war weariness at home. Churchill accepted because he wanted negotiations himself, but he had also come under pressure from new British Commonwealth members like India, Ceylon, and Pakistan.

In Geneva the expected deadlock on Korea and other issues ensued, while worldwide attention focused on the siege of Dien Bien Phu. In early April, Eisenhower considered and rejected a proposal for a massive air strike in relief of the fortress, which would have brought the United States into war in Vietnam a full decade earlier than actually happened. Efforts by Dulles to obtain British and French support for a program of collective action failed, even as President Eisenhower told the press that the loss of Indochina would be like the first of a row of falling dominoes: the rest of Southeast Asia would soon follow.

On May 7, while the meetings were in recess, Ho achieved what he had wanted: the surrender of the besieged French garrison at Dien Bien Phu. It was an enormous psychological victory, headlined in every newspaper around the world, and it came at just the right moment for North Vietnamese purposes: France would be bound to withdraw from Indochina. Complicated maneuvering at the Geneva Conference and pressures from China and the Soviet Union led to a series of agreements no one much wanted: Vietnam was divided for administrative purposes at the seventeenth parallel. The communists were located in the north and the non-communists in the south, with the proviso that a free transfer of those wanting to leave either area could take place, and that forces of each side would regroup in their

Map 6. **Vietnam and Its Neighbors**

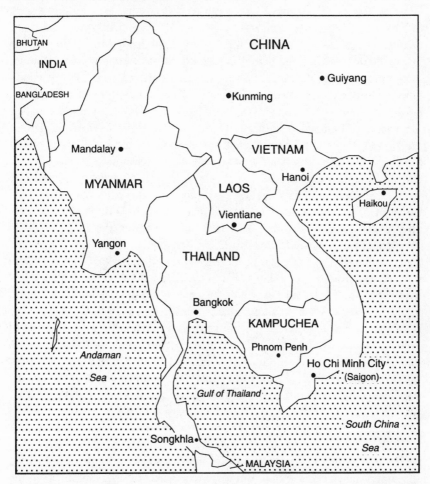

respective areas. No new troops or weapons were to be introduced into the area, and free, general, secret elections would take place within two years throughout the country under the supervision of an international commission composed of representatives from Canada, India, and Poland. Laos and Cambodia were to be neutralized and demilitarized.

Ho Chi Minh's representatives had demanded withdrawal of all foreign troops and immediate elections, which would have given them all of Vietnam. They accepted the agreements, however, because of their assurance that the regime in the south would collapse within a few years anyway and because Russia and China wanted to appear conciliatory before the new grouping of Asian states. But neither the new and fully independent

Vietnamese government in the south nor the Americans accepted all the Geneva agreements: conscious that partition was coming, unwilling to appear to have acquiesced in it, Dulles—the apostle of "liberation"—abandoned the conference and never signed the final act. Nor did Prime Minister Ngo Dinh Diem, the devout Catholic who now headed the southern government under the French-supported Emperor Bao Dai, sign: he was certain that the conditions for free elections could never be established in the Communist-controlled north, and he was also certain that he would be unable to create conditions for meaningful elections in the south within two years. As a result, neither the United States nor South Vietnam was really bound by any accord but the cease-fire. Records later showed that the Communists never expected elections to take place either.

In subsequent months some 850,000 refugees left the north, revealing the extent of opposition to the Communist takeover. Ngo Dinh Diem's government began to receive direct American aid, bypassing the French, and to everyone's surprise, the Nationalist Diem was able to consolidate his regime and incorporate the refugees. In the meantime, in mid-1955, Ho Chi Minh traveled to Moscow and Peking to sign trade and aid agreements that effectively coordinated the northern half of Vietnam with other Communist states. Many analysts saw the resulting situation as analogous to that of Korea and Germany, where a dividing line represented a division between spheres of influence that could be breached only at the peril of world peace. The war in Indochina was over, the French were gone, and instead of three successor states, there were four. What most people did not know was that the departing Communists left both cadres and hidden stocks of weapons in the south.

Taiwan and the Southeast Asia Treaty Organization

Nevertheless, by 1954, both the war in Korea and the struggle in Indochina appeared to have been settled. But there remained one area of conflict in the Far East: "It is imperative," declared Zhou En-lai soon after the Geneva Conference, "that the People's Republic of China liberate Taiwan and liquidate the traitorous Chiang Kai-shek group." President Eisenhower therefore served notice on the Chinese Communists that he would not permit an invasion of Taiwan to take place without American opposition: he secured a congressional resolution authorizing him to act in the event of an attack on Taiwan or the nearby Pescadore Islands, while at the same time reassuring everyone that the United States would not aid Chiang if he tried to attack the mainland. Another temporary and unstable Asian "settlement"—a two-Chinas arrangement unacceptable both to the Chinese Communists and to the Nationalists on Taiwan—had been reached.

At the same time, in order to deter further Communist expansion in Southeast Asia, the United States sponsored creation of a defensive alliance at Manila in September 1954. Pakistan, Thailand, and the Philippines joined Great Britain, France, Australia, New Zealand, and the United States in a pact that created the Southeast Asia Treaty Organization (SEATO). The pact was aimed at developing a collective capacity to resist armed attack and countersubversive activities. A protocol extended its provisions to cover the Indochinese states, which, as a result of the Geneva agreements, were not permitted to join. Countries like India, Burma, Indonesia, and Ceylon expressed their displeasure: the pact extended the Cold War to an area where it did not yet exist. For them the recently ended war in Indochina was clearly one between Nationalists and imperialists, and not one between the Communist bloc and the "free world."

As a part of the commitment to Southeast Asia, gradually, cautiously, the Eisenhower Administration also began to provide economic and military support to South Vietnam, where Ngo Dinh Diem appeared to be just the sort of incorruptible, non-Communist nationalist who could counter the appeal of communism. Just as in Korea before 1950, a commitment began to grow that it would be hard to abandon, as the issue of "credibility" would come into play—and play a key role in the 1960s, when the second Vietnamese War would have even more global repercussions than the first.

The Middle East

The "Middle East" is mainly a concept in people's minds. With borders that depend upon the criteria used, it encompasses diverse peoples of different languages, different religions, and different histories: it is a bridge between Europe, Asia, and Africa; and, through the Suez Canal, it provides the major passageway from Europe to South Asia, Southeast Asia, and East Asia. It also contains most of the world's supply of oil, which, under the notion of sovereignty, belongs to the state sitting on top of it. The oil, of course, meant nothing until the twentieth century. The Middle East was long under Turkish domination, but as Turkey weakened in the nineteenth century, the area became a focus of Russian and German ambitions—both were ultimately blocked—and of growing struggle between Britain and France in which Britain won control of the Suez Canal and domination of Egypt. The last vestiges of Turkish empire ended with Turkish defeat in World War I, and the areas under its domination became League of Nation mandates under French and British rule with arbitrarily drawn borders. Of the mandates, Iraq became independent in the interwar years, Syria, Lebanon, and Jordan at the end of World War II. Palestine posed more problems.

The Creation of Israel

Zionism—the movement to provide a national home for the dispersed Jews of the world in Palestine—grew rapidly in the first half of the twentieth century, as Ottoman control over the Middle East dissolved. During World War I, in order to get Jewish support in the war against the Central Powers, Britain issued the Balfour Declaration, promising the Jews a "national home" in "Palestine," a region that then also encompassed what is now Jordan and Syria. British leaders foresaw no conflict with the Arabs, whom they had stimulated to revolt against the Turks by promises of booty and independence, since the area in which the Jews would settle constituted only a sparsely settled 1 percent of the total area to be wrested from Turkey. In the interwar years Jewish immigration increased, and the well-organized Jewish community bought land and established its own institutions of self-government, stimulating overall development of a now much smaller area composing the Palestine Mandate. The Arab population of the area increased, and Arab agitation against Jewish immigration arose. Nazi persecution of the Jews intensified Jewish immigration, which the British tried to restrict while instituting a local government in which Arabs would predominate.

During World War II, Jews found increasing support from the American Jewish community through the American Zionist Organization, which in 1942 asked for the creation of a Jewish state in Palestine, unlimited immigration, and the formation of a Jewish army. Then, at the end of the war, the survivors of Hitler's extermination centers intensified the problem. President Roosevelt had told King Ibn Saud of Saudi Arabia that, although he thought more Jews should be admitted to Palestine, no step would be taken without consulting both Arabs and Jews. But following the war, President Truman pursued his demand for immediate admission of 100,000 Jewish refugees. When the winter of 1947 hit in Europe, the British, eager to get rid of the burden and under pressure from both Arabs and Jews, requested a special session of the UN General Assembly to consider the whole question. The session met from April 28 to May 15, 1947, and created the United Nations Special Committee on Palestine (UNSCOP), composed of eleven states. UNSCOP's assignment was to prepare and present a report to the regular fall session of the General Assembly.

In September 1947, by a vote of 33 to 13, with 10 abstentions, the General Assembly of the United Nations adopted the majority plan presented to it by UNSCOP to partition Palestine into two separate Arab and Jewish states, despite warnings by the minority that Arab states would never accept it. Everything was supposedly well planned out: a UN commission would effect partition, the Security Council would prevent any

Map 7. **Israel and Its Neighbors (1948)**

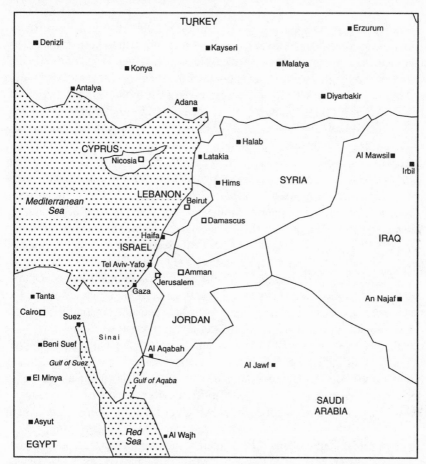

forcible attempt to alter it, the Economic and Social Council would effect an economic union between the Jewish and Arab states, and the Trusteeship Council would assume administration of an internationalized Jerusalem.

This plan was, many thought, an exciting example of how the new United Nations might function. For the first time, a state was to born not by force but legally, by a majority vote of the whole international community. It did not work. On May 14, 1948, when the British withdrew and the state of Israel was proclaimed (and immediately recognized by both the United States and the Soviet Union), Egyptian, Jordanian, Iraqi, Lebanese, and Syrian forces entered Palestine, while Arab refugees began to flee the fighting. The Security Council appointed a mediator, Count Folke Bernadotte, president of the Swedish Red Cross who, after a first short-lived truce broke down, was able to procure an armistice based on the current location of both sides' troops.

As a result of the fighting, the Jews considerably enlarged the territory allotted to them in the partition plan, and claimed the right to keep it: the Arabs had disregarded the UN plan, invaded illegally, and would have to take the consequences of their loss. Arab spokesmen maintained that the UN General Assembly had acted illegally in creating a new state in the first place. This, of course, hardened Jewish attitudes: in the face of Arabs implacably determined to destroy the new Jewish state, Israel needed all the territory it had gained.

Arab refugees, 600,000 of them, now crowded camps around the borders of Israel, in the Egyptian-administered Gaza Strip; on the Jordanian-administered West Bank of the Jordan River; and in southern Lebanon, where Arab states did little to resettle them, claiming, rather, a "right of return." The Israelis would not let the refugees return, fearing that they would form a "fifth column" devoted to the eventual destruction of Israel from within. In the ensuing years, hundreds of thousands of Jewish refugees left their homes in Arab countries to settle in Israel, effectively creating, in the Israeli view, a de facto exchange of population. The burden of Arab refugee relief was assumed by the United Nations and largely financed by the United States, and the refugees were taught that Israel must disappear. Palestinian nationalism began to emerge.

Arab leadership in several states was fatally weakened by the war. Abdullah of Transjordan proceeded to annex the West Bank, doubling the population of Jordan and transforming his Emirate into the Hashemite Kingdom of Jordan. By so doing, he weakened Palestinian claims to a separate state: he had incorporated most of what would be its territory. Two-thirds of Palestinians now lived within Jordan. In future years, when Israel occupied the West Bank after the second Middle East War (1967), and Palestinians now claimed it for their state, Israelis pointed out that the issue had never been raised when Jordan had annexed the West Bank, knowing, of course, that it was because the Palestinians had wanted not the West Bank, but Israel itself.

Like Israel, King Abdullah of Jordan had an interest in preempting a Palestinian nationalism that could destroy his state. It became common knowledge that he was ready to make peace with Israel. As a result, he was assassinated and the moment for a "Jordanian solution" to the problem of Palestine passed. After an interlude, Abdullah was succeeded by the present king, Hussein.

The Rise of Nasser

By 1950 disarray in the camp of the Arab League was complete. Projects for unity clashed with one another as Arab countries vied for leadership. In

Syria one coup succeeded another. In Egypt the defeat deepened the attitude that despite Western warnings, the Soviet Union was no threat—the West and Zionism were the real threat. The British bases around the vital Suez Canal were a source of festering resentment, along with continued British presence in the Anglo-Egyptian Sudan to the south. Hostility to Britain soon turned against the corrupt monarchy and the political parties that had betrayed Egyptian dignity. The "Free Officers" group overthrew the sybaritic King Farouk on July 23, 1952. After a brief period, Colonel Gamal Abdel Nasser emerged as prime minister and president, and he was to become the outstanding Arab leader of the 1950s.

The Revolutionary Command Council, which Nasser headed, initiated extensive internal reforms and inspired army leaders in other Arab states. In the foreign policy field, Nasser liquidated the Sudan issue by an agreement with the English that allowed the Sudanese a free choice between union with Egypt and complete independence—which the Sudanese eventually chose in 1955. He also negotiated a new Suez Canal treaty providing for gradual withdrawal of British troops and a British right of reentry in case of attack, but also a recognition that the canal was "an integral part of Egypt." It was another and vital step in the retreat of the West.

The Soviet Union Enters the Middle East

People throughout the Middle East hailed Nasser's diplomatic triumphs, and Western governments hoped for better relations now that a longstanding irritant had been removed. But the issue of Israel remained. France, England, and the United States had, in effect, imposed an arms embargo upon the Middle East, and they issued a May 1950 guarantee of existing armistice lines. It was of little help that the Americans tried to persuade the Israelis to limit immigration, and condemned it for retaliation in the face of Arab raids. An attempt to bridge the political conflict by stimulating and financing functional cooperation that would help both Arab and Jew—the so-called Johnson Plan for Jordan River development—collapsed over the basic issue: the Western powers acted on the assumption that Israel was there to stay. Arab leaders rejected it. The final straw was the Baghdad Pact of 1955, creating a Middle East alliance of the "northern tier" states—Turkey, Iraq, Iran, and Pakistan—with Britain. The pact, which was directed against the Soviet Union, enhanced the importance of conservative Iraq, whose monarch, King Faisal, was a cousin to King Hussein of Jordan.

Nasser accused Iraq of betraying the Arab cause and allying itself with the imperialists. Khrushchev saw in the pact an opportunity to change the whole political situation in the Middle East by a very simple move. In

September 1955, in the face of a falling world cotton market, he arranged to purchase Egyptian cotton for several years to come, in return for Soviet bloc arms. By this move he leapfrogged the Baghdad Pact to make Russia a force in any future Middle East dealings, gave the Arabs an alternative to their reliance upon the hated West, and in the process initiated an enduring arms race in the Middle East.

In the short run, Khrushchev's move was a brilliant one, making the Soviet Union a global player where it had never been before. Whether the Soviets benefited in the long run is something else again. Although Soviet capacity to project power in other parts of the world remained limited for the next two decades, the move was a forerunner of far more extensive Soviet involvement than had been true in Stalin's day.

Certainly by the mid-1950s the masses throughout the Middle East had found a hero in Gamal Abdel Nasser—the man who had triumphed over the Americans and British, and who had found a counter to the West in the Soviet Union. Together with Nehru, Sukarno, and Tito, he had begun to forge the new Non-Aligned Movement that would eclipse the West. Out of weakness and degradation had come both strength and glory.

The Suez War of 1956

To Eisenhower's Secretary of State John Foster Dulles, Nasser represented a tendency that must be curbed: the playing off of Russia against the West. To Anthony Eden (who had broken with the British government twenty years earlier over the issue of "appeasing" Hitler at Munich), Nasser represented—on a smaller scale—a new Hitler. To appease Nasser would mean permitting him to go from strength to strength, until the West lost all control over events in the Middle East to an absolute dictator. To French Premier Guy Mollet, Nasser represented intrusion into the nascent Algerian-French conflict; France had given up Tunisia and Morocco, but Algeria was French, and the terrorists bent on destroying the bond took heart—and received support—from Nasser. To Israel, surrounded by weak but hostile states, Nasser represented a new threat, that of Arab unity devoted to the destruction of Israel.

Dulles precipitated matters. On July 19, 1956, in order to curb the new game of playing off the Soviet Union against the West, he withdrew the American portion of funding for Nasser's great projected Aswan Dam, high on the Nile, symbol of Egypt's forthcoming modernization and independence from the West. For a week, Nasser—who was conferring with Tito and Nehru in Yugoslavia—remained quiet. Then, in an impassioned speech delivered at Alexandria, after telling the Americans to "Choke to death on

your own fury . . . ," he informed the delirious crowd that he was nationalizing the Suez Canal. He was retaking stolen property, and its profits would
enable Egyptians to forgo American aid and build the High Dam themselves. Third World countries and Moscow widely applauded the move;
among ecstatic Arabs his stock soared further. Dulles's "lesson" appeared
to have backfired completely.

To England, France, and Israel, Egyptian control of the vital canal, particularly under Nasser, was intolerable. They sought American support for
diplomatic, economic, or military sanctions, for some form of international
control through a users' association. Dulles gave them only mixed signals.
Certain now that they could not receive active support from their American
allies, but sure, too, that the Eisenhower Administration would not actively
oppose them, British and French leaders began building up their forces in
the eastern Mediterranean, secretly concerting their plans with the Israelis.

In the two years prior to nationalization of the Suez Canal, guerrilla
attacks upon Israel from the camps across the borders had increased in
scope and frequency. Palestinian hostility had been made bolder by
Nasser's successes on other fronts. Israel responded with retaliation in
force, for which it was condemned by UN border commissions and within
the Security Council. Nasser, with no international condemnation, blocked
Israeli cargoes from going through the Suez Canal (a violation of the treaty
he was bound to observe), while using his control of Sharm el Sheik, at the
southern tip of the Sinai Peninsula overlooking the southern exit of the Gulf
of Aqaba, to blockade the Israeli port of Elath, through which flowed oil
from the Persian Gulf.

On October 29, 1956—at the very moment when Russian tanks were
crossing into Hungary to suppress the Nagy government—the Israelis struck
rapidly across Egypt's Sinai Peninsula. The timing seemed ripe, since so
much world attention was focused on the events in Hungary; in the United
States, moreover, Eisenhower was busy winding up his presidential election
campaign. Israeli forces achieved rapid success, driving to the canal and
down the Sinai to seize Sharm el Sheik. The British and the French effected
a successful landing at the mouth of the Suez Canal on November 5—the
day after the reinforced Russian armies entered Budapest.

The results were completely unexpected. Nasser simply blocked the
canal by sinking ships that were already in passage. Pipelines in Syria from
oil-rich Iraq to Mediterranean ports were cut by Egyptian sympathizers in
Syria. All of Western Europe therefore faced severe oil shortages in the
winter ahead. Moreover, the French and the English had made another
monumental miscalculation: Eisenhower and Dulles were furious with their
allies. There must be no reward for aggression, lectured Eisenhower: "there

can be no law if we were to invoke one code of international conduct for those who oppose us and another for our friends." The administration refused to activate an emergency oil lift to Europe unless the French and the British withdrew from Egypt.

In the meantime, Khrushchev, busy assaulting Hungarian independence and neutrality, expressed outrage at the Western assault on Egypt; suggested joint military action with the United States; and, when rebuffed on this, offered to send volunteers to help Egypt. He also—somewhat implausibly—threatened to attack Britain and France with guided missiles. A run on the British pound and the French franc sealed the issue. A sick Anthony Eden (soon to resign) and a weary Guy Mollet, their plans dashed, agreed to withdraw.

A happy inspiration and improvisation by Lester Pearson of Canada provided a face-saving formula: the United Nations Emergency Force (UNEF), a small contingent of unarmed troops from neutral nations welded into a UN body, would be interposed between belligerents. When Nasser agreed to allow it to patrol the Israeli-Egyptian border and to be stationed at Sharm el Sheik, the English and the French could announce that they had obtained their original objective; and Israel, too, could agree to withdrawal.

Israel had at least demonstrated its power and secured its borders. But Nasser emerged greatly strengthened. Egyptian propaganda pictured the Egyptian army as having roundly defeated the invaders: they were, after all, forced to withdraw. Most countries of the world, including the Soviet Union, had supported him, and he gained unquestioned control of the canal. Khrushchev gained too, having successfully posed as the champion of the Arabs, ready to come to their aid when needed. And the Suez affair helped deflect attention from the invasion of Hungary, particularly among Third World states, who saw the Suez affair as a far more important reaffirmation of Western imperialism.

The United States seemed to have made gains in the area, too, having distinguished itself from the invaders and helped to force them out. Yet, in the aftermath, it dissipated what goodwill it may have amassed when Eisenhower appeared before Congress to ask for a joint resolution that would authorize the president to use U.S. armed forces "to protect any nation in the general region of the Middle East requesting such protection against overt armed aggression from any nation controlled by international Communism."

The "Eisenhower Doctrine," as it was called, immediately brought an angry Arab reaction. It was correctly interpreted as an attempt to substitute American influence for that of the departed British and French, but influence was viewed as domination. Not only was there no "vacuum" in the area—the Arab states were there—but the issue of international communism was fraudulent, too. The threat was not communism, but "imperialism, Zionism, and colonialism." Arab nationalism was the sole basis on which Arab policy was to be formulated.

The United Nations appeared to have gained, too. The events in the Middle East of these years appeared to presage a new, different, and prospectively widened role for the United Nations. "Collective security" was dead: the attempt to revive it in bastard form at the time of Korea had led to nothing, and when the General Assembly met to consider the Russian invasion of Hungary (any action in the Security Council being blocked by the Soviet Union), Third World spokesmen made it clear: the United Nations could do what it wanted, but they would support no collective measures such as most of them had supported at the time of Korea. It was best to try to keep the conflict localized; they would not be drawn into the conflict as they had been earlier. With that, the concept of collective security itself—that a conflict anywhere in the world is of concern to the whole international community—was buried.

But the quiet secretary-general, Dag Hammarskjold, had begun to grope toward something new: personal diplomacy based on use of his office as a symbol of the wider collective interest. As a diplomat, he would represent no state, but he could bring a genuinely disinterested view to existing conflicts, avoid taking sides, explore possible solutions with the parties involved, and build confidence in the office into the process. By discreetly seeking some measure of publicity, he would make it harder for parties to a conflict to ignore him, since the world media would be focusing on him. The UN Emergency Force represented his preventive diplomacy on a larger scale: by putting the "thin blue line" between belligerents—the soldiers wore blue helmets to identify themselves—he would make it difficult for the contending parties to resume hostilities: few states would want to attack unarmed Swedes, or Irish or Nigerian soldiers, who also symbolized the United Nations itself, and were backed by majority votes in the General Assembly. Eventually, such UN forces might resolve the old balance-of-power dilemma faced by the United States in the Mideast when it felt the need to use its influence to balance what it thought was growing Soviet influence in an area where states were weak. A UN presence might calm such fears and diminish the felt need for such balance-of-power policies—and might serve as a precedent for the future. The very first UN "peacekeeping" mission therefore had enormous symbolic importance.

The Promise and the Illusion of Arab Unity

Following the Suez War and for a dozen years until his death in 1970, Gamal Abdel Nasser and "Nasserism" strove to become the wave of the future in the Middle East and to give the area real unity. In 1958 Egypt and Syria formed the United Arab Republic (UAR). There was jubilation when a short-lived rival union between Jordan and Iraq broke up following violent revolution against the young Iraqi king: Iraq and Jordan would surely join the UAR once Hussein was also overthrown. There was, in fact, sufficient concern and fear of subversion in neighboring Lebanon and Jordan that the two countries appealed for Anglo-American intervention, and Eisenhower sent American marines wading ashore in Beirut, while British troops flew into Jordan. An angry Nasser conferred with Khrushchev, who blustered and thundered. But the Iraqi regime—which withdrew from the Western-sponsored Baghdad Pact—showed no tendency to join the United Arab Republic. As the sense of crisis simmered down, the American and British troops withdrew, and both the fragile Lebanese government and the Jordanian regime of King Hussein got a new lease on life.

Then, in 1961, the nucleus of true Arab unity split up, as Syrian political and military factions came to resent Egyptian domination. Nasser fulminated but could do nothing. Both Syria and Iraq would aspire to leadership of this part of the Arab world, known as the "fertile crescent," and both would receive substantial military aid from the Soviet Union. They remained hostile to each other, however. In 1963 the two engaged Nasser in a further attempt at union that sparked agitation for the overthrow of Hussein in Jordan, but despite their status as "liberated" radical states, contemptuous of older, traditional, Western-oriented regimes in other countries, nothing came of it.

One further problem was that many of the more traditional regimes were now beginning to really profit from growing world demand for their oil. These included countries like the British-protected Gulf states, Kuwait, Bahrain, and Qatar (the first of which became independent in 1961, the other two in 1971); the series of small states that formed the United Arab Emirates in 1971; and Saudi Arabia, the Kingdom of Libya, and Iran under the shah. These regimes (along with Iraq, the one Arab "socialist" state that had oil) now exported two-fifths of the world's oil. Despite much talk of imperialism, neocolonialism, and the growing power of multinationals such as the seven great international oil companies, these small states had already begun the process of imposing demands on the companies—a process that would eventually lead to the nationalization of the companies' operations within their borders in the 1970s. A power shift was in the making that no one had foreseen earlier: in 1956, at the time of the Suez War, the United States was still a major oil exporter, and could unilaterally affect the world's oil supply. By 1973, when yet another war broke out in the Middle East, Europe had shifted from a coal- to an oil-based economy and the

United States had become a large net importer of oil. This time, and in subsequent years, it was the oil-rich Arab exporters who held the upper hand and for a time were able to impose enormous oil price increases that sent the international economy into shock.

By this time, conservative Saudi Arabia had become the key player in the international oil game. At the southern tip of the peninsula, however, bordering the vital exit of the Red Sea into the Indian Ocean, and on the Indian Ocean itself, were a series of what had been British protectorates. As British power waned, these became an object of competition among Saudi Arabia, Egypt, and even the Soviet Union. From 1962 to 1969 a fierce civil war in Yemen found Saudi Arabia financing one side when Nasser, apparently trying a flanking move after the failure of the United Arab Republic, poured some 70,000 troops into the Yemen, whose new government had promised to unite the entire peninsula and liberate it from the "Saudi shame." Victory would give Nasser the key to control of world oil. He was forced, however, to pull out his troops after defeat in the 1967 war with Israel.

The British then disengaged from South Yemen (formerly the Federation of South Arabia), as part of their withdrawal from too expensive global responsibility. The winning faction in the subsequent struggle there called upon the Soviet Union for support, giving the Russians naval basing rights in Aden and adjacent islands. In future years South Yemen also aligned itself with Marxist Ethiopia and with Libya, and made frequent unsuccessful plans to unite with Yemen. Oman, to the east of South Yemen, asserted full independence in 1970; a Marxist faction supported from South Yemen tried to take over the government. It was defeated with British support. In subsequent years the southern tip of the Arabian peninsula remained divided, despite determination of Yemeni regimes to destabilize both the southeast coast and the east coast oil-rich states. Throughout the next two decades, a strong Russian presence continued to worry the west.

Iran: The First Crisis

Mohammad Reza Shah Pahlavi was twenty-two years old when his pro-Nazi father was deposed by the Soviets and the British in 1941 in order to establish a southern supply line to the embattled Soviet Union. In 1949, as he witnessed the outpouring of American economic and military aid to Western Europe, he approached the Truman Administration for aid for Iran. Truman advisers, however, likened Iran to China, where aid to Chiang's corrupt regime had been of no use, and the administration suggested to the shah that internal reforms must precede aid. The reform-minded shah acted, but no aid materialized, and in 1951, under leadership of Mohammad Mossadegh, the Iranian parliament nationalized the giant Anglo-Iranian Oil Company. Mossadegh became prime minister, while riots and disturbances erupted all over Iran in an upsurge of deeply felt nationalism.

Negotiations proved futile, and the British instituted an effective boycott of Iranian oil, counting on Iranian need for foreign income. Mossadegh, in turn, counted on world need for Iranian oil. Both proved wrong: the boycott had less effect than expected, since these were the years in which Saudi Arabian and Kuwaiti oil production began their enormous increase. The world could get along without Iranian oil.

As the crisis wore on without producing the expected revenues from nationalization, Mossadegh's disparate support began to disperse. He came to rely more and more on the Communist Tudeh Party, which had originally opposed him, and the incoming Eisenhower Administration in the United States became alarmed. Until this time, the United States had largely sided with Mossadegh in trying to arrange a compromise with the British. Now, in the face of growing chaos, and in concert with the British, the new administration provided financial backing to the Iranian army and to bazaar mobs who overthrew Mossadegh in August 1953, reinstalling the shah, who had fled the country.

Popular support and the army were the key. Despite myth, the U.S. Central Intelligence Agency (CIA) had only a relatively minor part. But the myths grew and played a growing future role: in Iran and elsewhere people felt that the United States had imposed a tyrant on a reluctant population; intelligence circles in the American government, on the other hand, concluded that quick, quiet covert action might be used to produce important political results. The shah, returned to his throne, relied on the army, and began a program of modernization that transformed his country. Never in the forefront of Third World movements, however, he made headlines again twenty-five years later when the upsurge of a new international movement, Islamic fundamentalism, finally did topple him from his throne (see chapter 7).

Bandung, 1955: Emergence of the "Third World"

In 1955 Eisenhower and Khrushchev met in Geneva and reassured each other that neither wanted nuclear war; West Germany achieved sovereignty and joined NATO, and the Warsaw Pact was created; Austria became sovereign and permanently neutralized; Khrushchev sought a rapprochement with Tito in Yugoslavia. That same year—dramatically—the leaders of twenty-four Afro-Asian countries met at Bandung, Indonesia, from April 18 to April 24, 1955.

There were no great substantive accomplishments at the conference, but Bandung symbolized the new states' emergence to independence and their leaders' determination to play a new role in a global system no longer dominated by Western Europe. It gave them an opportunity to meet one another and share views about the current international political scene. The final communique pleaded for world disarmament, nonintervention in the domestic affairs of states, increased UN membership, the end of colonialism, and cautiously criticized alliances: Prime Minister Nehru of India wanted a wholesale condemnation of all alliances, but several participants belonged to one or the other of the blocs. The big winner was undoubtedly Foreign Minister Zhou En-lai of the People's Republic of China, who came away from Bandung with an aura of great respectability.

Bandung hastened events elsewhere. The conservative government of Ceylon represented at Bandung was defeated in elections that brought to power the neutralist, Marxist-oriented S.W.R.D. Bandaranaike, who negotiated British withdrawal from its great Indian Ocean base at Trincomalee and established diplomatic relations with both Moscow and Peking. Indonesia abrogated its union with the Netherlands, and Sukarno visited Washington, Peking, and Moscow, from which he secured new credits. The new government of Prince Norodom Sihanouk of Cambodia withdrew from the French Union, in which it had remained after the 1954 Indochina settlement, and soon after, Tunisia and Morocco gained their independence. Habib Bourguiba of Tunisia declared that the independence of Algeria would have to follow soon.

Finally, at the United Nations, in December 1955, the longstanding deadlock over membership was broken, opening the gates to virtually universal membership. For years the Soviet Union had vetoed membership for other states so long as Eastern European states, viewed as puppets by the West, were not admitted. Under pressure from the Bandung grouping, the Western powers now dropped their opposition to a package deal, and sixteen states became members. In the future, all but the divided countries would almost automatically enter. As the march to independence speeded up in the late 1950s, a gradually self-conscious Third World virtually took over the United Nations and several specialized agencies, and made them its own.

Unrest and Independence in Africa

Change came more slowly to Africa than to other parts of the emerging Third World. Native societies south of the Sahara, while complex, were largely preliterate. In comparison to other colonial areas, the short European occupation had left much weaker governmental infrastructures and far fewer trained native elites able to operate a modern economy—a growing necessity in view of population growth and contact with the outside world. In Ghana, a country with a population of four million, there were perhaps 1,000 doctors, lawyers, and teachers with advanced professional degrees. In Nigeria, with forty million, there were only about 300 doctors and lawyers. Arbitrarily drawn boundaries, based largely on European exploration and European issues of balance-of-power politics, left interdependent populations spread across frontiers, while often enclosing hostile or competing tribal groupings within national boundaries. As a result of all these factors, the process of decolonization took longer and was frequently more bitter. It was most difficult where there was a large, white settler minority unwilling to give up power: in Algeria, the Portuguese colonies of Angola and Mozambique, Kenya, and Southern Rhodesia.

In the mid-1950s—apart from the special case of South Africa, independent under white minority rule since 1934—only Liberia, Egypt, Ethiopia, and Libya were independent, the latter two as a result of Mussolini's defeat in World War II. In 1949 the UN General Assembly resolved the issue of the former Italian colonies: Libya, the one Italian colony north of the Sahara, largely desert and with a population of less than three million, became an independent monarchy late in 1951. Discovery of rich oil deposits and the advent of a radical regime would catapult it into world politics in the future. Eritrea, on the Red Sea, was federated with the Ethiopia of Haile Selassie in 1952 (and its incorporation into a united Ethiopia ten years later led to secessionist guerrilla warfare that lasted until 1993, when it achieved independence). Somaliland was made a trust territory for a ten-year span, at the end of which it merged with British Somaliland to form Somalia. The new country announced its unfortunate goal of creation of a "Greater Somalia" that would include substantial areas of Ethiopia. Here, as in so many areas, there seemed real promise; instead, forty years later Somalia would be part of a new class of African areas: a geographical entity without statehood or a government.

Coastal states north of the Sahara—Tunisia, Algeria, and Morocco—were more Mediterranean than African, and were tied to the Middle East by religion and language. For the French, these countries were almost extensions of continental France: Algeria, in fact, sent departmental deputies to the French parliament. The other two were "protectorates," but their nationalist parties made much of how France had been unable to protect them during the war, and under the pressure of nationalist agitation, France granted independence to both in 1956.

The process was much harder in Algeria, where one million French Algerians insisted on integration of Algeria into France. An outburst of terrorist violence shortly after the Indochinese settlement in 1954 signaled the beginning of eight years of bitter warfare, of assassination and counterterrorism, and of fighting that ultimately involved 500,000 French troops and took 20,000 French lives and perhaps a million Algerian lives. It also brought the French Fourth Republic to an end in 1958, when the army that felt betrayed in Indochina and French Algerians banded together against the weakness of the Fourth Republic to help bring de Gaulle to power—only to be betrayed again, as they saw it, when de Gaulle himself negotiated independence for Algeria in 1962.

In the meanwhile, in the short span from 1957 to 1963, almost all the former British, French, and Belgian territories in the great arc sweeping from northwest Africa down to the Portuguese colonies and Southern Rhodesia became independent—sixteen in 1960 alone. Ghana was the first, under the leadership of Kwame Nkrumah, who devoted part of his energies to spurring independence elsewhere in Africa, but sought also—fruitlessly—to create a united Africa whose artificial colonial borders would disappear. Once the dam was broken there, the move to independence could hardly be blocked elsewhere. Other British colonies followed suit without too much trouble—countries like Tanganyika, Uganda, and Nigeria. The French, still trying to keep the postwar French Union together, attempted to create a status of quasi-independence within the Union. But by 1962, all the territories composing French West Africa and French Equatorial Africa opted for independence.

Growing Russian and Chinese interest in Africa both hastened and complicated the process of decolonization. When nationalists looked to the socialist bloc for support, they alarmed Western countries, which saw Communist influence flowing in. Khrushchev provided technicians and aid to Guinea, under Sékou Touré, leading to dire Western predictions of spreading Russian influence; a coup in newly independent Zanzibar in early 1964 led to proclamation of the People's Republic of Zanzibar, diplomatic relations with socialist countries, a variety of aid programs, and more dire predictions in Western media. At about the same time, in the former French Congo (Brazzaville) a series of coups followed one another, leading to a period in which Cuban troops were used to support one government and then expelled, a single governing party was created, and the country was established as the People's Republic of the Congo in 1969. It, too, established close ties with socialist bloc states.

The alarm over Soviet and Chinese influence proved to be a false one; within months, Zanzibar merged with Tanganyika under the leadership of the moderate nationalist Julius Nyerere, who continued to maintain close ties to China but followed an independent foreign policy. Sékou Touré followed an equally independent course in Guinea, expelling Russian personnel in 1961 for subversion; his relations with Western and socialist bloc countries followed a highly checkered course. Chinese Foreign Minister Zhou Enlai's visits to Africa in 1963 and 1965 did not sit too well: his declarations that Africa was ripe for revolution alienated some African leaders, who also felt that the growing Chinese-Russian conflict was being extended to Africa, where each of the two powers was vying for support.

Just as in Algeria, areas in Africa south of the Sahara with large white settler populations experienced far more strife than did others, Kenya and Rhodesia in particular.

A bitter conflict called the "Mau-Mau" rebellion erupted in Kenya, as the Kikuyu tribe, whose members claimed that white farmers had taken their rich uplands, attacked the British authorities. It lasted from 1952 until the mid-1950s and led to a British-imposed constitution with mixed-race representation and finally, in 1963, to independence under the leadership of Jomo Kenyatta, whom the British had formerly jailed for his association with the rebellion. To the south the British sponsored the economically rational Central African Federation of Northern and Southern Rhodesia and Nyasaland in 1953. It broke up in 1964 because blacks in the two northern states (which became Malawi and Zambia) argued that it perpetuated undue influence on the part of the powerful white Southern Rhodesian minority. Rhodesia, under a 1961 constitution that maintained white minority rule, declared independence from Britain unilaterally in 1965, when the British refused to accept any constitutional arrangement that did not provide for majority rule. British and then UN mandatory economic sanctions were imposed, and eventually, after many false starts, when the pressures proved too much for the white minority, Rhodesia became independent as Zimbabwe, under black majority rule, in 1980.

Independence of the giant Belgian Congo in June 1960 had even greater international repercussions. Belgians, still talking about a thirty-year period before independence, simply lost control. They were forced to negotiate an independence that would nevertheless protect Belgian economic interests and nationals in the Congo, where there were few trained elites to manage the giant state.

Chaos erupted when Congolese troops rebelled against their Belgian officers, and Belgium flew in paratroopers to protect its nationals. A brutal comic opera ensued, in which varying factions called for American or Soviet aid, while Third World countries looked to a UN intervention to preclude Cold War intervention and to secure the removal of Belgian troops. Secretary-General Dag Hammarskjold, with General Assembly (including U.S.) support, created a UN force modeled on the Middle Eastern UNEF. His unwillingness to actually send neutral UN troops into battle to force reintegration of the secessionist province of Katanga then earned him the opposition of African countries. Khrushchev, trying to take advantage of the Congolese chaos, attacked the secretary-general as a mere Westerner, proposing to replace him by a "troika"—a three-man secretary-generalship composed of one Westerner, one socialist bloc representative, and one representative from the Third World. He failed in this and in his overt military support of dissident Congolese factions through precarious Egyptian and Sudanese supply routes. Hammarskjold died in an airplane crash before the UN mission had accomplished its purpose of reestablishing general order, and his successor, U Nu of Burma (the first non-Western secretary-general), finally used the UN force to topple the Katanga government. A year after the force's withdrawal in 1964, Major General Joseph Mobutu seized power. He has never relinquished control, despite attempts to overthrow him and his resulting need to call upon American and Belgian intervention to support him—and despite the almost complete disintegration and degradation of the Congo over which he has nominally ruled.

The Congo imbroglio of the early 1960s greatly reduced the capacity of the United Nations to carry out subsequent peacekeeping missions: major states such as France and the Soviet Union, opposing the action for political reasons, refused to pay their share of its expenses, arguing that only the Security Council (where they had a veto) could carry out such measures. As a result, and until contemporary times, future secretary-generals had to be less ambitious and more circumspect.

In the course of the chaos, the erratic, radical nationalist leader and first Congolese Prime Minister Patrice Lumumba was murdered by another Congolese faction, giving African nationalism one of its most potent symbols of martyrdom. Years later it would develop that the Eisenhower Administration, fearing Lumumba's appeals to Russia, had planned his assassination but never carried it out (the Kennedy Administration reversed course, but too late). The Russians, cultivating African states, renamed their Moscow school for Third World students "Patrice Lumumba University."

The Congo incident divided African states into a radical "Casablanca group," led by Ghana and Guinea, which espoused both "socialism" and radical anticolonialism, and a more cautious "Monrovia group," which saw danger in Russian and Chinese attempts both to appeal to African revolutionary sentiments and to directly influence political events in several African states. In 1963, at the invitation of Emperor Haile Selassie of Ethiopia, a twenty-state summit conference of African leaders met to bridge the gap between the two groups, and created the Organization of African Unity (OAU), with headquarters in Addis Ababa. Twenty years later the OAU had fifty members and an elaborate institutional structure.

Map 8. **Africa in 1895**

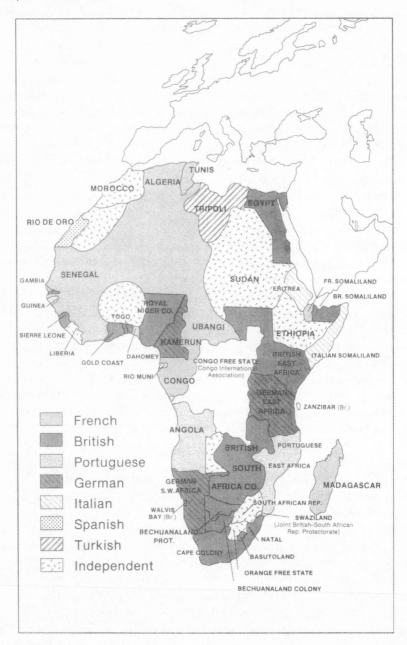

Source: Joseph Weatherby, Jr., et al., *The Other World: Issues and Politics in the Third World* (New York: Macmillan, 1987).

Map 9. **Africa Today**

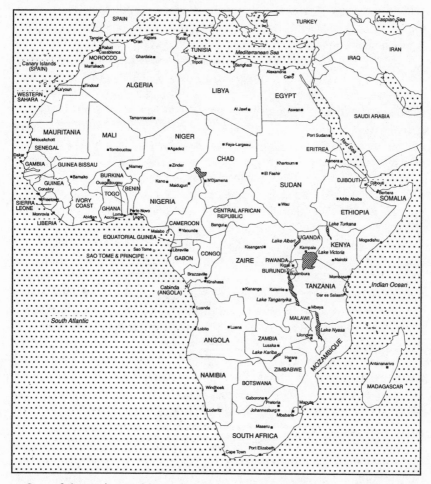

One of the major problems for African modernization is reflected in the fact that the OAU's official languages remain English, French, and, "if possible, African languages."

The Third World Captures the United Nations

Bandung in 1955 gave birth to the notion of the Third World. African and Asian states had been caucusing informally since 1950 at the United Nations, where they now followed suggestions made at Bandung to put the caucus on a permanent basis. By 1960, newly independent African states flooded into the General Assembly, greatly increasing the caucus's voting power and influence.

There was, for a time, a serious split between the Non-Aligned Movement and Afro-Asianism, prompted in part by the growing Russian-Chinese conflict. Tito of Yugoslavia, Egypt's Nasser, and Nehru of India called for a Non-Aligned Conference to convene in Belgrade, Yugoslavia, in September 1961. Sukarno and Zhou En-lai, however, supported Afro-Asianism as an alternative, and called for a purely Afro-Asian conference that would, incidentally, exclude Tito's Yugoslavia. The key was that Communist China—excluded from the Non-Aligned Movement—could belong to an Afro-Asian group, but Russia could not. Despite this, the Belgrade conference took place as scheduled, and the Non-Aligned Movement was put on a permanent basis, with a secretariat and periodic meetings. For Nehru, Nasser, and Tito, concerned with Chinese activities in Africa, the meeting was a public relations triumph. (It was also the high-water mark of Nasser's attempt to be an African leader.) The alternative, rival Afro-Asian movement subsequently collapsed over issues of membership.

At the United Nations itself, the various African and Afro-Asian caucuses then merged with Latin American representatives into the Group of 77 (G-77). It all came about because the United States moved to support the calling of an international conference on trade and development. Such a conference was by and large opposed by other Western states, which saw it as a futile diplomatic exercise that would take away from the importance of the Kennedy Round of tariff negotiations scheduled to start in Geneva in 1964, under the auspices of the General Agreement on Tariffs and Trade. GATT supporters argued that it was able to accommodate its rules to the needs of the less developed countries. The IBRD (the World Bank) had already added to its normal, commercial-rate loans a capacity to make "soft," or subsidized loans, and a capacity to provide guarantees to stimulate private financing through two new adjuncts created in 1958–59, the International Development Agency (IDA) and the International Finance Commission (IFC). Taken together, all of these moves should prove crucial to further opening up of the trading system to the newly independent Third World countries. The Third World General Assembly majority, however—now that it had American support—put through its own resolution in favor of the conference and organized itself as the Group of 77, to issue a manifesto on the historic importance of the forthcoming United Nations Conference on Trade and Development (UNCTAD).

UNCTAD, the largest international conference in history, met for three months in 1964 in Geneva. It was ambitious in scope: its sponsors wanted to create a new world trade organization that could make binding decisions on the basis of one state/one vote, to which GATT, the World Bank, and the International Monetary Fund (IMF) would be subsidiary. In the face of

Western refusal to join any such organization, the conference had to settle for much less: an UNCTAD organization in which Western countries would nominally participate, since it could only recommend. In subsequent years the UNCTAD Secretariat became essentially a secretariat for G-77, helping its members to prepare their positions and arguments. One result was the formalizing of the bloc system of voting at the United Nations generally; what had been merely agreement in the past on representational shares in various boards now became more formal, and the voting patterns followed suit, not always with the best consequences. As one French diplomat put it, "they think that votes in international organizations mean power," with the result that measures would be voted to attempt to force developed states into taking action they would not take, when negotiation might have produced at least limited but desirable results.

Bloc voting also lessened Western support for the United Nations, just when a truly global political system began to emerge. Western leaders charged the non-Western and socialist majority with developing a double standard that it applied throughout the UN and its family of organizations: the majority would condemn Western countries or call for action on the part of the West while remaining silent about Third World or socialist bloc violations of human rights, or peace and security. President de Gaulle of France referred contemptuously to the UN as a *machin*—a thing, or gadget—and crucial U.S. support began to fall off. The situation would worsen in the next three decades.

Guatemala and Things to Come

The term "Latin America"—like the term "Middle East"—is a misleading if useful shortcut. South America is divided into north and south by virtue of climate and economy, into east and west by the Andes; Central American countries differ from those to their south, while Mexico is actually a part of the North American continent. The term "Latin America" has come into use only in the twentieth century, and in particular since World War II. The presence of the "Colossus of the North" has played some part, although not all Latin American countries' leaders have shared the same view of the United States. Language and culture are perhaps the most unifying factors, although the postwar creation of international institutions such as the Organization of American States (OAS), bloc voting in UN agencies like UNCTAD, and the presence of the UN Economic Commission for Latin America all prompted the use of the notion of "Latin America," and acceptance of the idea of commonality.

Then too, there has been similarity of experience. Latin America was the only part of the non-Western world left physically untouched by both world wars. Although production increased in most Latin American countries in the years after World War II, by the early 1950s Latin American economies appeared radically unbalanced. Population increases tended to swallow up production increases, and imbalance could be seen in the contrast between the lavish new apartment buildings, hotels, and offices, and their surrounding slums, impoverished countryside, and somnolent villages. Considering these contrasts, radical politics flourished. American investments might raise the general level of the economies of the countries in which they were made, but the gains, many charged, went only to the wealthy few.

The United States also enlisted Latin governments in the Cold War, providing military aid and training, committing recipient countries to provide access to strategic materials, and getting them to limit trade with the Communist bloc. The policies were not popular, and increased anti-Americanism. A demand for change began to be articulated by intellectuals, college students, professional agitators, and labor leaders—occasionally joined by progressive-minded business leaders, churchmen, and officers.

The first explosion took place in 1954 in Guatemala, where a new regime moved steadily to the left, expropriated lands belonging to the U.S.-owned United Fruit Company, and moved to control the company's railroads and utilities. The Communist Party, entrenched in several ministries, claimed the favorably viewed radical reforms as its own, and the Guatemalan government of Colonel Jacobo Arbenz assumed foreign affairs positions more and more favorable to the Soviet Union.

Inevitably, the Eisenhower regime took alarm. Dulles referred to the "evil purpose of the Kremlin to destroy the inter-American system"; noted with alarm the arrival of a shipment of arms from the Soviet bloc; and finally, through the CIA, created an anti-Communist Guatemalan force under Colonel Castillo Armas to mount a successful intervention from neighboring Honduras. In essence, the United States had directly overthrown Arbenz and installed a none-too-savory successor. "Each one of the American states has cause for profound gratitude," said Dulles, praising the citizens of Guatemala who "had the courage and will to eliminate the traitorous tools of foreign despots."

Most Latin Americans did not see it the same way at all. The dangers of Russian Communist influence seemed far more remote than the dangers of American intervention against that influence. The United States had coerced Latin states at an OAS meeting in Venezuela in March 1954 into endorsing, with little enthusiasm, the "Caracas Declaration," condemning Communist efforts to gain control of any American state as a threat to regional security. This was, in a real sense, typical balance-of-power policy of an old style, with little regard to local sensibilities. To American policymakers, who had so recently helped restore the shah to his throne in Iran, where—as in Guatemala—it appeared that a local matter threatened to extend Russian influence, it also appeared to give further proof of how efficient and inexpensive quiet covert activities could be in maintaining the balance of power. It was perhaps the wrong lesson.*

Later in the decade, in 1958, when Eisenhower sent Vice-President Richard Nixon on a goodwill tour of Latin America, Nixon and his wife were physically attacked and had to cut the tour short, while Eisenhower alerted a force of a thousand marines in the Caribbean to protect the Nixons. The tour gave the American public an idea of how far relations had deteriorated. But the administration stayed with policies already in effect: extension of credit by the Import-Export Bank for the purchase of American exports, loans from the International Bank, Point Four technical aid programs, military aid, and suggestions to follow conservative fiscal policies that would avoid foreign exchange deficits and consequent import controls. It took the ascent to power in Cuba of a young, bearded, and radical guerrilla leader named Fidel Castro to prompt the Eisenhower Administration in its waning months to create the Inter-American Development Bank and to create a $500 million aid program for Latin America—for which Latin Americans ironically thanked Fidel Castro.

Conclusion

At the end of World War II, visionaries saw the shrinking globe as one that would, by force of circumstances, become more and more integrated. The imperfect United Nations was one small step in that direction.

What developed, instead, were divergent tendencies: one was toward a world divided in two—a "bipolar" world—while the other, as the old empires began to *dis*integrate, was toward a world with more and more states claiming the Western-developed attributes of sovereignty and independence, and seeing themselves as constituting a Third World.

There was also a third tendency: regions were hard to define, and conflicts usually took place between adjacent states, but regional solidarity began to manifest itself in several areas against global universalism. Euro-

---

*Attempts to show that the cause of American intervention was nationalization run afoul of successful nationalizations of other American properties with no subsequent threat of intervention: only two years earlier, Bolivian nationalization of American-owned tin mines failed to stop American economic aid to Bolivia. What set the Guatemalan case apart was the presence of the Communist Party with its direct tie to Moscow, and Arbenz's increasing reliance on possible Russian support.

pean regionalism aimed to increase European strength vis-à-vis both the Soviet Union and the United States. The region dominated by the Soviet Union itself excluded any UN action. In the Americas, where the inter-American system evolved under U.S. guidance, the UN-sponsored Economic Commission for Latin America—one of several Economic and Social Council regional commissions—had begun to enunciate a peculiarly Latin American view of relations between "developed" and "less developed" countries, reinforcing Latin American regional consciousness. The beginnings of an Afro-Asian grouping began to emerge, at Bandung, solidified into a non-aligned group at Belgrade, and then became the G-77 at the UN. While these countries, encompassing groupings throughout the world, hardly constituted a region, they became a new, highly organized bloc, espousing new policies.

Although the United States urged the French, for example, to grant genuine independence to the Indochinese, and the Dutch to accept independence for Indonesia, it also occasionally refrained from interfering in what England, France, or Belgium considered to be their sovereign prerogatives. These countries were, after all, American allies. As a result, the image of the United States among the leaders of new states was that it had never really done what it should have done to aid their independence. Whereas Americans tended to think of the United States as having been in the forefront of the anticolonial struggle, others did not see it that way. In contrast, Soviet support for independence was clear and unequivocal.

No one yet saw a pattern in the rise of Nasser in Egypt, the nationalization crisis in Iran, of the suppression of the radical government in Guatemala. Yet these events—along with Bandung—foreshadowed a link between the move to independence and demands for a revision in the very nature of the international system. For the first time in human history, it had become apparent that poor states lived side by side with rich states. Spokespersons for poor states might—and would—blame their poverty on rich states, thereby making it a moral *duty* for the wealthy to help close the growing gap in incomes. Spokespersons for the wealthier states would point, rather, to the centuries of social change preceding their own rapid growth in the nineteenth century, when the gap began to open up.

"Development" would become a central issue in the world of international organizations in the next decades, as one organization after another turned its attention to the matter, and as the impatient leaders of new states created new international organizations whose central purpose was to channel funds and technology to the new states. Perhaps most important was the proliferation of new analyses of why the gap existed, and what could and should be done about it. The gap became a clash no longer of national interests, but divergent theories—making agreement on policy much more difficult.

Development would also be complicated by horrendous conflicts within and between many of the new states, as well as, ultimately and unexpectedly to many, by the very success of many Third World states in joining the ranks of the developed, thereby breaking up Third World unity and once more shifting the terms of policy debate.

In any event, the breakup of the European empires and the emergence of a hundred new states was one of the most important of all changes in the fifty years following World War II.

Further Suggested Readings

A classic early survey of decolonization is Rupert Emerson, *From Empire to Nation* (Cambridge: Harvard University Press, 1960). David Kay, *The New Nations in the United Nations* (New York: Columbia University Press, 1970), reviews the initial impact of new nations on the UN. The first Indochina War is well reviewed in Ellen Hammer, *The Struggle for Indochina* (Stanford, CA: Stanford University Press, 1966), and on a more personal, more intense level by Bernard Fall, *Street Without Joy* (Harrisburg, PA: Stackpole, 1961). Fall was killed during the second Vietnam War. Lawrence K. Rosinger (ed.), *The State of Asia: A Contemporary Survey* (New York: Knopf, 1951), is an excellent collection on the early post–World War II years, while Charles Cremeans, *The Arabs and the World: Nasser's Arab Nationalist Policy* (New York: Praeger, 1963), gives the flavor of the early Arab revolt against predominantly Western influence. Hugh Thomas, *The Suez Affair* (Middlesex, England: Penguin Books, 1970), surveys the Middle East war of 1956, which marked the end of European influence in the Middle East. Cold War complications in Africa are recounted in Gerard Chaliand, *The Struggle for Africa: Conflict of the Great Powers* (New York: St. Martin's Press, 1982).

5

The Cold War in the 1960s and Beyond

If there was a brief détente during the mid-1950s, the early 1960s were dominated by crises in Berlin and over Cuba (when the world appeared to be on the brink of nuclear war), by a renewed arms race accompanied by a measure of stabilization through arms control, by a deepening of the conflict between Communist China and the Soviet Union, and by a futile and horrendous second war in Vietnam. Vietnam crystallized a series of attitudes and movements in the United States that destroyed the Cold War consensus. It also brought about a changed U.S. position in the world: the America that so many Europeans had admired and been attracted to in the postwar years seemed to begin crumbling before their eyes as it tried in vain to overthrow Fidel Castro (now a dynamic figure on the world scene); got mired in the bitter and brutal Vietnam War, invaded the Dominican Republic; and witnessed the assassination of its public figures, the explosion of racial issues, the decay of American cities, and the beginnings of a decline in American technological and economic leadership.

In the late 1950s Khrushchev talked of "competitive coexistence," of victory over capitalism by demonstration of communism's superior economic performance. He boasted of Russian technological and strategic superiority, as demonstrated by the first artificial satellite and the first intercontinental ballistic missile (ICBM). He claimed he was building ICBMs in great numbers, but this boast stimulated a hasty American buildup, evident by the time of the Cuban missile crisis of 1962. Khrushchev had seriously overreached himself both in Cuba and in Africa, and his successors vowed never again to be caught in such a weak position: the next quarter century produced a steady buildup of Soviet military power. By the decade of the 1970s, the Soviet leaders could congratulate themselves on "parity" with the United States, and on a global reach.

What was less evident was their double failure on the economic front: despite Khrushchev's earlier boasts, the Soviet economy grew only slowly;

in the 1980s per capita income would still be only about one-third that of the West. What was more, the new, global reach began to put an even greater strain on the economy, and Soviet leaders were forced to begin a desperate and ultimately unsuccessful attempt to shake up the whole sluggish system.

A Republican president, Nixon, was able to disengage from Vietnam, and belatedly to take advantage of the Russian-Chinese split. He did what no Democrat could have done: traveled to Peking to open relations with "Red China" and thereby put himself in a strong position to bring about a new détente with the Soviet Union. People talked of a new three-power world, but Nixon spoke of a five-power balance, consisting of the United States, the Soviet Union, China, Europe, and the Third World. The 1960s was certainly an era in which the organized Third World began to try to exert its influence, culminating in the first global oil crisis in 1973; it was a period, however, that showed how hard it would be to hold the Third World together.

By the early 1970s the world had become a very different and a very unexpected place—increasingly interdependent, yet more and more fragmented politically. The North Atlantic area, for hundreds of years the cockpit of major warfare, was now a zone of peace, where no major Western state threatened another with war. A relatively stable though shifting nuclear standoff appeared to have been reached by the Soviet Union and the United States, prelude to a new détente. The computer and communications revolution was at hand. But the use of force became endemic in the rest of the world.

From Eisenhower to Kennedy

Dwight D. Eisenhower retired from the presidency a disappointed and apprehensive man. He had secured peace in Korea and kept the United States out of further wars in Asia while completing a series of alliances he hoped would deter any others. He had successfully supported the shah in Iran and helped overthrow a radical government in Guatemala, secured German rearmament in the framework of NATO, and accepted a form of détente with Premier Khrushchev at Geneva in 1955. Against widespread opposition, he had managed to secure construction of military bases in Francisco Franco's Spain that would help protect NATO's southern flank. He had cut the increase in military spending brought about by the Korean War. But his own military had pushed creation of a nuclear strike force the size of which he thought was simply crazy. This led him, in his closing speech as president, to warn Americans against the dominance of a "military-industrial complex" that would distort American political life.

The Missile Gap

In part, Eisenhower's speech was also a warning to the Democrats, who had sought a 1960 presidential campaign advantage by attacking the Republican president for having let America weaken in the face of a growing Soviet threat: numerous groups in America took very seriously the assertive and bumptious Khrushchev's Russian space successes and his boasts of Russian technological superiority. Serious publications warned of a "missile gap" in favor of the Russians, and demonstrated that Russian growth might well lead in short order to a per capita income higher than that of Western Europe.

It later became a commonplace in America that the false "missile gap" of the late 1950s was concocted by the military-industrial complex about which Eisenhower had warned. The tendency of congress members with defense industries and military bases in their districts to support unneeded expenditures had joined with the military's tendency to overestimate Soviet military achievements in order to justify large American forces (and professional advancement). The two were buttressed by the industries' search for increased orders. In fact, however, Khrushchev and his cohort bore much of the responsibility. Khrushchev himself stated that a Soviet factory was manufacturing ICBMs at the rate of 200 a year: "We are turning them out like sausages!" he declared. In France, Communist Party boss Maurice Thorez trumpeted, "Anyone who does *not* believe that the Soviet Union is far ahead in nuclear missiles is a victim of lying capitalist propaganda!"

Since 1956 the United States had secretly been flying an extreme high-altitude surveillance airplane—the U-2—across Soviet territory. As a result of the U-2 overflights, which Eisenhower could not reveal, he knew that the Russians were not emplacing intercontinental missiles at any great rate, that Khrushchev was actually bluffing. On the other hand, it was also true that, while the Russians worked at developing second-generation intercontinental missiles rather than deploying their clumsy first-generation missiles, they were producing large numbers of intermediate-range missiles, directed at Western Europe. It appeared that, by one means or another, Khrushchev hoped to detach Western Europe from the United States.

The End of the First Détente

In fact, Khrushchev managed to make Eisenhower's last years as president uncomfortable in a number of ways. In November 1958 he proposed turning over access routes to Berlin to East Germany. He then called for "general and complete disarmament" before the UN General Assembly—a propaganda ploy disturbing to those hoping for real results from current talks. As a followup, he announced he would cut Soviet armed forces by one-third—a genuine move. On a trip to Asia he offered large aid packages while denouncing Western exploitation. And then, shortly before a much-touted May 1960 summit meeting in Paris with Eisenhower, he announced that Russia had shot down an American U-2 spy plane.

The United States was poorly prepared for the eventuality and was caught out in a lie about a strayed weather flight when Khrushchev dramatically produced both the pilot, Francis Gary Powers, and parts of the plane, and threatened to attack bases used by the planes in Turkey and Pakistan with showers of rockets. Belatedly, Eisenhower took responsibility for authorizing the flights. Khrushchev flew to Paris, where he delivered a blistering attack and demanded a personal apology. He had staked his position on growing friendship and good relations with the United States. Now, he said, negotiations with the United States were meaningless until the fall elections had replaced a moribund leadership.

That month he also opened diplomatic relations with the new Cuban revolutionary leader, Fidel Castro, and threatened anyone who attacked Castro with a rain of rockets—a threat which he later amended, saying he had meant it "symbolically." A month later, after shooting down an American RB-47 observation plane flying over the Barents Sea, claiming it had violated Soviet air space, he canceled a planned Eisenhower visit to the Soviet Union. (Eisenhower's planned trip to Japan was also "postponed" by Japanese authorities, on the basis that they could not guarantee his security.) A little later, Khrushchev told the United States that it would be wise to abandon the nuclear test ban talks that had been going on. It was that fall that he came to the UN General Assembly meeting in New York and publicly embraced Fidel Castro at the Hotel Theresa in Harlem. The embrace represented a decisive commitment, made before the whole world, to support the revolutionary romantic nationalist ninety miles off the U.S. coast. It would have fateful consequences for all concerned.

Kennedy, Castro, Khrushchev, and the Future

Castro's Cuba

Two years earlier, in 1958, the unsavory regime of Fulgencio Batista crumbled in Cuba. In January 1959, Castro and his *barbudos*—"bearded ones"—swaggered into Havana and gained a control of the Cuban government that Castro would never relinquish. In the next year and a half, Castro abandoned the liberal aims of his earlier July 1957 Manifesto from the Sierra

Maestra, which called for free elections and constitutional government, and was designed to attract the middle and professional classes while he was still garnering support to overthrow Batista. Circuslike trials and executions of Batista followers were followed by imprisonment or exile of those who disagreed with him on the course of the revolution (including many of his earliest supporters), by rapid nationalization of the means of production, and by increases in authority of the central government over all aspects of life. Trade and aid agreements with socialist countries were followed by subsequent orders for military equipment.

A heretofore friendly but wary Eisenhower administration responded by cutting Cuba's sugar quota, and when Castro nationalized American oil companies, with great irony, he made compensation dependent upon continued sugar exports to the United States. In the fall of 1960, while attending the UN General Assembly meeting where he and Khrushchev embraced, Castro called Nixon and Kennedy, the 1960 presidential candidates, "beardless, brainless, youths." By the end of 1960, Castro had endorsed Soviet foreign policy in a joint communiqué and Eisenhower had embargoed all exports to Cuba except for nonsubsidized foodstuffs and medical supplies. On January 2, 1961, Castro ordered that the American embassy staff be reduced from eighty-seven to eleven within forty-eight hours, and Eisenhower broke off all diplomatic relations with Castro. Diplomatic relations between Cuba and the United States have never been resumed.

Castro's desire to rid Cuba of American influence was profound, and he refused all early considerations of American aid. Eisenhower was genuinely puzzled at the hostility Castro and especially his brother Raul and his close adviser Che Guevara displayed toward the United States. With others in the United States, he concluded that it could only be explained by the increasing role the Cuban Communists were playing in the Castro government. In fact, Eisenhower was not seeing "reds under the bed": Castro was deliberately giving Communists a role as he discarded supporters from his own July 26 Movement. For the first year and a half that the Cuban leader was in power, it was he who took the lead in creating alienation between the United States and Cuba. After March 1960, the Eisenhower Administration concluded that Castro was intent on exporting Marxist-Leninist revolution throughout Latin America, with Russian backing. As a result, the president moved to an active policy of confrontation, imposing economic sanctions and using the CIA to arm and train anti-Castro guerrillas. He based this policy on the 1954 success in Guatemala—where the CIA now set up the training bases for Cubans. At the same time, Eisenhower moved to enlist the support of other Latin American nations.

Map 10. Cuba and the Eastern Caribbean

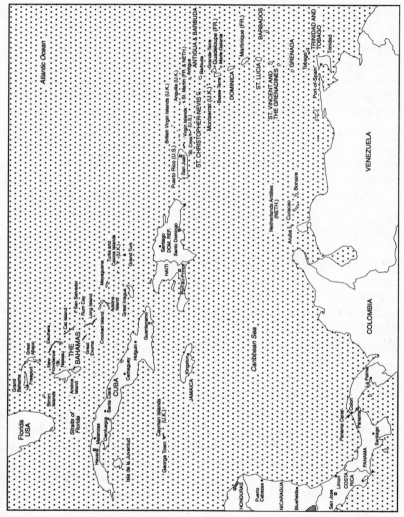

John F. Kennedy

These were the circumstances when the youthful, handsome, seemingly vigorous John F. Kennedy strode center stage to be inaugurated as president of the United States in January 1961. The promises of America would be kept, a sense of national purpose would be evoked, and the world would look to America as an example and a leader. NATO was to be reinvigorated, the Berlin issue would be settled; and Khrushchev, impressed with American power, would be met with unflinchingly firm but friendly resolve. Instead of a race for the allegiance of the Third World—whose development would be encouraged by the presence of benevolent, technologically sophisticated American "Peace Corps" volunteers—there would be a peaceful race to see who would get to the moon first. Instead of radical, populist, dictatorial revolutionaries like Castro being allowed to come to power, reform underwritten by America would encourage progressive democratic trends and forestall revolution.

Achieving all this would take time. In the interim the United States had to see to getting rid of the annoying Castro. Most Americans failed to see the hubris in all these goals.

The Bay of Pigs and the Alliance for Progress

Kennedy faced a dilemma: his campaign had focused on Eisenhower's weakness in allowing a Communist regime to be established ninety miles from Florida. Now he discovered the secret Eisenhower support for Cuban refugees at bases in Guatemala, as well as Florida and Louisiana, and the plan for their landing in Cuba that would presumably spark an uprising among the supposedly oppressed Cubans. The Central Intelligence Agency and the armed forces assured a hesitant Kennedy that no overt military action by the United States would be required, and told him time was of the essence: Cuban pilots were being trained in Czechoslovakia to fly Soviet-supplied jets, and the president of Guatemala came under pressure to close the bases there. Perhaps most important, what would be the domestic consequences for Kennedy when—not if—it became known that he had forgone the use of Cubans to oust a Castro now aligned with the Soviet bloc? Democrats were still tarred by the "soft-on-Communism" charges of the McCarthy period.

In the circumstances, the U.S. president authorized an invasion that turned out to be a perfect failure. Fifteen hundred men landed at a spot called the "Bay of Pigs" and were overwhelmed by Castro's enormous militia force, while his air force kept them from being resupplied. There was no internal uprising, nor were there multiple diversionary landings. Kennedy, reminding his advisers they had told him there would be no need for direct American participation, refused to authorize an air strike at the time the invasion was palpably failing. American spokesman Adlai Stevenson was embarrassed at the UN, and worldwide reaction mounted against the American-sponsored invasion, especially in Latin America, where the Cuban revolution with its defiance of the "Colossus of the North" had touched wellsprings of emotion never tapped during the Guatemala affair.

The failure was not just a terrible blow to anti-Castro Cubans, but also to the Kennedy image at the very start of his administration. It did, however, help persuade Kennedy to adopt the grandiose "Alliance for Progress," a scheme based on the view that help in spurring economic development coupled with extensive domestic reform could produce peaceful change in the direction of liberal democratic institutions. At Punte del Este, Uruguay, in August 1961, the American states signed a series of multilateral agreements promising $20 billion in U.S. aid over a ten-year period, commitment to fundamental social change on the part of participating governments, and coordination of long-range development plans. The Kennedy Administration also persuaded a majority of OAS foreign ministers to vote to exclude Castro from the inter-American system, although the important states of Brazil, Argentina, Chile, and Mexico, among others, abstained.

In the meantime, the world was treated to Castro's wooing of a rather reluctant Khrushchev, for whom the somewhat erratic, bearded revolutionary could be a danger to any détente with a new American administration. Confounding American media supporters of Castro's revolution, in mid-1961 Castro's aide Che Guevara declared that the revolution had been a Marxist-Leninist one all along, and in December Castro himself declared that he had always been a Marxist-Leninist.*

The chastened President Kennedy, with a major defeat behind him, went to Vienna in early June to meet Khrushchev—who could boast that in the week of the failed American Bay of Pigs invasion, his Russian government had sent Yuri Gagarin into space to be the first man to orbit the earth. In Vienna, despite Kennedy's efforts to charm, Khrushchev bullied and blustered about Berlin, UN reorganization, and a nuclear test ban on Russian terms.

---

*In Tad Szulc's *Fidel: A Critical Portrait* (New York: Morrow, 1986), the veteran Castro watcher reports that Castro long concealed his Marxist-Leninism and his desire from the outset to transform Cuba into a Communist state, creating a temporary, powerless, transitional government while his secret parallel government seized the levers of power. Fidel Castro's brother Raul had been a Communist since 1953.

The Berlin Wall

Six weeks later, on August 13, 1961, Khrushchev resolved the Berlin crisis by building the Berlin Wall, dividing East Berlin from West Berlin, dividing families and friends and people from their workplace, and effectively blocking the hemorrhage of skilled manpower from the East. It was a shocking move. In subsequent years, hundreds would be killed trying to cross the Wall from East to West Berlin. Khrushchev's move led to much bluster on the Western side and solemn resolve that "the Wall must come down." President Kennedy was criticized again for not taking decisive action, but the West was not ready to risk war for freedom of movement between the two halves of Berlin. To the West it seemed a brutal and aggressive move; to Khrushchev it must have seemed a minimal solution, one that—unlike his earlier proposals—did not encroach on Western rights. He appeared to have been trying to use Berlin to extract general agreement from the West on Germany and nuclear weapons; the Wall, in retrospect, represented a failure of this attempt.

In July, he had rescinded his proposed cuts in Soviet armed forces. Two weeks after the Vienna meeting—despite having told Kennedy he would not do so—he announced the resumption of nuclear tests. On October 30 he exploded the largest nuclear device ever—in the vicinity of *fifty* megatons. If it was intended as a threat to the Americans, it was probably also aimed at the Chinese, for the Russian-Chinese split had become public that month at the Twenty-Second Party Congress, when Khrushchev's attack upon Stalin and his henchman became even more violent, and during which Stalin's body was moved outside the Kremlin walls. A few months later, in mid-1962, Khrushchev boasted to reporters that the Soviet Union now possessed an antimissile missile that could "hit a fly in space" and proceeded with another giant thermonuclear explosion.

Shortly after Vienna, Kennedy, shaken, moved to increase defense spending and the size of the armed forces, while initiating a countrywide fallout shelter plan. Then came the Cuban missile crisis.

The Cuban Missile Crisis

The missile crisis of 1962 did much to restore the image of a decisive, courageous, realistic Kennedy. It all came about unexpectedly: Khrushchev, while repeatedly assuring the American administration that he would never put offensive missiles in Cuba and would never embarrass Kennedy during a congressional election campaign, installed bases for some sixty-four nuclear intermediate- and medium-range ballistic missiles on the island—that is, deep within what had been the American sphere of influence. As the Chinese were later to say, Khrushchev, without consulting anybody—neither the Chinese, nor other Communist leaders, nor Castro—had embarked on a reckless course that endangered the lives of hundreds of millions of people. It was as though the United States had installed missiles in Hungary in 1956. No one thought Khrushchev would take the risk of putting the missiles in Cuba since they would serve little obvious purpose: the rational Secretary of Defense Robert McNamara thought they changed nothing. As liquid-fueled above-ground missiles, slow to launch, they could not be used for deterrence, since they would be destroyed in a first strike. Nor could Khrushchev threaten to use them first, knowing the United States could retaliate and destroy the Soviet Union. (It was reasoning of this sort that led McNamara and others to doubt the possibility Khrushchev was installing the missiles in Cuba until hard evidence made it clear he was.)

Kennedy's advisers discussed the alternative courses of action during several tension-laden days without any sense of *why* Khrushchev had put them there, and therefore what the stakes of the gamble really were. All were agreed: the missiles and the bombers had to go. The differences were on how to get them out.

One group sought to temporize, to offer to withdraw American medium-range Jupiter missiles in Turkey in return for the withdrawal of those in Cuba, and to publicize the matter at the UN and use world pressure there. (The American missiles had been installed in Turkey at the time of Khrushchev's boasts of missile superiority. Kennedy had already decided on their withdrawal.) Another group wanted an immediate air strike or invasion: to offer an exchange would open the administration to blackmail under other circumstances; the reckless prime minister must be taught an immediate lesson, even at the risk of war. A third group sought an intermediate course, using the threat of invasion or air strike and a naval blockade to pressure the Russians to withdraw. (Since "blockade" is a term in international law for action taken by belligerents in war, the blockade was always referred to as a "quarantine.")

Ultimately, Kennedy, who had announced the presence of the missiles over television, chose the third course, privately letting the prime minister know that the Jupiter missiles were being withdrawn from Turkey anyway. American invasion forces were mustered in Florida and strategic forces were placed on alert; in the midst of the days of waiting to see how Khrushchev would respond to the quarantine, whether he would order Russian ships to stop or not, one U-2 plane strayed over Russian territory and another was shot down over Cuba, causing the "hawks" among Kennedy's advisers to argue for a strike against the Russian surface-to-air missile bases in Cuba. In the end, Kennedy received two messages from Khrushchev: one, emotional and rambling, offered withdrawal in return for a pledge not to invade Cuba; the other, received somewhat later, called for mutual missile withdrawal, from Cuba and Turkey. The president chose to respond to the first one and ignore the second, letting Khrushchev know about the planned withdrawal. By doing this—and with Russian acceptance of UN personnel in Cuba to observe the dismantling of the bases—Kennedy gave the premier a face-saving way out, allowing him to claim that the missiles had been placed there to protect Cuba in the first place, and that, with the American pledge not to invade, they had served their purpose.

Castro, furious at not being consulted, refused to allow UN observers in.

There is still controversy over all aspects of the crisis. In retrospect the hard-liners felt that the danger of war was much lower than thought at the time. Khrushchev could not have sacrificed all of Russia over the issue, and he was thoroughly aware of the awesome nature of the American nuclear force. (By this time the United States had 300 intercontinental and submarine ballistic missiles to the Russians' 80.) Castro could have been toppled and the missile sites destroyed by swift military action. The others felt the right course had been taken: unforeseen events always play a part, and the situation could have escalated to beyond what anyone wanted, just as it did in August 1914. Besides, there were only contingency plans for an invasion, and U.S. forces were not really ready for a large-scale attack. What would follow Castro? Some analysts always remained critical of Kennedy for risking nuclear war at all: the situation itself was not worth it. (But later Khrushchev in his own memoirs wrote that he recognized and deliberately took the risk of confrontation in order to bludgeon the United States into recognizing that the balance of power favored the Soviet Union.)

The Beginning of Arms Control and the Soviet Buildup

In any event, a learning process took place. Within a year, Khrushchev and Kennedy signed a partial nuclear test ban agreement, long under negotiation, which had been stalled over the issue of whether underground tests could be detected. The issue was temporarily resolved by exempting underground tests from the ban, and banning those in the air, from which fallout had been poisoning the atmosphere. Perhaps even more important, on June 20, 1963, their representatives signed a memorandum of understanding establishing the "Hot Line"—a direct communications link between Washington and Moscow that could be used in time of crisis. The two superpowers could thus reassure one another about their intentions in a moment of tension. Never again would they wait the long hours of the Cuban missile crisis to find out what the other party intended to do, nor depend on channels that could too easily be interrupted. At Geneva, in 1955, both sides had presumably but tacitly recognized a two countries' common interest in avoiding nuclear war. Until now, however, both had still occasionally been willing to threaten the use of nuclear weapons. The Hot Line institutionalized the two countries' common interest in avoiding any nuclear confrontation.

The Russians learned another lesson, however. Following the missile crisis—coming hard on the heels of U-2 revelations about Khrushchev's missile bluff, along with his failure to enforce his will over Berlin, and his weakness in trying to support a faction in the far-off Congo—Khrushchev himself had to change course, realizing that his military policies had failed. His means were inadequate for his ends. During the height of the missile crisis negotiations, one Russian told American negotiator John J. McCloy that "the Soviet Union will never again face a 4 to 1 missile inferiority." In 1964 the Russians began a massive arms buildup that only occasionally slowed down, but never really faltered until after 1989. Khrushchev's successor Leonid Brezhnev gave the various military services virtually all they wanted. Like the partial test ban and the Hot Line agreement, the Russian buildup was an unanticipated result of the American tactical victory in Cuba. It may also, in retrospect and in the long run, have fatally overburdened the sluggish Russian economy.

Cuban-American relations would not improve in the next decades. Castro continued active support of antigovernment revolutionary parties in the seventeen Latin countries that broke relations with him; the United States, for several years, carried out inept assassination attempts ("Operation Mongoose") and provided support to anti-Castro guerrillas. Most of Castro's trade was with the Soviet bloc, and the Soviet Union began a heavy subsidy of the Cuban economy which, by the early 1980s amounted to some $4 billion dollars a year (and again, like the military buildup, constituted a drain on the Soviet economy). In the meantime, Cuba became the most heavily militarized state in the Western Hemisphere, and even deployed tens of thousands of Cuban troops in African countries in furtherance of joint Soviet-Cuban aims.

Dominican Interlude

John F. Kennedy died at the hands of an assassin in Dallas, Texas, on November 22, 1963, and something more died with him: the sense that an active American government could help bring about a better world. "His actual, tangible impact on history," wrote one observer, "was not significant enough to explain his enormous psychological impact, the indefinable way in which John F. Kennedy touched people throughout the world." She also noted that, in Indian villages on the other side of the globe, pictures of Gandhi, Nehru, and Kennedy could be found side by side.[1]

Kennedy's vice-president and successor, Lyndon B. Johnson, was able to move further and faster in the direction Kennedy had begun to head in domestic politics, in the interest of civil rights and a more just society. But he—and America with him—were undone in the quicksands of Vietnam and to a lesser extent in the Dominican Republic.

Castro had sensitized the Americans to developments in the Caribbean. When, in 1963, a military junta overthrew a mildly leftist government in the Dominican Republic, the Kennedy Administration, angry about a tide of military coups in Guatemala, Ecuador, and Honduras, withheld recognition and suspended economic aid. Johnson, succeeding Kennedy, feared that the attempt to punish military regimes would both fail and lead to charges of intervention. He therefore resumed relations with the junta. On April 24, 1964, a revolt against the junta led to bloody conflict, and Johnson threw his weight on the side of the counterrevolution: 21,000 American troops were ashore by May 6, with 9,000 more on nearby ships. Johnson feared being charged with allowing another unfriendly Castro-and-Communist-influenced regime to come to power, close to the American shores.

An almost universal uproar followed, both in Latin America and in Europe, echoing in the halls of the United Nations and in the American press. The administration thereupon forced out some less savory members of the junta and cooperated with OAS and UN mediators in creating a provisional coalition government that included rebel elements. The next year, following relatively free elections, the troops were withdrawn. (Earlier, with specific reference to the Dominican Republic, Kennedy himself had summed up how he viewed the dilemma of Latin America: "There are three possibilities in descending order of preference: a decent democratic regime, a continuation of the Trujillo regime or a Castro regime. We ought to aim at the first, but we can't really renounce the second until we are sure we can avoid the third.")

But by 1964 American attention had largely turned away from its Caribbean obsessions with Cuba and the Dominican Republic, and toward Southeast Asia.

Vietnam

Laos and Cambodia

Southeast Asia did not, in fact, figure large in the original agenda of the Kennedy Administration; Berlin, Cuba, and the Congo loomed much larger.

Even Laos appeared more important than Vietnam: there the fragile 1954 Geneva settlement came unstuck by 1960. Despite international efforts to create and support a coalition government of royalists, neutralists, and Communists throughout the 1960s, when South Vietnam finally collapsed in 1975 the Communist-led Pathet Lao took over the whole country, and Vietnamese troops who had used it as a supply route all through the late 1960s remained.

Cambodia, ultimately, suffered a worse fate than either of its neighbors. In the 1950s it was viewed by foreigners as something of an oasis of neutral peace in an area of widespread conflict. Its erratic ruler, Prince Norodom Sihanouk, who became head of state in 1960, trod warily between the right and various left factions. Rightists, drawing upon a history of imperialist pressures by neighboring Thailand and Vietnam (curbed in the past by the French), now looked to the United States to resist pressures from either North Vietnam or South Vietnam, while some leftist factions looked to North Vietnam or to China for support in their efforts to gain power. In the early 1960s Sihanouk broke relations with the United States, apparently feeling he should accommodate to potentially dominant Vietnamese Communists. In 1969, fearing growing Communist-Vietnamese influence within Cambodia itself, and more confident of a military stalemate in South Vietnam as a result of newly elected President Nixon's policies, he resumed relations and fairly intimate cooperation with the United States. Secretly, he sanctioned U.S. bombing of North Vietnamese forces and supply routes in eastern Cambodia, and suppressed a leftist coup.

In March 1970 a rightist coup overthrew Sihanouk while he was abroad, and he fled to China. American withdrawal from Vietnam and withdrawal of support for the rightist Cambodian government then brought about a victory of the Communist Khmer Rouge—and a totally unforeseen, hideous holocaust. The most knowledgeable observers of Cambodian politics were at first unwilling to give credence to the reports of the horrific policies of the Khmer Rouge and their results: as the cities were deliberately emptied of their inhabitants, hundreds of thousands—or perhaps between one and two million—Cambodians perished miserably at the hands of the new Khmer Rouge government under the leadership of the little-known Pol Pot, pursuing rigidly ideologically determined policies. Border clashes between Vietnam and what was now called "Democratic Kampuchea" began in 1976 (Vietnam, as the Cambodians had feared, had annexed border areas), and in 1978 a full-scale Vietnamese invasion led to installation of a Vietnam-supported People's Republic of Kampuchea, while the pro-Chinese Khmer Rouge fled west, to the borders with Thailand. Only the changed circumstances of the 1990s would bring some measure of relief and a coalition government to the unhappy country (see chapter 11).

The Second Vietnam War

The main war in Southeast Asia, of course, took place in Vietnam, growing gradually, year by year, from the late 1950s. It lasted for some seventeen years, until the collapse of South Vietnam in 1975, following American withdrawal. By Western estimates, 1,300,000 died in the war. (Recent Vietnamese estimates are much higher: three million.) Of these, perhaps one-third were civilians. The rest were military, more Northerners than Southerners. Of the total, about 4,000 were Korean troops; 400 were Australians and New Zealanders; and 300 were Thai, fighting under American command. Fifty-six thousand were Americans, who died in a war whose purposes few understood and many rejected, and which ultimately, the mighty United States lost to North Vietnam. Politics in the United States has never been the same since.

When the obscure, ascetic Catholic Ngo Dinh Diem became prime minister of the Republic of Vietnam in 1954 and president in 1956, he made unforeseen progress in consolidating the government in the South. Within a year and a half, the flood of refugees from the North was largely integrated, private armies were disarmed, and land reform was initiated. Diem was a man of integrity, free of any taint of collaboration with the French or the Japanese, and South Vietnam appeared to be doing far better under his direction than many other newly independent countries. If his rule was occasionally arbitrary and repressive, there was good reason for it: a large contingent of Communist cadres had remained in the South, ready to act in the future.

With the ascetic nationalist Diem, Eisenhower had found the place to draw the line in Southeast Asia. Years before he became president, John F. Kennedy, then a young Democratic senator from Massachusetts, spelled out his agreement in a speech to the American Friends of Vietnam:

> Vietnam represents the cornerstone of the Free World in Southeast Asia, the keystone to the arch, the finger in the dike. . . . Vietnam represents a proving ground for democracy in Asia . . . the alternative to Communist dictatorship. . . . The United States is directly responsible. . . . We cannot afford to permit that experiment to fail . . . we cannot abandon it, we cannot ignore its needs. And if it falls victim to any of the perils that threaten its existence . . . our prestige in Asia will sink to a new low.

Kennedy opposed the elections envisaged by the Geneva agreements as impossible in the circumstances, and urged more military and economic aid for Vietnam.

By the time Kennedy became president, the situation had deteriorated, as the Diem government became more and more repressive. Communist leader Ho Chi Minh, in the North, had his own troubles: overly brutal and harsh administration, purges, executions, and abuse in his land collectivization program had provoked a revolt that had to be crushed at the expense of thousands of lives. Nevertheless, in 1957 he ordered the Vietminh in the South to regroup into new military units, and in 1959, conscious of the opportune situation that had developed, he gave orders to begin the insurrection in the South, where the reorganized cadres formed the National Liberation Front in 1960 in conjunction with disaffected Southerners. (Most Western observers—including this one—wrote that Southerners began the insurrection and that eventually the North came to their aid. They were wrong: it was a case of successful deception on the part of the Communists, who later spoke openly about it.)

The American Commitment

The North Vietnamese hoped to complete the conquest without provoking American intervention, thinking that the possibility of Russian or Chinese reaction and disapproval by America's European allies might deter the United States. But several factors were to influence Kennedy that would prove them wrong. One was simply the felt need to regain a prestige that had slipped badly at the Bay of Pigs and in Berlin. The second was in part produced by Khrushchev himself when he redefined the world situation in a speech on January 6, 1961. Thermonuclear weapons, he said, had worked a fundamental change. All-out war could, in fact, destroy communist as well as capitalist society, and must therefore be avoided at all cost. Large-scale conventional war could escalate into nuclear war, and must therefore also be avoided. The only way in which force could play its necessary part in the onward march of communism was through guerrilla-type wars of national liberation, and it was the duty of the Soviet Union to support them wherever they might be.

Unfortunately, what he said fit right in with what a series of American generals had been saying and writing about Eisenhower Administration strategy. Generals Maxwell Taylor, James Gavin, and Matthew B. Ridgway—among the most distinguished of American military men—had all written critiques of undue reliance upon nuclear weapons, when the real threats to American security would be nonnuclear, in what might seem to be peripheral areas, and when a nuclear response would be impossible, given the new Russian nuclear capacities. All had advocated a rebuilding of conventional forces and of special forces that could be used in counterguerrilla warfare. After all, guerrillas had been successfully defeated by the British in

Malaysia and by joint Philippine-American efforts against the Hukbalahaps in the Philippines. It was necessary, now, to show Khrushchev that he could be beaten at his game.

The "loss" of China by a Democratic administration still played a part in American politics: no Democratic president wanted to be accused of "losing" more countries in the Far East to communism. The sense that such a charge would gravely weaken Democratic capacities to put through domestic programs in the fields of civil rights and welfare played a strong role in Kennedy's decision to up the ante in Vietnam.

Kennedy received innumerable reports on the situation. Some suggested large-scale military aid and action, including military pressure on the North, while others proposed more limited support. An extraordinary memo from the Joint Chiefs of Staff, breathtaking in the inadequacy of its world view, called the war "a planned phase in the Communist timetable for world domination."[2] The president opted for limited support, hoping to deter the North Vietnamese by convincing them of the American commitment. By the end of 1963, there were 16,000 Americans advisers and support personnel in South Vietnam.

The Vietcong, as the insurrectionary forces were now called, dominated increasing areas of the countryside, using an astute combination of terror and assassination of government officials on the one hand, and populist administration on the other. In the face of what appeared to be imminent administrative and military collapse, South Vietnamese military leaders sounded out the Americans: what would the United States do if a coup deposed Diem? The Americans replied that they would support any government that could carry out necessary reforms. On November 1, 1963, Diem and his hated brother-in-law and closest adviser Ngo Dinh Nhu were both assassinated. Three weeks later President Kennedy was assassinated in Dallas. The next month the North Vietnamese Communist Party Central Committee resolved to step up the tempo of the insurgency.

President Lyndon B. Johnson's first briefings revealed disaster in the making. CIA Director John McCone told him that the optimistic reports about the success of counterinsurgency emanating from Hanoi over the last year were grossly in error.

The political situation in South Vietnam continued to deteriorate during 1964, as one government succeeded another. Facing Republican charges of failure to win in Vietnam, Johnson increased military pressure on the North, seeking and receiving overwhelming approval from the Congress in the form of the so-called Tonkin Gulf Resolution, in support of his Vietnam policy. Following his decisive defeat of Republican conservative Barry Goldwater in the presidential election of 1964, Johnson began the first program of measured and limited air action against selected military targets in North Vietnam. In June 1965 the American Commanding General William Westmoreland was authorized to use American troops in combat, and on July 27 Johnson authorized a deployment of 100,000 combat troops to Vietnam by the end of the year. The United States was at war.

The next three years witnessed a continuous growth in the American effort, an increased involvement of North Vietnam in the actual fighting, continual efforts by third parties to get negotiations started, and growing and bitter opposition to the war within and outside the United States. B-52 intercontinental bombers dropped more tons of bombs on the tiny hamlets and jungle trails of Vietnam than were dropped in all of World War II. Carrying on the war while maintaining relative normality at home meant that one small segment of the population faced combat duty while the rest of the populace went about their business as usual and watched the war on their television sets at night. There was no sense of common necessity and effort. Divisions deepened. In 1967 black leader Martin Luther King, Jr., linked the civil rights struggle to the war in Vietnam: the "Movement" was born, directed against the institutions and policies that had led the United States down a pathway to disaster for all concerned, especially the Vietnamese who were fighting for unity and independence.

To the supporters of the war, Vietnam was a test case for defeating Russian-supported wars of national liberation; it was an international war in which North Vietnam was the aggressor against South Vietnam. To the North Vietnamese, the war had become an effort to defeat a foreign power that had intervened in a civil, not an international, war. Many states on the Asian perimeter hoped for a continued American presence (including even India, when it found its forces under attack by the Chinese in 1962; see below, page 147), but the nature of the Vietnam intervention with its divisive influence in the United States seemed to guarantee a lessened U.S. involvement in the future.

American intervention brought greatly increased Russian and Chinese material aid to the North Vietnamese, and the bombing of the relatively primitive economy did less to inflict material damage than it did to give the North Vietnamese moral stature. Suddenly, in 1968, at the time of Tet, the Vietnamese New Year, the Vietcong launched an offensive against the South Vietnamese capital city of Saigon, against a series of provincial cities, and all through supposedly secure rural areas. In Saigon they actually penetrated the American Embassy compound, and only three days of bitter fighting rooted them out. Civilian casualties piled up. These developments seemed inexplicable in the light of what American spokespersons had been saying, and when the news leaked out that the American commander in Vietnam was calling for 206,000 more men—above the 500,000 already there—the die was cast. In the early period of the war, the American media and Congress had strongly supported the idea of drawing the line in Vietnam. Now the administration found itself under the strongest fire.

The "Tet offensive" cost the Vietcong enormous casualties, and their main expectation—that the South Vietnamese population would rise up and join them—was dashed. But it was a great propaganda success. In the United States, antiwar candidates began to pile up large votes in 1968 primary election campaigns, and the late President Kennedy's brother, Robert Kennedy, entered the race for the presidency. Still, it came as a surprise on March 31, 1968, that President Johnson announced a partial bombing halt in the hope of starting negotiations, as well as his own withdrawal from the presidential race. Hanoi replied promptly, and after a long-drawn-out argument over the site of negotiations, the shape of the negotiating table, and who the participants would be, the talks got under way.

In the meantime, 1968—that year of worldwide upheaval—bore out its terrible promises when an Arab assassin removed Bobby Kennedy from the scene and a white supremacist in Memphis, Tennessee, assassinated Martin Luther King, Jr. Hubert Humphrey of Minnesota, Johnson's long-suffering vice-president, was nominated by the Democrats in Chicago—but not until after the nation and the world were treated on their television screens to incredible battles between demonstrators in the streets and the Chicago police force. Under the impact of Vietnam, the fabric of American political life was unraveling before everybody's eyes; to the demonstrators and millions of their sympathizers, Vietnam had revealed the sham of American democracy.

In the election that followed, there was no clear antiwar candidate. Humphrey could not distance himself fully from the Johnson Administration, and no one was sure where the Republican candidate, Richard Nixon, stood. He had built his career on anti-Communism. As he triumphantly reentered the American political scene, people remembered that it was he who had launched the trial balloon of American intervention at the time of Dien Bien Phu, back in 1954, and he who had strongly backed support for an invasion of Cuba by Cuban refugees in the waning years of the Eisenhower Administration. Campaigning now, he pledged that he would "end the war and win the peace." He won the election by a tiny plurality, but no one was sure what he would do.

The Nixon Strategy

Nineteen hundred and sixty-eight, the year of Nixon's election in the midst of American turmoil, was also the year of revolutionary May upheavals in

France. Though these upheavals ultimately failed, they fatally weakened de Gaulle's hold on power. It was the year Greek colonels consolidated their brutally repressive regime in their hapless country, the year of the bitterest fighting in the Nigerian civil war, the year freedom broke out in Prague only to be crushed by Warsaw Pact tanks, the year the Great Proletarian Revolution wound down in China—and the year Russian-Chinese relations grew so tense that, three months later, in March 1969, border warfare would erupt along the Ussuri River. Furthermore, France—the country where the Vietnam peace talks now began—exploded its first thermonuclear weapon.

Nixon's strategy in this rapidly changing world unfolded only gradually. It emerged from a balance-of-power world view. Nixon took account of the limits of American power, he had a sense that the United States must maintain a reputation of being willing to use that power when necessary, and he knew there was no longer any "world Communist movement." There were no absolutes of black and white, good and evil. He meant to carry out phased withdrawal of American troops from Vietnam, timed so that the South Vietnamese would be ready to take over their own defense; he would continue pressure on the North to force it into reaching an agreement that would give South Vietnam a chance to survive on its own; he would simultaneously provide diplomatic inducements to the Russians to diminish their support for a North Vietnamese victory by offering them the fruits of détente—trade and stability. It was the only alternative to a quick pullout, a collapse of South Vietnam, and an uncertain future for all the rest of Southeast Asia.

In the early stages of his administration, Nixon hoped that a greater negotiating flexibility on his part and announcement of the first troop withdrawals combined with continued pressure—along with an implied threat to resume the bombing of North Vietnam unless progress ensued in Paris—would result in a quick end to the war. But the North Vietnamese were more determined to win than he had realized. "Vietnamization" did not go smoothly, and the gradual shift in strategy and withdrawal of American troops took time. Massive protests continued throughout the United States, as casualties continued to pile up in Vietnam.

By the end of 1971, American troop strength in Vietnam had fallen by three-quarters, the countryside appeared considerably more secure, and the Vietcong were on the defensive. The legendary Ho Chi Minh had died in 1969. In the last week of February 1972, President Nixon made his historic visit to Mao Zedong in Beijing (see pages 153–154). The day after he left China, the North Vietnamese launched a massive invasion of the South. They had decided to end the stalemate in the South, presumably to improve their negotiating position in Paris.

That the Easter invasion did not defeat the South was mainly a result of the heavy air support given to the South by the United States and aerial mining of the northern harbor of Haiphong, through which flooded Russian supplies.

In the three weeks before the 1972 elections, in which Nixon faced Democratic candidate George McGovern, the stalled peace talks were renewed in Paris when Hanoi made several concessions. Nixon suspended bombing north of the Twentieth Parallel, and on October 26 Secretary of State Henry Kissinger told the press that "peace is at hand." Ten days later, Nixon was reelected by an overwhelming majority. But Kissinger's announcement proved premature, and further deadlock in the peace talks led to resumption of massive bombing beginning December 19, 1972, during which fifteen B-52s were lost to sophisticated Soviet-supplied surface-to-air missiles— though North Vietnamese air defenses were devastated. Nixon's opposition charged that the October announcement was an obvious election trick. It appears, rather, that Hanoi pulled back on several points of agreement, hoping to pressure Nixon into accepting them because of the forthcoming election and the announcement that Kissinger had made. In the eyes of many Americans, the American government could no longer do anything right.

On January 27, 1973, a cease-fire was finally signed. It provided that all American troops would leave within sixty days after the cease-fire, American prisoners of war would be released, and the United States would remove any mines it had sown in Northern harbors. The dividing line would remain between North and South; but North, South, and the National Liberation Front in the South would work for reconciliation. Free elections would be held in the South, where Northern troops would be allowed to regroup. The agreement called for creation of the four-nation International Control Commission, to supervise the enactment of the agreement.

Nixon forced President Nguyen Van Thieu of South Vietnam to sign the agreement on the basis that unless he did, the United States would no longer provide him with aid. The commander of the Australian army advisory team in Vietnam called it "a shameless bug-out." But Nixon, fresh from his electoral victory, had promised Thieu continued aid for his army and speedy reaction (in the form of renewed bombing) if the North Vietnamese violated the accords.

The End in Vietnam

Congressional reaction against what had come to be called the "imperial presidency" and the spreading domestic "Watergate" scandal that entangled the president and eventually forced him to resign prevented Nixon from carrying out his pledges. Congress cut off funds. Brezhnev, in the face of the weakened American presidency, continued to pour heavy military equipment into North Vietnam in preparation for the offensive the North had decided, by late 1973, to resume as soon as feasible. In early March 1975, six months after President Nixon's resignation, Northern armies joined National Liberation Front (FLN) forces in the South to rout the deteriorating South Vietnamese armies, whose movements were hampered by the hundreds of thousands of refugees fleeing the combat zones, and who felt little inclination to fight and die for a collapsing and ineffective regime. On April 21, Communist troops marched into Saigon, the last Americans were evacuated by helicopter from the roof of the American Embassy, and South Vietnam surrendered. On July 2, 1976, a National Assembly meeting in Saigon—renamed Ho Chi Minh City—proclaimed the reunification of North and South, and creation of the Socialist Republic of Vietnam. Hundreds of thousands of refugees fled the Communist state, including 500,000 ethnic Chinese forced out by the new Vietnamese government.

North Vietnam had defeated not only South Vietnam, but also the United States of America. (Twenty-five years later, having fallen far behind the economic development of surrounding non-Communist states, the Vietnamese would be seeking an American return.)

The Great Realignment: Communist China and the United States

Even as the United States pulled out of Vietnam, Nixon and Mao Zedong engineered a major realignment in world politics. To understand how this took place, we must turn to prior events in South Asia and the Middle East in the 1960s.

War in the Subcontinent

India and the People's Republic of China established good relations in the mid-1950s. But in 1959 China crushed a revolt in Tibet, sending thousands of refugees across the border into India, where the Dalai Lama settled to become a permanent rallying figure for dissident Tibetans and unsettling Chinese relations with India. In the fall of 1962, following a series of border clashes, the Chinese, unexpectedly, launched large-scale attacks in Assam in the east, and Ladakh in the west, overrunning ineffective and ill-equipped Indian troops. In India there was panic, dismay, and recrimination. Prime Minister Nehru, long a leader of nonalignment, declared a state of emer-

Map 11. **South Asia**

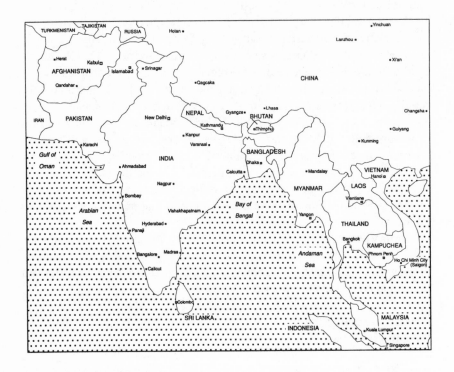

gency and sought arms aid from Britain and the United States as well as limited American military guarantees.

The effect on Pakistan was unfortunate: Pakistan, a staunch American ally, saw its Indian antagonist receive arms despite India's record of non-alignment and general anti-Americanism—and despite the fact that it was India that held on to disputed Kashmir. As a result, Pakistan in turn sought and received substantial arms aid from China and then the Soviet Union, even as the Americans and the British vainly sought to work out some resolution of the Kashmir problem. In short order, Pakistanis signed their own border agreement with the Chinese.

The Chinese, within a month or so of their initial attacks, withdrew from most of the area they had overrun in the east and held on to most of the barren area of Ladakh in the west. There the matter rested. India's rearmament, however, coupled to Pakistan's amassing of arms from China and the Soviet Union, heightened tension between the two countries over the unresolved issue of Kashmir. Nehru, worn by his exertions, died in May 1964, six months after the assassination of President Kennedy. Nehru's successor, Lal Bahadur Shastri, perhaps to cement domestic political support, further integrated the Indian sectors of Kashmir into Indian political life. In 1965, border incidents flared into outright war. China openly backed Pakistan, while Western countries and the United Nations desperately sought a ceasefire and stopped economic and military aid to both countries. Exhausted by the brief but bitter fighting, both sides accepted a third UN call for a ceasefire on November 22, 1965.

Under Soviet mediation, India and Pakistan signed an agreement to withdraw troops and resume diplomatic relations. The frail Shastri's death within hours of the signing brought Nehru's daughter, Indira Gandhi, to power in India; she promised to uphold the agreement, although Kashmir remained at issue. It was internal developments in Pakistan, rather than in Kashmir, that led to the second Indian-Pakistan war, in December 1971.

East and West Pakistan were separated by a thousand miles of Indian territory. In East Pakistan, where officials had a series of grievances against the central government situated in Karachi, in the West, an autonomy movement arose. Elections in 1971 were disastrous for unity. Sheik Mujibur Rahman's separatist Awami League swept to victory in East Pakistan, obtaining a majority in the National Assembly. In March 1971 the Pakistani army struck against the independence movement in East Pakistan, and by the end of the year *ten million* refugees had crossed the border into densely populated and poverty-stricken East Bengal, in India. Indira Gandhi obtained international support for her position that India could neither simply stand by nor absorb the ten million refugees; by early December, open warfare broke out once more between India and Pakistan. On December 6, India recognized East Pakistan as the independent state of Bangladesh. The outnumbered Pakistani troops surrendered in mid-December. Bangladesh and Pakistan faced innumerable problems. So did India, though it had emerged as the sole real power in South Asia.

The Soviet Navy's New Worldwide Role

Russia had obviously placed its own bet: on August 9, 1971, shortly before the war, it had signed the Twenty Year Treaty of Peace, Friendship and Cooperation with India, which, among other matters, granted the Russians docking and port facilities. This was not, said Indira Gandhi, a reversal of nonalignment. It just looked like one. The Chinese, seeing Russian influence supplant the long-departed British, called the Red Navy a tool for establishing the supremacy of a new colonial empire. When the Russians became principal arms suppliers to North Vietnam and found their route blocked across China, they had to resort to ocean shipping. Their experience here, coming after Khrushchev's inability to support Soviet interests in the Congo and to deal with Kennedy's quarantine of Cuba, served as further confirmation of the necessity for Russia to become a maritime as well as continental power.

Other events encouraged the spread of Russian commitments. In 1967, after another brief war between Israel and its Arab neighbors (see chapter 6), known as the "Six Day War," the Russians reequipped the armies of Egypt, Syria, and Iraq with several billion dollars' worth of arms. Intermittent warfare continued between Israel and its neighbors. In April 1970 the Israelis announced that Russian crews manned the new surface-to-air missiles being supplied to Egypt, while Russian pilots flew the new MIG-21 fighters. In the course of a cease-fire during which neither the Israelis nor the Egyptians and the Russians were to construct new military installations in a zone near the Suez Canal, the Russians proceeded to install several hundred SAM missiles in the prohibited area—"the most advanced missile system in the world," said the Israeli prime minister. The incident reinforced Israeli views that international guarantees meant little, and increased Russian prestige among Arabs.

It also highlighted the increased Russian presence in the Eastern Mediterranean as well as in the Indian Ocean, focusing attention on the changing nature of the Soviet navy. Under Stalin and Khrushchev, in the tradition of a continental power, the Soviet Union had built a vast submarine fleet designed to cut American communications to the Eurasian rim lands in case of war (the USSR had over 300 attack submarines, compared to fewer than 70 for the United States). By the late 1960s, under the leadership of Admiral Sergei Georgievich Gorshkov, the Soviet Union had created what it called "naval infantry," expanded its amphibious landing capabilities, launched two helicopter carriers, and had begun construction of its first attack carrier. In addition, and with its new missile-equipped surface vessels, it had begun to "show the flag" in ports all over the world. It made the decision to put a substantial part of its strategic nuclear power into submarine-launched ballistic missiles: until 1967 the West outbuilt the Soviet Union in nuclear submarines, but in that year the Soviet delivery rate doubled.

By the 1970s, the Soviets had more, though smaller, ships in the Atlantic than NATO, and more ships in the Mediterranean than the American Sixth Fleet. Russian naval yards were outbuilding the United States. Russian forces now conducted joint maneuvers with Cuban units in the hitherto inviolable Gulf of Mexico, and naval units routinely came to call at Cuban ports. If, in the late 1950s, the United States had overestimated what the Soviet Union would build in the way of bombers and intercontinental missiles, it also, in the 1960s, persistently underestimated the speed and extent of both the Soviet missile buildup and the Soviet naval buildup. By the end of 1969, the Soviet Union had more ICBMs than the United States, and while a pause took place in the early 1970s, the mid-1970s witnessed deployment of a whole new series.

China in Turmoil

In the meantime, upheaval in China had an enormous effect on Chinese relations with the rest of the world.

Mao's "Great Leap Forward" of the late 1950s represented a radical attempt to move beyond conventional forms, to mobilize the masses, and to disarm domestic Communist opponents. His ideological claims that it represented a direct move into the Communist stage, and thus put China ahead of Russia, added fuel to the conflict with Khrushchev. Subsequent data revealed that it was an economic disaster, buttressed by widespread falsification of production statistics, general productive disruption, and suppression of evidence of far-ranging famine in which millions died. Khrushchev's removal in 1964 sparked hope for Chinese-Russian détente, but brief talks proved fruitless: the conflict was too deep. Chinese explosion of its first nuclear device only a day after Khrushchev's dismissal hardly pleased the Russians; earlier in the year Mao had complained about Russian massing of troops on the frontier, apparently fearing a Russian preventive strike against Chinese nuclear installations. In future years the Chinese, like the French, refused to participate in nuclear arms control agreements, arguing that these agreements left intact the Russian and American forces and thus their joint hegemony. One result was to induce closer Russian-Indian cooperation, as China's neighbor to the south looked for support. In 1974 the Indians exploded their own first nuclear device, though they have apparently exploded none since.

But it was the explosion of the Great Proletarian Cultural Revolution, beginning in 1965, that startled the world, with millions of rampaging young Red Guards studying and waving their Little Red Books *(Quotations from Chairman Mao)*, and with the spectacle of the humiliation and imprisonment of old-line Communist leaders. The reality behind the spectacle was factional politics within China: Mao, pushed aside by more pragmatic, order-oriented leaders after the failure of the Great Leap Forward, launched the Red Guard movement, mobilizing millions of young people to attack

the universities and schools, and then the party and the government apparatus. Ordering the army to provide the young Red Guards with food, lodging,
and free railroad transportation, he sent them to roam and rampage throughout the country, where they attacked anything linked to the past or to the
West. They used physical violence against anyone attached to Mao's opponents or infected with bourgeois ideology, and they destroyed vast numbers
of books and works of art. Late in 1967, in alliance with his right-hand man,
the moderate Zhou Enlai (whose staying capacity through all this amazed
onlookers), Mao began a purge of the party designed to bring it back into
power. Over the next three years, many reeducated bureaucrats returned to
their jobs, while the army broke up any remaining Red Guard units. On the
right, people like Deng Xiaoping were expelled from the party, while on the
left, others were condemned as "ultra-left" extremists who had abused their
power. By early 1969, some measure of order was restored and General Lin
Biao was named as Mao's designated successor.

The Proletarian Revolution and Chinese Foreign Policy

This extraordinary spectacle did much to inspire young radicals of 1968 in
the rest of the world, among whom it became popular to be a "Maoist." It
also set back economic development and science in China by a decade. In
the meantime, in the course of the Cultural Revolution, China virtually
severed diplomatic relations with the rest of the world, abandoned its effort
to build a powerful bloc of anti-Russian Communist Parties, and engaged in
military skirmishes with Russia along their 4,500-mile border, while the
Russians took the occasion to resume leadership of the world Communist
movement. Fidel Castro declared that Cuban-Chinese relations would get
better when China rid itself of "senile leaders." Kim Il Sung of North Korea
reknit relations with Russia and refused to accede to Chinese insistence that
all true Marxist-Leninists must take a stand against the revisionism of the
Russians.

  While the upheaval lasted, Red Guards sacked the Foreign Ministry,
while all ambassadors but one were recalled. Most aid programs faded
away, foreign embassies in Beijing were attacked and invaded, and diplomats were manhandled. Only when the Cultural Revolution petered out did
Chinese relations with the rest of the world begin to return to normal. It was
the supple Zhou Enlai, taking charge of foreign policy, who restored normal
relations—including, significantly, relations with Yugoslavia and Romania—
and reestablished various aid programs.

  The border skirmishes with Russia stimulated conjecture that a real war
might break out. China claimed territories to the north and in central Asia

totaling some 700,000 square miles, taken by Russia through a series of "unequal treaties" in the mid-nineteenth century. In March and May 1969 serious border clashes and hundreds of border violations occurred on the Ussuri River, along the Manchurian border, and in China's far west. Both countries massed hundreds of thousands of their most modern troops along the frontier. "World War III," the Chinese government told their people, might well break out "before October." Brezhnev's attempt to get a formal condemnation of China at the Moscow-sponsored world conference of Communist Parties in June 1969 failed.

In mid-September, though, Premier Aleksei Kosygin made a surprise visit to Beijing on his way home from Ho Chi Minh's funeral in Hanoi, and met with Zhou, who agreed to diplomatic talks. Although the polemics resumed shortly after, the situation appeared to have been defused.

Nixon Visits Mao

Chinese condemnation of Russia's "wolfish social imperialism" was usually linked with attacks upon American imperialism and the charge that both superpowers were trying to divide the world between them. For twenty years the United States had refused to recognize the Chinese Communists as the legitimate government for China: to conservative Americans—organized in the "Committee of One Million to Keep China out of the UN"—Mao Zedong was virtually the devil incarnate. It was therefore astonishing in February 1972 to see Republican President Richard Nixon, after a week of talks in Beijing with Mao and Zhou Enlai, getting up from a banquet table in Beijing to clink glasses with and toast Mao, proclaiming, "This was the week that changed the world!" He was right. The inconceivable had happened, and people could watch it on television all over the globe. In simple terms, balance-of-power principles had triumphed over ideology. It was not quite what in older times would have been called a shift in alliances, but it was a major diplomatic realignment.

The Nixon Administration had relaxed some longstanding trade and travel restrictions to China as early as 1969, and there had been quiet diplomatic communication through Pakistan indicating that, despite differences, the Chinese would welcome a rapprochement with the United States. Following the meeting in early 1971 of an American ping-pong team with Zhou Enlai, who solemnly proclaimed that their visit had turned a "new page in American-Chinese relations," Nixon lifted all travel curbs to China, and relaxed commercial and financial restrictions. A presidential commission recommended that the United States work for admission of the People's Republic of China to the UN, while retaining Taiwan as a member.

On July 15, 1971, most startling of all, President Nixon announced on television that he had accepted Zhou's invitation to visit China, where he would seek a normalization of relations. Obliquely, he told the Chinese Nationalists on Taiwan that his action "was not at the expense of old friends" and the Russians that it was "not directed against any other nation." And in fact, three months later, he announced that he would visit Moscow in 1972.

On October 25, 1971, in New York, the UN General Assembly voted to seat the delegation of the People's Republic of China and to unseat Taiwan, and other international organizations followed suit.* From February 21 to February 28, President Nixon and his wife visited Communist China, where Nixon spent long hours in conversation with Zhou.

The carefully crafted Shanghai Communique issued upon Nixon's departure listed agreements and disagreements, particularly over Vietnam and Taiwan. A formula was found by which China and the United States agreed that China constituted a single entity, that the problem of Taiwan would be resolved peacefully, and that American troops there would be gradually removed, while normalization of Sino-American relations would take place. In what Nixon called the "most vitally important section," both accepted that neither nation "should seek hegemony in the Asia Pacific region and each is opposed to efforts by any other country or group of countries to establish such hegemony." This was a clear warning to Brezhnev's Russia, with its million troops on the frontier with China, and the beginnings of its Pacific naval buildup.

Nixon and Kissinger and their Chinese counterparts had made a basic change in the political map of the world.

Détente

The Soviet Union under Brezhnev already faced the need to rethink policy. Paradoxically, parity in nuclear missiles made possible serious, stabilizing arms control negotiations with the United States. On the negative side, Eastern Europe remained in an uneasy state, Brezhnev Doctrine or no. In 1970, popular discontent with the economic situation in Poland led to rioting and the replacement of Premier Wladyslaw Gomulka. The Soviet economy had shown a slowdown in growth since the 1950s. Russia's far-off global commitments were proving difficult to handle. Brezhnev appeared to

---

*As of the end of July 1972, there is no longer any mention of Taiwan in UN documents, including statistical reports—although Taiwan, as of this writing, has probably the largest foreign exchange reserves in the world.

need détente and to be willing to sacrifice some interests to obtain it, but rapprochement between the United States and China placed Nixon and Kissinger in a much better bargaining position than before—as they had planned.

In 1971, at the Soviet Union's Twenty-Fourth Communist Party Congress, Brezhnev defined a basic need: the final recognition of the territorial changes that took place in Europe as a result of World War II. Socialist Chancellor Willy Brandt of West Germany had already abandoned the goal of unification, as well as the "Hallstein doctrine" to the effect that West Germany would not establish diplomatic relations with countries that recognized East Germany. In Moscow on August 12, 1970, he signed a treaty confirming the division of Germany into two states, and ratifying the transfer of land to Poland in the east. Four months later, Brandt signed the Treaty of Warsaw, ratifying the land transfer and the Oder-Neisse border directly with Poland. Having given the Soviet Union what it had so long sought in Germany—legitimacy for the East German regime and the Polish borders—Brandt asked for and received a clarification of the status of Berlin. In June 1972 Moscow assured him it would assume the guarantee of free transit to and from Berlin, that the special ties between West Berlin and West Germany would be maintained, and that more freedom of movement of East and West Berliners would be stimulated. In December the two Germanies regularized their relations (without a final de jure definition). A year later, both were admitted to the UN.

Willy Brandt, a politician of unusual integrity, had reversed twenty years of West German foreign policy by recognizing the situation in the East in what was called *Ostpolitik*. This reversal seemed, at the time, both courageous and realistic. Twenty years later, however, people debated whether or not *Ostpolitik* had simply helped postpone the collapse of communism.

President Nixon's visit to Moscow was fixed for May 1972, and a number of issues, all involving détente, hung upon the visit. The North Vietnamese full-scale conventional attack, Nixon's mining of the harbor of Haiphong (where Russian vessels docked), and resumption of heavy bombing all preceded the visit. Many Americans viewed Nixon's response in Vietnam as a direct challenge to Moscow, which would jeopardize the summit. It did not. In the face of Nixon's warm reception in Rumania and his rapprochement with Mao, Brezhnev appeared to want détente even more than the Americans did.

The summit produced numerous agreements, of which the most important were the Anti-Ballistic Missile Treaty (ABM treaty) limiting deployment of antiballistic missiles, and the first Strategic Arms Limitation Treaty (SALT I) interim agreement, putting a cap on numbers of strategic ballistic missiles (see chapter 7). SALT I was designed to be the first of a series of strategic arms limitation agreements that would finally bring about genuine disarmament. In addition, negotiators laid the basis for an important commercial agreement that would settle the old World War II Lend-Lease debts, accord the Soviet Union most favored nation (MFN) tariff treatment, and provide for extended credits that would enable it to buy much-needed American grain and technology.

In a world vastly different from Khrushchev's day, a real détente appeared to have replaced the Cold War.

Conclusion

When Kennedy became president, Americans by and large shared a Cold War consensus: the United States had to act to block the aggressive Soviet Union. There were differences on how this must be implemented, and there were Democrats who were more "hawkish" than Republicans, especially since they still feared being tarnished as "soft on Communism." By the end of the decade, when Nixon became president, the consensus had largely disappeared: large segments of the population, especially among the young, blamed the United States—not just for the horrors it had perpetrated in Vietnam and its support of repressive governments elsewhere, but for the Cold War itself, the premises of which had led directly to Vietnam. They could find little good to say about American society.

The Western bloc, too, fractured, as de Gaulle sought to distance himself from the United States as well as England. But Europeans recognized in Richard Nixon one of their own, one who could forgo ideology and act in balance-of-power terms. When he visited Bucharest, where Nicolae Ceausescu gave him a big parade; when he clinked glasses with Mao Zedong (as no Democratic president could have done), when he then visited Moscow to sign numerous agreements that would stabilize the Cold War and result in a real détente, Europeans could cheer. Even his strategy of only gradual extrication from Vietnam secured their approval, despite the losses incurred. They applauded, too, the Nixon Doctrine, which would mean that America would not waste its resources in far-off places. Here, finally, was an American president they could understand and work with, even if they had differing interests.

For the Soviet Union the decade started off with Khrushchev trying to go too far. The gray men who succeeded him in the Kremlin in 1964 were grimly determined to abandon bluff and to build their military power to the point that they would not be found in the same position Khrushchev put them in at the time of the Cuban missile crisis. For Brezhnev the crackdown on Czechoslovakia in 1968 was routine, and useful in demonstrating Soviet power and determination. The Soviet navy now cruised the world in support of far-flung interests that could never have existed in Stalin's time.

The attempt to mend the break with China, however, was perfunctory. The break split the world Communist movement and gave Nixon the chance at promoting the great realignment, then to travel to Moscow to enshrine détente. What subsequent chapters will show is that Soviet leaders had a very different conception of détente: détente provided the opportunity to continue the struggle with the West on a safer basis. As a result of distrust of Soviet intentions, the American government backed off from many of détente's provisions—reinforcing Soviet suspicions.

Notes

1. Louise FitzSimons, cited in David Burner and Thomas R. West, *The Torch is Passed: The Kennedy Brothers and American Liberalism* (New York: Atheneum, 1984), p. 187.
2. Quoted in William J. Rust, *Kennedy in Vietnam* (New York: Scribner, 1985), p. 63.

Further Suggested Readings

No one book on the Vietnam War can be singled out. The best procedure for a student wishing to learn more is to use the well-annotated James S. Olson, *The Vietnam War: Handbook of the Literature and Research* (Westport, CT: Greenwood Press, 1993). Two books by Adam Ulam are useful for this period, the first is cited in chapter 2, and the second is *Dangerous Relations: The Soviet Union in World Politics, 1970–1982* (New York: Oxford University Press, 1983). Nelson L. Keith, *The Making of Detente: Soviet–American Relations in the Shadow of Vietnam* (Baltimore: Johns Hopkins University Press, 1995), is also useful. James A. Nathan (ed.), *The Cuban Missile Crisis Revisited* (New York: St. Martin's Press, 1992), adds considerably to contemporary accounts. Richard C. Thornton, *The Nixon-Kissinger Years: Reshaping American Foreign Policy* (New York: Paragon House, 1989), is a good survey.

6

Cooperation and Conflict in the Third World

The idea of the "Third World" implied that all non-Western and non–Soviet bloc countries shared the experience of having been objects of the international politics conducted by the Western powers in the past. They had been exploited and impoverished, and as a result were in need of aid to overcome the handicaps of poor infrastructure, poor communications, and lack of capital. They were mainly raw material exporters, and they were importers of manufactured goods. All too often, they had single-crop export economies subject to continued unequal relationships with the developed countries. In the 1960s and the 1970s, these countries forged a unity based largely on these notions, and they directed much of their efforts in international politics toward trying to redefine relations between them and the First World.

It was all rather misleading. As chapter 4 has shown, this emerging Third World was, in fact, made up of highly dissimilar countries with very different historical experiences and geographical settings. The conflicts between them often burst out in open warfare, or were papered over and blamed on First World countries. The oil-exporting countries of the Middle East, which had among the highest per capita incomes in the world, invested heavily in First World countries (rather than in other Third World countries). When, in the 1970s, they were able to greatly increase the price of their oil exports, the countries they hurt most were other Third World countries that depended on oil imports. Although Third World unity was based largely on what was viewed as a constantly growing gap between incomes in Third World countries and those in the First World, at least forty Third World countries came to have the highest growth rates of any countries in history in the 1960s and 1970s, while some industrialized more rapidly than any Western countries had done in the past, and a number became primarily exporters of industrial goods. On the other hand, some forty countries in the grouping—mostly in Africa and South Asia—were among the poorest states in the world. In UN agencies they came to be called the "Fourth World" or "MSA" countries—those most seriously affected by the oil price rise of the 1970s.

In the earliest, optimistic, years, "independence" was very largely equated with "freedom." Reality proved to be different, as military coups and dictatorships succeeded one another in too many Third World countries, where ethnic, religious, or tribal rivalries produced repressive regimes dominated by one group or another, or led to bitter warfare. In poor states, access to political power too often proved a pathway to enrichment and corruption. Improvement in agricultural productivity—the basis for economic development—often languished.

Governments and rulers usually heralded economic development as their prime aim, and their foreign policy stance in international organizations was usually dictated by an agreed-upon list of what was needed for development: more aid, aid on easier terms, more investment (though many insisted on the right to nationalize existing investment—hardly an inducement to investors), and special trade advantages. Again, reality was often very different, as many ruling elites carried out policies that contributed little to development and much to the maintenance of their political power, or else tried to cope with ethnic, religious, and nationality conflicts that inhibited any strong development effort. As background to all these developments, the poorest states continued to have the highest population growth rates in the world.

If the pathway to independence was not easy, as chapter 4 showed, the pathway to freedom, justice, and economic development proved rockier than most people had imagined. Intervention by the Soviet Union, China, and the United States—often requested by warring parties—did not always help matters.

Africa After Independence

Taken as a whole, Africa showed considerable growth in the 1950s, as countries sought independence. Although independence was accompanied by major conflicts such as the one in the former Belgian Congo, it brought a surge of elation and optimism, and the 1960s still showed promise, though other wars erupted. By the 1970s, shadows of the grim future began to lengthen, and people began to write of a continent that had lost its way.

The Spread of Conflict

Some of the warfare on the African continent dragged on interminably. The brutal conflict between the black south and the Arab north of the giant

Sudan persisted until March 1972, when it came to an end as a result of mediation. After a series of coups in the 1980s, the two regions found themselves once again at war and generating hundreds of thousands of hungry refugees.

Conflict also became endemic after what seemed a good start in the horn of Africa. Somalia sought accession of French Somaliland and Somali-inhabited regions of neighboring Kenya and Ethiopia. In 1967, however, the inhabitants of French Somaliland, now called Djibouti, rejected any union with Somalia and ultimately chose independence, a decade later. Somalia sought and received extensive Chinese and Russian help, and numerous Cuban advisers arrived when Somalia began to aid Somali guerrillas within Kenya and Ethiopia; full-scale war erupted between Ethiopia and Somalia in 1977. In an ironic twist, a Marxist revolution that overthrew Emperor Haile Selassie in Ethiopia in 1974* presented Russia with a new opportunity it could not turn down: Ethiopia was simply more important than Somalia, despite Russia's strategically valuable Indian Ocean naval base on the Somali coast at Berbera.

Two billion dollars worth of Soviet tanks, artillery, and modern jets were dispatched to the new government of Mengistu Haile Mariam along with a large contingent of Cuban troops and a Soviet general, who led them to victory in the Ogaden. It all prompted Somali renunciation of its treaty of friendship with the USSR. Russian support also helped Ethiopia resist the largely Marxist-led Muslim independence movements in Eritrea in a war that broke out shortly after Haile Selassie's government ended Eritrea's autonomous status in 1962. The conflict dragged on for thirty years, until 1991. By this time Russian support for the Mengistu regime had ended. After years of guerrilla warfare Mengistu fled, and on May 28, 1991, rebels from the northern and eastern provinces entered Addis Ababa. With American mediation a relatively peaceful transition took place, and Eritrea became independent in 1993.

There were other conflicts, with fewer international implications—between Algeria and Morocco, between Morocco and Mauritania (which Morocco briefly claimed in its entirety), between Chad and its neighbors, and between Uganda and Tanzania (a conflict that had particularly long-lasting effects). The erratic and ferocious General Idi Amin seized power in Uganda in early

---

*According to testimony in the mass murder trial of the Marxist leaders in 1994, the emperor was strangled in his bed on August 26, 1975, "most cruelly." It was a sad end for the slim man who had stood so dramatically before the Assembly of the League of Nations almost forty years earlier to appeal for sanctions against Italy—symbolizing both the hope placed in the League and its fatal weakness.

Map 12. **The Horn of Africa**

1971 and unleashed a reign of terror that led to the death or disappearance of several hundred thousand people. African leaders at first approved of his expulsion of 80,000 hapless Asians who dominated small
businesses: the brutal move appealed because it would turn over the
economy to Africans. Yet Julius Nyerere of Tanzania called it "racist," and
the move's appeal was short-lived, as terror spread throughout the country.
Amin, who continued to wear the Israeli paratrooper wings he had won in
training there, broke with Israel and declared that Hitler had done the right
thing in killing six million Jews. (When Palestinian hijackers landed an El
Al airliner at Uganda's Entebbe airfield in 1976, Israeli commandos
mounted an attack that liberated most of the hostages, destroyed much of
Amin's air force, and set an example others would hope to emulate in the

future.) Eventually, in 1979, Tanzania, harboring thousands of Ugandan refugees, intervened directly. Nyerere's troops drove Amin out of the country, along with his few supporters and a number of Libyan troops that had been sent to help him. Tanzanian soldiers withdrew in 1981, but the damage had been done. Tribal hatreds and distrust were compounded, coup followed coup, and attempts to rebuild both the governmental system and the ravaged economy seemed unavailing in the years ahead.

Independence came late to the Portuguese "overseas provinces" of Angola and Mozambique, where Portugal still maintained an army of 100,000 in 1970. The situation appeared relatively stable. But developments in the rest of Africa and the flow of African nations into the United Nations were bound to affect both areas. Guerrilla movements grew, supported by the Soviet Union, the United States, and China. Ironically, as the relatively small Portuguese army came to rely on conscripts to maintain colonial power, the army itself became radicalized and helped overthrow Portuguese dictator Salazar's successor, Marcello Caetano, establishing a democratic regime in Portugal and negotiating a withdrawal from the colonies in 1974-75. The Soviet-supported Popular Movement for the Liberation of Angola (MPLA), consolidated its power, helped by 20,000 Cuban troops airlifted in by the Russians. The American Congress forced President Gerald Ford to discontinue aid to a rival faction, the National Front for the Liberation of Angola, which promptly collapsed. But a third grouping, UNITA, (the National Union for the Total Independence of Angola) led by Jonas Savimby (who had a Ph.D. in political science from the University of Lausanne in Switzerland) received support first from China, then from South Africa, and eventually from the United States. UNITA continued to wage guerrilla warfare against the MPLA government, now recognized by the OAS. Only in the 1990s, finally, did a UN-brokered peace seem to hold.

Mozambique was simpler. Only FRELIMO (the Front for the Liberation of Mozambique) fought the Portuguese from its base within neighboring Tanzania. Led by a hard-line Marxist, it negotiated independence with Portugal after a period of harsh warfare; 250,000 whites fled, and on July 25, 1975, the new government proclaimed independence as the People's Republic of Mozambique. In the next few years it received substantial aid from the Soviet Union, East Germany, and Cuba. (Later, though, South Africa supported a rival guerrilla movement that spread terror and civil war through the state until 1994, following the end of apartheid in South Africa.)

Other conflicts were shorter, but equally ferocious. The giant Federation of Nigeria, with a population equal to that of France and Great Britain together, was one of sixteen African nations to become independent in 1960. It was widely viewed as probably the most viable of the new states, a showcase for how federalism could reconcile tribalism with strong central government. Ethnic, religious, and regional cleavages nevertheless overcame the advantages it appeared to possess, and internal war broke out on May 30, 1967, when one of the four Nigerian regions peopled primarily by the Ibo declared independence as the state of Biafra, under the leadership of General Odumego Ojukwu, and the central government moved to suppress it. Initial Biafran successes were soon overcome, the war settled down to a prolonged siege during which thousands of Biafrans starved to death, and in January 1970 the last Biafran enclave fell. To the surprise of many, the Nigerian government followed a generous policy in reintegrating the region.

Biafra received extensive support: even four African states—Tanzania, Gabon, the Ivory Coast, and Zambia—recognized its independence despite the general African fear that splintering of African states would fatally weaken them. The Ibo of Biafra, the Tanzanian declaration said, had earned their right to independence. Aid from outside Africa—including large-scale aid from the Soviet Union to the Nigerian government—poured in for both sides; some analysts depicted the war as an imperialist one over control of oil resources located in Biafra. Efforts at mediation by the UN, the pope, neutral countries, and the Organization of African Unity (OAU), all failed because Nigeria would negotiate only on the basis of Nigerian unity, Biafra on the basis of independence. By the time the war ground to its end in 1970, an estimated million and a half to two million Africans had perished. Britain, which had created the Federation of Nigeria, continued to back its unity—and therefore, unofficially, like many other states, to block aid to Biafra. Said Labour Prime Minister Sir Harold Wilson, musing on the necessities of strategy and realpolitik, "If a million Ibos had . . . to die to preserve the unity of Nigeria, well, that was not too high a price to pay." This war was perhaps a portent of horrors to come in Ethiopia, Bangladesh, Cambodia, and the Sudan.

Nigeria has never really stabilized nor lived up to its potential, although the state has held together.

Regionalism in Africa

Africa has little coherence as a continent. In 1984, according to the president of the Congo, intra-African trade composed only 2.9 percent of total African trade. The idea that Africa north of the Sahara is a part of a Mediterranean region, linked by trade, common interests, and a Mediterranean civilization that includes southern Europe, keeps returning. North Africa, in this view, has little in common with Africa south of the Sahara. Egyptian President Nasser flirted briefly with being an African leader, but Egyptian ties to other Arab states overwhelmed the attempt. The North African area of Tunisia, Algeria, and Morocco—called the "Maghreb"—appears by many criteria to constitute a region, yet attempts at any sort of unity have foundered on national differences. West African countries have few contacts with East Africa, and both of these areas are internally divided. Southern Africa, also divided, appears to be very different from other parts of the continent.

If the new African states were to become "sovereign" and "independent" in order to fit into what had been the Western state system, their new leaders had to create a sense of nationhood to support the claim to legitimacy of their new governments. Nevertheless, and in spite of their differences, they sought to create broader, more "natural" regional groupings, or associations based on ideology and common interests—groupings designed to keep Africa from being a collection of small, fragile states that would continue to fall prey to more powerful nations.

The march to independence was therefore accompanied in those euphoric early years both by all-African meetings and by innumerable attempts at regional organization and integration. Customs unions and common markets followed one another in rapid profusion. Most of them proved to be ephemeral, meeting the same fate as the East African Community (EAC)—the outgrowth of a common services organization created in 1961 by the British for Kenya, Uganda, and Tanganyika. The EAC had a common currency, a railroad network, telecommunications and postal services, a common market, and an airline. It all seemed to make economic sense, and in 1963 leaders of the three states declared their intention to create a genuine federation. But the EAC itself couldn't last: the other two states complained that Kenya benefited the most economically; Kenyans came to feel that their membership had become an economic burden; political strains erupted once Idi Amin seized power in Uganda; Tanzania's own particular economic policies and interests conflicted with those of the others. The EAC finally broke up in 1978, well after many of the other more ephemeral but often widely proclaimed "economic unions."

In more recent years a series of regional groupings and regional development banks have been created on the basis of more sober expectations. Some are primarily Francophone, some English-speaking. One early division has been bridged: five years after creation of the European Economic Community (EEC) in 1958, an agreement of association signed at Yaoundé, Cameroon, linked seventeen Francophone states with the Community. Other African countries complained that the agreement shut them out of the European market, but in 1968, Kenya, Tanzania, and Uganda signed a similar agreement with the EEC at Arusha, Tanzania. The Yaoundé and

Arusha pacts were followed by the series of Lomé, Togo, agreements with forty-six (later sixty-six) African, Pacific, and Caribbean (APC) countries, with the result that this particular split disappeared.

The Organization of African Unity has faced the same basic dilemma troubling the United Nations: "sovereignty" formally precludes outside intervention, but devotion to promotion of human rights often means that an outside party may want to intervene in order to prevent gross violation of human rights by a sovereign government (as Tanzania eventually did unilaterally in Uganda). In the case of South Africa or Rhodesia, where white minorities repressed black African majorities, African governments rejected the notion that sovereignty prevents outside intervention. In the cases of the two tiny, densely populated landlocked states of Rwanda and Burundi, however—to choose two out of numerous cases—the OAU could do little when internal upheaval led to massacres of tens of thousands and sent hundreds of thousands of refugees across borders into neighboring Tanzania, Zaire, and Uganda. Both Rwanda and Burundi had been German- and then Belgian-ruled, and both achieved independence in 1962; but in the case of Burundi it was ruling minority Tutsi tribesmen who repressed a Hutu uprising in 1972 (causing, the UN secretary-general estimated, 200,000 deaths), while in Rwanda the majority Hutu sent Tutsi into flight. (The scene would be repeated in the late 1980s and most horrifically in 1994, when a million Hutu refugees would end up in poverty-stricken Zaire, following a planned genocidal attack on Tutsi by a Hutu faction and a Tutsi victory in the ensuing conflict.)

In the meantime, African leaders tended to focus more and more on the need to get rid of white rule in Angola, Mozambique, Rhodesia, Namibia, and, most of all, South Africa, whose government dug in to resist what eventually, in the 1980s, turned out to be an irresistible tide.

Asian Turmoil

Throughout South Asia and the Far East, the decades of the 1960s and 1970s brought change at a dizzying pace. As we have seen in chapter 5, democratic India, aligned with the Soviet Union, emerged as the main power in southern Asia when Pakistan, aligned with the United States, split in two. War in Vietnam ensured that all of formerly French Indochina would become Communist, but rather than Communist Indochina being an extension of Chinese Communist power, the two were instead in bitter conflict. One result was reassessment of security threats in the area: American air bases built in Thailand under South East Asian Treaty Organization (SEATO) auspices were phased out, and in 1977, the organization itself came to an end. In the meantime Bangkok, the capital of Thailand, became something of an international center, hosting the headquarters of several regional UN bodies, and the city in which the Association of Southeast Asian Nations (ASEAN) was created in August 1967. ASEAN was to be devoted primarily to economic development, but it also gained a somewhat unexpected prominence as a diplomatic grouping, particularly as some of its members—Thailand, Malaysia, and Indonesia—began in the 1980s to emulate another of its members, Singapore, in achieving extraordinary rates of economic growth.

Sukarno's Indonesia and a New World Order

Two other states in the area took a very different path. One, Burma—independent since 1948—followed its own unique, somewhat isolationist path under single-party authoritarian rule, and participated minimally in international organizations. It even withdrew from the Non-Aligned Movement in late 1979.

The other was Indonesia under the charismatic Ahmed Sukarno. For a brief period in the years after the Bandung Conference of 1955 he dominated world headlines about Southeast Asia, and played a larger-than-life role on the world scene. Yet in the long run he had little impact.

In 1956 he dissolved the Netherlands-Indonesian Union under the Dutch crown, toured the capitals of the Communist world, invited the president of the Soviet Union for an extended stay, and proclaimed the desirability of "guided democracy" in which political parties would be dissolved and he would exercise quasidictatorial rule. Western governments were disturbed by his increasing reliance upon the previously rebellious and outlawed Communist Party, which had close links to Communist China.

In the meantime, he created a prolonged international crisis by laying claim to Western New Guinea, or "West Irian," as a remnant of Dutch colonialism. Eventually, a face-saving formula was devised by the UN to turn the area over to Indonesia, regardless of the inhabitants' wishes. By this time, Sukarno had enunciated his ambition to create a Southeast Asian sphere embracing Malaya, the Philippines, and Indonesia—"Maphilindo"—under Indonesian leadership. In the early 1960s, following British-sponsored creation of a federation of Malaysia to include Singapore and several colonies on the northwest coast of Borneo, Sukarno acted swiftly to prevent it coming about, and began a guerrilla campaign to "crush Malaysia." Unable to block the new state's admission to the United Nations, Sukarno proceeded to withdraw from the UN.

This was a startling move that provoked headlines the world over. Su-

Map 13. Indonesia and Its Neighbors

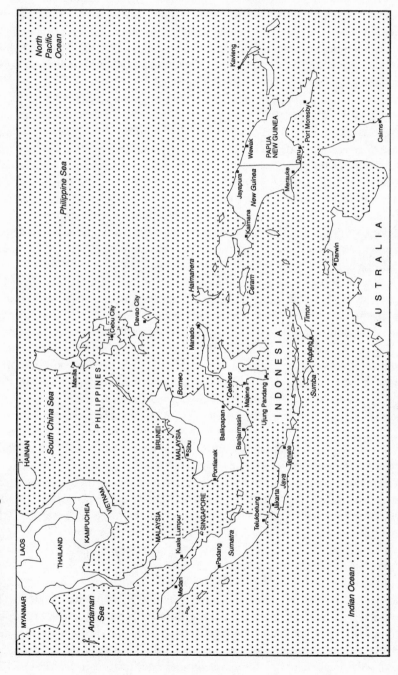

karno now declared that the UN represented the domination of the Old Established Forces (OLDEFO)—while Indonesia, with other new Third World states following suit, would replace it with one that represented the New Emerging Forces (NEFO).

Sukarno's attempt to change the very structure of world politics, to make Indonesia the leader of a coalition of new radical states, failed. No one, not even the People's Republic of China, joined in. In late 1965, Sukarno's time ran out. With his foreknowledge and apparent acquiescence, pro-Communist army officers tried to assassinate a group of leading army generals, hoping then to cooperate with the Communist Party and to neutralize any possible army opposition to a Communist takeover. The conspiracy misfired; the generals rallied the army against the young officers' movement and destroyed the Communist Party apparatus in the process. The countercoup unleashed longstanding resentment against economically dominant Chinese minorities (associated in the popular mind both with the party and with Communist China), and several hundred thousand people were killed in the resulting bloodbath.

A new regime, led by General Suharto, moved quietly to redirect Indonesian foreign policy into cooperation with the West, easing out Sukarno before he could assert some of his old magic. The new Indonesian leaders ended the confrontation with Malaysia (permitting Britain to withdraw most of its troops based in Singapore) and established diplomatic relations with both Malaysia and Singapore. They arranged for consolidation and deferment of the enormous debt incurred by Sukarno, curbed hyperinflation, met conditions for resumption of investment, and began to develop again the export markets that once existed for Indonesia (and for the next quarter century Indonesia had one of the highest per capita income growth rates in the world). In 1966 Indonesia resumed its place in the United Nations, and when the Association of Southeast Asian Nations was founded in 1967, its headquarters was located in Djakarta. In 1970 Sukarno died quietly; Indonesia celebrates his earlier years, when he fought for independence from the Dutch and helped create a nation out of a far-flung archipelago. (Indonesians also continue to live under authoritarian rule.)

Japan's Reemergence in Southeast Asia

Concern arose in Southeast Asia as America faltered in Vietnam, but abated in the face of mutual hostility between the Chinese and Vietnamese. With the growth of vigorous economies outside Indochina, a new confidence replaced the old concerns. It was, in fact, Japan—the defeated conqueror of 1942—that reappeared as the largest trader and investor in Southeast Asia as a whole. Instead of brutal soldiers sent by a militarist government bent on securing access to the tin, rubber, and oil of the region, now it was Japanese businessmen and bureaucrats who were sent out by one of the wealthiest nations in the world. In 1968 the Japanese gross national product surpassed that of Germany, making the Japanese economy second only to that of the United States and the Soviet Union. The Japanese presence raised apprehension and, on occasion, led to much irritation. It also raised the issue of whether Japan might implement some kind of security interest in the region.

The Japanese certainly had an interest in the free flow of trade in the area. Among other things, 90 percent of Japan's oil flowed through the Straits of Malacca from the Middle East. But after the end of Sukarno and the end of the second Vietnam War there seemed little in the way of a security threat. Indonesia gave up most of its imperial ambitions. (In 1975, when Portugal gave up its African colonies, a brief civil war broke out in Portuguese Timor, which occupied half of the island of Timor. The other half had belonged to Holland and had become a part of Indonesia in 1950, and Indonesia now intervened to annex the second half.) As a result, Japan seemed content to extend its economic interests, and to leave security matters to others. For a variety of reasons, but in part to underline how different its role was from in the past, it took an active part in the creation and management of the Asian Development Bank, inaugurated in Tokyo and located in Manila in 1966, and which has become an important and influential presence on the Asian scene.

The Middle East: More Wars

Nowhere was Third World unity more tenuous than in the Middle East. Even being able to join in hostility to Israel and imperialism was not enough. The decades following the Suez War of 1956 and the gradual withdrawal of Western influence were ones of dashed hopes, small, bitter wars, military coups, irredentist claims, and civil strife.

The Palestine Liberation Organization and the Third Round, 1967

The growing number of Arab "revolutionary" regimes rejected both Western liberal institutions and traditional societies that had allowed themselves to be dominated or humiliated by the West. The Soviet Union offered something of a model—a powerful anti-Western state that joined a single, mobilizing party to a strong military. It also offered arms aid and diplomatic support for those hostile to the West and to Israel, having few qualms about upsetting the Middle East balance that Western powers had tried to maintain earlier. In the 1960s and the 1970s Moscow expended considerable diplomatic effort in cultivating ties to as many Middle East and North African states as possible.

In 1964 Arab leaders met at a summit conference in Cairo that created the Palestine Liberation Organization (PLO) under Ahmed Shukairy. The PLO organized itself as a quasi government, based on its Covenant and Fundamental Law and capable of acting independently of other Arab states. (The Covenant, until amended thirty-two years later, in 1996, effectively rejected the existence of the state of Israel.) A year later, in 1965, a new and radical Baath leadership in Syria encouraged Palestinian commandos to go on the attack against Israel. Nasser, to maintain his leadership, joined Syria in a new military pact, and in berating King Hussein of Jordan for his attempts to restrain the Palestinians. An explosion of raids and counterraids took place across Israeli frontiers, further jeopardizing the Jordanian king.

Rumors circulated—fired by the Soviet Union, which vetoed even the mildest UN resolutions calling for conciliation—that Israel was preparing to attack Syria. Nasser, under mounting public ferment, made his fatal moves in mid-May 1967. He mobilized his army on the Israeli borders, reoccupied Sharm el Sheikh at the tip of the Gulf of Aqaba, and ordered out UN troops who had patrolled both areas since the 1956 war, maintaining a precarious cease-fire and Israeli freedom of navigation. UN Secretary-General U Thant felt he had no excuse to refuse the order to withdraw the UN forces, and Israel's pleas at the UN went unheeded.

Israel had declared that a blockade of Sharm el Sheikh would be a casus belli (a legitimate cause for war): the gulf was Israel's pathway to the Indian Ocean, and also allowed it access to the oil it imported from the Persian Gulf. In the next two weeks, Syria, Iraq, and Jordan—whose king now rejoined the military alliance to keep from being overthrown—moved troops to the Israeli borders. On June 5, 1967, Israel mounted a swift pre-emptive air strike that caught and destroyed most Egyptian aircraft on the ground. Within less than a week, it had seized the Gaza Strip and the entire Sinai Peninsula, and its troops patrolled the Suez Canal; it took the entire West Bank area from Jordan; and it drove Syrian troops from the Golan Heights area, a raised ridge overlooking northeast Israel from which, for two years, hundreds of Syrian guns had lobbed shells into Israeli collective farms.

The "Six-Day War" of 1967 was both a startling victory for Israel and a crushing defeat for the surrounding Arab states. Several of these states broke relations with the United States when Nasser falsely accused the United States of having provided pilots for the Israeli planes.

The Israelis were, however, unable to turn military victory into political gain. They were willing to negotiate a return of the Sinai, the Gaza Strip, most of the West Bank, and the Golan Heights (with some rectifications: the rapid withdrawal of the UN Emergency Force had demonstrated to them the weakness of international guarantees, and they wanted to be able to provide for their own security). They would not, however, return the Arab half of Jerusalem, nor Sharm el Sheikh, overlooking the vital straits of Tiran. In exchange, they wanted peace. To this the Arabs would not agree. They looked instead to diplomatic pressure to force an Israeli withdrawal; their expectations were raised when French President de Gaulle condemned the Israelis and embargoed arms shipments. (France had been Israel's chief arms supplier since the Soviet Union had started supplying Egypt in 1956.) Arab leaders also looked to a Russian return in force to the area and were not disappointed: the Russians made up the arms they had lost in the war, and broke diplomatic relations with Israel (resumed only in 1991, after the crumbling of the Soviet empire). At a meeting in Khartoum the Arabs were able to agree on the principle of "no peace with Israel, no negotiations with Israel, no recognition of Israel, and maintenance of the rights of the Palestinian people in their nation." (The declaration would bedevil Arab leaders in later years when they sought Western support for their positions on relations with Israel.)

In other words, Israel would negotiate the return of most territories and would also negotiate about other matters directly with countries that recognized its right to exist and that would establish normal diplomatic relations with it. This the Arabs refused to do. (And this most people have forgotten that Israel was willing to do.)

The situation festered while Israel hardened its stance and its new defense lines. In November 1967 British representatives devised the slightly ambiguous UN Security Council Resolution 242, calling for Israel's withdrawal from the occupied areas, but linking this to acceptance of principles for a lasting peace and providing for designation of a special representative of the secretary-general to assist the parties to effect it. The prolonged efforts of UN mediator Gunnar Jarring, however, proved fruitless. In the meantime, the Soviet Union supplied Arab belligerents with arms equivalent to the amount they had supplied in the previous twelve years.

A major new factor in the equation was the increased sense of selfhood of the Palestine Arabs, now grouped in the Palestine Liberation Organization, which came under the leadership of Yasir Arafat in 1969. The PLO Council assumed a stance more favorable to guerrilla activities, insisted upon greater independence from the Arab states, and called for the creation of a Palestinian state that would harbor Christians, Muslims, and Jews who had been in the area in 1948—thus still rejecting the existence of the state of Israel.

To dramatize their cause, Palestinians began a series of terrorist acts and hijackings outside the Palestine area: in September 1970 one radical faction blew up a giant Pan American Airlines 747 jet at Cairo airport to protest Egyptian (and Jordanian) acquiescence in exploring a new American peace plan for the Middle East. A few days later they destroyed Swissair, British Airways, and TWA jets outside Amman, Jordan, in an effort to get release of terrorists held in Western Europe. Increase in their armed activities in Jordan led to outright civil war, as Hussein found it necessary to disarm them to protect his throne.

In the meantime, in retaliation for attack on an Israeli airliner in Athens and to show that countries harboring terrorists were liable to attack, Israeli commandos destroyed thirteen Lebanese airliners in Beirut, where the terrorists were based. But Arab terrorist acts multiplied: terrorists murdered the American ambassador to the Sudan and launched a letter bomb campaign; Arabs in ski masks massacred eleven members of the Israeli Olympic team in Munich in 1972; and three Japanese associates disembarking from an aircraft sprayed the Tel Aviv airport with machine-gun fire, killing and wounding a hundred people. Soviet leaders, wary of terrorism, nevertheless began to cultivate relations with the PLO and to support its aims.

The cease-fire between Israel and Egypt following the Six-Day War was never very stable, and in 1969 violence escalated in what became known as the ''War of Attrition''—a series of raids and counterraids—as new Soviet arms flooded into Egypt. Israel, Egypt, and Russia accepted a new cease-fire and a standstill on the introduction of new arms into the Suez Canal zone in 1970. When the Russians secretly used the occasion to ship and deploy their advanced antiaircraft missile system into the zone, it reinforced Israeli views on the worthlessness of international guarantees. Nevertheless, the cease-fire was maintained.

Anwar Sadat and the Fourth Round, 1973

On September 28, 1970, Gamal Abdel Nasser died of a heart attack. Delirious masses had restored him to power in 1967 when he resigned as a result of failure in the Six-Day War. Now five million witnessed his funeral cortege and many of them wept. Nasser, unable to fulfill a dream of Pan-Arabism, nevertheless represented Arab pride and honor. Anwar Sadat, his successor, seemed to many merely a stopgap. He vowed to continue Nasser's policies: Arab unity, support for Palestinians and opposition to Zionism, nonalignment but friendship with Russia, and support for Afro-Asian peoples and for liberation movements.

Throughout 1971, Sadat found himself having to make excuses for not resuming hostilities with Israel. Suddenly, in July 1972, the Egyptian leader ordered Soviet advisers and experts to leave Egypt, and to turn over Russian bases and materiel to exclusive Egyptian control. He explained that Russia had hindered him from resolving the Israeli question by the end of 1971, as he had publicly and popularly announced he would do. Brezhnev, it seemed, had put a priority upon détente with the United States.

In ensuing months, carrying out a general diplomatic and economic opening to the West, Sadat tried to persuade the United States to bring pressure on Israel to withdraw from the Sinai. In this, predictably, he failed. As a result, Sadat turned to support from Libya, Syria, and Saudi Arabia, and carefully prepared for the surprise attack he launched against Israel on October 6, 1973, the day of Atonement—Yom Kippur—the holiest day in the Jewish calendar. The Fourth Middle East War between Arabs and Israelis had begun (though the Egyptians always said they had not started the war, merely renewed the hostilities that had never really ended in 1967).

The Arab armies attained an unforeseen measure of surprise, and were initially successful: an Egyptian army crossed the Suez Canal and drove into the Sinai. But the Israelis counterattacked; cut off the Egyptian army; and repulsed the Syrians, bent on retaking the Golan Heights. In the course of the war, the Soviet Union, which had advance warning of the hostilities against which it had counseled, resupplied the Arabs by a massive airlift, and the United States resupplied Israel (using bases in the Azores, supplied by the dictatorship in Portugal—for other NATO countries refused to cooperate). Tension mounted as the Egyptian front faced complete military collapse, and Brezhnev suggested to the Americans a joint intervention, failing which he would be prepared to send Soviet forces to bring peace to the area. At this juncture, American Secretary of State Kissinger, putting American strategic forces on the alert as a signal, warned the Russians to keep out, in return for which he would force the Israelis to stop, thus saving Russia's client states from worse defeat. A United Nations cease-fire resolution that included introduction of a new UN peacekeeping force brought an uneasy end to the crisis. Wrote Tunisian Cecil Hourani in *Am Nahar*, a Lebanese newspaper,

> Another consequence of our unwillingness to accept as real what we do not like is that when reality catches up with us, it is always too late. At every debacle we regret that we did not accept a situation which no longer exists. In 1948 we regretted that we had not accepted the 1947 UN plan for partition. In May 1967 we were trying to get back to pre-Suez. Today we would be happy—and are actually demanding at the UN—to go back to things as they were before 5 June. From every defeat we reap a new regret and a new nostalgia, but never seem to learn a new lesson.[1]

Russia, the Arabs' friend, could supply them with arms, but it was an uncertain friend that clearly had other priorities besides backing them in a war of liberation against the Jews. The United States was hardly the Arabs' friend, backing Israel as it did, but it was the one state that could secure Israeli withdrawal and stop Israel from achieving total military victory. Arabs were angered at what they saw as East-West collusion in the affair, but the Nixon people were angered at what they saw as Russia's giving in to temptation to profit at the West's expense when the opportunity arose: it seemed a first, clear violation of the implicit rules of détente, and it had led to war.

Colonel Qaddafi

When Sadat made his first mark by resuming hostilities with Israel, he received support from his new neighbor, Colonel Muammar al-Qaddafi, leader of sparsely populated but oil-rich Libya, who would also make his mark on the world scene. In 1969 army officers overthrew the conservative Western-oriented king, who had ruled Libya since independence in 1951. Colonel Qaddafi became head of government; quickly closed British and American air bases the king had allowed to remain; and soon identified America and Israel as Libya's main enemies, despite American overtures. He committed himself to the Palestinian cause and took upon himself the mantle of Nasserism, seeking union with other Arab states (and as quickly condemning them for not adhering to his own ideas). He crushed frequent attempts to oust him by rival factions, arranged to murder opponents who had fled abroad, and—although he was leading a state with a population one-tenth that of Egypt—became an international figure on a grand scale through sponsorship of worldwide terrorism and his offers of full support to Egypt in the Middle East struggle. Europeans were loath to oppose him, since light Libyan oil—which was comparatively easy to refine—did not have to come through the Suez Canal or around Africa, as most other Middle-East oil did. In the last decades of the century, Libya became the fourth Arab oil producer.

The end of the fourth round over Israel led to only an unstable peace; Palestinian opposition to the existence of Israel was now a deep-rooted factor in the equation; Sadat had shown his own hostility. With people like Colonel Qaddafi on the scene, anything could happen, and the world depended on a steady supply of Middle East oil.

Struggle in Latin America

Latin America seemed far from the pyrotechnics of the Middle East or the travail of new states in Africa. Most Latin nations differed in that they had been independent for a lengthy period. Yet they, too, felt the impact of global change.

Once the United States had created the Inter-American System, however, it paid attention to Latin American affairs only when jolted into doing so—in Guatemala in 1954; or when U.S. Vice-President Richard Nixon and his wife Pat were endangered by mobs in 1958; or when Castro broke with the United States and introduced Soviet power into the Caribbean, promising to spread revolution throughout Latin America. By the late 1960s, less fearful of any Soviet "threat" to the region, the United States again paid less attention to Latin American affairs, and the organized Inter-American System faded in significance. The Nixon-Kissinger Administration was preoccupied by the complex structure of détente, Middle East crises, and oil. Only when a genuinely Marxist government came to power in Chile in 1971 did it react.

Nevertheless, the groundwork for change was being laid. In the 1960s the restoration of Europe, the rise of Japan, and the possibility of contact with a more outward-looking Soviet Union gave Latin American states more opportunities for varied contacts. Many of them began to take the initative in cultivating these contacts. Latin Americans also produced a new set of ideas that soon gained widespread acceptance under the rubric of "dependency." Dependency theory argued that peripheral, Third World states were functionally linked to the international economy in such a way that their economies served the purposes of the advanced economies, while their own needs were not met and they were kept in permanent subjection by elites within their own borders who profited from the relationship. This was, in theoretical terms, a call for breaking away from U.S. economic ties. Despite its seeming explanatory power, the theory tried to explain too much, and the countries to which it was supposed to apply were far too diverse.

In the 1960s and the 1970s Latin American countries as a whole actually grew twice as fast as Western countries, including the United States; large numbers of American investments were nationalized with little fuss; industrialization increased at an extraordinary pace. Exports of manufactured goods from Brazil, Mexico, Argentina, and Colombia grew at an average annual rate of more than 30 percent. The share of Brazil's exports represented by manufactured goods rose from 2 percent in 1960 to more than 65 percent twenty-five years later. The United States' share of investment in South America dropped sharply, while that of Europe and Japan expanded. The Soviet Union increased its diplomatic representation from three countries in 1960 to nineteen, and Latin dependence on the United States for arms gave way to purchases from diversified sources and to domestic production.

Population also grew, however, as life expectancy at birth rose rapidly in these years. In 1960 South American population was roughly equal to that of the United States. Despite a falling birthrate, it would be twice as large by the year 2000. Population increases in the poorer countries swallowed up much of the increased production, while in even the wealthier ones gains were very unequally distributed, leading to charges that there had been "growth without development."

The rise of Fidel Castro and his effect on U.S.–Latin American relations has already been described (see chapter 5). The attempt to counter Castro's appeal through the well-intentioned Alliance for Progress and the Dominican intervention to "prevent another Castro" near American shores were both results of Castro's move to align himself with the Socialist bloc while fomenting revolution wherever he could. So were the technocrats of the Kennedy Administration who sought to spread their own brand of progress. At the same time, they helped train police forces and armies to counter the revolutionary guerrilla warfare that Castro supported in so many countries—the Dominican Republic, Haiti, Nicaragua, Panama, Guatemala, Colombia, Venezuela, Peru, and Bolivia. Castro sent guerrilla bands to the last five of these to spark revolutions not yet in process. It was in Bolivia that Castro's comrade Che Guevara met his end in October 1967 and became a cult figure for revolutionaries everywhere.

For a brief period in the mid-1960s, Castro found himself cut off from other Latin states that objected to his sponsorship of guerrilla warfare. As Brezhnev moved to improve his relations with Latin American states, he forced Castro to subdue his revolutionary activity, with the result that in subsequent years most of the governments that had broken relations with Cuba in 1964 reestablished them.

In theory, the alliance's insistence on coupling reforms to the provision of large-scale credit was supposed to support and hasten the trend toward constitutional government perceived in the late 1950s. Stable democratic systems allowing popular participation would forestall the revolutionary urge. The United States supported the 1961 coup that ended the long reign of dictator Rafael Trujillo in the Dominican Republic and prevented a countercoup a few months later; in 1963 it made an abortive attempt to help indigenous forces overthrow the unsavory dictatorship of "Papa Doc" Duvalier in Haiti. But democratically elected governments began to topple in the 1960s in Argentina, Peru, Guatemala, Bolivia, Brazil, and Guyana. In the case of the last two, in fact, the U.S. administration, fearing the leftward slant of these governments, had authorized CIA financing of opposition parties and groups, though it did not actually overthrow their governments. As already noted, in 1965 the United States did intervene directly in the Dominican Republic.

By this time, in the Johnson years, the early optimism of the Alliance for Progress was gone, and so was the emphasis on structural and political reform. President Eduardo Frei Montalva of Chile wrote of it as "the alliance that lost its way." Latin American governments, he argued, now avoided all reform, all attempts at more democracy, with the result that the alliance was merely a flow of aid dollars from the United States.

Ironically enough, it was in Frei's state, Chile, that American intervention, originally on behalf of democracy, ultimately helped bring a harsh military regime into power. Frei had carried out partial nationalizations of American properties, but it was he whom the American government supported financially in the elections of 1964 and 1970 when it feared a possible government under one of his opponents, Marxist Salvador Allende. When Allende won a plurality in a three-way race in 1970, Kissinger and Nixon first tried to prevent him from being named president by the Congress, then supplied funds to opposition parties and blocked credits through international agencies. Allende found credits elsewhere, but internal opposition mounted—primarily a result of his own errors in alienating the middle and lower-middle classes that were originally ready to support him. In 1973 he was overthrown in a military coup that brought a brutal, unsavory regime to power under General Augusto Pinochet. It was an unhappy ending to what had been one of the longest, most stable democracies in South America. Allende himself died a suicide, and became another martyr, though his administration was marked by ruinous policies and inflation. Left to himself, he might well not have lasted, but the United States reaped a deserved opprobrium for having helped hasten his demise.

Conclusion

By 1960, as the old European empires broke up, it became evident that the superpowers could no longer simply treat minor countries as either for or against them. Yet both, for a while, acted as though the Cold War would be decisively fought out in terms of the allegiance of this new Third World. The situation became even more complex when China decisively broke with Russia, and posed as an alternative leader in Third World politics. Throughout the 1960s, China sought and was denied entry to the United Nations. Some diplomats suggested that G-77 would gain real clout when China joined and lent its weight to Third World demands for restructuring the global system, but the effects of the Great Proletarian Cultural Revolution on Chinese foreign policy ended such speculation. In 1971, when mainland China's representatives finally replaced those of Nationalist China at the UN, China played a relatively minor role.

European influence declined in Asia and the Middle East, less in Africa. Soviet and American power was frequently extended, usually drawn in by demands from local powers. Regional successors rose and fell: Sukarno's Indonesia, Nasser's Egypt, Kwame Nkrumah's Ghana, each trying—and failing—to create a larger regional unity following Western withdrawal. Some states split, as Pakistan did, leaving India as the major South Asian power; the Federation of Rhodesia and Nyasaland is another example. Others split and repaired the split at great cost, as Nigeria did. Some began an unprecedented economic growth that precipitated them into their own forms of modernity; others lagged and failed, as their populations grew, requiring a wrenching abandonment of their old ways and an economic growth they found hard to come by. Some—like Castro's Cuba; Sukarno's Indonesia; and, for a brief period, the People's Republic of China—called for world revolution and the overthrow of older elites who tried to fit new states into the old, established order: "one, two, many Vietnams...." The Soviet Union itself muted its own efforts, seeking rather to align itself with existing governments.

By the early 1970s the Third World, despite its diversity, existed in organized form at the United Nations. At the UN and in outside meetings, its leaders began to voice strong—some said strident—demands for changes in the Western-dominated world system. Events in the next decade lent urgency to Third World demands, but also increased the differences between Third World countries. The new global system emerging out of bipolarism lent itself to little simplistic analysis.

Note

1. Quoted in Irving Howe and Carl Gershman (eds.), *Israel, the Arabs, and the Middle East* (New York: Bantam, 1972), p. 152.

Further Suggested Readings

In addition to works previously cited, Steven R. David discusses shifting alliances in *Choosing Sides: Alignment and Realignment in the Third World* (Baltimore: Johns Hopkins University Press, 1991), and William Zartman reviews the era after independence in *International Relations in the New Africa* (Englewood Cliffs, NJ: Prentice Hall, 1966). Kwame Nkrumah, who failed in his mission, argues for a united Africa in *Africa Must Unite* (New York: Praeger, 1963). Federico Gil offers a good discussion of the period in *Latin-American–United States Relations* (New York: Harcourt, 1971). Don Peretz, *The Middle East Today*, 5th ed. (New York: Praeger, 1988), carries us beyond the period in this chapter, but is always a good introduction to developments in the area. In an influential book, Robert Packenham argues that the United States is inherently limited by ideology in its approach to the Third World: *Liberal America and the Third World* (Princeton: Princeton University Press, 1973).

Part III

Global Politics

7

Toward a Politics of the Planet Earth

The League of Nations and the United Nations both embodied the idea that, despite the sovereign state, humankind was one—that the globe itself needed to be considered as one. The family of UN agencies testified to the extent to which problems needed to be tackled globally. In the 1970s, this old idea began to be reinforced, as a flood of books and articles argued that many issues could no longer be attacked within the purview of national politics but needed urgent global attention.*

Since the time of genocide in Nazi Germany, human rights could no longer be considered simply a matter of domestic jurisdiction, and the matter was enshrined in numerous international conventions and declarations. Yet everywhere violations were taking place that only global action could take care of. Population growth had now become accepted as a global problem, along with pollution and resource and species depletion, especially of the seas. Soon these problems were joined by such matters as prospective global warming and the thinning of the protective ozone layer. Equally important was the effect of cheap, instant global communications combined with computers in producing new global patterns of production and massive, uncontrollable financial flows that undermined the sovereignty of the state and its capacity to regulate its own economy. Local communities began to realize that employment was at the mercy of developments on the other side of the globe. International politics appeared to have been fundamentally altered and "realist" power politics analyses outmoded.

On the policy level, all this led to more urgent calls for global action. Détente between the West and the Soviet bloc seemed to offer the opportu-

*The title of this chapter reveals the change in thinking: in 1945 Harold and Margaret Sprout published their first, widely used international relations textbook, *Foundations of National Power*. Their next version, in 1961, was entitled *Foundations of International Politics*. The final version, published in 1971, was called *Toward a Politics of the Planet Earth*.

nity for turning attention away from security issues to these other concerns. Balance-of-power politics based on the existence of the sovereign, independent state had to be superseded by recognition of interdependence, by a "reinvention of global politics."

As this chapter shows, however, politics is not invented; it unfolds. The call for fundamental change took place against complicated developments and conflicts: international monetary disorder, oil crises and resultant North-South conflict, the rise of new economic powers, and the Soviet Union's attempt under Brezhnev to use emerging détente for its own, expansionist purposes. Even arms control and reduction, seen as a prerequisite for global cooperation, took a back seat. James Earl Carter, the Georgia peanut farmer who had risen to the presidency of the United States with an evident personal desire to reorient American foreign policy away from security issues and toward resolution of global agenda issues, found himself caught up in security policy.

The global agenda was there, and numerous international conferences testified to the attempts to come to grips with it. It was not easy.

High Politics and Low Politics

The End of Bretton Woods

At the end of World War II the United States performed an unusual service to the world when it led in establishing the liberal trade and monetary institutions that underlay the enormous expansion of the postwar economic order. This was an act of enlightened self-interest. By the 1970s, when world population had doubled, trade expansion had contributed substantially to the fact that far more people were living better and longer lives than anyone could have expected earlier, that many Third World countries were growing at historically extraordinary rates, and that countries devastated in World War II now had living standards far above those that prevailed before the war. Countries that had fought one another for centuries around the Atlantic basin now adjusted their differences without threatening the use of force against one another, constituting an area of peace.

Nevertheless, increased growth in population and production began to produce doomsday predictions: in 1972, for example, an international group, the Club of Rome, sponsored a report prepared at the Massachusetts Institute of Technology called *The Limits to Growth*, which predicted the end of industrial civilization some time early in the twenty-first century, given present trends: "The basic behavior mode of the world system is exponential growth of population and capital, followed by collapse."[1] The report was widely criticized, especially by economists, as building in few feedback effects, that is, the ways people would respond to trends to change them as their effects became noticeable.

Traditionally, statesmen concerned themselves with grand strategy, diplomacy, alliances, and balance-of-power politics: "high politics." Left to their underlings were the more routine day-to-day dealings in the realm of trade relations: "low politics." By the time Nixon and Kissinger launched their grand strategy—alignment with China, détente with the Soviet Union, and a Middle East peace settlement—all this had begun to change. For the two men with grand plans, "low politics" became "high politics."

Until the late 1960s the United States essentially managed the international monetary system in consultation with others. But the growth of international banking and of international financial markets meant that monetary interdependence increased rapidly: No state could simply raise interest rates to restrict its domestic money supply, since this would draw in foreign funds. Nor could a state simply lower rates to stimulate investment, since this could lead to an outflow of funds to take advantage of higher rates elsewhere. When other major states acted by raising or lowering rates, it affected one's own economy. In other words, sovereign control over the state of the economy was rapidly disappearing.

In addition, Europe and Japan came to rival the United States as financial and economic powers whose policies could affect the international monetary system. By 1970 the United States—largely because it had fought a war in Vietnam without raising taxes—was running the balance-of-payments deficit that brought heavy pressure on the dollar, and that brought Richard Nixon to the devaluation of 1971 (see chapter 3, page 90). The Bretton Woods system of relatively fixed exchange rates with flexibility under international supervision was dead.

A number of ad hoc arrangements and more formal agreements linked central banks of major trading states and their finance ministries, through which they could communicate their concerns and develop common measures. By 1975 these no longer seemed adequate. That year, outside Paris at Rambouillet, the first annual heads-of-state meeting devoted to economic affairs took place. Presidents and prime ministers of five—later seven—leading non-Communist, industrial states agreed on how to tackle global inflation and recession without resorting to the kind of protectionist measures used so disastrously in the 1930s. Although subsequent meetings of this Group of Seven (G-7) tended to become public relations affairs and their effects were limited, the very act of preparing for them promoted greater dialogue between the economic bureaucracies, and G-7 tended to become a managerial group for the world economy (to the objections of a number of non-Western states). The extent to which the United States had now become one player among many was underlined when the world was treated to the startling spectacle of American President Carter, for example, virtually begging German and Japanese prime ministers to follow a more expansionist economic policy so as to attract more imports and provide stimulus to other economies, including that of the mighty United States.

The Rise and Impact of OPEC

The Middle East War of October 1973 has already been described (chapter 6). Within five months, by March 1974, the price of oil on the world market quadrupled. Six years later the same thing happened again when the shah of Iran was overthrown.

These events were a result of another major structural change in the world economy: world consumption of petroleum rose from 9 million barrels per day in 1950 to 48 million by 1973. The United States, long an oil exporter, had been able to help Europe when the Suez Canal was closed in 1956. By the 1970s, it *imported* 40 percent of the 15 million barrels of oil it consumed every day, and while new sources other than the Middle East had appeared, most known world oil reserves existed under the sovereign control of a handful of countries with a relatively small total population.

Until the 1970s, world oil production, transportation, refining, and marketing were largely under the control of seven international oil companies. In the early 1970s all this changed. The producing nations proceeded to nationalize many of the production facilities of the supposedly impregnable oil companies. In 1970 the seven companies owned 61 percent of crude oil produced outside the Communist world; by 1979, they owned only 25 percent. (This was a remarkable episode, falsifying many of the observations about the power of multinationals and their relations to their home countries: potentially hostile, small, militarily weak host countries had simply taken over control of the wealthy, developed countries' most vital necessary resource without anyone so much as raising a hand.)

The Organization of Petroleum Exporting Countries (OPEC) was formed in 1960. The changed market of the 1970s, the Middle East War, and American aid to Israel gave OPEC both the opportunity and the motive, first to embargo oil to the United States, Canada, and Holland (whose port at Rotterdam was the most important transshipment point) and then, jointly, to successfully quadruple the price of oil in 1974. Despite inflated rhetoric about "energy independence" on the part of the Nixon Administration, and despite Jimmy Carter's declaration that the energy crisis was "the moral equivalent of war," U.S. energy policy remained incoherent in the next few

Figure 1. **World Distribution of Proved Oil Reserves**

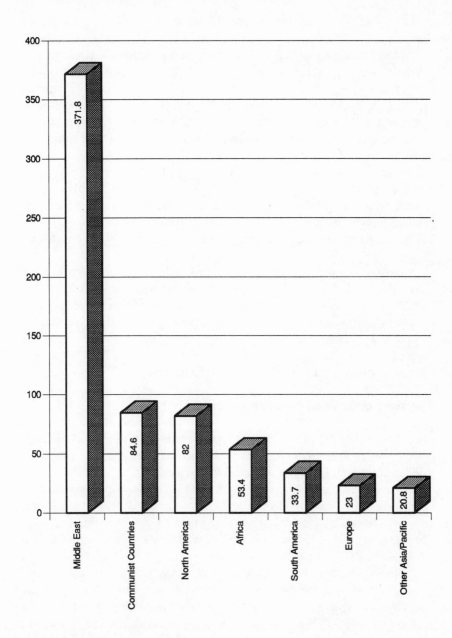

Source: Oil and Gas Journal, 1984.

years. From 1974 until the fall of the shah of Iran in 1979, U.S. oil imports continued to rise.

Western efforts to coordinate policy and to face OPEC with a united front largely failed. Never before in history was there such a large, immediate shift in financial resources from one part of the world to another. Within twelve months, the share of fuels in world trade rose in value from 12 percent to 20 percent, and the current account balance of OPEC countries increased sevenfold, to $60 billion in 1974. Part of this enormous economic windfall was well handled; some OPEC members squandered it in grandiose or overly expansive programs. Much of what was not used for increased imports was "recycled"—that is, deposited in European banks which loaned it out to countries with oil import bills that had increased drastically, but which did not want to cut imports for fear that this would hamper economic growth. As a result, many countries, such as Brazil, Argentina, Taiwan, Korea, and Mexico, continued to grow rapidly during the 1970s, but some built up a debt that would burden them in the future (see chapter 10).

Western countries, though hard hit, were able to absorb the price rise more easily. The real price of oil drifted back downward until 1979, and OPEC's surplus in that year amounted to only $6 billion. In 1979 came another dramatic oil shock. But in the intervening years global institutions had come to be burdened with a peculiar result of the first oil crisis, something called the "New International Economic Order" (the NIEO), perhaps the most misunderstood of calls for global change.

The New International Economic Order

The 1960s were years of high growth rates for many less developed countries (LDCs), but of little progress in the institutional changes these countries demanded at the UN. Despite gathering data that showed real progress, dissatisfaction over what had been proclaimed as the "UN Development Decade" became the norm, accompanied by accusations that the developed world was directly responsible for the deplorable state of the Third World—an accusation that found fertile ground among the disenchanted post-Vietnam generation in the West.

Following the Six-Day War in late 1973, American Secretary of State Kissinger tried to use the resulting oil crisis to break up the unity of the Third World: oil-importing Third World states (the poorest of which were now known at the UN as the most seriously affected, or MSA, states or, alternatively, as the Fourth World) were the ones most injured by the oil price rise engineered by other Third World states, the oil exporters. In

February 1974, Kissinger invited the MSA oil-importing countries to join Japan and the Western countries in the Energy Coordinating Group, the consumers' answer to OPEC.

Fearing a split in the Third World, Algeria countered rapidly by proposing the grandiose-sounding New International Economic Order, which enshrined a series of new demands. These were then reinforced in the Charter of Economic Rights and Duties of States, passed by the UN General Assembly in December 1974. Both of these documents, adopted over the general opposition of developed countries, became the basis of UN development orthodoxy in the next decade, deflecting attention, many thought, from the real issues. They demonstrated a new, confrontational stance on the part of the organized Third World.

In essence, in addition to traditional demands, they stressed the absolute sovereign right over subsoil resources, the right to nationalize control over these without recourse to international agreement or arbitration or to prior contracts, the right to form producer cartels like OPEC (rather than commodity agreements in which both producers and consumers agree on marketing strategies for their mutual benefit), and the duty of consuming states to work with rather than against such producer cartels. The NIEO belittled contractual rights, and called for restitution for developed countries' stripping of Third World countries' resources in the past, as well as for the creation of central planning under UN control (i.e., on the basis of one state/one vote) in substitution for the existing market institutions. UN bureaucracies would presumably set prices and direct production and marketing, independently of market forces. It was an incredible and unrealistic set of demands, but many took it seriously.

For the next half-dozen years, virtually all UN resolutions on economic matters made reference to "the need for the NIEO," with the result that Western countries inevitably voted against them. Few commentators observed that the origin of the NIEO lay in a maneuver on the part of the oil exporters, led by Algeria and Venezuela, to keep oil-importing LDCs from reacting against them, to deflect them from Kissinger's suggestion that they join in on the consumers' side in the International Energy Agency. In essence it said to them, "Instead of worrying about your increased oil bill, do what we did, nationalize your subsoil resources on your own terms, form export cartels, and extract a high price for your raw materials." This was the main point of the high-sounding NIEO, which exhausted international negotiators for the next few years and, essentially, deflected attention from attainable reforms, while bringing the UN with its socialist bloc/Third World majority into disrepute among the nations that might have acted to improve North–South relations. (Skeptics pointed out that among other dubious aspects of the NIEO was that many

Third World countries were large importers of raw materials, and many were becoming exporters of manufactured goods, while the United States was the largest raw material exporter in the world.)

The major problem with the NIEO maneuver soon became apparent: it couldn't work. No other resource was as vital as oil and lent itself to cartelization the way oil did. In the meantime, LDC oil bills increased, while organizations like the IMF provided special funds. European banks continued to "recycle" petrodollars deposited in them by OPEC members into loans to the LDCs, who in turn paid the money to the oil producers—while amassing large debts to the banks that had recycled the money to them.

Given the unworkability of the NIEO strategy, oil country leaders then tried to use oil power not merely to extract a higher price, but as a lever with which to extract Western concessions to older, long-existent LDC demands. Under OPEC pressure, the West ceded and agreed to the convening of the Conference on International Economic Cooperation, which met off and on from late 1975 until June 1977. Despite exhaustive negotiations, it accomplished little. Western leaders argued that the basic postwar economic system was sound and needed only incremental changes that would improve and strengthen the free market. The remarkable LDC growth of the 1960s and 1970s was the best evidence, and the LDCs themselves had to make domestic reforms. They had to improve their economic performance by eliminating bureaucratic corruption; increasing market efficiency; providing more equity; observing human rights; improving agricultural productivity; and providing an atmosphere that would attract, rather than repel, investment. The very last thing one could want was a kind of international economic planning under irresponsible and undemocratic UN bureaucrats. And while LDC representatives had many measures in mind, the very heterogeneity of Third World national interests made it difficult for them to bargain as a group.

The result was a series of agreements to provide more aid on easier terms, especially to the poorest, MSA countries, and to finance commodity agreements. There were some broad agreements on a number of less controversial issues, and there were disagreement and deadlock on others. What blocked more general agreement was not so much that participants had different interests as that they disagreed fundamentally on what the problems were; with how they should be dealt; and, it must be said, with the red herring of the NIEO.

Iran, 1979

Between 1973 and 1979, LDCs grew three times faster than industrial countries, while expanding their external indebtedness from $100 billion at the end of 1973 to $400 billion by 1979—an amount close to their increased oil bills over the same period. (Five LDCs—Brazil, Mexico, Argentina, South Korea, and the Philippines—accounted for 40 percent of the debt.) At the same time, Eastern European socialist bloc countries' hard currency debt also rose, from $6 billion to $60 billion. Given some accompanying increases in production, the debt appeared manageable. Unfortunately for all these countries, the U.S. Federal Reserve Bank raised interest rates in the United States to combat late-1970s double-digit inflation, with the result that interest rates soared worldwide, greatly increasing the payments debtors would have to make over time. In mid-January 1979, the troubled government of the shah of Iran collapsed as the shah fled the country and the Islamic Republic under the leadership of the heretofore exiled, Muslim fundamentalist Ayatollah Khomeini emerged (see page 197). In the expectation that Iranian oil exports would collapse, the world price of oil shot up once more, to as much as $40 a barrel on the spot market.

The increase was smaller in percentage terms than the increase of 1974, but its impact was greater, partly as a result of the success of the earlier recycling effort: now debtors' ability to borrow and lenders' capacity to lend were both decreased. The industrial countries, following American-led anti-inflationary policies, fell into a recession that contracted demand and world trade. By 1982, raw material prices were a third lower than at the end of 1980, and LDC foreign exchange receipts fell far more sharply than the overall costs of LDC imports. Forced to borrow just to maintain imports necessary to their economies, LDCs saw their debts soar, especially as they borrowed at higher interest rates. Growth rates in most areas fell, actually becoming negative in countries such as Brazil, Argentina, and Chile and continuing on their downward course in sub-Saharan Africa.

Interdependence had its benefits. It also, clearly, had its costs. So far as numerous Third World countries were concerned, the decade of the 1980s was a lost decade. Events, however, moved apace in other parts of the world.

New Economic Players: The EEC, Japan, and the NICs

Enlarging the EEC

On July 1, 1967, a new treaty created common organs for the European Communities (EC) out of the European Economic Community (EEC), the European Coal and Steel Community (ECSC), and the European Atomic Energy Community (EURATOM). The EC, with its headquarters in Brussels, had a Council of Ministers from member governments; an Executive Commission; a European Parliament (first directly elected in 1979), which supervised the work of the Commission and the Communities and met in Luxembourg; and a Court of Justice.

Greece signed an association agreement with the EEC in 1962, and then Turkey signed in 1964, Malta in 1971, and Cyprus in 1973. When the United Kingdom, Denmark, and Ireland left the European Free Trade Association (EFTA) to join the EEC in 1973, Norwegians rejected Norwegian membership in a referendum. Greece became a full member in 1981, and Spain and Portugal, with whom negotiations began in 1979, were finally admitted in 1986. In addition, Portugal was admitted to the Council of Europe in 1976 and Spain was admitted in 1977, while Spain became a member of NATO in 1982. (Negotiation of membership in the EEC for all the southern tier countries was complicated by issues of excess capacity in certain industries; by increased competition in other fields; by these countries' relative poverty, with a concomitant necessity for EEC financing of development, at great cost; by language problems that increased the cumbersomeness of decision making; and by fear that their presence would, in sum, dilute the possibilities for further integration. The same issues would arise in the 1990s when Eastern European states sought membership.)

Behind the enlargement of the Common Market lay major political changes in Europe: the collapse of authoritarian dictatorships in Portugal in 1974 and in Spain in 1975, with the death of Franco and these countries' adoption of Western-style democracy, and the rise and fall of military dictatorship in Greece, whose longstanding conflicts with Turkey complicated matters.

Both Greece and Turkey became members of NATO in 1951, and both sought EEC membership in the 1960s, but events on the island of Cyprus, forty miles to the south of Turkey, intruded.

In 1967, two years of political crisis in Greece led to a military coup and an unsavory and repressive military regime in that ancient country—a regime that lasted for seven years. (Long American support for the military in Greece in the name of NATO necessities led to charges that the United States instigated the coup to forestall leftists. It did not; but it continued to supply military aid and maintain relations with the regime.) In 1974, seeking a foreign policy success, elements in the Greek government gave backing to a radical group's attempt to seize power in Cyprus in the name of *enosis*, or union with Greece. Turkey promptly invaded the north of the island, where a large Turkish minority lived, securing at least a third of it against feeble resistance; Greeks in the north fled south, and Turks in the south moved north. A de facto division of the island resulted, with UN troops policing a dividing line (which was still there twenty years later). Legitimate Cypriot rule was restored in the south.

Discredited by the Cyprus affair, the Greek colonels' regime collapsed and democracy was restored. The new government, under pressure from a wave of anti-Americanism, temporarily withdrew from the NATO command structure, while remaining a party to the treaty and reluctantly allowing American bases to remain; on the other hand, it was allowed to rejoin the Council of Europe from which the military regime had been expelled, and it successfully negotiated entrance into the EEC in 1981. Although the Cyprus affair exacerbated relations with Turkey (always in turmoil over control of the seas in the Aegean, where other Greek islands lie close off the Turkish coast), and delayed EEC expansion, the European Community loomed large. Its success in these years contrasted with stagnation in Eastern Europe.

Japan Inc. and the NICs

The return of Japan as a world power highlights a trend: a growing number of states in the international system have come to depend upon trade without resorting to the presence of military force to protect their continued access to trade needs as a part of their overall security. While the United States, the Soviet Union, Western European states, and Middle Eastern states—among others—spent 5 percent or more of their gross domestic product on arms in the decades of the 1960s and the 1970s, and while the United States devoted 50 percent of its research and development funds to military purposes, Japan kept its military budget to 1 percent, and 99 percent of its research funds were going to civilian purposes.

The Japan that was firebombed into ruins in 1945 began its period of spectacular economic growth in the early 1960s. Japanese enterprises were assisted by their government in undertaking export drives targeted at specific product markets, and rapidly moved into areas of higher and higher technology. Japan's share of world trade in manufactured goods increased from 5.6 percent in 1960 to 20 percent in the mid-1980s. By 1980, Japan's automobile production exceeded that of the United States. In the 1980s, as other newly industrializing countries (NICs) moved into traditional manufacturing fields, Japan became a leader in telecommunications and computers.

Following World War II and until the early 1970s, it was the United States that provided most foreign investment in the world at large. After the early 1970s European and then Japanese funds began to flow into the United States in such quantities that European investments in the United States soon became roughly equal to American investments there. By the mid-1980s, Japan's investments surpassed those of Western Europe. (It was these investments that permitted the United States to run a large current account deficit, importing more than it exported, and consuming rather than investing.) The ten largest banks in the world were Japanese. Japanese society and practices, on the other hand, hindered foreign investment within Japan as well as imports.

Article IX of the Japanese Constitution of 1947 renounced war, "the threat or use of force," and the maintenance of "land, sea and air forces, as well as other war potential," but has been interpreted since the end of the American occupation in 1952 to allow "Self Defense Forces" totaling some 250,000 men. Over time, the Japanese accepted certain principles: they would acquire no "offensive" weapons such as intermediate-range or intercontinental missiles, long-range bombers, attack aircraft carriers, or nuclear weapons. The "Self Defense Forces" would not be sent overseas (though this has been recently modified to permit participation in UN peacekeeping operations); they would accept no obligation to come to the defense of another country. The security treaty with the United States which allowed American bases (but no nuclear weapons) on the mainland and in Okinawa, provided deterrence to any direct attack upon Japan.

As U.S. relations developed with China in the 1970s, the Chinese let it be known that the U.S.-Japanese security treaty seemed to them a useful counter to Soviet power. As a result, Japanese left-wing opposition to the treaty diminished—and then diminished even more following the Russian invasion of Afghanistan in 1979, the development of the Soviet Pacific Fleet into a major force in the 1980s, and the stationing of new Russian SS-20 missiles within range of Japan. Russian use of the great American supply ports at Cam Rahn Bay and Danang, in Vietnam, and the oil crises of 1973 and 1979 considerably increased the Japanese sense of vulnerability. As a result, American President Carter's abortive suggestion for withdrawal of U.S. forces from South Korea in 1976 aroused considerable apprehension in Japan.

Japan, admitted to the UN in 1956, is a member of a number of "Western" institutions, such as the Organization for Economic Cooperation and Development (OECD) and the Group of Seven (G-7). It joined the Inter-American Development Bank as a nonregional member in 1976, signifying its growing interests in Latin America. Its economic presence is pervasive throughout Southeast Asia. It established diplomatic relations with the People's Republic of China in 1972, while continuing to maintain important trading relations with Taiwan. Attempts to negotiate—finally—a World War II peace treaty with the Soviet Union, begun in 1972, have consistently faltered over the issue of sovereignty over the Kuriles islands to the immediate north of Japan proper, which have been occupied by Russia since the war.

In the 1970s, Japan, now with the second largest national economy in the world, became a world player. As a nominally nonmilitary power, its role was far from clear. Changes in the Soviet Union would raise more questions about it in the 1980s and the 1990s.

Emergence of the newly industrialized countries (NICs) constituted another remarkable, related development of the 1970s. During the decade, South Korea's manufactured exports grew at an incredible average annual rate of 33 percent, followed closely by those of the three other "Asian Tigers": Singapore, Taiwan, and Hong Kong. All four started with labor-intensive lines of standard production in which their abundant, readily trained, literate, and low-cost labor forces gave them an advantage over older industrialized countries. In Latin America, Brazil showed a similar pattern, with Mexico not far behind. In the next decade, others began to join them: India, Malaysia, Thailand, Indonesia, and Colombia. The four Tigers themselves began to move into higher-technology goods. Their economic growth began to have an impact on the economies of other countries as they displaced other, older industries; the nature of their growth brought into question a number of accepted notions about Third World countries; the idea of dependence; and that of peripheral economies whose development was presumably prevented by older, core economies. By the mid-1980s, American transpacific trade had outpaced transatlantic trade.

The United States in Retreat?

Both superpowers retained their great military establishments and nuclear strike forces during the 1970s, although American nuclear weapons and overall megatonnage (i.e., explosive power of its nuclear weaponry) continued to decline sharply from earlier peaks, while the number of smaller, more accurate warheads increased. The United States' spending for its military establishment remained essentially flat in terms of constant dollars from the mid-1950s to 1980, with the exception of the temporary increase for the Vietnam War between 1965 and 1975. Given the tripling of gross domestic product (GDP) during those years, military spending declined by two-thirds as a percentage of GDP, from between 15 percent and 18 percent to just under 5 percent. With the increased cost of a volunteer army and of more complex weaponry, the military establishment itself declined in size. It was harder to estimate Soviet expenditures, though they were certainly much larger as a percentage of Russian GDP, and they produced larger numbers of weapons, while universal military service provided enormous trained reserves at relatively low cost.

Following the Vietnam debacle, Nixon attempted to redefine American commitments abroad in a more limited way, to bring them into line with domestic resistance to the American global role. In the so-called Nixon Doctrine, announced in Guam in 1971, he posited that the United States from now on would basically only help countries that were willing to defend themselves. The oil crisis and resultant problems further highlighted the limits to the use of America's military force: access to its most vital resource was swiftly limited by relatively small, weak countries without any real possibility that it could act, and America's subsequent attempts to become import-independent failed miserably. (We may note that while it seemed impossible to act in 1973 and 1979, in 1990 when Iraq invaded Kuwait and threatened to control much of Middle East oil, President George Bush was able to send 500,000 Americans to the Persian Gulf. To those who supported the action, it showed that the United States had finally overcome the "Vietnam syndrome," which had inhibited action earlier.) Military power remained important for extended deterrence, and presumably for keeping order in other parts of the world; but many thought it had little to do with what were becoming some of the most pressing international issues: the economic, financial, and ecological issues that had come to the fore. People who thought this way helped to elect U.S. President Jimmy Carter in 1976.

Carter and the Reorientation of American Foreign Policy

"We are now free of . . . inordinate fear of Communism," newly elected President Jimmy Carter declared in a speech at Notre Dame University in 1977. As a result the United States could cut back on armaments and on arms sales, withdraw troops from abroad, reorient foreign aid toward satisfaction of basic human needs and, perhaps most important, use diplomatic and economic pressures on governments to observe human rights. The United States, the president argued, could tolerate leftist revolutionary nationalism. The Nixon Administration had—to its credit—encouraged détente with the Soviet Union (enshrined in the SALT talks and their accompanying agreements) and created the opening to Mao's Communist China. But it had been less concerned with the global agenda and not at all with human rights, and Carter was determined both to further détente while making these the foundation of American foreign policy.

Two years earlier, at the Helsinki Conference of August 1975, President Ford, Secretary Brezhnev, and the heads of state of thirty-three European states and Canada had signed the Final Act, which provided something the Soviet leaders had long sought—a guarantee of the post–World War II European frontiers—in return for agreements to observe fundamental human rights, along with a series of cultural and economic agreements. The Soviet leaders may have thought they were signing another innocuous agreement when it came to human rights, but the Helsinki accord would bedevil them at future review conferences. (Some analysts have even argued that it contributed to the final collapse of the Soviet Union.)

The contradictions in Carter's aims soon caught up with him. Human rights policies clashed with détente in the case of the Soviet Union, with the strengthening of relations with China, and with strategic necessities in the cases of Iran and South Korea—in all of which human rights were not being scrupulously observed. Arms sales to friendly Arab oil-producing states increased, matched by sales to Israel to maintain balance (with the result that arms sales actually increased in the Carter years). Leftist revolutionary regimes often turned into tyrannies even worse than those of the right: in 1978 Vietnam expelled 500,000 ethnic Chinese, some 100,000 of whom died in the process. Then Carter (like the rulers of China) found himself supporting the remnants of the murderous Pol Pot Khmer Rouge regime in Kampuchea when Vietnam could no longer stand the horror on its borders and invaded the hapless country to oust its barbarous government.

Economic necessity at home limited concessions to Third World states; the desire to cut American troops in Western Europe and Korea gave way to Europe's insistence on their presumed deterrent effect; even the Chinese Communists wanted American troops in Korea as a stabilizing force. Carter had to pull out all stops to secure a wary Senate's ratification of the treaty turning control of the Panama Canal over to Panama. The treaty was ratified on April 18, 1978, by a close vote, but it cost Carter heavily. When SALT II was signed in June 1979 the Senate was in a fractious mood, made distrustful by the Russian buildup and introduction of its new SS-20 mobile, multiple-warhead missiles in Europe and its activities throughout the world (see below). Russian invasion of Afghanistan in December killed the treaty: Carter wisely withdrew it from the Senate.

Everything seemed to conspire against Carter's wishes in his last years. The attempt at a cohesive energy policy failed. Then the Soviet Union invaded Afghanistan and Vietnam invaded Kampuchea. A seeming Carter triumph, the Camp David agreements that finally brought peace between Anwar Sadat's Egypt and Israel, signed on September 17, 1978 (see chapter 12), brought angry condemnation from other Arab countries as a betrayal of the Arab cause. Carter wavered when public resistance to placing new neutron weapons in West Germany grew, and ultimately he "delayed" any decision. In the meantime, Russian deployment of the new SS-20s aimed at Western Europe led NATO leaders to devise the "dual-track" strategy that called for talks with the Russians to reduce such intermediate-range weapons, but also for deployment of equivalent new American weapons until such time as the Russians agreed to reductions. The threat of the new weapons, presumably, would be the bargaining chip that would bring the Russians to the conference table before the weapons were actually put into place. All this was hardly in line with Carter's original intention of cutting forces, rather than augmenting them.

Brezhnev counted upon public opinion in Western Europe to prevent Western deployment of new weapons without the necessity for the Russians to cut their own intermediate nuclear forces: a coalition of political groups in Germany, Holland, and England—encouraged and supported in many cases by the Russians—mustered hundreds of thousands of demonstrators against the weapons. It fell upon Carter's successor, Ronald Reagan, to actually deploy them in 1983, and then—surprisingly, but in justification of the expensive dual-track decision—negotiate them all away (see chapter 9).

Relations worsened over other issues during Carter's years: Soviet armed intervention in Angola, in Yemen on the Arabian peninsula, and in Ethiopia angered Americans and Europeans. Carter's establishment of full diplomatic relations with China in January 1979 brought vigorous Soviet protests. Ultimately, events in Iran, Central America, and Afghanistan—along with the growth of domestic double-digit inflation—were Carter's undoing, bringing a sharp reaction in American policies, and icy relations with the Soviet Union. The brief period of global détente initiated by President Nixon was over.

Revolution in Iran

The United States discovered Iran only during World War II, when it helped to depose the old shah and install his son in his place, helped to open a supply route to the Soviet Union, and then helped the young shah expel the Soviet-supported separatist government in Azerbaijan province in the north after the war. In 1953 it helped the shah oust the Mossadegh regime. In current Iranian mythology, the United States now became—instead of a somewhat benevolent protector of Iran against other, traditional great power pressures—the new great power that could intervene directly and effectively to manipulate governments in Iran.

In reality, however, on the whole it was the shah who manipulated successive American governments. Fueled by a tenfold increase in oil revenues, and determined to modernize Iran and make it capable both of resisting great power pressures and of being the sole great regional power, the shah set out upon both a social revolution and an enormous buildup of the armed forces. He launched what he called the "White Revolution," leading Iran into an enormous and chaotic spurt of construction and modernization that drew heavily upon Western technology and institutions. In line with the Nixon Doctrine, which encouraged regional powers, Nixon and Kissinger gave the shah virtual carte blanche to order any nonnuclear military technology he wanted.

The advent of the Carter Administration could hardly be welcomed by the shah, given Carter's campaign pledges that human rights and reduction of arms sales would be at the forefront of his foreign policy. But the shah effected some reforms in the next year; arms sales continued, and in 1977, at a meeting in Teheran, Carter incautiously referred to Iran as an "island of stability in a turbulent corner of the world."

The stability was deceptive: opposition to the shah was deep and growing as the strains and unevenness of his program of modernization grew. From exile as a leader of the conservative clergy, the Ayatollah (the name means "reflection of God") Ruhollah Khomeini orchestrated a growing, implacable opposition.

In January 1978, massive street demonstrations in the Ayatollah's favor erupted throughout Iran. Some of the shah's advisers advocated the "iron fist"—martial law during which ruthless force would crush opposition to the shah. Others advocated reform and a widening of political power. The shah never resorted to the iron fist, and his supporters were overwhelmed. On January 16, 1979, the shah was forced into ignominious flight.

The United States first sought accommodation to the new, moderate successor regime. Some observers thought there would be a drift of the revolutionary regime toward democracy; others thought it would move left and toward a Marxist-Leninist regime. The ten months following Ayatollah Khomeini's return to Iran determined its actual direction, as the implacable Ayatollah and his followers undermined and decimated all the other groups in Iran. In late October 1979, the shah's admission to the United States for cancer treatment sealed the fate of the revolution in Iran: radical Khomeini supporters seized upon it as an excuse to overrun the U.S. Embassy and make hostages of everyone in it. Khomeini immediately issued a statement of support for the "students" who had carried out the takeover, against all the international laws of diplomatic immunity. In so doing, he silenced those opposing his program, diverted domestic attention from domestic disputes, and launched a major confrontation with the United States that galvanized public opinion behind him. No one knew it yet, for it would take a year, but by this simple move he had won supreme power against all opposition.

At the outset, American leaders could not believe that the crisis would last for more than a short time, that a sovereign government would flout international norms accepted as useful and necessary by all states, and that a quiet diplomatic approach would not work to secure release of the hostages. They underestimated both the fury against the America that had supported the shah—as demonstrated every night on television by the Iranian mobs— and its usefulness to the revolutionary regime. An unbelievable year of frustration followed, as the U.S. government did the right thing: it presented its case to the International Court of Justice at the Hague, which ruled on December 15, 1979, that whatever the shah might have done or been, Iran had no right to imprison people with diplomatic immunity. The UN Security Council condemned the hostage taking by a vote of 10 to 2, but most U.S. allies were unwilling to go along with the idea of sanctions against Iran. UN Secretary-General Kurt Waldheim's visit to Teheran produced nothing more than his statement that he was glad to get out alive. The Soviet invasion of neighboring Afghanistan on December 27 did nothing to make the Ayatollah seek to mend fences with the United States. The shah's departure from the United States (he went first to Panama and then to Egypt; no other state would give the dying man sanctuary) had no effect on the situation.

More and more Americans chafed at their government's impotence. It had exhibited continued restraint, to no effect but to receive more abuse. When Muslim radicals seized the Great Mosque at Mecca, in Saudi Arabia, in November 1979, rumors that it was Americans who had done it led to an attack upon the American Embassy in Islamabad, Pakistan, in which the embassy was burned and two Americans and four Pakistanis were killed. In April 1980 the Carter Administration finally adopted economic and diplomatic sanctions against Iran. On April 24, it launched a carefully prepared helicopter rescue mission—which had to be aborted when three of the helicopters registered mechanical problems.

Disaster in the desert, widely shown on television, was a crushing and embarrassing blow to Carter and to U.S. prestige. It also led to the resignation of Carter's secretary of state, Cyrus Vance, who had counseled continued restraint. The situation quieted for several months as political forces struggled and sorted themselves out in Iran, now at war with Iraq. The American election drew near, and American allies finally legislated limited sanctions. The shah's death in July, in Cairo, made no mark. Carter went down to defeat in the November elections before a Ronald Reagan who capitalized on American frustration. Finally, in the waning months of 1980, a deal was worked out through Algerian mediators. It involved complicated bargaining over Iranian assets frozen in the United States and various debts. On January 20, inauguration day in the United States, the hostages were finally flown from Iran to Germany, shortly after Carter had turned the White House over to the new American president, Ronald Reagan.

Central America in Upheaval

Brezhnev's assertive foreign policy was one blow to Carter, and to his early, nonconfrontational orientation toward foreign affairs and his desire to attend to the global agenda. The Iranian hostage crisis was another. Central America was a third.

Carter had his eye on Latin American states as he proposed to pay less attention to strategic issues, more to human rights, and to show a willingness to accept revolutionary regimes. He would try to funnel development funds through multilateral institutions, and his administration would divest itself of the Panama Canal and strive to normalize relations with Castro's Cuba. It would cease American support to regimes that used it to destroy political opponents. In line with this, the president reduced aid to and supported sanctions against countries accused of particularly harsh human rights violations: Chile, Argentina, Uruguay, and Brazil. There seems little question but that the pressures had some effect.

The opening of dialogue with Cuba—including the exchange of diplomatic interest sections—ran into the security considerations that Carter tried to ignore at his peril. Both Kennedy in 1963 and Ford in the mid-1970s had made tentative overtures, hoping to detach Castro from the Soviet Union and turn him into a kind of Caribbean Tito. The first attempt foundered following Kennedy's death* and Johnson's unwillingness to appear "soft" in an election year; the second foundered on the introduction of Cuban troops into Angola. Carter's attempt foundered on Cuban troops sent to Ethiopia, on greatly increased Russian military presence in the Caribbean area, on growing Cuban aid to other Caribbean revolutionary forces, and on a flurry in Congress over the discovery of a Soviet "combat brigade" in Cuba.

In March 1979, a coup on the tiny island of Grenada, 100 miles to the north of Venezuela, deposed its unpopular elected government, and installed the Grenadan People's Revolutionary Government under the leadership of the New Jewel Movement, a Marxist-Leninist party. The new government turned to Cuba for military aid, and Cuba rapidly became a conduit for Grenada's relations with the Soviet Union. Carter paid little heed to the tiny island, where Cuban and Russian aid went toward the building of an airport supposedly devoted to increasing the tourist trade, but

---

*French journalist Jean Daniel, one of Kennedy's two channels to Castro, was dining with Castro when news came of Kennedy's assassination. Castro muttered, again and again, "Es una mala noticia" ("This is bad news") and told Daniel, "there is the end of your mission of peace."

which government leaders themselves said might be useful for airlifts to help head off fascist governments in neighboring states.

Much more U.S. attention was being paid to the situation playing itself out in Nicaragua, a far larger state strategically situated near the Panama Canal. Here the forty-year, highly personal dictatorship of the Somoza family came to an end four months after the coup in Grenada. When Somoza was forced to leave on July 17, 1979, a junta took over as the Provisional Government of National Reconstruction. The Sandinista National Liberation Front (FSLN) was the best-organized political group in the junta and had a virtual monopoly of armed force. Carter policy was to work with the FSLN, to try to help maintain the pluralist structure of the government and of society, and to fund some measure of reconstruction, but the government eventually drove out many of its earlier supporters.

Within weeks, several hundred Russian, Cuban, and Bulgarian security and military advisers were attached to the government. In early 1980, a series of technical, economic, and military aid agreements were signed with socialist bloc countries. Although Castro apparently advised against the move because it would agitate the imperialists, Soviet arms, including tanks and other armored vehicles, began to be shipped to Nicaragua. At the Moscow Institute of Latin America, experts lauded the Nicaraguan experience, saying it marked a return to Cuban revolutionary hero Che Guevara's long-discredited guerrilla warfare tactics as a potentially successful means to create Marxist-Leninist regimes in strategic locations.

Sandinista spokesmen talked of the spread of revolution to El Salvador: here there were severe rural poverty, economic dominance by a small oligarchy, and a military-dominated political system that led to pervasive, indiscriminate violence by guerrillas, by the government, by paramilitary death squads, by vigilantes, and by spontaneous "defense" squads. Carter policy, in desperation, had been to try to get a center to hold in El Salvador, so as to bring the military and the reformist Christian Democrats to re-form a consensus that would block both the rightist death squads and an extreme left guerrilla takeover. Aid to El Salvador, cut off in 1977 because of human rights violations, was resumed after a reformist coup in 1979. It was cut off again in December 1980 after the murder of three American nuns and a lay social worker, and then was resumed again in January 1981 (four days before Ronald Reagan assumed the presidency), because of the increased flow of Soviet-supplied arms to rebels who were in the midst of a "final offensive" to try to seize power before the new, presumably tougher, Reagan Administration came to power.

In this the rebels failed, but thanks to Cuban support, disparate Marxist-Leninist groups were brought together into the Farabundo Marti Liberation

Front, which external forces could support. Once again, the Carter Administration seemed, in the eyes of many Americans, to have revealed its fundamental weakness in the face of a renewed, concerted, Russian-backed Cuban effort in the Caribbean and Central American basin.

Carter and the Russian Invasion of Afghanistan

Soviet-backed Cuban troops in Africa were bad enough; the Iranian hostage crisis was worse; Communism in the Caribbean and in Central America—areas that many Americans considered their own backyard—seemed worse yet. The worst, however, followed: starting on December 25, 1979, with an airlift of 5,000 Russian troops into the capital city of Kabul, came what eventually turned into a large-scale military invasion of Afghanistan—the first use of Soviet ground troops in large numbers, outside what had previously been accepted as the Russian sphere. Within months, 100,000 Russian soldiers were in Afghanistan. The occasion was the growing inability of the Marxist regime of Hafizullah Amin to control a countryside in insurrection. The model for action seems to have been successful Russian invasion of Czechoslovakia in 1968, when a sullen population was rapidly forced to acquiesce to a new government as a result of naked Russian force.

For Carter, this was perhaps the final straw. Strategists pointed out that invasion brought Russian troops much closer to the Straits of Hormuz, gateway to the unsettled Persian Gulf area, from which the West and Japan got most of their oil. Pakistani leaders feared the effect on their northern frontier, where a separatist movement had long been supported by Afghan governments and the Soviet Union. (In retrospect, actually, it appears that such considerations played little part in the Soviet decision to intervene.)

There was widespread condemnation. The UN General Assembly called for an immediate and unconditional withdrawal of the Soviet forces by a vote of 104 to 18 with 18 abstentions, and the thirty-six-state Islamic Conference denounced the Russian move and suspended Afghanistan from membership.

Carter announced a series of punitive measures: an embargo on grain sales to the Soviet Union (mostly made up by other countries' sales to the USSR, especially Argentina), a halt in the sale of certain high-technology products, and (harking back to the 1936 Berlin Olympic Games that helped give Adolf Hitler respectability) a controversial boycott of the 1980 Moscow Olympics. Perhaps more important, the invasion led to the first substantial, projected increases in American military spending since the decline initiated in the Nixon years after withdrawal from Vietnam.

In January, following the invasion, the president announced to the Congress that the Persian Gulf represented a "vital interest" which the United States would be prepared to defend against any outside power by force. It meant an increase of America's capacity to use its armed forces in power projection, largely through assigning existing and enlarged forces to a new command that came to be called the "Rapid Deployment Force." To make more credible the capacity to control escalation in the face of probably superior enemy forces, Carter also adopted a new nuclear missile targeting strategy: According to Presidential Directive 59 (PD59), retaliation would be directed first against missile bases, not against cities, so that, after a first exchange, in a nuclear war, a pause and negotiations to end the war could take place. In line with this, he moved to procure the giant, mobile MX intercontinental ballistic missile (ICBM).

Thanks to the Soviet Union, Carter had come a long way from his earlier stance, and the American mood was far more assertive than it had been in the years following Vietnam. To an uncomfortable West, the Cold War seemed alive and well, and the benefits of détente appeared to be receding at a rapid rate. Ronald Reagan had plenty of ammunition for his 1980 presidential campaign. Global events of the end of the decade provided a sorry ending to the Carter attempt to adapt American foreign policy to a changing and more interdependent world in which balance-of-power security concerns would have a lesser role.

Brezhnev: Détente, Soviet Expansion, and Soviet Decay

As the foregoing shows, Brezhnev followed an assertive foreign policy on numerous fronts. At the start of the 1970s, however, Nixon and Kissinger appear to have thought Brezhnev would interpret détente in the same way they did, and arms control talks seemed to substantiate this.

Disarmament and Arms Control

Several major arms control agreements had been negotiated before the 1970s in an effort to prevent a nuclear war no one country wanted but in a situation in which no one quite trusted the other to avoid seeking some sort of advantage. The 1959 agreement promising to keep the Antarctic free of nuclear weapons was followed, after the Cuban missile crisis of 1962, by a partial test ban, permitting only underground testing and prohibiting tests in the air, the seas, or outer space. That same year saw installation of the Hot Line. In 1967 the two superpowers signed a convention agreeing to ban the placing of weapons of mass destruction in outer space. A smaller number of countries also signed the Treaty of Tlatelolco, banning nuclear weapons in

South America and the Caribbean. (Cuba was not a party to the treaty until 1995.) A year later, the Nuclear Non-Proliferation Treaty banned countries from obtaining nuclear weapons that did not already have them, while countries that had them pledged not to transfer them to others and to take measures to reduce their own arsenals.

The realities of nonproliferation proved complex: once India exploded a nuclear device in 1974, Pakistani governments became intent on developing their own, and knowledge that Israel had constructed its own weapons led Arab hard-line states to try to acquire a nuclear capacity. In June 1981 Israel launched a daring long-range raid across other Arab states to attack and destroy the Iraqi Osirak nuclear reactor, which Israeli intelligence claimed was intended for nuclear weapons production; a decade later the Iraqi program would be back in full swing, and suspicion arose that North Korea was engaged in nuclear weapons production. The nuclear fuel cycle is a complicated one, and the International Atomic Energy Agency had a hard time tracking nuclear materials and maintaining the nonproliferation regime. The fall of the Soviet Union in 1991 made it far more difficult: the traffic in nuclear materials greatly increased.

Nevertheless, the numerous arms control agreements were testimony to willingness to stabilize matters. By the 1970s, Soviet strategic weapons parity made the Russians ready to negotiate on the basis of equality. Nixon, for his part, saw such controls as part of his overall attempt to establish a new and more stable structure of world peace. SALT I (the first Strategic Arms Limitation agreement) itself hardly stopped the arms race: signed May 26, 1972, it was an interim agreement (not a treaty) that put a cap on numbers and classes of certain strategic weapons, while still allowing a variety of qualitative improvements to take place. But it envisioned the more rapid completion of a SALT II and a SALT III, which would begin real reductions, and it underlined its seriousness by being linked to a treaty signed at the same time: the ABM treaty, which limited further development of antiballistic missiles (defensive weapons designed to destroy incoming missiles). By that stroke, each country gave its own population to the other as a hostage for its good behavior: in abjuring a defense against the other's missiles, each effectively made itself unable to threaten a first use of nuclear weapons, since retaliation by the other would entail the loss of its population. Defense, in other words, seemed destabilizing, offering the possibility of use of nuclear weapons. The ABM treaty would stabilize deterrence through the probability of "mutual assured destruction"—the acronym for which was, of course, MAD. It had, indeed, become a MAD world, when defensive capability was more dangerous than offensive capability.

In the meantime, the Hot Line was upgraded, and the powers signed the

Seabed Arms Control Treaty, which forbade placing weapons of mass destruction on the seabed, and negotiated a convention banning the production and use of biological weapons. The two superpowers also agreed on measures to lessen the possibility of accidents that might lead to nuclear war. The United States retired large numbers of older, more powerful, but vulnerable weapons. SALT I had set up the Standing Consultative Commission to verify issues of implementation and compliance, and clear up misunderstanding. To add to all this, in 1972 the United States and the Soviet Union signed a trade treaty that settled the debt situation left over from World War II, gave the Soviet Union most favored nation (MFN) trade treatment, and promised the Russians large import credits. It appeared that a new era of cooperation had been inaugurated; the Cold War had come to an end; détente was truly at hand.

Third World countries complained, however, that they had seen no signs of disarmament, nor the savings it would provide—a so-called peace dividend to be used for development aid.

The End of Arms Control

Despite summit meetings in Washington a year after SALT I and in Moscow in 1974 (following President Nixon's resignation), SALT II moved slowly. The Russians began to build a new class of heavy missiles with multiple warheads—within the provisions of SALT I—missiles that could presumably destroy American retaliatory missiles in their silos in a first strike. By the time a SALT II treaty came before the U.S. Senate for ratification after several missteps, it was dubbed "fatally flawed" by opponents; all momentum was lost. The Russians had begun large-scale deployment of the SS-20 in Europe, and NATO, as we have seen, decided on its two-track strategy: to install its own new intermediate-range missiles unless the Soviet Union accepted its offer to negotiate away the Russian missiles. That same month, the Russians invaded Afghanistan, killing all possibility of SALT ratification—and helping to kill the possibility of Carter's reelection, despite his sharp increases in spending for new strategic weapons.

Brezhnev's Global Foreign Policy

Despite the advantages the United States tried to present to him with détente, Brezhnev faced too many opportunities he could seize in the world at large, now that the Soviet buildup since 1963 had taken effect. If 1975 was the year for victory throughout Indochina, 1976 was the year for Angola, 1977 for Mozambique and Ethiopia, 1978 for Yemen and Afghanistan, and 1979 for Grenada and Nicaragua. Détente represented an opportunity, not a limitation.

Despite the Paris accords, the Brezhnev regime continued to pour arms into North Vietnam, just when the United States Congress cut off aid to South Vietnam. As a result, in 1975 North Vietnam took advantage of Nixon's fall and the vacuum in leadership that resulted from a weakened presidency. It launched an all-out attack on South Vietnam, in violation of the Paris accords that had gained American Secretary of State Henry Kissinger and Vietnamese negotiator Le Duc Tho the Nobel Peace Prize only two years earlier. The North Vietnamese and Brezhnev could be sure now that the United States would not help the Vietnamese as Nixon had promised them he would. In April 1975 the world was treated on television to the degrading sight of Americans scrambling to board the last helicopter leaving the roof of the embassy in Saigon. There, a year later, a reunified Vietnam was proclaimed. In the meantime, the dominoes fell in Laos and Cambodia, where the world witnessed a bloodbath no one had thought possible. All of former French Indochina was now, finally, under the control of Communist Parties. Russian spokesmen boasted of how successful Russian support for wars of liberation could be, of how the imperialists were everywhere in retreat.

The collapse of the Portuguese African empire has already been referred to (see chapter 6). In Angola it was Russian support and Russian-supported Cuban troops that helped put the Popular Movement for the Liberation of Angola (MPLA) into power when President Gerald Ford was forced by Congress to abandon aid to the American-supported National Front for the Liberation of Angola. Clearly, it appeared—as in the case of Vietnam—that Marxist-Leninist movements could count upon support from the Soviet Union, but their opponents could count upon little from the United States. Soviet-bloc aid also went to the Front for the Liberation of Mozambique (FRELIMO), and Soviet aid enabled the Ethiopian regime of Mengistu Haile Mariam to repel the rebels in the north and defeat Somalia in the south.

In 1978 the Soviet Union signed a treaty of friendship with the Marxist-Leninist government of South Yemen, where there were already substantial numbers of Russian, Cuban, and East German advisers, and where its port rights on the island of Socotra in the Indian Ocean at the mouth of the Red Sea were reinforced. Together with port rights in Vietnam and new rights at Assaba and Massawa in Ethiopia, the agreement gave the Soviet Union the ability to service the substantial naval forces it now maintained in the Indian Ocean.

Then, in December 1979, came the invasion of Afghanistan and the Soviet decisions to support the new regime in the tiny island of Grenada as well as the Sandinistas in Nicaragua.

The Russian air and naval presence in the Caribbean had increased all through the 1970s, when Brezhnev also completely reequipped the Cuban armed forces, many units of which then saw service abroad. In the process, Cuba became far and away the most heavily armed state in Latin America. Russian reconnaissance and antisubmarine warfare planes began to use Cuban bases. By the early 1980s, many Russian planes were permanently based in Cuba. Russian submarines began to pay regular port calls in the mid-1970s, and later they began to operate out of the well-equipped Cienfuegos naval base. A submarine rescue ship was stationed in Cuba, and in 1976 the Russian navy and the Russian-equipped Cuban navy began annual joint maneuvers in the Caribbean, while Russian naval units operating out of Cienfuegos conducted antisubmarine maneuvers on their own. When Grenada and Nicaragua opened up opportunities, the Russians supplied Cuba with new squadrons of military transport aircraft. Some 2,000 Russian personnel operated a giant electronic intelligence collection facility at Lourdes, outside Havana, monitoring American communications, both military and civilian.

By this time, however, Soviet expansion raised a real issue of whether it might not cost the socialist bloc too much.

Socialist Economies in Difficulty

Reconstruction after World War II had proceeded relatively rapidly. In the 1950s and the 1960s the socialist economies achieved high rates of growth, but the limits of extensive growth were reached by the end of the 1960s, when growth rates began to slow. Efficiency of production—increased productivity based on advanced technology and sophisticated management— became necessary. The overcentralized Stalinist economies proved singularly unsuccessful at reform, despite attempts at some measure of decentralization in the late 1960s that ran up against heavy bureaucratic resistance. As a result, Comecon turned to the capitalist West for solutions.

Western European countries were willing to reopen trade and extend credit, and the United States tended to follow suit. But socialist bloc countries had little the West wanted to buy: raw materials were available, at world market prices, but manufactured goods, by and large, were not at the level of quality set by Western manufacturers or the new Far Eastern competitors. Nevertheless, in the 1970s German, Japanese, and American exports to the Soviet Union expanded tenfold, partly financed by a new Soviet policy of trying to produce for export. But they were also financed by borrowing, in the hope that the new imported technology would increase productivity sufficiently to increase export capacity substantially. By 1980, socialist bloc debt to the West reached $70.5 billion, with Poland owing almost a third of the total.

Eastern bloc experts themselves blamed the continued slowdown in growth on the unwieldiness of their centrally planned economies, on management failures, and on lack of incentives. Throughout the bloc, experiments in "market socialism" of various forms were tried out. Little seemed to work, and within the bloc, any enthusiasm for "building socialism" on Marxist-Leninist lines disappeared. To the east of the USSR, successive upheavals in China had much to do with economic failures.

American policy toward Eastern European countries had shown a marked shift since the early 1950s, when there had been talk of "liberation." The move toward détente with the Soviet Union inevitably left the countries within the Soviet sphere, although Nixon had used his visit to Romania to show the Russians he was willing to deal with any Communist country that wanted to deal, and Romania, in fact, was granted MFN trading status to reward and encourage it for its relatively independent foreign policy stance. Carter, in line with his human rights emphasis, had adopted a policy of "differentiation": Eastern bloc countries would be rewarded for liberalization and independence in foreign policy, and Hungary followed Romania in receiving MFN treatment.

All the Eastern bloc suffered declines in growth rates in the late 1970s; Poland and Romania were forced to reschedule their debts, Hungary barely avoided doing so, and all three had to cut imports and introduce austerity programs. In Poland a new force, Solidarity, emerged—the first independent workers' movement in the supposedly workers' states—and grew to a membership of eight million. This movement joined forces with intellectuals and the church to demand real, substantive change. In September 1981 the Soviet Union issued a series of warnings of dangers to the Polish state, calling for a crackdown on Solidarity and, in the pages of *Pravda*, reminding readers of the 1956 Hungarian and the 1968 Czech crises—and the resultant Soviet interventions.

All through 1980 and 1981, agitation and negotiation accompanied one another, while the economic situation grew more and more precarious. On December 13, 1981, to preserve "People's Democracy" against rule by the people, General Wojciech Jaruzelski, the new head of the Communist Party, proclaimed martial law, established a military council to run the country, and outlawed Solidarity. To forestall the Russians from doing it, Poles had saved Communism in Poland.

By this time, the expenses of empire had become heavy for the USSR. Castro's Cuba was costing the Soviet Union several billion dollars a year by 1980, and aid to and military support for other states also grew rapidly.

When Americans referring to Nicaragua said that they didn't want it to become "another Cuba," they were in good company: some Russians said the same thing. They could not afford it. Afghanistan was becoming a heavy drain. The year 1980 was another in a series of disastrous years for grain production, necessitating enormous hard-currency grain imports. Brezhnev was an old and ailing man in 1980, and Russia was ruled by a gerontocracy in the Politburo, out of touch with major underlying changes taking place in Soviet society. Repression of a handful of dissident writers and an underground press was easy enough, though it provoked a foreign outcry; but repression of a widespread underground economy, consequent corruption, and ethnic rivalries on a grand scale was less possible. Ronald Reagan in the United States was cranking up the pace of the arms race again. The situation cried out for reappraisal. Brezhnev finally died on November 10, 1982, but he was replaced by the aged Yuri Andropov, and then by Konstantin Chernenko. Both were dead by March 10, 1985. Only when Mikhail Gorbachev became prime minister did a new era dawn in Soviet and Soviet bloc politics; only then did a new Russian leadership seriously reconsider the relationship between ends and means in Soviet foreign policy.

The Global Agenda

This chapter began with the emergence of a "global agenda" in the decade of the 1970s. In the face of all the tumult of the decade just described—much of it a product of growing interdependence—how effective could attempts be to deal with this global agenda? The list of global problems grew longer through the decade: population growth; resource depletion; pollution in the oceans and the atmosphere; availability and distribution of world food supplies; urbanization in the Third World; refugees; fresh water supply and use; desertification; new and renewable energy supplies; peaceful use and development of outer space; making science and technology available to, and suitable for, poorer nations; deforestation; new concerns about global warming (in the 1980s) as a result of the "greenhouse effect"; and ozone depletion in the stratosphere. Promotion of human rights and consideration of the role of women in development assumed new urgency.

All these problems were beyond the capacity of any single state or even a group of states to handle. A higher level of global policy making—of cooperation and coordination—was needed, a level that would be hard to achieve in a world embroiled in political and economic conflicts. New tasks were coming to the fore at a time when many international organizations were in disarray and public support for them was minimal.

Figure 2. **World Population Growth**

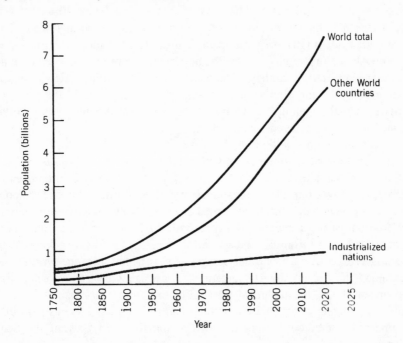

Source: Josepth Weatherby, Jr., et al., *The Other World: Issues and Politics in the Third World* (New York: Macmillan, 1987).

The Role of International Organizations

Nevertheless, international organizations played a key role. A pattern developed: discussion within one or more organizations led to enough of a consensus that a world conference could be called which could then set a program and create a new organization or charge older ones with carrying it out and with persuading states to cooperate. The United Nations Educational, Scientific, and Cultural Organization (UNESCO) Conference on the Biosphere in 1968 led to the UN Conference on the Human Environment, which was held in Stockholm in 1972. The conference adopted a Declaration of Principles on environment and pollution, and in its Action Plan called for creation of what became the UN Environment Program, with a small organization primarily devoted to spurring governments and other international organizations into supporting the principles developed at Stockholm. The principles enshrined the view that no state could claim a sovereign right to produce pollution that affected other states: all bore a responsibility to conduct themselves in such a way as to not damage the environment of other states or areas beyond the national jurisdiction, such as the high seas or the atmosphere. Politics at various levels, however, was never absent. The Soviet bloc boycotted the conference because East Germany was not invited to participate. Third World countries campaigned vigorously against having control of pollution take priority over economic development activities; they argued that major industrial states were the prime polluters and should bear most of the costs, and that the goals of environmentalists should not hamper their own necessary increase in pollution as a result of delayed development.

Implementation would hardly be easy.

The pattern was similar in the other issue areas. In the 1950s and the 1960s, for example, there had been UN Law of the Seas Conferences to update what was one of the most ancient bodies of international law: contemporary technology has transformed use of the seas, and the old principle of freedom of the seas beyond a three-mile limit was no longer adequate. Countries began to tap oil and gas on the continental shelves, long-range fishing vessels using sonar and enormous nets began to range worldwide, depleting the fish in the 10 percent of the ocean where they occur. For advanced states, the technical possibility of mining the seabed for rich mineral deposits developed. Something had to be done. Treaties painfully hammered out of conflicting interests at the first two Law of the Seas Conferences failed to be ratified by enough states.

Finally, in 1973, UN Law of the Sea Conference III (UNCLOS III) convened, basing itself, ultimately, on a new conception of the high seas as the "common heritage of mankind." It reflected a degree of consensus on several issues: simply letting states use the seas freely was rapidly depleting its hitherto vast seafood resources; a scramble to use seabed resources would benefit only the rich few who could afford the enormous capital investments required, and would be to the detriment of Third World mineral exporters; all states, even the landlocked, should benefit from an orderly use of the commons. More and more states had been extending their jurisdiction out beyond the traditional 3-mile limit, first to 12 miles, then to 200 miles. Order had to be brought out of this chaos, reflecting goals of production, equity, and conservation.

It took UNCLOS III nine years to produce a 200-page treaty, which needed ratification by sixty states. Most of it represented consensus on a series of compromises, but several key states remained opposed to articles setting up the relatively powerful International Seabed Authority to provide some international management of the high seas. Eleven more years passed before the sixtieth state ratified the treaty, and it came into force in December 1993. The Law of the Sea Treaty may yet come to be regarded as the forerunner of much more, as an exemplar of how global issues should be globally managed. It may also show how far states still are from being able to make policy on a global basis.

There were innumerable other conferences, each striving to create new global policies, each inevitably colored by international politics. The first World Population Conference at Bucharest in 1974 found itself divided between those who argued that government-sponsored population control policies were fundamentally necessary for economic development, and representatives from some Third World countries who argued that economic development, spurred by Western aid, must come first: it would then lead to a decline in population growth rates. The World Food Conference in Rome that same year set up the World Food Council to coordinate the work of the dozens of international agencies involved. Food production, food distribution, and food security in times of shortage are all complicated by the interdependent food networks now existing in the world. Whole regions depend on imports from surplus areas at prices that they can afford but that will not undercut and thereby destroy local production. 1973 had been a crisis year, during which world production fell, reserve stocks were drawn down, and famine struck Ethiopia. The situation in that unhappy country highlighted a persistent political problem: that of weak governments that cannot admit to failure, or governments unwilling to accept that their own domestic policies are wrong.

Innumerable other world conferences followed, dealing with different aspects of the global agenda. There would be follow-up conferences a decade later, to assess progress. A second population conference was held in 1984, in Mexico City, a third in Cairo in 1994. In 1985 a conference in Nairobi assessed women's rights, a decade after the first 1975 conference on women, and this was followed by another in China in 1995. By the time of the 1975 conference, politics began to intrude in new forms, both on strictly economic topics and in the area of human rights. On the economic side, G-77 countries insisted that reference to the need for the New International Economic Order be inserted into virtually every set of resolutions as part of the solution to any problem; Western countries refused, G-77 used its automatic majority, and consensus disappeared into recrimination.

On the human rights side, there had been conflict almost from 1948, when the UN General Assembly adopted the Universal Declaration of Human Rights, pursuant to the UN Charter, incorporating the view that civil and political rights were necessary to the preservation of all individual and minority rights. Several UN treaties drafted after the Universal Declaration and a large number of conventions sponsored by other international organizations spelled out individual rights in great detail. Socialist bloc countries that curbed civil and political rights then insisted that economic and social rights—to employment, to medical care, and so on—were more important than civil rights. As the colonial empires broke up, new states in which one-party or military regimes eventually emerged sided with the Soviet Union, and the issue became more and more politicized, with Third World states ready to criticize Western states, along with Israel and South Africa, for their violations of human rights while ignoring massive violations in other Third World countries or in the socialist bloc. In 1975, following upon a carefully orchestrated campaign associated with a general attack upon racism, the General Assembly overwhelmingly adopted a resolution condemning Zionism as "a form of racism and racial discrimination."

Western nations could well decry the picture of states that were massacring groups of their own peoples with little international recrimination solemnly voting for the "Zionism is racism" resolution. Ritual reference to Zionism as racism helped embroil conferences on other global concerns. At the 1977 General Assembly that took up further international action to support human rights, a majority voted that the NIEO was essential to improvement in human rights. Confrontation had become an integral part of any attempt to deal with global problems.

Conclusion

The 1970s did not see the diminution of conflict that so many expected early in the decade. Instead, détente collapsed—in part because many Americans in and out of government distrusted the Soviet Union and felt that détente strengthened it, but in larger part because Leonid Brezhnev and his cohort perceived a growing weakness in American leadership, and could see no alternative but to try to take advantage of it. It collapsed because, during the decade, the Warsaw Pact nations consistently outbuilt NATO nations in all realms of conventional weaponry. It collapsed because of Western fears about the continued advances in Soviet nuclear missiles. It collapsed because, for the first time in history, Soviet naval forces other than submarines now ranged the oceans and had basing rights in the Caribbean, Africa, Arabia, and Southeast Asia, enabling the Soviet Union to support the far-flung commitments it undertook in the Brezhnev years.

The American economic and political position in the world had undoubtedly changed. The United States faced powerful competition; it was now more dependent on the economic actions of others and therefore more subject to the necessity of adjusting to short-term changes and imbalances in international trade and financial flows. It could no longer minimize the cost factor in the conduct of foreign policy. In the face of the continued nuclear standoff, Japanese and Western European leaders more often felt that they could act independently of the United States—as long as it remained committed in Europe—and Third World leaders by and large felt no compunctions in opposing the United States.

American government leaders, separated into the competing institutions of the presidency and of Congress, were divided on how to face the change in their world role. As a result, they often appeared to be vacillating and weak. Europeans, bordering on the socialist bloc, were torn: they felt they had a stronger interest in the benefits of détente than did the Americans, yet their governments wanted steady American leadership and the continued American military commitment to extended deterrence. The Japanese shared this European view, while the Chinese scolded the Americans for not reacting strongly enough to the Soviet Union. The Europeans had recognized in Richard Nixon one of their own, cognizant of balance-of-power realities. The sober French political commentator Raymond Aron wrote, "In twenty five years the United States has perhaps not yet learned what it took the European states centuries to grasp . . . it is on Richard Nixon and Henry Kissinger that a European pins his hopes for a foreign policy governed by reason . . . ."[2] President Jimmy Carter remained a puzzling figure.

The real impact of Russian-American relations came in the 1980 election in the United States, when Carter, who believed until the day before the election that he would be reelected, lost to conservative Republican Ronald Reagan, former movie star and former governor of the state of California. As usual, domestic dissatisfaction, especially over double-digit inflation, played the major role in deciding the election. But the main set of campaign ideas differentiating Reagan from Carter in the realm of foreign policy was fairly simple: American weakness (displayed in Central America, in Africa, Iran, and over imprisoned hostages) was what had led Russia into its imperial ventures at the time when the West should be taking advantage of Russia's growing stagnation. A strong America would rectify this.

What of global concerns? At the beginning of the decade, many had thought that fundamental change in international politics was under way, that traditional balance-of-power politics was increasingly irrelevant as states became less sovereign. Attempts to cope with the emerging global agenda were real, attested to by the increasing numbers of international conferences recommending global plans of action in numerous fields. They were marked, however, by the impact of the calls for an NIEO and the "Zionism is racism" resolution, both repeated and included by majority vote in virtually all world agenda forums, alienating the Western powers and Western public opinion that might otherwise have looked more favorably upon the important initiatives taken. The number of international governmental and nongovernmental international organizations performing useful tasks proliferated, but most of the public in most countries remained largely unaware of the vital work they performed.

Yet the decades of the 1970s and the 1980s demonstrated repeatedly that the imperatives of integration could not be ignored. The ecological consequences of population growth and economic development appeared evident even if they were far from clear, and even if events gave the lie to gloomy forecasts of shortages. The communications and computer revolution began to make real the "one world" forecast earlier, tying financial markets and global production in ways undreamed of heretofore. Parts manufactured in several countries could be coordinated with components assembled in others and with final assembly in yet another to produce what came to be called the "global factory." Early in the decade of the 1970s multinational enterprises came under attack as the tentacles of the octopus of American capitalism. It soon became evident that companies engaged in mineral extraction, such as oil companies, could be easily nationalized and controlled, since the sources of their production were rooted in the land. Manufacturing and services, however, could be shifted around. It was hardly American capitalism that had produced them: it was the opportunities offered by cheap communications and transportation, and the necessity to overcome tariff barriers of other countries. Major enterprises of other countries soon followed suit: Japanese automobiles began to be produced within the United States to escape import quotas, and within England for sale throughout the Common Market. People in small communities found themselves depending on far-off production and political developments, their own livelihood often affected directly by events over which they could have no control. Facsimile transmission of documents and satellite and fiberoptic transmission of images led to a concomitant globalization of media and television.

Thirty-five years earlier, the United States could provide leadership to the attempt to create a new world order, following upon the destructive crisis of the previous thirty years. Stalin's Russia sought to provide an alternative pattern, claiming that it represented the next stage in the inevitable unfolding of world history. The result—briefly—was bipolarism. By 1960, a new Third World had arisen to dilute the bipolar pattern, and the return of Europe and Japan complicated American policy, while the Soviet Union–Chinese conflict reflected other fissures in the socialist bloc. In the 1970s, attention turned to the globe itself, but it was a globe beset by conflict.

Notes

1. Donnella Meadows et al., *The Limits to Growth* (New York: New American Library, 1972), pp. 125–26.

2. Raymond Aron, *The Imperial Republic* (Cambridge, MA: Winthrop Publishers, 1974), pp. x–xi.

Further Suggested Readings

The challenge of global policy took place against a continued Soviet-American arms race that can be traced in Lawrence Freedman, *The Evolution of Nuclear Strategy* (New York: St. Martin's Press, 1981); in David Glantz, *The Military Strategy of the Soviet Union: A History* (Portland, OR: Frank Cass, 1993); and in John Newhouse, *Cold Dawn: The Story of SALT* (New York: Holt, Rinehart and Winston, 1973). A followup to the earlier Club of Rome report gives the flavor of growing awareness of the global agenda in the 1970s: Jan Tinbergen et al., *Reshaping the International Order: A Report to the Club of Rome* (New York: Dutton, 1976). Two later books reflect on the changing international economy: Robert Keohane, *After Hegemony: Cooperation and Discord in the World Economy* (Princeton: Princeton University Press, 1984); and Marvin Soroos, *Beyond Sovereignty: The Challenge of Global Policy* (Columbia: University of South Carolina Press, 1986). Charles W. Kegley, Jr., and Eugene Wittkopf have edited a useful reader, *The Global Agenda* (New York: Random House, 1984). On the NIEO, see the thoughtful critique in Stephen Krasner, *Structural Conflict: The Third World Against Global Liberalism* (Berkeley: University of California Press, 1985).

Part IV

The End of the Cold War

8

The Collapse of the Communist World

We shall cease to be Communists when shrimps learn to whistle.
—Premier Nikita Khrushchev

In 1979 the two superpowers faced each other with new intercontinental superweapons, with enormous opposing NATO and Warsaw Pact armies along a boundary running through central Europe, and with costly world-wide commitments. The Cold War was alive and well. This was a familiar picture of relatively stable global politics to everyone who had lived through the last forty years, and most people expected it to last indefinitely.

Incredibly enough, fifteen years later the Soviet bloc and the Warsaw Pact no longer existed, all Russian troops were at home, and most startling of all, the Soviet Union—one of the two superpowers—no longer existed either. Eastern Europe had thrown off its Communist governments, and American forces in NATO were only a sixth the size they had been. Both the United States and Russia had destroyed quantities of their nuclear weapons and canceled deployment of new ones. Most of the constituent republics of the USSR had become independent and joined the United Nations. Marxism-Leninism, one of the two major answers to modernization, lay in discredited tatters as the weaknesses that long existed behind the façade of Soviet power were revealed for all the world to see. Some in the West crowed that the West had "won the Cold War" and that containment had succeeded, but a good case could be made that it was the *failures* of containment that made the Soviet Union collapse—each Soviet "victory" bringing costs its floundering economy could no longer meet—and that, given the costs incurred, nobody had "won" the Cold War.

The first non-Communist government in Eastern Europe since Stalin's time was formed in Poland in mid-1989. But it was the opening of the Berlin Wall—that symbol of separation between the two blocs—on the night of November 9, 1989, that let loose the flood. It was a date to be likened to that of November 11, 1918, or August 14, 1945, the dates on which the two world wars had ended. Despite numerous solemn declarations that unity between West Germany and East Germany was not yet in the cards, it was—almost fantastically—formally effected less than a year later, on October 3, 1990. In December 1991 Mikhail Gorbachev, the man who had tried to modernize and maintain Communism was gone, and the Soviet Union with him. On September 1, 1994, the last Russian troops left Berlin, and Russian President Boris Yeltsin declared "Today is the last day of the past." World War II was finally over, and the last remnants of the Cold War were gone.

The prospect of bringing Eastern European countries and even Russia back into the Europe that existed before 1914 was immensely enticing, both to East and to West. Gorbachev had talked grandly of a "Common European Home," and successor governments in Eastern Europe had made known their desire to join the European Community. How to do it all proved to be an enormous puzzle, as early euphoria following the fall of Communist governments evaporated and hard realities took hold, such that large segments began to look back to the Communist era with nostalgia. In the meanwhile, to the horror of onlookers, Yugoslavia—that state cobbled out of the remnants of Austria-Hungary at the end of World War I—broke up, to the accompaniment of unusually bitter warfare between its constituent units, and the inability of Europe to bring the war to a halt brought discredit to the United Nations, to European institutions, and to NATO.

Transatlantic ties remained strained, as usual.

By the 1990s, it was all a whole new ball game, but few people knew the rules or who was on what side.

The Soviet Union Changes Course

Glasnost and Perestroika

Until the mid-1980s, official Soviet pronouncements and analyses of political and social matters continued to follow the old ideological line. Khrushchev, the man who destroyed the myth of Stalin and opened up to the world's gaze Stalinism's myriad horrors, nevertheless confidently forecast the triumph of socialism. When he told the Americans, "We will bury you," he meant it: Communism's historically inevitable superiority would become so apparent through the better life it would provide that capitalism would transform itself. The 1961 Party Program not only declared that "Socialism will succeed capitalism everywhere," but provided forecasts of how much greater Soviet per capita production of consumer goods would be in the next two decades compared to that of the United States. The forecasts were very soon set aside, but the official optimism was not—until Mikhail Gorbachev succeeded Chernenko in March 1985, and a breath of realism swept through the Kremlin and the party. In short order, Gorbachev determined that he had inherited a system both atrophied and overextended. In the past those who had dared to question its premises were crushed, and those who had wanted to do things differently were swept aside. Now discussion of everything would have to be opened up; this was "glasnost." And clearly the society would have to be restructured; this was "perestroika." How much and how were still to be determined, but the import was quite clear when Gorbachev spoke to the party faithful in the summer of 1986:

> The current restructuring embraces not only the economy but all other facets of public life: social relations, the political system, the spiritual and ideological sphere, and the style and the methods of the work of the party and all of our cadres. . . . I would equate the word "restructuring" with the word "revolution." . . . The tremendous scale and volume of the work ahead is coming to light more fully.

The Fatal Blow: Afghanistan

Failure in Afghanistan may well have been the straw that broke the camel's back, coming as it did on top of the failure to block deployment of American missiles in Germany, the new American military buildup—which might require a new round of military expenditures—and the increasing costs of commitment in Africa, Latin America, and Asia.

The Soviet invasion of Afghanistan in late December 1979, occasioned by conflict within the Afghan Communist Party, appeared to climax Brezhnev's decade of assertiveness. With a new government installed in power, followed by a withdrawal of most Russian forces, international condemnation would fade away once it proved useless: most countries had to get along with the Soviet Union, whatever it did. The Brezhnev government, however, miscalculated the extent of Afghan resistance, the extent to which outside parties would support it, and how long it would last. The longer it lasted, the more international attention it received: despite strong Russian lobbying, the annual UN General Assembly call for the withdrawal of "foreign troops" received increasing votes.

By late 1987, as the war began to become a drain and casualties mounted, growing hostility to the war within the Soviet Union began to tell. A divided leadership had already made the decision for withdrawal when peace talks began in November. To everyone's surprise, peace agreements were signed on April 14, 1988. Soviet troop withdrawals began soon after, and on February 15, 1989, the last Soviet units left Afghanistan. "The troop withdrawal is not a defeat," declared departing Soviet General Gromov. "In spite of our sacrifices and losses, we have totally fulfilled our internationalist duty." Reflecting the growth of glasnost, he also said, "The day that millions of Soviet people have waited for has come." A remarkable commentary in *Pravda* stated, "One can say that in the future such vital issues as the use of troops must not be decided in secrecy, without the approval of the country's Parliament."

The Najibullah regime installed by the Russians in Afghanistan before their departure held on until April 1992. It was unable to negotiate a peace with the rebels, to whom Kabul now fell. Russian troops were gone, but the devastated land found no peace. Rebel forces exploded into bitter infighting, with support for different factions from Iran, Pakistan, Saudi Arabia, and Uzbekistan to the north. By 1994, a few areas were secure enough that some of the millions of refugees in Iran and Pakistan began to return, but fighting continued. Afghanistan was perhaps the last victim of the Cold War.

In 1989, the same year that Russian troops left Afghanistan, Vietnamese troops supported by the Russians left Cambodia, and Cuban troops—also supported by the Russians—were preparing to leave Ethiopia and Angola, where another precarious settlement had been reached (see chapter 13). It was all hardly coincidental: it represented in action what had come to be called "new thinking" about foreign policy in the Soviet Union.

The Breakup of the Soviet Empire

The official view of "détente" in Brezhnev's time—contrary to the American view of it—was that there had been a dynamic shift in worldwide class conflict, not an easing of it. The world "correlation of forces" had shifted in the direction of the socialist bloc. Now Gorbachev, in a radical departure from this and its Leninist basis, stressed in numerous speeches that the historical dialectic was leading to more cooperation and interdependence rather than to conflict and division. Mutual security would be achieved by political agreement, not by military power. A real détente would free economic resources and promote trade that would restore growth to the stagnant economy and dynamism to Soviet society.

How far the economic basis for policy had eroded was becoming fairly evident, but at the June 1988 Party Congress government spokesman after government spokesman made it explicit. Gorbachev led off: "We underestimated the depth and gravity of the distortions and stagnations of the past."

Said the minister of health, "In the past . . . we kept quiet about the fact that we were in 50th place in the world for infant mortality, after Mauritius and Barbados . . . that our life expectancy ranks 32nd in the world." An education official told the party that half the schools in the Soviet Union "do not have central heating, running water or a sewerage system," while another official told it that rural people were fleeing to the cities because of failure of local authorities "to resolve the three most important tasks: providing heat, constructing roads and providing running water and sewerage." "Science," said the rector of Moscow State University, "has been a hollow word in our country . . . we have done very little for its development," while the editor of *Izvestia* told the conference that the reason for failure was mainly that those who made decisions had no responsibility for their results, and those who had responsibility made no decisions. "We have made one contribution," said another. "We have taught the world what *not* to do." Clearly, the Soviet Union was no longer "the wave of the future."

Every day of the late 1980s brought reports of ethnic unrest, clashes with police, strikes, industrial accidents, or disasters—of which the nuclear accident at Chernobyl in April 1986, with its horrendous local effects and its widespread milder effects throughout Europe was only the worst example. Previously, such matters were concealed. Now the widespread ecological disasters were fully reported: Chernobyl brought a pervasive crisis of confidence in established authority. A conference of leading economists in June 1989 called the economic situation "critical" and foresaw economic disaster unless the pace of change was greatly hastened.

For countries outside the Soviet sphere, the issue was in the main how all this would affect Soviet foreign policy. In Gorbachev's first years, the Soviet Union had continued a major naval buildup in the Far East and in the north; both its deployment of new classes of quieter submarines with longer-range missiles, and its continued construction of three large-deck aircraft carriers that could provide air cover for task forces in distant waters testified to a seeming continued determination to remain a global power, not merely a continental one. Gorbachev, in the face of Russian economic woes, quickly reached the conclusion that it could not do this.

It is impossible to avoid following developments without the hindsight of 1996, for each difficult step deemed so important at the time was followed by others that almost immediately made it insignificant.

Gorbachev began by radically shifting the Russian position on a number of issues concerning the Intermediate Nuclear Forces treaty, and finally signing it. This led to actual destruction of *all* Soviet SS-20 missiles, under verification agreements that contradicted virtually every earlier Russian position on on-site inspection (including views made known by leading military figures shortly before the negotiations). By 1987, the Russian forces in Europe began to shift to a defensive operational strategy instead of one based on their traditional combination of mobility and concentrated fire-power for exploitation of breakthroughs. (East German government files have since revealed that earlier Soviet operational plans included the first use of over 500 tactical nuclear weapons, enabling capture of Denmark, the Netherlands and Belgium within two weeks and open access to the Atlantic within four.) Over the next two years, step by step, Gorbachev proposed larger and larger reductions of forces in Europe, leading finally to the No-vember 1990 Treaty on Conventional Forces in Europe. Four years later, one might indeed wonder what the complicated calculations and negotia-tions had been all about: the Russians had unilaterally withdrawn *all* their troops.

As a result of his first radical shifts, Gorbachev was at center stage on the world scene. His domestic problems might appear overwhelming, but European and American leaders vied with each other in visiting him in Moscow, while he made triumphant trips abroad. The Russian leader was still seeking Western European economic support to help maintain the erod-ing Soviet empire, and he wanted expanded ties before 1992, the date for European unity, when the East might find itself squeezed out. While still on this quest, in Paris in July 1989, he faced some hard questioning about the Russian relationship to changes in Eastern Europe. He reacted quickly. Addressing the Council of Europe in Strasbourg a day later, where he renewed his appeal for a "Common European Home" stretching from the Atlantic to the Urals—that is, for a situation in which the Soviet Union would have newly normalized and mutually profitable relations with West-ern Europe—he assured his listeners that Eastern European countries could develop as they wished. The Brezhnev doctrine was, essentially, dead.

With that simple declaration the floodgates opened, Communist control over Eastern Europe collapsed, the Warsaw Pact and the Council on Mutual Economic Assistance (Comecon) were doomed, and real arms reduction in Europe was assured. It appears that Gorbachev still hoped to be able to steer change in Eastern Europe, but it was not to be. No one quite realized it at the time, but his policy, essentially, collapsed as he was rapidly forced into a far different path than the one he had been following—making Western policies obsolete into the bargain.

Poland led the way for the rest of Eastern Europe. In February 1989, in the face of stagnation and enormous debt, President Jaruzelski finally ac-cepted demands for changes in the structure of government. The Roman Catholic Church, which had continued to flourish in a twilight of illegality, was given legal status. (The fact of a Polish Pope in Rome had much to do with the continued strength of the Catholic Church in opposition in Poland.) That summer came the first partial, free elections since World War II, and in August 1989, for the first time since shortly after the war, an East European state found itself with a non-Communist government: Tadeusz Mazowiecki of Solidarity formed a coalition government. A year later Lech Walesa, the trade-unionist leader of Solidarity, would become president, and the outgoing President Jaruzelski would apologize for the "harm, pain and injustice" suffered by Poles during his nine years in office. Poland, for the next few years, would face economic penury as it struggled to throw off the vestiges of a socialist economy.

Hungary, with a population only a third that of Poland, had done better under Janos Kadar, installed by the Russians in 1956. But the economy went sour in the mid-1980s. The aging Kadar retired as head of government in 1988, and in June 1989, a Hungarian politburo member declared that the discredited Communist Party was largely the cause of the current crisis. Imre Nagy, the executed leader of the 1956 revolt, suddenly became a symbol: on June 16, 1989—only one year after a pro-Nagy demonstration had been brutally broken up—came the reburial of Nagy and several of his companions in Budapest's Heroes' Square, in front of a throng of 250,000, while books, lapel pins, and large photographs of the former leader blossomed throughout Hungary. For more than thirty years, the events of 1956 had scarcely been mentioned, and the Russian invasion had been justified as a legitimate help against counterrevolution. Now, finally, the myth was dismissed. In March 1990, the first free elections brought to power a center-right coalition, whose foreign policy aim, along with that of the new governments of Poland and Czechoslovakia, was a rapid integration with Western Europe.

Events in each of the countries affected those in others. The Czechoslovak and East German governments, knowing well the extent of subterranean opposition, tried to follow a hard line, using the autonomy granted by Gorbachev to publicly oppose all he stood for. Czech spokesmen, along with Rumanians, were the most bitter critics of the rehabilitation of Nagy in Hungary, and of the nature of the demonstrations at the time of his reburial. But it was from Czech dissidents that the obvious and discomforting question came: the Russian invasion of 1968 had taken place because the Czechs had tried to do what the Russians were doing now, twenty years later. What then could be said of the legitimacy of the present Czech government—which cracked down hard on demonstrators as events played themselves out elsewhere?

In the meantime, the Erich Honecker government in East Germany followed the same hard line as the Czechs, stressing order and criticizing

Gorbachev. Starting in July 1989, however, East Germans in large numbers began to vote with their feet, to flee through Austria and Hungary. Gorbachev used the occasion of the fortieth anniversary of the establishment of the East German People's Republic on October 6 to visit Berlin and tell the East Germans to adopt Soviet-style reforms, and the floodgates opened. Subsequent demonstrations in Berlin, Dresden, and Leipzig were broken up by police, but a few days later, 50,000 and then 100,000 demonstrators marched in Leipzig without opposition. Honecker's instructions to fire on the demonstrators were apparently personally countermanded by State Security Chief Egon Krentz. On October 18, Honecker resigned. More demonstrations followed: 500,000 marched in East Berlin on November 4. The entire cabinet resigned on November 7; the Wall opened up on November 9, establishing free passage between East and West Germany; and in December, to all intents and purposes, East Germany abandoned Communism. Numerous leaders were arrested for various forms of corruption, and a roundtable of remaining party and opposition leaders agreed to hold free elections within six months.

In Moscow, in early February 1990, Chancellor Helmut Kohl of West Germany found Gorbachev ready to concede that it was up to the Germans to decide about reunification. Gorbachev now told Kohl that a united Germany could remain in NATO, in return for which Kohl agreed to accept continued German weapons limitations and also to accept the presence of Russian troops for another four years. (The German government would later pay $8.2 billion to help rehouse Russian soldiers in Russia.) On July 17, in Paris, the two Germanies and the four previous occupying powers—France, the United Kingdom, the United States, and the Soviet Union—guaranteed the Polish borders. On September 12, in Moscow, the four powers plus the two Germanies signed the "Treaty on the final settlement with respect to Germany." On October 3, 1990, what had been unthinkable for so long took place: the formal reunification of Germany. Gorbachev had abruptly reversed forty years of Soviet policy, in which East Germany was a key player in the Warsaw Pact—or in which, as an alternative, Germany might be united, but only as a disarmed neutral, outside NATO—a position he had reiterated as late as June 1990 in an address at Stanford University.

Many unbelieving Western commentators were still unable to grasp that Communism was finished in Eastern Europe. When, in the autumn of 1989, the demonstrations began that would bring down the German Democratic Republic, many noted that the Czechs, as they expected, were simply more passive before their own repressive government, which cracked down hard on relatively small numbers of demonstrators in early November—there were 1,500 students at one demonstration, and then 2,000 at a subsequent one protesting the death of a student at the first. On November 20, as if to give the lie to foreign observers, 200,000 marched in Prague to demand free elections and the resignation of the Communist Party leader. Civic Forum, an opposition organization formed by playwright Vaclav Havel and others, now met with the government. Within a few days, Havel addressed a crowd of 800,000 in Prague to denounce attempts by the government to hang on through resignations and reorganizations. By the end of November, the leading role of the Communist Party was gone. Within a month, a returned Alexander Dubcek—the leader of the Prague Spring of 1968—was chairman of the newly elected Parliament, and Vaclav Havel was its president, in what came to be called the "velvet revolution." Free elections were to be held in June 1990, and negotiations began for the withdrawal of Soviet troops—whose entry into Czechoslovakia in 1968 was declared "not justified" by the Parliament.

Civic Forum and its allied party in Slovakia swept the June elections in 1990. Slovak separatism nevertheless intruded: proposals for political restructuring involving either confederation or federation fell by the wayside, and in June planning began for splitting the country in two. Negotiations leading to a constitutional amendment in November brought a difficult independence to Slovakia on January 1, 1993; late in the month, Vaclav Havel was elected president of the new and more Western-oriented Czech Republic.

By mid-June 1991, the last Russian troops left both Hungary and Czechoslovakia.

In Romania the long-lived Ceausescu regime, which had received Richard Nixon with such enthusiasm twenty years earlier and had followed a path of resistance to Soviet foreign policy (condemning the invasion of Czechoslovakia in 1968), became increasingly repressive across the years. Nicolae Ceausescu and his wife Elena instituted a cult of personality that outdid even that of Stalin. But an extraordinary scenario played itself out over a six-week period in the last months of 1989. Seemingly impervious to what was going on in the rest of Eastern Europe, Ceausescu spoke for a full five hours to the Fourteenth Congress of the Romanian Communist Party on November 12, 1989—three days after the Wall came down in Berlin—calling the party the "vital center" of Romanian political life, and receiving unanimous reelection as party general-secretary. On December 18, while demonstrators battled security forces in the town of Timisoara, Ceausescu still felt free to fly to Iran for a state visit. Returning earlier than planned, on December 20, he denounced the demonstrators on television as "fascist reactionary groups."

Then, the next day, the unbelieving Great Leader found himself shouted down as he addressed an open-air meeting in front of the Presidential Palace in Bucharest. When the army joined demonstrators a day later, it was all over. Ceausescu and his wife fled into hiding, but were arrested after twenty-four hours. They were tried and executed by a special military tribunal on Christmas Day. Fighting between security forces and the army ended, and opposition leader Ion Iliescu, a former Central Committee member ousted by Ceausescu, formed a government pledged to hold free elections in April 1990.

In contrast to events in other Eastern European countries, however, this was a palace coup rather than a revolution, and Iliescu used the state apparatus to repress dissent and destroy opposition party headquarters. Old members of the nomenklatura remained in place; unrest continued as right-wing nationalist parties emerged, laying claims to areas inhabited by Romanians in Moldavia and the Ukraine (both of which became independent when the Soviet Union broke up in 1991). The economy did badly. But Iliescu hung on; was accepted as a member of the Council of Europe in 1993; and aligned himself with a traditional ally, Serbia, following the breakup of Yugoslavia (see below).

Communist authorities in Bulgaria were traditionally readier to follow Soviet leadership than were those in other Eastern European states. They gave some lip service to glasnost and reform within the party, ejecting long-time leaders and renaming the Communist Party the Bulgarian Socialist Party (BSP). Other parties were allowed to organize. June 1990 elections gave the ruling BSP 47 percent of votes, but opposition parties soon formed an unstable but long-lasting coalition, while former Communist administrators managed to keep some measure of hold over the economy. As in other former Communist countries, there was an early plunge in the economy and then there were the beginnings of recovery. By 1994, the government was agitating to join NATO and thereby to form a "security triangle" in the Balkans with Greece and Turkey. Late in the year it assumed the six-month presidency of the Council of Europe, to which it had been admitted earlier.

Tiny Albania remained the last Stalinist country. In past years it had broken both with the Soviet Union and then with China over the issue of revisionism. Following the death of its long-time leader Enver Hoxha, it could finally no longer resist the tides of change in either the Soviet Union or Eastern Europe. Liberalization began in 1990; the Democratic Party of Albania took over the shaky reins of government in the impoverished state following elections in 1992. Tensions with Greece over minorities and over the fate of newly independent Macedonia—formerly a part of Yugoslavia—remained high, but not as high as those over another remnant of Yugoslavia, the Albanian-populated region of Kosovo, which threatened to become an area of open conflict with the Serbian-dominated successor state, the unrecognized Federation of Yugoslavia.

Ironically, Albania was the first Eastern European country to formally request admission to NATO and to initiate close military cooperation with the United States.

The End of Comecon and the Warsaw Pact

The Council on Mutual Economic Assistance had been created in 1949, as the Russian-sponsored answer to the Marshall Plan. On June 28, 1991, members signed an agreement in Budapest to put Comecon out of business. On July 1 in Prague the Eastern Europeans and the USSR agreed to disband the Warsaw Pact. Within the next three years, 540,000 Red Army soldiers and civilians left East Germany—the last of them on September 1, 1994— along with 2,600,000 tons of equipment, including thousands of tanks, artillery pieces, and airplanes, and 700,000 tons of ammunition. Only the monuments to Russian defeat of the Nazis remained.

It was all a little hard to digest. In 1989 Gorbachev still hoped that the Soviet Union would remain a central European power. But his repudiation of the Brezhnev Doctrine eviscerated the logic of his unfolding military strategy and arms control initiatives of 1989. By mid-1991, it was all over: the Eastern European bloc so long under Soviet domination was gone.

The Demise of Yugoslavia

Yugoslavia, it has been said, consisted of six republics, five peoples, four languages, three religions, two alphabets, and one party. It was created following World War I out of an assemblage of mainly disparate South Slavs. It lay across the fault line between, on the one hand, Catholics and Orthodox Christians, most of whom had been under Austro-Hungarian control, and, on the other, Muslims, whose presence was a legacy of Ottoman Turkish control of much of the region until the war. What had been from 1918 to 1929 the Kingdom of Serbs, Croats and Slovenes became in 1945 a union of five peoples, as Montenegrins and Macedonians, previously subsumed as Slavs, took on their own identity. In 1967 it became a union of six, when Bosnia was added, as the term "Muslim" became official for Muslims who spoke Serbo-Croat in the country—perhaps because of Tito's wooing of the primarily Muslim Third World. In the interwar period, a unitary state existed under Serb domination. During World War II, Bulgarian, Italian, and Hungarian claims over Yugoslavia brought dismemberment and fratricidal warfare, in which a million died. In Croatia, the Catholic fascist satellite state of Nazi Germany, the Ustashi militia carried out horrific repression of the Serb minority within the state.

The genius of Marshal Tito, in the post–World War II years, lay in his capacity to run a federal, largely decentralized state under the domination of the single Communist League, which he headed, despite Soviet attempts to subvert him through appeals to Serb resentment of other nationalities (Tito himself was of Croat and Slovene origin), and despite the complex legacy of rivalries of the past. Tito successfully defied Stalin, flirted with NATO membership, and became a globally recognized Third World leader while encouraging Yugoslav ties to the West. At the time of his death in 1980, Yugoslavia appeared to be prosperous and stable, a world leader, with almost a quarter century of economic growth, and with a 1974 constitution that would create a new, collegial presidency.

Unfortunately, the image covered a reality of deep foreign indebtedness as a result of domestic failure to invest and a resulting economic decline that put strains on relations between the wealthier republics within the country—particularly Slovenia in the north—and the poorer ones. Bipolarism and the Soviet threat and then the opportunity of Third World leadership were among the main unifying factors Tito could use to keep rival particularisms from emerging. Where he failed was in creating an institutional basis to keep ethnic hostilities in check. Following his death and the end of Communism, all the rivalries rose again, and the nature of the federation came into question.

The wealthier Slovenia and Croatia both wanted a loose confederation. Serbia argued for a tighter federation for reasons of economic necessity (but its leader, Slobodan Milosevic, was suspected, correctly, of hegemonic aspirations by the others). Bosnia and Macedonia, attached to keeping the country together and fearful of their fate if it broke up, tried to mediate. In addition, Serbia disputed territorial boundaries, arguing that the substantial Serbian minorities within Croatia and Bosnia should be able to choose their own destinies. (Bosnia was 44 percent Muslim, 31 percent Serb, and 18 percent Croat.) The weak existing federal government, democratically elected and market-oriented, was supported by both the British and the Bush Administration, who thought it better to keep Yugoslavia intact.

When talks about the nature of the federation failed in 1991, Slovenia and Croatia opted for independence. The move sealed the fate of Bosnia, which could either remain under what would clearly be Serb domination in a truncated Yugoslavia, or could opt for independence, which it ultimately chose to do.

Chaos erupted as the Serbs moved to create a greater Serbia. In Croatia the Serb-dominated Yugoslav army moved in rapidly to help Serb minorities and occupy a quarter of the area (which had never belonged to Serbia). Bosnia, where a more tolerant government would have certainly granted a

Map 14. Yugoslavia's Constituent Republics and the Distribution of Ethnic Groups (Pre-Conflict)

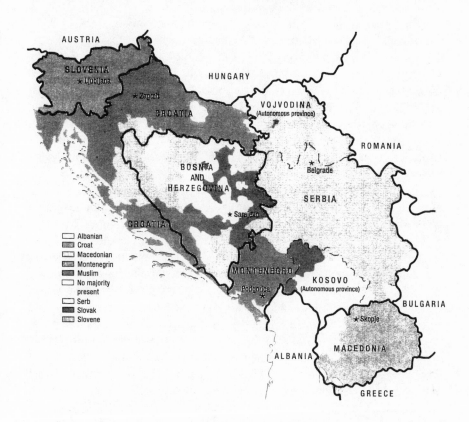

Source: CIA

measure of autonomy to its Serb minorities, now found itself invaded by Serbs supported from Belgrade and a resulting uprising by its own Serbs, who declared several areas "Serb Autonomous Regions." In justification, it must be said that Serbs in Croatia bore vivid memories of the wartime horrors perpetrated by the Croatian Ustashi; there are commentators who believe Bosnian Muslims might not have been as tolerant as some believe.

In December 1991, the European Community, under German pressure, recognized Croatia and Slovenia and offered recognition to Bosnia and Macedonia. Bosnians voted in favor of independence on February 29, 1992, and the European Community recognized it on April 6. Serbia used the occasion to loose its irregulars; to arm them; and, as the Croatian fighting died down, to release more federal troops to support the Bosnian Serbs. In March 1992, before any country had recognized Bosnian independence, Bosnian Serbs declared a "Serbian Republic."

Over the next three years the fighting in Bosnia between Bosnian Serbs and Bosnian Muslims continued almost unchecked—along with mass rape; the creation of concentration camps; and "ethnic cleansing," the terrorizing of civilian populations to make them flee. A fairly early count reported 250,000 Muslim refugees in Germany and 600,000 in Croatia. Further complications were provided by warfare between Croatians and Muslim Bosnians, and by other elements: tacit Russian support for their old Slavic friends the Serbs, Middle Eastern charges that the West was leaving Bosnia to its fate because it was Muslim, and the fact that fighting groups were under little centralized command or control.

The international community failed to resolve the complicated issues. Humanitarian aid saved thousands of lives. Threats from the administration of President Bill Clinton may have kept the Serbs from military action in Kosovo (whose autonomy within the rump Yugoslav Federation, however, the federal government formally ended). The United Nations also voted an arms embargo into the region, which did little to stop the flow of arms into Serbia. (As the Bosnian war shows, the end of the Cold War has released enormous quantities of weapons of all kinds onto the world scene to feed local conflicts.) In all else it failed, despite a public outcry for some form of multilateral intervention to stop the horrors taking place in Bosnia. (How, people asked, could a war in Europe be tolerated now that the Soviet threat was gone—a war that they could watch on television every night and, what was worse, a war that was directed against civilians?) Wary Bush and Clinton administrations stood aside, using the excuse that there would be little congressional support for an uncertain intervention that would cost American lives. They were convinced that it was up to Europe, now that the Russian threat had waned, to put its own house in order. Americans rejected European and UN plans for a division of Bosnia, which were thought to "reward aggression." But rejection of partition meant that any intervention would be to restore all of Bosnia—a formula for large-scale warfare in unsuitable territory.

Despite all the superstructure of supranationalism, war in Bosnia showed that "Europe" did not yet really exist: Western countries had different policy orientations and followed different policies. Germany, by pushing hasty action to recognize Slovenia and Croatia, gave rise to renewed fears of German hegemony in old spheres of influence; France retained old ties to Serbia, although President François Mitterrand sought to ease foreign fears by his symbolic visit to the besieged Bosnian capital of Sarajevo in mid-

1992; Britain sought to mediate in a way that would avoid any continental intervention—but that would, inevitably, "reward Serbian aggression" unless unified sanctions or pressures could be brought against Serbia.

For humanitarian aid to get through to isolated communities required armed protection against marauders. The UN sought to provide this, as well as to send peacekeeping forces: between mid 1992 and the end of 1994, a total of 44,000 troops, observers, and civilian personnel were sent to the area. Critics warned that without a peace, "peacekeeping" troops could serve as hostages. They were proved right when on several occasions Serbs seized UN troops. Six "security zones" for civilians were created and frequently violated: in mid-1995, when Bosnian Serbs overran several of these while lightly armed UN troops stood helplessly by, they slaughtered thousands of civilians. In the meantime, the UN War Crimes Tribunal had been created in The Hague, seat of the International Court, and the principal Bosnian Serb leaders had been indicted (making compromise with them somewhat difficult).

In March 1994, following an uneasy truce, a shaky Muslim-Croat federation was created. In 1995 Croats drove Bosnian Serbs from several strong points, heartening and strengthening Bosnian Muslim resistance. UN economic sanctions—frequently observed in the breach—had been voted against Serbia earlier, and Serbia tried to get them removed by promising to stop the flow of arms to the Bosnian Serbs. NATO, in a complicated command arrangement that now involved the United States (stung to move, finally, when Americans by the millions saw the results of the shelling of a central marketplace in Sarajevo, the long-besieged Bosnian capital), carried out isolated air strikes against Serb strong points that violated cease-fire agreements.

By late 1995, with Croat and some Bosnian Serb military successes, and Serbian desire to end its isolation, and in the face of manifest impossibility for European action, the Clinton Administration opted to intervene. In essence, it was ready to enforce a partition plan which it had earlier rejected. At a meeting in Dayton, Ohio, it pressured all the parties to accept unwelcome partition lines within a loosely structured confederation, and to accept the replacement of lightly armed UN forces with much more heavily armed NATO troops who could respond to provocation as the UN forces had been unable to do. NATO forces, including 20,000 Americans, were to stay only until the end of 1996. International aid was to help rebuild the shattered economy of the area; the Bosnian Muslim armed forces were to be equipped and retrained; joint governmental institutions were to be created for the Muslim and Serbian parts of Bosnia. It appeared, as in the past, that without American leadership, little could be accomplished in resolving many conflicts.

As of this writing, the outcome of these Dayton Peace Accords is still uncertain.

Dissolution of the Soviet Union

Although the Soviet empire dissolved in 1989, the Soviet Union lived on— as a very different country from that of Stalin's time. Khrushchev had largely destroyed one pillar of Stalinist Russia, mass terror. Substantial economic growth in the 1950s and 1960s slowed sharply by the late 1970s, but many people lived relatively comfortably. Few people believed in official propaganda anymore, corruption was endemic, and cynicism ran rampant, particularly among the intelligentsia. Power had become somewhat decentralized; the existence of a parallel market to that of regular channels meant that a good part of the economy was not under central control. The change was accompanied by the emergence of a managerial class and of sophisticated technological experts who had access to Western information. It all gave rise to analysis in the West that "convergence" between Western and Soviet societies would eventually take place: they would become more and more alike. Most observers concluded that the Soviet Union was on fairly solid ground.

"Gorby! Gorby! Gorby!"

In 1989, when the Russians withdrew from Afghanistan and the Vietnamese from Cambodia, large numbers of Soviet troops pulled back from the Chinese border. As a result, Soviet Premier Mikhail Gorbachev visited Beijing in mid-1989 to renew friendly relations with China. A million students and workers interrupted the visit to demonstrate in favor of democracy, which Gorbachev seemed to represent. When Gorbachev went to West Germany a month later, he was greeted with shouts of "Gorby! Gorby! Gorby" by masses in the streets, and in a public opinion poll, Germans voted him the most trustworthy politician and world leader. Yet, a year and a half after the demise of Communism in Eastern Europe, the Soviet Union that had existed for seventy years, and had withstood the mighty Nazi onslaught to become a global power of unprecedented military strength, suddenly and completely collapsed. Communism disappeared, and Marxism-Leninism largely disappeared with it. It was, in a word, extraordinary.

Both glasnost—open discussion—and perestroika—restructuring—had much to do with the collapse. Glasnost allowed the whole system and its past to come into question. The collapse of governments in Eastern Europe contributed. Rather than energize the system, Gorbachev's erratic domestic policies and reforms led to chaos, recession, inflation, and shortages by mid-1990. In 1991, production dropped disastrously. In the end, it appears that while all these developments eroded the power of Moscow, it was resurgent nationalism and ethnic assertion in the constituent republics—and the hostility of Boris Yeltsin when he was elected president of the Russian Federation—that sealed the fate of Gorbachev and of the Soviet Union in December 1991.

Resurgent Nationalism

In 1989, as glasnost produced more and more revelations about the past, the Soviet Union finally acknowledged one historical reality it had long denied: that the Hitler-Stalin pact of August 1939 had indeed had (as everyone outside the Soviet bloc knew) a secret protocol handing over the independent Baltic states of Latvia, Lithuania and Estonia to the Russians. The Soviet Union formally annexed these states in May 1940. Now, the fiction that they had simply joined the USSR because they wanted to could no longer be maintained.*

On August 24, 1989, fifty years to the day after the signing of the Nazi-Soviet pact, a 400-mile-long human chain of more than a million citizens of the three countries linked their capital cities, demonstrating in favor of independence. During the years of the Cold War, no one in the West had taken very seriously the notion that these three small countries could ever again become independent of the Soviet Union: unlike the other countries of Eastern Europe, they had been directly incorporated into the USSR. Now, with extraordinary rapidity, the movement gained such strength that it posed a major problem for Gorbachev. His conservative opposition saw it as a direct result of glasnost, a threat to the unity of the Soviet Union that could be emulated elsewhere—in the Ukraine, where latent nationalism had always challenged Russian hegemony; in Uzbekistan, where rioting in the spring of 1989 left a hundred dead and thousands homeless; in Transcaucasia, where ethnic groups were at each other's throats. In the space of a few short months, Baltic leaders began to debate not whether they could achieve independence, but how to proceed, blurring the whole picture of politics within the Soviet Union.

---

*There were other shocking revelations as archives opened up: Foreign Minister Shevardnaze acknowledged that the Katyn Massacre of the Polish officer corps was carried out by Russia, not by the Nazis, as the Russians had long tried to prove; Russia had simply lied about items long in dispute during arms control negotiations, such as a giant radar array at Krasnoyarsk that violated the ABM treaty; it had almost always lied about numbers of weapons.

Within the Soviet Union, hundreds of informal groups began to take a political stance, and to create parties that were still formally illegal. Gorbachev himself was responsible: he had supported freedom of action of informal groups in order to bolster perestroika against his conservative opponents. On March 26, 1989, partially free local elections brought dissidents to power in many cities. By the end of 1989, events had moved beyond Gorbachev, who was still trying to reform the Communist Party and keep it in control. In Moscow, the rehabilitated nuclear physicist Andrei Sakharov called for a debate on the leading role of the Party in the Soviet Union, a debate only temporarily averted by Gorbachev, who also ruled out secession of any constituent republic. Within a month, however, in the face of massive demonstrations in Moscow, he reversed course and led the Congress of People's Deputies, whose members were intimidated by the demonstrators, to accept a multiparty system in the Soviet Union.

All through 1990, upheaval in non-Russian areas affected a now-emerging battle between Boris Yeltsin—a somewhat erratic former member of the Politburo, elected to the Russian Parliament and soon named as its speaker—and Gorbachev. In March 1990 Gorbachev had brought sanctions against Lithuania for its parliamentary declaration of independence (and George Bush had backed off from sanctions against the USSR for so doing, provoking the Lithuanian president to call Bush's action "a new Munich"); in May he made a demonstration of military force in Latvia. There were riots in Tajikistan and Kyrghyzia; unrest began in the Ukraine, continued in Georgia, and led the Moldavian government to make Moldavian the official language and to plan for its own special defense force.

Despite his trouble at home, Gorbachev still traveled abroad: early in December 1990 he met with the pope in Rome. The pope endorsed Gorbachev's reforms, and Gorbachev, in return, promised legalization of full religious rights and a move to establishing diplomatic relations. In a new blow, however, on December 20, Foreign Minister Eduard Shevardnaze resigned, saying that he foresaw a dictatorship emerging in Russia; three weeks later, Russian armed forces were ordered by Gorbachev to begin a military crackdown in Lithuania, and Boris Yeltsin proposed that Russia recognize the Lithuanian government as independent. The battle was now in the open. Two months later, Yeltsin called on Gorbachev to resign for trying to hold onto the system, for not allowing independence for the constituent republics, and for leading the country toward a dictatorship under the guise of a strong presidency.

In April 1991 Gorbachev again traveled abroad, this time to Japan and Korea, where he promised to reduce the Soviet military presence in Asia, called for investment in the Soviet Union, and agreed to a tenfold increase in trade with South Korea. That same month, the parliament of Georgia voted unanimously for independence, provoking Gorbachev—who was still trying to hold the Union together—into a new attempt at concessions in a painfully drafted new Union treaty. In July, the parliament suggested a new program for the Communist Party that would wholly change its ideology—calling for a free market economy, for individual rights, and for private ownership of property. In the meantime, on June 12, 1991, Boris Yeltsin became the first freely elected president of the Russian Federated Republic and walked out of the Communist Party along with the mayors of Moscow and Leningrad (which was soon, to the astonishment of the outside world, to be renamed St. Petersburg).

While Yeltsin in the Russian Federated Republic drafted a radical 500-day privatization plan and called for creation of a loose confederation to replace the USSR, Gorbachev—telling the Supreme Soviet that "the system is no longer there; it's gone"—tried hard to come up with acceptable alternatives.

The August 1991 Coup

In the face of internal chaos and the decline of any Soviet presence on the world scene, on August 19, 1991, disgruntled conservatives overthrew Gorbachev. They proclaimed a state of emergency, banned demonstrations, closed newspapers, and outlawed political parties. The eight-man junta included Gorbachev's vice-president, the chairman of the secret police, the prime minister, the ministers of defense and of the interior, and others. They were representatives of what should have been the most powerful remaining groups from the past; their remaining power would have been stripped by the loose new Union treaty. Their coup failed dismally. Although they kept Gorbachev sequestered in Crimea and seized control of radio and television in Moscow, they failed to realize how much glasnost had freed communications from central control, how much power had devolved to other centers. The Red Army, long a pillar of the regime, stood by as Boris Yeltsin mounted the opposition to the coup, gathered a crowd of a 100,000 before the parliament building, and had the junta arrested. In the process, he sealed the death warrant of the Soviet Union, for it was he, as president of the Russian Republic, who had demonstrated the real power, not Gorbachev.

Gorbachev, still with the support of Western powers, returned to Moscow; resigned from the Communist Party, whose upper echelons had supported the junta; and suspended its activities throughout the country. He was still trying to keep the Union together, but on August 20 all three Baltic states declared independence; on December 3 the Ukraine followed suit. On December 8 Yeltsin, as president of the Russian Federation, and the presidents of the Ukraine and Byelorussia (now Belarus)—the core of the "Slavic Union" that exiled writer Aleksandr Solzhenitsyn had long called for—announced the formation of the Commonwealth of Independent States (CIS): acting on behalf of the republics that had founded the Soviet Union in 1922, they declared an end to the "fiction" of its existence. They were soon joined by other Soviet republics. The move meant the demise of the Union of Soviet Socialist Republics and its replacement by the new, loose, undefined Commonwealth. On December 25, 1991, bowing to the inevitable, Mikhail Gorbachev resigned as president of the Soviet Union in a grim, live television broadcast. He relinquished his command over the Soviet armed forces and conferred upon Yeltsin command over 28,000 nuclear weapons. The red hammer-and-sickle banner was hauled down throughout Moscow, to be replaced by the white, blue, and red Russian flag.

The Soviet Union was gone. All over the world people wept, laughed, celebrated, and mourned for the millions of dead. They mourned, too, the death of an ideal so many had believed in and fought for, but against which so many had ultimately turned as its awful reality and its failure became apparent.

The Commonwealth of Independent States

The death of the Soviet Union led to years of upheaval throughout the territory formerly within its purview, and little can be understood without looking at a map.

Russia lost its borders with Eastern Europe: Belarus and the Ukraine and Moldavia (now Moldova) now separated it from Poland, Slovakia, and Romania. To the southwest, it was separated from Turkey and Iran by the Transcaucasian states of Georgia, Armenia, and Azerbaijan, while to the south it no longer had borders with Iran or Afghanistan, and its border with China was much reduced: the Central Asian successor states of Kazakhstan, Turkmenistan, Uzbekistan, Tajikistan, and Kyrgyzstan were the new border states. Most of the new states were landlocked, which meant that their ties to the rest of the world crossed other countries. Only a handful bordered the Russian Republic, which meant their ties to Russia crossed other CIS states. Geopolitically, their hard-won independence and sovereignty looked fragile.

The Nature of the CIS

Enormous problems and numerous issues accompanied the dissolution of the USSR—problems and issues concerning such matters as: whether the

Map 15. The Commonwealth of Independent States

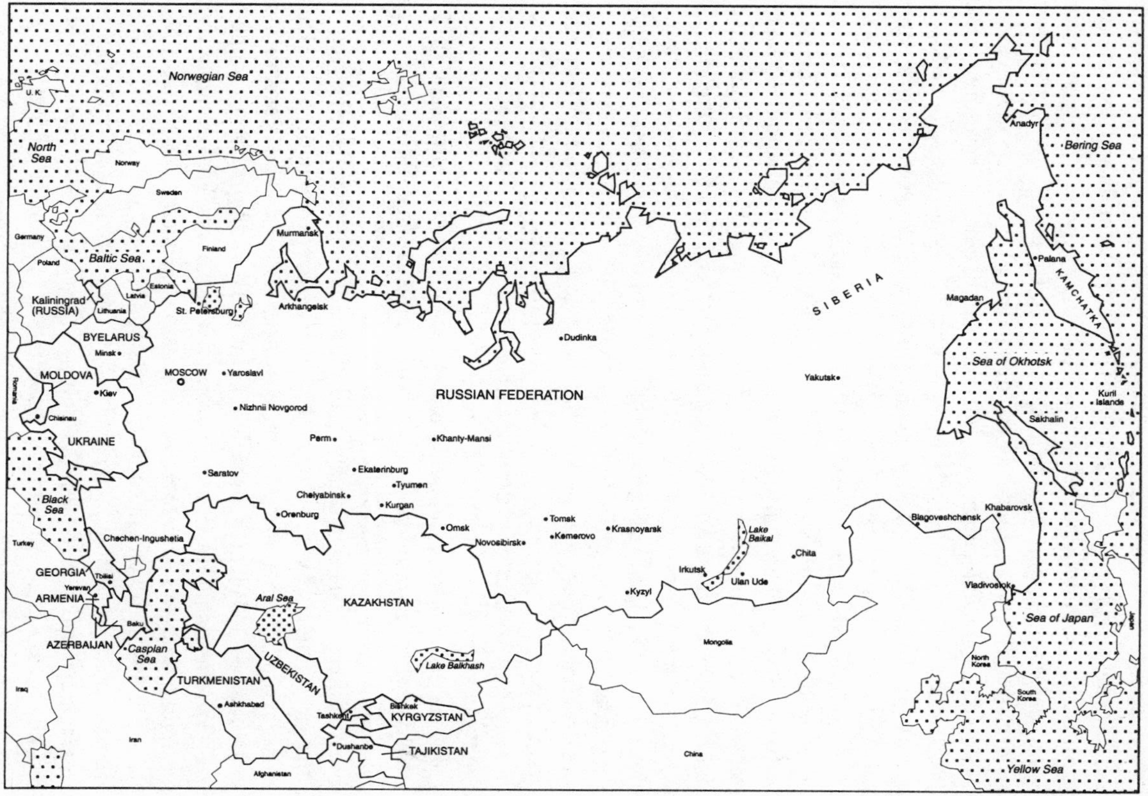

new states would have their own armed forces; whether specifically Russian forces would be withdrawn from the successor states; who would control nuclear forces and who would decide whether strategic weapons would be moved back to Russia; and how weapons agreements signed by Russia would apply to successor states. Twenty-six million Russians living as minorities within the successor states loomed large as a problem: minorities issues haunted almost all the successors. Border issues would have to be settled and governmental assets divided, and the issue of whether the CIS could establish a common ruble zone would have to be resolved. Moreover, groups within the largely Muslim Central Asian states looked to relations with Turkey, Iran, and Afghanistan to balance relations with Russia, while pro-Russians opposed them.

Yet, for all the member states of the CIS, including Russia, the major problem was that not only must a new, legitimate political order be created but there must also be a different economic order which would allow these states to find their place in the global economy. One development that surprised observers but should have been foreseen was that many old Communist functionaries—members of the nomenklatura—would maintain, move into, or reclaim key roles within a short time: they were the ones with know-how. It was significant, too, that throughout Eastern Europe and the former Soviet Union, there was little retribution against former Communist leaders and activists, whatever their roles had been in the repressive regimes. Many soon resumed political roles and reconstituted local Communist Parties under new names.

Latvia, Estonia, and Lithuania never contemplated joining the CIS. They looked toward Germany and Scandinavia, and Latvia and Estonia had trouble with Russia over the large Russian minorities within their borders. In token of their Western orientation, all three, having established a free trade zone among themselves in April 1994, also became members of the Council of Europe, and adhered to the Partnership for Peace, which was proposed on December 3, 1993, by President Clinton as an alternative to immediate NATO membership for Eastern European nations. The Partnership provided for a limited degree of cooperation that would be acceptable to the Russians (see page 244). Lithuanian soldiers and ships actually participated in NATO exercises in 1994. On January 1, 1995, the free trade agreement that these three nations had signed with the European Union in 1994 came into effect, and all three sought an ultimate association agreement similar to that of Eastern European countries. Of the three, Estonia was much the most prosperous (and looked more toward Finland and Sweden), and Lithuania was the poorest (and tended to exploit its historic ties to Poland and central Europe).

In a somewhat euphoric period following the collapse of the USSR in December 1991, all kinds of possibilities seemed open: with substantial help from the west, Russia would rejoin that "Common European Home" Gorbachev had talked about, CIS states would become market-oriented democracies that would share in Western prosperity and join Western institutions like NATO or the European Union. It was exhilarating and misleading. Western aid was substantial—though European recession and American deficits limited it—but CIS states had to create stable monetary systems and institute market reforms, with new legal norms to ensure the efficacy of whatever aid was provided. This was no easy task, particularly given the seventy years of socialism and the weakness of, and struggles over, new political systems. In several states, open conflicts precluded economic progress. In addition, Russia gradually reasserted its primacy in what it came to call "the near abroad"—the territory of much of the former Soviet Union as well as Eastern Europe.

Until June 15, 1993, eighteen months after the demise of the Soviet Union, the army under the CIS Joint Armed Forces Command remained the last all-Union institution in the former USSR. It did not last, as CIS members began to create their own armed forces, but the primacy of Russia and of Russian armed forces has since been reasserted: Russia insisted before the UN that it had primary responsibility for peacekeeping within the region of the CIS and planned its own Rapid Deployment Force.

Conflict in the CIS

In early 1995, in a move that gravely weakened reform in Russia, Yeltsin launched an ill-prepared Russian army against separatism in the territory of Chechnya (see page 244). At the same time, as Eastern European states looked to the West for trade, aid, and support for their new regimes—including, as several insisted, inclusion in NATO as a precaution against a possibly resurgent Russia—the Russian regime hardened its position against such a development. It would view membership in NATO as a hostile move. (Only in mid-1996, following Boris Yeltsin's reelection as president, were there hints that it might accept East European states accession to NATO if the West accepted certain conditions.)

In the meantime, there occurred severe conflicts within several successor states: in Georgia, once one of the richest and most cosmopolitan of Soviet republics; in the Ukraine with its rich agricultural lands and numerous Black Sea ports; in Armenia and Azerbaijan, where there was bitter fighting over the Armenian-inhabited enclave of Nagorno-Karabakh, deep in Azerbaijan; and in Tajikistan. In all these states, ethnic conflicts were accompanied by separatist tendencies, often linked to differences in levels of economic development.

Ukrainian leaders had looked forward to making the Republic a bridge between West and East, and the hope of Western aid helped bring the massive vote for independence on December 1, 1991—despite trade dependence on the Soviet Union and despite the fact that the latter provided all the oil and gas necessary for Ukrainian industry. (After a rocky start in relations with the United States, by 1995 the Ukraine became the fourth-largest recipient of U.S. foreign aid, after Israel, Egypt, and Russia.) Khrushchev, who was of Ukrainian origin, had made Ukraine the dubious gift of the Crimean Peninsula in 1954, unknowingly complicating the future forty years later: the largest Russian Black Sea naval base was located on the peninsula, and its predominantly Russian population sought an autonomy denied by the Ukraine but supported by Russia. Division of the Black Sea Fleet proved a thorny issue, with most of it ending back up in Russian hands, while the status of Crimea remained under dispute.

Attempts by several CIS states to create their own currencies failed: they ended up within the ruble bloc. In January 1994 a summit meeting of Turkish-language states failed to take place as a result of Russian pressures. The effort of several successor states to use Turkish influence to balance that of Russia seemed to have been checked. The emergence of right-wing nationalism in Russia had much to do with Russian reassertion of its sphere of influence.

All this represented a shift within the former Soviet Union, from the first heady days when liberals accepted the independence of the Baltic states and looked to their own partnership with the West.

Winding Down the Cold War

Before the collapse of the Soviet Union, at the end of June 1991, Gorbachev and President Bush had signed the first agreement on actual reduction of strategic weapons, a reduction of 30 percent over a seven-year period. Two months later, both leaders called for even greater reductions in strategic weapons, and Bush, arguing that a Soviet invasion of Western Europe was "no longer a realistic threat," announced the withdrawal of tactical nuclear weapons from Europe and Asia.

With the Soviet Union dead and gone, Bush met with Yeltsin in June 1992; they agreed to further reductions, and their agreement was turned into a formal treaty in December. The treaty was signed on January 3, 1993. Called START II (for Strategic Arms Reduction Talks—a follow-up to START I), it promised a two-thirds reduction in strategic weapons, the elimination of land-based multiple warhead missiles, and warhead reductions to 3,500 for the United States and to 3,000 for the Soviet Union by the year 2003. The Ukraine, Belarus, and Kazakhstan agreed at a meeting in Lisbon in May 1992 to give up Soviet weapons in their territories (which they had seen as a bargaining chip). The Ukraine stalled and finally consented to carry out the agreement only in January 1994, in return for a joint territorial guarantee and the cancellation of its enormous debt to Moscow. The United States was prepared to spend well over a billion dollars to help the four republics destroy the weapons (a delicate and costly operation). Bureaucratic politics on both sides greatly slowed the process.

A critical consequence of the collapse of the Soviet Union is that arms control agreements will result in liberating close to 500,000 kilograms of enriched uranium and 60,000 kilograms of plutonium. It takes fifteen kilograms of uranium or six of plutonium to make a nuclear weapon, and the temptation to sell the enormously valuable stock is very great, given the economic problems and the degree of corruption within the CIS. (In addition, in 1995, American Senator Jesse Helms of North Carolina single-handedly held up Senate consideration of the SALT II treaty until such time as the Department of State undertook administrative reorganizations upon which he personally insisted.)

Yeltsin's Russia

Boris Yeltsin was determined to press forward with the economic and political reforms he had accused Gorbachev of dragging his feet on: privatization and the creation of a market economy with Western help, and the creation of democratic institutions. In the countryside, the peasantry and existing institutions resisted; in the cities, some people enriched themselves enormously, and others fell into poverty, while crime became a way of life. Foreign investors were justifiably wary. Hyperinflation had all its usual effects on savings and fixed incomes. Anger and dissension increased, and the Communist period began to look rosy.

With the complex legacy of an ancient Russian past and a long-lasting Communist system, there was little agreement over what kind of society Russia should develop: even the reemerged Russian Orthodox Church was divided over whether to cooperate with a secular state or to insist on reestablishing a theocracy, and whether to tolerate Protestants and Catholics. Western aid was resented: it humiliated many Russians who felt they had now assumed the role of the Africans whom they themselves had been proudly helping in the past. Moreover, Russia itself was a federation of some eighty-nine states and felt the kind of secessionist pressures and resistance to central control that had developed earlier in the Soviet bloc. Old Communists harking back to Lenin and Stalin and the glory of the Soviet Union, and conservatives harking back to the glory of Czarist Russia and the Orthodox Church, were joined in an awkward opposition to reform.

Surprisingly, Yeltsin received a largely favorable response in a referendum he called in April 1993 on reform. He tried to capitalize on this response by convening a convention to draft a new, democratic constitution. In September 1994 he announced that he was dissolving parliament and calling for new elections. Parliament retaliated by dismissing Yeltsin and replacing him with his conservative vice-president. Besieged in the parliament building—the White House—the conservatives called for an assault on the Kremlin. Under a state of emergency, troops bombarded the White House, forcing out the insurgents. Yeltsin, now able to rule by decree, suspended local governments, privatized the land, and set new legislative elections for December.

The results were disastrous for Yeltsin, and largely unforeseen. All the accumulated grievances and dissatisfactions came to the surface. Though the democratic constitution passed by a tiny majority, old Communists and new nationalists took over the parliament in a "red-brown" alliance. The outstanding winner, who received 25 percent of votes, was the anti-Semitic, openly imperialist Vladimir Zhirinovski, now a force to be reckoned with.

Bit by bit, Yeltsin backed off from his reformist colleagues. Russia began to insist on the prerogatives of a great power again, asserting its special rights and responsibilities as the largest military, political, and economic power in the region. It moved to recreate a ruble zone. Foreign Minister Andrei Kozyrev, having expressed in numerous forums Russian intentions to carry out peacekeeping and mediation activities in the CIS, sent 20,000 troops into Tajikistan to support the president against Islamic fundamentalists; obtained UN support for the presence of Russian forces in Georgia, separating dissident Abkhazis from the rest of Georgia; and sent peacekeeping troops under UN aegis into Yugoslavia. Kozyrev and the military gave frequently repeated warnings to the West and to Eastern European leaders that NATO should not be extended to incorporate countries like Poland, Hungary, and the Czech Republic; they also reiterated their deep interest in the situation of the Russian minorities in the Baltic states. It was all far from the optimistic, Western-oriented stance of two years earlier.

War in Chechnya

Then, on December 12, 1994, after three years of inconclusive talks, Yeltsin ordered Russian troops to take over the tiny breakaway Chechen Republic in the Caucausus. Western countries, especially the United States, hesitated to criticize the move, terming it an internal matter, for Chechnya was one of Russia's eighty-eight constituent units. But as the people in the republic fought back and indiscriminate bombing of the capital Grozny turned it into a smoking ruin, the conflict became, inescapably, Boris Yeltsin's war. It was unpopular in Russia and roundly condemned abroad. The ill-paid army was unprepared for the ferocious resistance it encountered from the Chechens, an independent people who had been deported en masse under Stalin and returned to their homeland only after World War II. As criticism of indiscriminate killing of civilians mounted, the European Union suspended implementation of a trade treaty recently negotiated with Russia. In mid-January 1995, the Council of Europe tabled the Russian application for membership on the basis of violation of human rights in Chechnya. Angry Russian leaders lashed out in reply, clamping down on domestic critics. Conservatives attacked Yeltsin and the government for having allowed the revered Red Army to fall into decay, and army leaders themselves voiced their dismay.

The brutal repression in Chechnya was certainly carried out as a lesson to other states within the Russian Federation that might contemplate secession. In several Eastern European countries, the issue of NATO membership came back to the fore as fear of Russian reaction mounted. The Chechen affair put into grave doubt both the progress of reform in Russia and improvement of relations with the West. In December 1995, in new parliamentary elections, Yeltsin received another rebuff, as the reconstituted Communist Party received more than 20 percent of votes and called for a brake on reform and a return to many institutions of the Communist past. In the summer of 1996, however, President Yeltsin secured reelection in a runoff with the Communist candidate, partly as a consequence of an alliance he forged with a tough former Red Army general, whose political views were none too clear. The future path of the former Soviet Union was none too clear either, particularly in the light of Yeltsin's ill health.

Gorbachev secured 0.5 percent of the vote.

Conclusion

The Soviet Union was the last great multinational empire to collapse before the forces of national assertion—the Soviet Union that had existed for seventy years and had withstood the mighty Nazi onslaught to become a global power of unprecedented military strength.

In the eyes of history, Gorbachev will be the man responsible for the collapse, although the Brezhnev regime set the stage with its overly ambi-

246 THE END OF THE COLD WAR

tious expansiveness. Some will blame Gorbachev, as many Russians do now, for having opened a Pandora's box and released the troubles of the present; order under a somewhat repressive Communism was preferable to the present brutal chaos. Others will credit Gorbachev with having foreseen that matters could not go on, and with managing a peaceful transition, even though virtually all his holding policies failed.

The global effect of such a change could only be enormous. Unfortunately, the first elated sense that Russia and the other successor states would now become "normal" members of what Gorbachev had called the "Common European Home" dissipated rapidly. Nevertheless, Western European nations curtailed their armed forces while keeping their powder dry, and the United States continued to maintain a diminished military presence in Western Europe. NATO was formed back in 1949, as a NATO secretary-general once put it, "to keep the U.S. in, the Germans down, and the USSR out." Now the USSR no longer existed and the Germans were no longer down. Western foreign policies, the NATO mission, and security strategies had to be completely reassessed. Much depended upon what new successor states did, especially Russia.

In the rest of the world, where local conflicts had often been seen by Western powers within the context of an East-West balance, the issue of the balance was gone, as the Soviet Union pulled out. The results were not always what people hoped for. Struggles became once again only local conflicts; parties could no longer look to the Soviet Union for help, with the result that Americans themselves lost interest in many areas. On another plane, when Iraq invaded Kuwait and then itself came under attack by an American-organized coalition, Iraq could no longer look to the Soviet Union for support, as Arab states had done ever since Khrushchev's move to support Egypt in 1955. The playing off of East against West by third parties was no longer possible. Less developed countries' leaders complained that the West was now ready to help Eastern Europe or Russia at the expense of aid to their much more needy peoples. Marxist-Leninist solutions to problems of development lost much of their attractiveness.

Russia still retained the potential of being a great power. It was still the one country, apart from the United States, that possessed intercontinental nuclear weapons. What kind of policies it might follow as Russians struggled to build a new system remained a troubling puzzle. European leaders spent innumerable hours with their Eastern counterparts determining—soberly—the kind of relations that could be established in the new, reunited Europe, and built several halfway houses. In the meantime, Russia reasserted its interests in the area of the former Soviet Union, and tried to impress upon Eastern European states that they could not simply join Western European institutions without considering Russian reaction. A "cold peace" appeared to have replaced the Cold War, while local conflicts grew.

As the next chapters will show, the world had become a very different place.

Further Suggested Readings

For a Soviet view of NATO in the pre-Gorbachev years, see Anatoly Grishchenko et al., *Danger—NATO* (Moscow: Progress Publishers, 1985). There are enormous numbers of books on the collapse of the Soviet Union and its empire. Among the most interesting are Hélène Carrère D'Encausse, *The End of the Soviet Empire* (New York: Basic Books, 1993), and Anatoly Khazanov, *After the Soviet Empire: Ethnicity, Nationalism, and Politics in the CIS* (Madison: University of Wisconsin Press, 1995). On the collapse of Yugoslavia, see Richard West, *Tito and the Rise and Fall of Yugoslavia* (New York: Carroll and Graf, 1995), and Warren Zimmerman, *Origins of a Catastrophe: Yugoslavia and Its Destroyers* (New York: Times Books, 1996).

9

"The Winner"

At the outset of the 1980s, Brezhnev boasted that a third of the world's people now lived under Marxist-Leninist socialism. American President Jimmy Carter's humiliation over the Iranian hostage crisis only underscored the Europeans' fears that weakened and erratic American leadership against an expansionist Soviet Union was faltering badly, just when it was most needed.

This chapter moves backward in time to recount a strange story: how in the 1980s Western leaders reacted to the image of a triumphant Soviet Union by joining to take a hard line against it. The Cold War took on a new life just as Soviet economic weakness began to manifest itself. In the United States, President Ronald Reagan initiated the greatest military buildup in peacetime history and launched his startling and enormously expensive Strategic Defense Initiative (SDI), a program of defense against intercontinental ballistic missiles (ICBMs). Yet, as we have seen in the last chapter, the Soviet Union was overextended. Only the devices of propaganda covered the inherent weaknesses of its economy, weaknesses that could be glimpsed on a smaller scale in an Eastern Europe still under Soviet domination. It is still a matter of contention as to how much the Reagan buildup may have helped force the Soviet Union into bankruptcy.

In his first year Gorbachev reinforced Western views when he tried to maintain the impetus of Brezhnev's global thrust. But his rapid retrenchment caught Western leadership by surprise. In the latter half of the 1980s, Western leaders struggled to adjust to the downward spiral of Soviet power and to deal with a world in which the Soviet Union no longer supported radicals and revolutionaries who could offer them strategic advantage. The arch hard-liner, Ronald Reagan, surprised everyone by taking Gorbachev at his word, not only signing the first genuine disarmament agreement since 1922, but seeming to agree with the Russian that *all* nuclear missiles should be done away with.

With the unexpected dissolution of the Soviet empire and then of the Soviet Union itself, Western leaders floundered. NATO "downsized" and tried to redefine its mission, while in America the radical right now took up the cry of the radical left of the late 1960s: bring American soldiers home. But President George Bush took advantage of vanished Soviet presence in the Middle East to orchestrate a successful coalition war against Iraq following its invasion of Kuwait, and spoke grandly of a "New World Order"—which was not to be.

Everywhere leaders tried to adapt to changing reality. In Europe, under the leadership of EU Commission Chairman Jacques Delors, integration took a new lease on life, and the European Union wrestled with the issue of how and whether Eastern European countries and even Russia could be associated with it. Early optimism dissipated, and the limits of "Europe" became apparent when Europeans were unable to deal with a conflict on their own doorstep, in Yugoslavia. Domestic problems such as unemployment in Western Europe and deficits and race relations in the United States began to appear insuperable. It was hardly clear that the West had emerged as the "winner."

In Asia the decline of the Soviet presence allowed the economic dynamism of Japan and the newly industrialized countries (NICs) full sway. Unburdened by heavy defense expenditures, they wove a Pacific-wide web of interlocking economic and financial interests that soon extended to Western Europe. But the roles of post-Maoist China and of North Korea in a world without the Soviet Union remained an enigma.

Ronald Reagan and the New Cold War

Ronald Reagan was inaugurated as president a year after Conservative Margaret Thatcher became English prime minister, two years before conservative Helmut Kohl came into power in Germany, and a year before Socialist François Mitterrand's triumph in France. These were the last years of Brezhnev's foreign policy assertiveness. Revolutionary Iran had just released the American hostages held for over a year, Russia was now fully engaged in Afghanistan, the radical Sandinistas had come to power in Nicaragua and Communist-led insurrection persisted in El Salvador. Cuban troops supported several Marxist regimes in Africa. Domestically, the United States was digesting the second oil shock, and was suffering from double-digit inflation, high interest rates, and a high level of unemployment. Conservative frustration about both foreign and domestic ills elected Ronald Reagan.

Reagan found a staunch ally in Prime Minister Thatcher and, oddly enough, another in Socialist President Mitterrand. Both, like Reagan, espoused a hard line toward Russia, which Reagan characterized as the "Evil Empire." The Cold War he called "a struggle between right and wrong, good and evil." He brought into his administration those who shared his view that the Soviet Union had gained a superiority in the strategic arms race that had opened a "window of vulnerability." He set aside arms control while he launched a weapons buildup to surpass Brezhnev's, expanded the navy to counter the Soviet Union's new global role, promised to roll back Marxist gains in Central America and the Caribbean (the United States' "backyard"), and downplayed Carter's human rights emphasis as a policy that had hurt governments friendly to America while doing nothing to help individuals within totalitarian Communist states. "Constructive engagement," for example, was to be substituted for confrontation with South Africa; quiet diplomacy and persuasion could ease inevitable change.

Over time, policy toward Marxist-Leninist states supported by Russia in the Third World evolved into what became known as the "Reagan Doctrine." Support was now to be given to anti-Communist forces to help reverse the tide that had begun to flow during the Brezhnev era. His supporters argued that the doctrine actually extended and corrected Carter's human rights policy. Like the Nixon Doctrine before it, the Reagan Doctrine would not bring direct American military involvement. When, in the late 1980s, Soviet support for foreign insurrections and governments faded away, so, of course, did the Reagan Doctrine.

Reagan the Cautious Militarist

Despite the limits of the Reagan Doctrine, the president—some thought deliberately, some thought carelessly—gave the impression that America, having recovered its self-esteem and thrown off the "Vietnam syndrome," would again be quickly ready to use force to back up its interests and preserve world order against the disorder being sown by the Soviet Union and its regional Communist allies. In the long run, it turned out that Reagan talked a harder line than he used.

Nicaragua and El Salvador represented the Reagan Doctrine in action. In fact, Reagan told the American people, Nicaragua would be the "litmus test" of the Reagan Doctrine.

The administration mustered aid for the "Contras"—the armed opponents of the Soviet-supported Sandinista regime (see chapter 7), sent troops to maneuvers in neighboring Honduras where most of the Contras were quartered, mounted an economic blockade, and ultimately mined Nicaraguan harbors—but never sent the four to five divisions the Pentagon estimated would be necessary to overthrow the Nicaraguan government. By the time an exasperated Congress—not knowing what the aims of Reagan's policies were and opposing intervention—cut off military aid to the Contras, White House aides were reduced to the expedient that brought about the Iran-Contra scandal in Reagan's last year: against all announced policy, working through shady intermediaries, they tried to ransom American hostages held by Iran-backed Islamic extremists in Lebanon, promising arms sales to presumably moderate factions in Iran, in return for which the Iranians would see to the release of the hostages. (Declared policy stated that ransom would never be paid for hostages, for the simple reason that any such payment would stimulate terrorists and kidnappers into seizing more hostages.) Proceeds from the arms sales were to be funneled in "laundered" form to the Nicaraguan Contras. When it all broke out into the open, the administration retreated in considerable embarrassment.

Yet in the long run, support for the Contras paid off. The Sandinista government, increasingly radicalized and driven to extreme measures, began to weaken as Soviet support disappeared under Gorbachev (who, by 1989 had begun to warn Soviet clients to seek political compromises). Driven by increasing opposition and economic chaos, the Sandinista government accepted elections in 1990 under a plan proposed by President Oscar Arias Sanchez of Costa Rica, under which the Contras would be disarmed in return for free, internationally supervised elections. Sandinista President Daniel Ortega, convinced by his own propaganda and by polls that showed his inevitable victory against a disorganized, fractured opposition, took the gamble. To almost everyone's surprise, and certainly their own, the Sandinistas suffered electoral defeat. With thousands of observers present, there was no question of the validity of the election. A resulting coalition government worked hard at restoring social order, and with the Cold War over, Nicaragua dropped out of international sight.

The United States also viewed a Marxist-led revolt in neighboring El Salvador in the context of the Cold War, and $3.3 billion of publicly acknowledged American aid flowed to the centrist, democratically-elected government in power for most of the 1980s, prodded to reform by the United States. Despite repeated fears among congressmen and other elites in the United States that the Reagan Administration might send in troops, it did not do so. El Salvador might be vital, but not that vital. Eventually, facing stalemate and, as in Nicaragua, the end of Communist aid, the rebels and the government agreed to elections supervised by the United Nations. They were successfully carried out in 1993. Once again, the Reagan Administration could have, in retrospect, claimed some measure of success, though the decline of the Soviet Union appeared to be more important.

If the Reagan Administration forbore using force in Nicaragua or El Salvador, it did use it on Grenada, in 1983, where it could neither fail nor get bogged down. In October 1983 President Ronald Reagan sent 6,500 American paratroopers and marines storming ashore to overthrow the unruly four-year-old Marxist-Leninist government of the tiny island of Grenada (population 90,000!), a hundred miles off the coast of Venezuela. The quiet neighboring islands of the Caribbean had appealed for support against the Grenada regime from the United States, and the Reagan Administration, declaring that the invasion was to protect the lives of American citizens and to restore democratic rule and order, clearly wanted to show that it would curb further growth of Soviet and Cuban influence in the Caribbean. The invasion, in other words, was a signal, one that did not carry the dangers of armed intervention in either Nicaragua or El Salvador, but designed to show that the United States would and could still resort to force to protect its interests and citizens. (It had the merit, for the Reagan Administration, of being relatively risk free—which also undercut the impact of the message it was designed to convey.)

On the other hand, when another small American force suffered a horrifying blow halfway around the globe, in Lebanon, Reagan retreated.

The civil war that began in 1975 in what had previously been the most prosperous country in the Middle East dragged on from bad to worse (see chapter 12). Syria and Israel occupied parts of the country, and so did remnants of the Palestine Liberation Organization (PLO). The Reagan Administration, in the process of trying to broker a wholesale Middle East peace deal, attempted to get Israel, Syria, and what was left of Arafat's PLO out of Lebanon, and to build a consensus of the warring groups within the war-torn state.

A multinational peace force of Americans, British, French, and Italians secured removal of PLO armed forces, whose presence had provided the rationale for the 1982 Israeli invasion. Fighting continued, however, and the United States attempted to back a new "legitimate" government of Lebanon, which it now supported, by means of naval gunfire and air strikes from the Sixth Fleet against Syrian strong points. In response, on October 23, 1983, a Syrian-backed terrorist drove a suicide truck-bomb into U.S. marine headquarters, killing 241 American servicemen in their barracks. An attack on a French compound killed 58; two weeks later, a similar attack destroyed Israeli headquarters in Tyre, killing another 60 men. In the face of stalemate among Lebanese factions, the risk of greater conflict with Syria, and confused public opinion at home, President Reagan, on February 7, 1984, announced the forthcoming withdrawal of the American forces.

Four months earlier, in late October 1983, President Reagan had declared the issue of a sovereign independent Lebanon a "vital interest" of the United States. Now he had abandoned it. The incident displayed how much harder it was for the United States to decisively use force to affect events in far reaches of the globe than it had been in Eisenhower's time—and the extent to which Reagan and his advisers appreciated this, despite their rhetoric.

Somewhat more risk free was the other occasion on which the president used force, this time in North Africa, against Libya, in mid-April 1986.

The phenomenal rise of terrorism in the 1970s and 1980s is primarily a subject for chapter 10. Terrorist actions appeared to have the backing of a number of governments, prominent among which was that of Libya's Colonel Muammar Qaddafi, who, among other actions, arranged the murder of political opponents abroad through his embassies. Following particularly violent bombing incidents at the Rome and Vienna airports in December 1985, Reagan—who called Qaddafi "the mad dog of the Middle East"—decided to make an example of him. American Sixth Fleet vessels began maneuvers close to Libya, shots were exchanged, and pressures were brought to bear upon European allies to restrict their Libyan contacts. On April 15, 1986, American carrier jets and planes from bases in England struck at a series of military targets in Libya.

Although the air strike caused some collateral damage, it was a limited and fairly precise attack, and the administration later claimed that the raid cooled Libyan ardor for more terrorist action.

Even when war broke out in September 1980 between Iraq and fundamentalist Iran, threatening to spread to the whole Persian Gulf area—which Jimmy Carter had declared to be of vital interest to the United States—the Reagan Administration's response remained measured. In the first years of what became a bloody but stalemated war, costing over a million dead and far larger numbers of wounded, and $400 billion in resources, the United States essentially did little but back UN diplomatic efforts to end the war. When Iran began to attack neutral shipping to disrupt the economies of countries that supported Iraq, notably Kuwait and Saudi Arabia, the Reagan Administration responded to a Kuwaiti request, sending a flotilla to shield neutral shipping and "reflagging" Kuwaiti ships as American ships. Even a misguided Iraqi attack on the USS *Stark*, bringing twenty-nine American deaths, failed to stop the administration's "tilt" toward Iraq. The mistaken downing of an Iranian airbus, with the deaths of 290 civilians on board, by the USS *Vincennes* in mid-1987, brought merely an American expression of regret and an offer of compensation.

But it also brought, within two weeks, a reversal of the Ayatollah Khomeini's long-held view that the war would only end with the removal of President Saddam Hussein of Iraq. The resulting cease-fire meant that the United States' gamble had paid off: a limited naval presence was all that was required of it. Later, when Iraq invaded Kuwait in August 1990, the benefits of the earlier "tilt" toward Iraq began to look more dubious (see page 261).

Reagan and Europe

NATO matters got off to a bad start in 1981 when the Reagan Administration seemed not to know what NATO strategy actually was. Secretary of State Alexander Haig, a former NATO Commander in Chief, told the press that in case of a Warsaw Pact attack, NATO was prepared to let off a single atomic explosion as a warning to the Russians. Secretary of Defense Caspar Weinberger said there was no such plan. President Reagan suggested that a nuclear war might be limited to Europe. Europeans were greatly upset, and the antinuclear forces in Western Europe gained renewed vitality.

It was the time of the Soviet invasion of Afghanistan, of its deployment of SS-20 mobile missiles in Europe and of emplacement of two new classes of giant ICBMs. SALT II was dead, and the lengthy European Mutual Balanced Force Reduction talks on conventional arms were moribund: no one could agree on what "balance" was, since they couldn't agree on what to count nor how to count it. NATO members had committed themselves to a progressive yearly increase in their military budgets, and the Reagan Administration's buildup increased the military budget in real terms from 1980 to 1984 by 26 percent. Arms control was on hold.

Reagan Administration strategy was to deploy enough new weapons to show the Soviet Union's leaders that they could not hope to achieve superiority in a race with the Americans. Only then would it move to negotiations—but this time in the interest of reductions, not mere limitations. When the new talks materialized, they were to be called Strategic Arms *Reduction* Talks (START) instead of Strategic Arms Limitation Talks (SALT).

In the meantime, the loose talk among administration officials about keeping nuclear war limited to the continent served to scare Europeans; they were angered when the administration tried to pressure them not to help build a gas pipeline from Russia, particularly when it tried to forbid American subsidiaries in Europe from participating (Reagan officials argued it would make the continent too dependent on Russia). Invasion of the tiny island of Grenada made Reagan look like a bully.

The Falklands War

During his years in office, Reagan did much to scare and annoy Europeans. But he had several firm friends in Europe, including British Prime Minister Margaret Thatcher, who agreed with the president about much that he was trying to do domestically. For one thing, she remained grateful for his support during the dramatic Falklands War, which erupted in April 1982, when the Argentine government of General Leopoldo Galtieri interrupted talks with Britain about sovereignty over the tiny Falkland Islands by invading them and overcoming the opposition of some 100 Royal Marines. Argentina's claim dated from 1820 (though it was never buttressed by "effective occupation"), and the British had occupied the islands since 1833. The 2,000 inhabitants of British descent had secured a British promise that there would be no transfer of sovereignty without their consent. The unpopular and repressive Argentine military government had taken advantage of the decline of British power in order to buttress support at home.

There was considerable diplomatic maneuvering at the United Nations and the Organization of American States, to very little effect. Margaret Thatcher, securing full European Community support, was not one to take the seizure lying down. Despite the fact that the closest staging area was on Ascension Island, 3,400 miles away, the British mounted a successful counterattack, and while losing several ships to Argentine airplanes (using, ironically, French-made Exocet cruise missiles) retook the islands by June 14, 1982.

One serendipitous result was the fall of the unsavory, discredited, Argentine military government and the return of Argentina to civilian government. Another was the cementing of Ronald Reagan's relations with Margaret Thatcher. Despite pressures from Latin American governments and after intense attempts at negotiating a solution, Reagan provided full and generous support for the British. Although Margaret Thatcher would be annoyed by his subsequent invasion of Grenada, previously a British island, she would not forget his help. To some analysts, the whole episode reaffirmed the value of Atlantic ties, at a period when they were under constant strain.

The Strategic Defense Initiative

Perhaps the most startling of Reagan's military moves while in office was the president's declaration in a speech on March 23, 1983, that he intended to deploy a defensive system that would make intercontinental ballistic missiles obsolete and eventually lead to their abolition. The administration called the multi-billion-dollar plan the Strategic Defense Initiative (SDI), but journalists promptly and derisively dubbed it "Star Wars," after the popular science fiction movie. In its initial stages, SDI would be a research and development program, but after several years it was to result in a multilayered capacity, partly ground-based and partly space-based, to detect and destroy enemy-launched missiles either shortly after they were launched, while they soared through outer space, or shortly before they hit their targets. It would use exotic new technologies like hydrogen-explosion pumped lasers and particle beams, and would take advantage of the newest computer advances. (As opponents pointed out, no mention was made of either incoming cruise or submarine-launched ballistic missiles, which might require very different forms of defense.)

The Anti Ballistic Missile Treaty (ABM treaty) of 1971 was specifically designed to prohibit deployment of such a defense: the argument had been that deployment would be inherently unstabilizing, since a real defense might tempt its possessor to use nuclear weapons first, secure in the knowledge that no one could successfully retaliate. Deterrence through mutual assured destruction (MAD) was both less costly and more stable. But the Russians had always acted as though defensive measures could pay off, and deployment of the huge, accurate, MIRVed SS-18 missiles (i.e., missiles equipped with multiple independently targeted reentry vehicles) had led to the suspicion that a capacity to threaten to use them to destroy not cities but American missile sites might be translated into political pressure. Hence the Carter Administration's decision in 1979, with Presidential Directive 59 (PD59), to officially establish a new strategy: weapons could be targeted against the weapons systems of the other side, so that a limited nuclear response *could* be threatened against a limited attack by the other side. While such a response could be viewed as a modified form of deterrence, its proponents were always uncomfortably aware that it also implied a nuclear war–fighting capacity, and that civil defense—abandoned in the mid-1960s—might reenter the picture.

In a sense, this is what happened. President Reagan's SDI was a logical outgrowth of President Carter's PD59. But the SDI occasioned an enormous outcry and an outpouring of literature that increased in rough proportion to the increasing yearly outlays of billions of dollars for SDI research and development.

Opponents argued that a sure defense was technically impossible, impossibly expensive, and dreadfully destabilizing, and that it would merely bring forth Russian countermeasures and therefore stimulate a new stage in the arms race. To test some of the myriad components envisaged would require renouncing one of the most important arms control agreements, the ABM treaty. Said Nobel Prize physicist Hans Bethe, "it is difficult to imagine a system more likely to induce catastrophe than one that requires critical decisions by the second, is itself untested and fragile, and yet is threatening to the other side's retaliatory capability."

Proponents argued that technical advances made it absurd to call the project impossible before all the advances had been explored, that success would make the cost bearable, that the Russians had been working on such defense measures all along, and that defensive systems would be adopted only if it could be shown that countermeasures would be more costly. The ABM treaty was not an end in itself: the purpose of military strategy and arms control was to provide a more secure environment, and if defense was once more possible, making MAD obsolete, then the treaty was outmoded, and a safer world would result.

The waters were further muddied when some proponents admitted that a perfect defense was not feasible, and that a partial defense was all that could be hoped for. It could be installed around the vulnerable land-based missiles, and could thus improve deterrence. This was a direct contradiction of what the President had proposed, and raised the question of what SDI was really all about. (In addition, it turned out much later that SDI directors had faked a widely shown successful test of a missile intercept!)

INF and Reykjavik

In the meantime, in desultory talks through 1982, the United States stuck to a position on intermediate-range nuclear forces (INF) that was viewed as unrealistic by domestic and European opponents: it would forgo deployment of its new European missiles if the Soviet Union did away with its substantial and continually growing number of SS-20 missiles—the so-called "zero option." The Russians ridiculed it: why should they give up what they already had in return for what the West didn't yet have? As the time for Western deployment approached in December 1983, Soviet negotiators walked out on both the INF and the START talks.

In the meantime, relations were further embittered when Korean airliner 007 was shot down by a Soviet fighter in September 1983, killing 269 people. It had strayed over Russian airspace in somewhat suspicious circumstances, which were never thoroughly explained. Reagan Administration spokesmen at the UN took the opportunity to excoriate the brutal Russians for having shot down a civilian plane in cold blood (although they knew the Russians had mistaken it for a military plane). While American overkill dissipated the effect, the brutality of the Russian act and the Russians' failure to make any amends were striking.

The all-around stalemate was deceptive. The decision to deploy the SS-20 had been made on military-technical grounds, and Russian political leaders now saw it as a serious miscalculation that had led to Western deployment of threatening weapons. Then along came Gorbachev.

Despite Gorbachev's tough first-year stance, arms talks subsequently resumed, with a number of seemingly attractive proposals put on the table.

Reagan then accepted an invitation from Gorbachev, who proposed that the two hold a meeting in Reykjavik, Iceland, in mid-October 1987, prior to a summit scheduled for a little later. Here an almost incredible series of events took place. With little preparation beforehand, and without consultation with his allies, President Reagan at first reached a remarkable tentative understanding with Gorbachev. The two would reduce long-range nuclear weapons by 50 percent within five years; remove all their intermediate-range weapons from Europe, maintaining only 100 in Asia and 100 in the United States; and—although the Americans created confusion by at first denying it—apparently do away with all nuclear missiles within ten years. In one stroke the president appeared to have committed himself to destroying the most reliable retaliatory weapons, upon which deterrence and extended deterrence had so long depended, and to eliminating the European theatre weapons over whose emplacement European governments had virtually mortgaged their lives. To top it off, the exercise then ended in recrimination because the president refused to consider what Gorbachev wanted in return for sacrificing Soviet missiles: the abandoning of Star Wars—a collection of, as one caustic commentator put it, "technical experiments and distant hopes."

Administration supporters tried to put a good face on Reykjavik, but European leaders were angered and appalled that such far-reaching changes could be considered without consultation, strategists were unnerved, and others were simply puzzled at the whole ill-prepared exercise.

Yet, in the months that followed, while Gorbachev shifted to far more daring moves in both the domestic and the foreign fields, confounding early commentators, negotiators did the impossible: in the fall of 1987 they agreed that the United States would destroy 859 medium- and short-range missiles, while the Soviet Union would break up 1,752. Reagan and Gorbachev signed the agreement in a brief summit conference in Washington, on December 8, 1987. For the first time since the Washington Naval Conference of 1922, an agreement actually produced cuts in weapons, not merely agreed limits or other types of arms control measures, and was accompanied by far-reaching and precedent-setting verification: the world was treated to the spectacle of American inspectors in Siberia and Russian inspectors in Colorado supervising the destruction of each other's recently built intermediate-range ballistic missiles. For a Soviet Union that had previously balked at almost any inspection, it was an astounding turnaround—but in the light of past congressional attitudes, it was almost as surprising on the part of the United States.

Reagan Administration supporters pointed out that by sticking to his guns, the president had obtained elimination of the new Soviet weapons in return for elimination of American ones, whereas earlier he had been pressured by an enormous campaign in the United States to renounce the American missiles while leaving intact large numbers of Russian ones. But without the new Soviet leadership, there might have been no treaty. What many observers failed to see, reflecting on the Reykjavik affair in the light of Reagan's arms buildup, was the president's fundamental antipathy to a peace based on a balance of terror, on mutual assured destruction, on the threat to civilian populations. That we lived under it, he once said, was "a sad commentary on the human condition." His opponents did not understand that he was genuinely interested in doing away with nuclear weapons. The president who presided over the biggest peacetime arms buildup was therefore also the man to negotiate the first real arms reduction treaty since 1922.

NATO in the 1990s

Now events in the Russian sphere simply took over. Gorbachev's December 1988 announcement of a series of unilateral cuts and withdrawals was, as we have seen, quickly outmoded by the collapse of Communism in Eastern Europe in the fall of 1989 and by subsequent dismantling of the Warsaw Pact, which in turn led to the withdrawal of all Soviet troops in Eastern Europe. By the time Bill Clinton became president of the United States in 1993, the incredibly time-consuming, exhausting wrangling over arms control all seemed a distant memory.*

In the meantime a NATO summit in Rome in November 1991, only a month before the dissolution of the Soviet Union, reached an agreement that a smaller NATO of more mobile forces was still necessary in the face of instability in Eastern Europe and the threat of spread of nuclear weapons. President Bush told other members that as long as they wanted American forces in Europe, the Americans would remain, albeit in far smaller numbers. Many predicted the demise of NATO as a result of the demise of the Soviet bloc and the Soviet Union, but the organization served too many other purposes than merely facing the Soviet menace.

The Gulf War and the New World Order

If anything symbolized the changed nature of international politics under the impact of Soviet withdrawal from global commitments, it was the war

---

*There were interesting revelations, though. Domestic critics of administration policy had often accused it of exaggerating Soviet numbers, or of wrongly accusing the Soviet Union of violations of earlier agreements. But Foreign Minister Shevardnaze admitted to several such violations, and it turned out that in Eastern Europe large numbers of weapons had been successfully concealed, so that the numbers put forward by the Soviet Union in the Mutual Balanced Force Reduction talks were, in fact, frequently false.

in the Persian Gulf in January 1991. George Bush, who succeeded Ronald Reagan in 1989, essentially promised more of the same in the realm of foreign policy—pragmatic dealings with the changing Soviet Union; an attempt to maintain some measure of Atlantic unity in the face of a shifting world scene; and a general, cautious, nonideological preference for order. Like many European leaders, he was thus wary when Eastern European states moved toward independence from Moscow, tentative in his support for German unity, and careful not to offer too much in support of change in the Soviet sphere.

Initially he looked even more cautious than Ronald Reagan had proved to be in practice. Nevertheless, goaded by a thuggish drug lord and former CIA collaborator who had overthrown the civilian government of Panama, Manuel Noriega, Bush sent a force of 26,000 men into Panama in December 1989 to seize Noriega and restore civilian rule.

Noriega was later tried and convicted for drug smuggling and racketeering in American courts. The OAS condemned the invasion, and the United States had to veto a resolution criticizing it in the Security Council. Bush may have hoped not to be as critically involved in the Panama–Nicaragua–El Salvador triangle, but Noriega's prominent role in the drug-smuggling operations the administration was trying to thwart—in cooperation with other Latin American states—seemed to him to leave him little choice. The invasion would show he was serious.

The Gulf War of 1991 against Saddam Hussein's Iraq was much more dramatic. It is, however, necessary to backtrack a decade and shift the focus temporarily to Iran and Iraq.

The Iran-Iraqi War

For years, Iran and Iraq were at odds over frontiers and minorities, but the revolution in Iran that brought the Ayatollah Khomeini to power in 1979 precipitated matters. Khomeini's determination to spread his brand of Shiite Muslim fundamentalism disturbed relations with smaller Gulf states and Saudi Arabia, but particularly with Iraq, whose President Saddam Hussein was a Sunni Muslim in a country primarily Shiite in orientation. In late 1979, Saddam Hussein, seeing Iran torn by revolution and its army leadership decimated by purges, thought the time was ripe to crush Iran once and for all, to bring to an end Shiite agitation for his overthrow emanating from Iran, and to settle border issues in his own way.

Iran rejected his demands to renegotiate the status of the vital Shatt-al-arab waterway and of Arabs in Iran, and on September 12 Saddam sent the much smaller but well-equipped Iraqi armies across the border, where they quickly seized substantial Iranian territories.

But Saddam had miscalculated. Instead of crumbling before his on-slaught, the revolutionary government of Iran was able to muster both na-tionalist sentiment and large numbers of young men, and within two years it regained all the territory Iraq had seized in its first offensives. Both sides resorted to outlawed chemical weapons, and thanks to an influx of Soviet weapons after 1984, Iraq was able to return to more mobile tactics which its better organization and morale permitted. Iran suffered enormous casual-ties, but Iraq could not prevail. Both then attacked each other's cities with Soviet-built missiles, while Iran attempted to intimidate two Iraqi support-ers, Kuwait and Saudi Arabia. Both sides resorted to economic warfare, blocking one another's exports of oil, ultimately leading to the "tanker war" in the Persian Gulf, where Iran laid mines and attacked tankers.

Iran's Ayatollah Khomeini long resisted calls for a cease-fire: the only acceptable peace would be one in which the anti-Islamic, heretical, and satanic Iraqi government was replaced. Circumstances were against him: the international presence in the Gulf, Iraqi success in repulsing a new Iranian offensive in the north, falling oil revenues and the drain on his economy, and lack of almost any foreign support but that of Syria, finally led Khomeini to a decision that was, he said, "more deadly than taking poison." In July 1988, to preserve the revolution, he accepted a UN-sponsored cease-fire and a ten-point peace plan. The war was finally over. A million had died, one and a half million were wounded, and an equal number were refugees; the borders were almost exactly where they had been at the beginning; and the two countries had poured perhaps $400 billion into the war. Iraq emerged with its army strengthened, thanks to both Soviet and Western arms and aid.

The Gulf War

On August 2, 1990, three years after the end of the costly Iran-Iraqi War, Saddam Hussein tried again. This time he invaded the tiny, bordering emir-ate of Kuwait, which he formally annexed six days later. It was the first time since World War II that any country had simply taken over another sovereign state.

There was no excuse for the invasion. The Iraqi dictator, whose regime had no scruples about slaughtering its own domestic opponents in large numbers, owed enormous sums to Kuwait for its support during the Iran-Iraqi War. He wanted access to Kuwaiti oil fields and to Kuwaiti port facilities on the Persian Gulf, and made clear that he disagreed with current timid OPEC policy, led largely by Saudi Arabia. Engaged in talks with Kuwait before the invasion, Saddam assured other Arab leaders that he would not invade. They in turn assured the United States he would not attack an Arab brother. The U.S. State Department continued to support and even arm Iraq as a preferable alternative to Iran as a dominant Persian Gulf power. In the face of Iraqi troop movements toward the Kuwait border, American diplomats gave Saddam ambiguous signals about what might happen if he moved further.

The unexpected invasion changed the whole equation in the Middle East and raised what Saddam may not have anticipated—a worldwide storm. Iraqi troops were now massed on the northern border of Saudi Arabia, the country that still had the largest proven oil reserves in the world, and Iraqi control of Kuwaiti oil already made it a much larger player. Suddenly Saddam loomed as a threatening figure both in the Middle East and on the world scene: while some Arabs chanted his praises, most Arab leaders reacted angrily, with the result that on the very day of the invasion, August 2, the UN Security Council was able to pass a resolution of condemnation and a call for Iraqi withdrawal with only Yemen abstaining. Mandatory economic sanctions were voted a week later, and the resolution invalidating Iraq's annexation of Kuwait three days later received unanimous support. A series of further resolutions followed. On November 29, 1990, in the face of obdurate refusals to comply, the UN Security Council authorized member states to "use all necessary means" to implement the first resolution if Iraq had not withdrawn by January 15, 1991.

By this time, thousands of American troops were in Saudi Arabia, ready to block any Iraqi attack. Within a short time, hundreds of thousands more would be on the scene, along with naval and air forces, backed by British and French forces and contingents from a dozen other countries, including several Arab ones. Saddam Hussein's attempt to split off the Arabs by linking a possible withdrawal from Kuwait to Israeli withdrawal from the Gaza Strip and the West Bank failed. He drew back from an open attempt to use Western civilians caught in the invasion as hostages. By September 1990, 600,000 refugees from Kuwait had passed over into Jordan, and Saddam threatened to attack Saudi Arabia, other Arab countries, and Israel if the economic sanctions strangled Iraq. Visiting Kuwait, now "Province 19," he vowed that he would never compromise, never give up an inch of the new province.

Bush, despite public pressures and the advice of some of those closest to him, did not hesitate. Urged on by Margaret Thatcher, he succeeded in organizing the whole enterprise. All but three members of the Arab League backed him. On January 16, 1991, having obtained a congressional resolution of support, he launched an air attack upon Iraq that lasted for five weeks. Then, in spite of a last-minute Soviet suggestion for mediation, he launched a ground attack that lasted for four days, cost the allied forces few casualties, and destroyed most of Iraq's armed forces (with the exception of half of Saddam Hussein's Republican Guard, the bulwark of his regime). The retreating Iraqi forces left hundreds of Kuwaiti oil wells afire and the ravaged country blanketed in heavy black smoke.

In subsequent months Saddam reconsolidated his power and used it to crush revolts by Shiites in the south and Kurds in the north, who fled by the hundreds of thousands, while thousands died of hunger and exposure. At first ready to stand by, hoping the Iraqi military would overthrow Hussein, the Bush Administration, under French and Turkish pressure, eventually moved to support relief and peacekeeping efforts, to establish no-fly zones for Iraqi aircraft over both north and south, and to organize aid for Kurds in the north and in Turkey. Acting under terms of the armistice accord, UN inspectors— frequently harassed and hampered by Iraqi authorities—discovered that Iraq had progressed much further in the production of nuclear weapons than anyone had suspected. Bacterial and chemical weapons facilities also came under UN scrutiny, and inspectors reported that Iraq had four times as many chemical weapons as earlier reported.

In the next three years, under American pressures, UN sanctions continued as Saddam resisted full implementation of UN resolutions. The Clinton Administration saw in his behavior a continued threat to precarious Middle East stability. In the meantime, the fundamentalist Iranian regime began to regain regional strength.

The short war produced much self-congratulation over a remarkable victory, in which the allies had suffered few casualties. (There were no reliable estimates of the much higher Iraqi casualties). It turned out, however, that gross overestimates of Iraqi strength had led to gross overestimates of what allied casualties might be. As one later analyst put it, "A relatively weak and isolated Third World country, whose gross national product was perhaps a third the size of the U.S. defense budget, took on the world's only superpower, which was funded by the entire developed world and assisted by several major military powers."[1] Nevertheless, George Bush, at the height of his popularity for having forged allied unity, reported proudly to Congress in March 1992 that with the Cold War over, the Gulf War would bring about a "New World Order," since it had shown how the United Nations could now act in the face of aggression. Few shared his optimism, and these were soon disenchanted.

The Gulf War had the side effect of putting the spotlight on the problem of the Kurds: some twenty million people spread primarily across Turkey, Iran, and Iraq. Tribal independence and grants of autonomy in the past had kept a Kurdish nationalism from asserting itself in the form of demands for a Kurdish state. The drawing of state boundaries in the area at the end of

World War I distributed the Kurds among the modern states whose territories would have to be amputated if an independent Kurdistan was to be created. Kurdish resort to terrorism in Turkey and against Turks in Germany muddied the image of the Kurds, but the aftermath of the Gulf War once again raised the issue of the Kurdish future.

Somalia

President Bush was unable to translate his short-lived Gulf War popularity into electoral success, and in November 1992 Bill Clinton, former Governor of Arkansas, defeated him. Before Clinton was inaugurated, however, in December 1992, Bush moved to reassure people about the New World Order. In Somalia, central government had collapsed in the face of repeated drought, defeat by Ethiopia in 1981 (when the Soviet Union had switched to support of Ethiopia from support of Somalia), and resultant clan warfare that led to the flight of President Siyaad Barre in 1991. The UN Security Council, at the urging of the new secretary-general, Boutros Boutros-Ghali, was preparing to send a UN force of some 3,500 Pakistani and other soldiers to ensure that food relief would reach some of the masses of starving people (who were being seen worldwide on television), instead of falling into the hands of warring militia. Three weeks following the election of Clinton, the Bush Administration offered to send another 30,000 American soldiers to help in the task.

On December 3, 1992, the UN Security Council authorized intervening forces to use all necessary means to deliver food and to stop war between the Somali clans. This was the first "humanitarian" UN intervention, designed to prevent mass starvation, and it was widely hailed. Presumably it would be followed by more such interventions, as the UN could now turn its attention to local conflicts, unhampered by Cold War considerations. A week later, 1,700 U.S. marines were in Somalia, and at the end of December, to underline the American commitment, President Bush visited the U.S. Embassy in Mogadishu as well as some Somali schools and orphanages. Despite the signing of a cease-fire by fourteen factions in mid-January 1993 and of another agreement at the end of March to create a representative group to run the country until a national government could be formed, fighting broke out between clans and UN peacekeeping forces.

In effect, the United Nations, with U.S. support, had been trying to recreate government for the state of Somalia. But attacks upon (and retaliation by) Pakistani peacekeepers, the death of several American soldiers, and spreading violence brought an American about-face. Clinton faced heavy opposition in Congress to the American involvement: what business was it of the United States to try to create a government in the far-off Horn of Africa, to try to trap a leading Somali warlord, to have American men killed in the process? In response, the president temporarily increased the number of America troops, in hopes that the larger numbers could bring about a resolution to the conflict, while promising to bring all American troops out by March 31, 1994. Conflict resolution failed and the Americans left. A year later, 2,000 would be sent back in to cover the final retreat of what remained of the UN peacekeeping force, mainly from Pakistan and Bangladesh.

Hundreds of thousands were saved from starvation, but America's role in the New World Order was badly blurred, and so was the concept of UN peacekeeping. As the UN debated the situation in Bosnia in September 1993, Clinton himself warned its members that in the future the United States would support peacekeeping only if the organization became more selective in its tasks, defined its missions more clearly, and reduced the U.S. share of its costs. In the meantime, continuation of the war in Bosnia demonstrated that without U.S. leadership its allies would do little.

Europe 1992

While differences over policies to follow vis-à-vis the Soviet Union and other parts of the world clouded American relations with Western European governments in the 1980s and 1990s, economic affairs remained a primary source of tension. At the end of the Carter years, in 1979, the U.S. Federal Reserve successfully imposed high interest rates to curb domestic double-digit inflation. The action had worldwide repercussions: at a critical time, Third World countries had to pay more to borrow, and European countries had to keep interest rates high and forgo expansion to keep capital from flowing to the United States. Then Reagan's deficit spending kept the rates high.

One result of the transatlantic economic discord was to give a boost to the flagging efforts at European unity, as Europeans once more sought to lessen their increasing vulnerability to American economic policy.

In early December 1985, as a result of EC Commission President Jacques Delors's initiatives, members of the European Community announced their intention to eliminate remaining internal barriers to free movement of labor, capital, goods, and communications within the European Community by 1992. A detailed white paper recommended that some 300 measures be taken in the fields of physical, technical, and fiscal barriers. With this, an enormous wave of activity began that replaced years of inertia and false starts. These developments raised hopes that finally, after almost thirty years, the European Community might begin to approach the goals set by its founders in the Treaty of Rome, while also revealing how difficult the operation was going to be: it would require harmonization of hundreds of regulations and laws in vastly different spheres, all of which reflected different social priorities in the different countries. In 1987 the Single European Act came into force, the first major amendment to the Treaty of Rome of 1957, easing procedures for making the necessary changes, and demonstrating the renewed impetus. By the target date, December 31, 1992, 95 percent of the legislative program required in the individual member states had been completed, in what one report described as "the biggest democratic lawmaking program in the history of civilization."

All this did not occur without strain, as old ways had to be modified, and the unexpected unification of Germany changed the context, adding financial stresses to the process. In the middle of all the activity, an old issue reappeared: what had defined "Europe" in good part in the previous thirty years had been the Soviet threat and the division between East and West. With this gone, all the questions reappeared: Was Europe defined by geography? If so, was Turkey—a country whose population had increased from seventeen million to fifty million in fifty years—really a part of Europe? How far to the east did Europe extend? (Turkey signed a free trade agreement with the EU in March 1995, after thirty years of waiting. But the rising Islamic tide within Turkey, and its bad human rights record in dealing with a Kurdish uprising, still put the accord in question.) Was Europe defined by level of economy, by form of government, by adherence to human rights, or by common adherence to welfare policies? All these questions bore on both the deepening and the widening of the European Community, now called the European Union (EU).

Maastricht

In April 1989, EU Commission Chairman Jacques Delors presented a plan to member states to create a single central bank to set monetary policy, intervene in currency markets, hold reserves, and eventually create a single Europe-wide currency.

Delors and his supporters saw the ambitious plan as a fundamental part of the move to 1992. Clearly it would remove from sovereign control a large measure of crucial governmental functions, since countries would have to adhere to common macroeconomic and budgetary policies.

Political reaction set in immediately. Prime Minister Thatcher led the charge: no British government could abrogate its autonomy to this extent. Yet the issue of a central bank and common currency was crucial. Those in favor of the drastic move argued that without it there could never be a genuine single, common market. The bull had to be taken by the horns. In fact, it had been known since earlier theoretical works on customs unions that this was ultimately what would have to take place, and Jean Monnet, the prime mover in creation of the Common Market, had expected it—forty years earlier. Europe, with its 320 million inhabitants and its recovered economic and technological dynamism, could truly compete with the United States and Japan only if it became a single economic unit. (Competition with the Soviet Union was no longer a crucial issue, as it had been for so long.)

On December 11, 1991, the contemplated single currency system was embodied in a treaty signed at Maastricht in the Netherlands. The treaty also proposed a common European foreign policy. "Maastricht" became a rallying cry for Europeans, and the target of all opponents. The treaty only barely received the necessary ratification by member states.

The timetable for creation of a European currency would probably have to be modified. The Maastricht treaty requirements for moving through the stages toward a single currency were not easy. Germany, in the fall of 1994, suggested a Europe at two speeds: a core would move forward as suggested by Maastricht, and the rest would proceed at their own pace. As a result, another debate began. Several monetary crises, in 1992, 1993, and 1995, resulting from internal political crises, demonstrated how hard it would be to align policies sufficiently to make a single money possible; some concluded that the single money was necessary in order to force states into appropriate policies.

Two contradictory forces remained at work. European industries and firms were scrambling to position themselves to be competitive in the new Europe, merging and acquiring partners in other countries, setting up Europe-wide production and distribution systems. Airbus Industrie, for example, a firm producing jet transports with parts from all over Europe, had proved to be the only real competitor on world markets to the American aircraft industry. Work proceeded on combining the growing national networks of high-speed trains into a Europe-wide network. And after a century and a half of talk, in 1994 Britain and France had actually completed a Channel tunnel—sometimes called the Eurotunnel, but more often inelegantly referred to as the "Chunnel."

On the other side was the intractable fact that tax systems in 1990, for example, took from 30 percent of GNP in Spain to 52 percent in Denmark, and there was no federal body to begin to harmonize these systems. Yet for 1992 to really work and for Maastricht to take effect, this and much more would have to be done, requiring enormous adjustment of national policies long entrenched in law. In the mid-1990s, attempts to achieve common policies on rising unemployment and lagging economic growth failed miserably. (Overall, official unemployment in Western Europe hovered around 11 percent, whereas for much of the postwar period it had been around 2 percent. In the United States it remained between 5 percent and 6 percent.)

The European Union and the World

In the last decades of the century, intra-European trade increased much faster than European trade with the rest of the world, and other countries reacted as a result. One result was a new round of worldwide trade talks under GATT auspices. These talks were launched at Punte del Este, Uruguay, in the fall of 1985, in an attempt to keep the world trading system open. (Many economists had expressed a fear that the globe would break up into several great trading blocs—European, American, and East Asian—with others left out in the cold.) The talks would also tackle many of the new kinds of issues cropping up in the fields of services and nontariff barriers. The arduous negotiations finally culminated in a treaty signed nine years later, in 1994, to which the EU was a party.

The remaining members of the European Free Trade Association (EFTA)—Norway, Sweden, Iceland, Finland, Switzerland, and Austria—had signed a free trade agreement with the European Community in 1973, along with numerous other cooperative agreements; trade with EFTA countries represented a quarter of EC overall trade with the outside world, while the EC represented almost half of EFTA country trade. In the light of the changing world situation, Austria, Finland, and Sweden applied for EC membership, and Norway, which had rejected it by referendum in 1971, reapplied. The first three became members as of January 1, 1995, but once again Norwegian voters turned down membership. This left Norway, Iceland, and Switzerland to negotiate complicated bilateral agreements with the now-enlarged European Union. Eastern European countries were still seeking a form of association with the EU or, ultimately, full membership. By 1995, the Czech Republic, Poland, Hungary, and Estonia had signed association agreements.

For years the Soviet Union itself had fulminated against the European Economic Community—as an extension of NATO, or of American capitalist domination of Europe. When trade and financial ties increased in the 1970s the theme faded, as Eastern bloc countries, the People's Republic of China, and eventually, in 1988, the Soviet Union itself signed agreements with the EC and sent ambassadors to Brussels.

A hundred and thirty other countries had diplomatic relations with the

European Union as such in the early 1990s (and not just with its member nations), while the EU spoke for its members in trade negotiations. The EU had observer status at the United Nations and some of its specialized agencies, and it negotiated at some of the major global conferences mentioned in chapter 7. There was, as yet, no EU foreign policy as distinct from the foreign policies of member states: the debacle in trying to deal with war in the former Yugoslavia was evidence of this. But for some issues at least, the move toward a common foreign policy had begun, and Maastricht promised more.

The European Community's share of world trade in 1988 stood at 19 percent (much of it growing intra-European trade), against 17 percent for the United States and 10 percent for Japan. If, indeed, 1992 and Maastricht took hold (and by 1996 some important areas of 1992 implementation were still not completed), Western Europe would become a formidable player on the world scene. A Europe of over 300 million people would be a larger economic unit than the United States, Japan, or Russia. It would—if finally brought into being—represent a remarkable reversal of the distribution of power forty years earlier.

Yet, as the wealthy states in Europe maneuvered to find a balance between national distinctions and centralized powers, between new membership and greater depth, and as they sought to define a European foreign policy, war in Bosnia mocked all their efforts. The almost moribund Western European Union (WEU) which had been created earlier and resurrected in 1955 at the time of German rearmament was once more resurrected as the organization that might help create European defense policy. Some eight different accords—mostly out of the public eye—created European military units, some under NATO aegis, but several under the WEU. They might, in the future, be used to prevent another Bosnia, or to act outside Europe. The German army, downsized from 700,000 men to 330,000, was now reorganized and empowered to carry out missions outside Germany (and a unit was used in the UN mission in Somalia in 1993). The use of European units, nevertheless, would require the kind of common political will that eluded everyone as Yugoslavia crumbled into the warfare of the 1990s. Whether that will could be established in the foreseeable future remained open to severe doubt after the Balkan debacle. Only an American decision to act in Yugoslavia mobilized the Europeans in late 1995.

The Pacific Grows Narrower

Japan and the NICs

In 1954 American Secretary of State John Foster Dulles told a congressional committee that Japan lacked the skills to export much of anything to the United States. As late as 1980, Japan still had an overall trade deficit. But during the 1980s its trade surplus with almost all areas of the world except the oil-rich Middle East soared, despite a continual rise in the value of the yen.

Stock markets boomed throughout East Asia as the decade of the 1980s wore on, aided by a flow of foreign funds. Economies soared. South Korea, one of the world's biggest debtors at the end of the 1970s, had become an international creditor a decade later. (Analysts cited this remarkable feat to compare it to the crippling effect debt seemed to have on other newly industrializing countries in the 1980s. Korea showed that debt need not have such drastic consequences.) By the early 1990s, East Asia produced more than 20 percent of the world's GNP, not far behind North America's 27 percent. In 1968 European Community imports from the United States were one-third more than Pacific basin imports of $6.8 billion; twenty years later, in 1988, Pacific basin imports from the United States totaled $104 billion, compared to $80 billion for the European Union—and most of the American exports to Asia were high-technology and manufactured goods.

As Japan joined the ranks of the rich, its labor costs soared, and its companies moved labor-intensive manufacturing and capital to other labor-rich areas of Sinic culture, such as Taiwan, Hong Kong, and Singapore. These in turn faced the same labor cost squeeze and began to shift labor-intensive production to still other areas. The spread effect worked, and incomes in the areas not affected by political upheaval grew along with the network of trade. (The exceptions were Indochina and the Philippines.) Latin American countries began to get drawn into the network, although demographic and cultural factors and the debt crisis of the 1980s slowed their incorporation.

Japanese success engendered conflict with other countries: they insisted that a mature Japanese economy must now change its ways. Its joint government/industry export-oriented strategy had worked, bringing it into the ranks of the wealthy countries of the world in a remarkably short time. Now, to avoid perturbing the global economy, it must make drastic internal readjustments—increasing wages and incomes; allowing more imports and foreign investments; improving its infrastructure; and using its financial power to help resolve debt issues, add to IMF assets, and increase foreign aid. All this, if it were to happen, would involve a virtual social revolution and an internal political upheaval that would decrease the power of the barons of the Liberal Democratic Party and their financial allies who had run matters since the postwar U.S. occupation.

Disputes with the United States were often bitter. American companies charged Japanese companies with all kinds of unfair trade practices; journalists argued that Japan systematically undermined Western industries through "adversarial trade" and through the creation of global monopolies in highly specialized areas. The status of American armed forces still stationed in Japan and Okinawa came into question, and political crises rocked Japanese government.

Post-Mao China

There were also real and potential political conflicts within the broader Pacific area. The future of now-wealthy Taiwan remained uncertain: its trade and tourism with, and investment in, mainland China had greatly increased. In 1987, forty years of military rule came to an end; in 1995, it held its first completely free legislative elections, and in March 1996, its first free presidential elections. As it moved toward democracy domestically, it began to seek greater international recognition. As a result, in 1995 China took steps to underline its claim that Taiwan was still a part of the mainland. It strongly protested an unofficial visit to the United States by Taiwanese President Lee Teng-hui. In 1996, when presidential elections took place, China made numerous threatening moves: it held naval maneuvers close to the coast of Taiwan, "tested" missiles in the Taiwan straits, and provoked the United States into sending two aircraft carriers into the area to insist upon freedom of the high seas—and to notify mainland China not to attack Taiwan, an unlikely eventuality at this point. (State Department spokespersons revealed that no thought had been given to the fact one of the carriers was the USS *Independence*. The administration had used what was available in the area, but within China many people thought use of the *Independence* was a direct signal to China that the United States backed independence for Taiwan. Such are the cultural differences in perception.) Clearly, the bond of strategic interest that bound China, Japan, and the United States against a militarily assertive Soviet Union in the 1970s and 1980s was gone; in April 1996, the Chinese began to mend their relations with the new Russia, to give to Japan and the United States some food for thought.

China itself grew rapidly but unevenly under tight political control, following the suppression of the democracy movement in Tiananmen Square in 1989. China's future aims were uncertain, but its immense population meant that inevitably, in whatever manner its authoritarian political system developed, it would become a great Asian Pacific power. It modernized its armed forces, increased its navy, and claimed large areas of the rather distant, oil-rich South China Seas, where other countries in the area also had claims. By the mid-1990s, it had come into conflict with the United States

Map 16. **Current and Possible Chinese Boundaries**

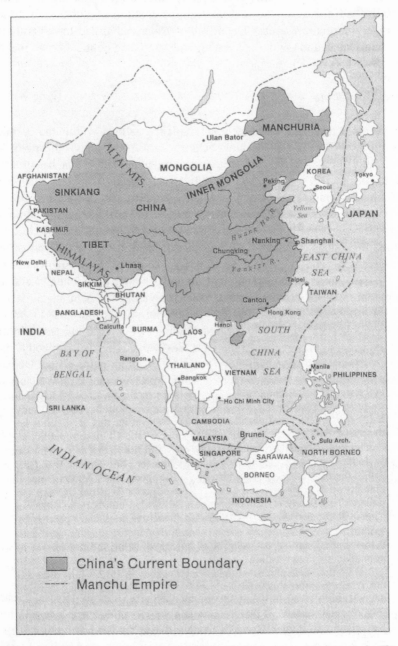

China's Current Boundary

---- Manchu Empire

Source: Joseph Weatherby, Jr., et al., *The Other World: Issues and Politics in the Third World* (New York: Macmillan, 1987).

over its sales of advanced weapons to Middle East countries, its shipment of nuclear materials to states thought to be building bombs, and its human rights record. Its continued nuclear testing irritated numerous countries. Its exports soared, and so did its trade balance. In oblique fashion, China warned the wary Japanese not to make common cause with the United States against it.

China faced an uncertain political succession as the aging Deng Xiaoping faded from the scene. To foreign analysts it appeared that its foreign assertiveness must be tied to the struggle for succession. Some analysts argued that China was merely asserting what had been traditional interests which it felt were threatened by those around it. Some believed in a continued policy of "constructive engagement," such as Nixon and Kissinger had followed with respect to South Africa, arguing that the United States must avoid alienating China. Such a policy would provide discrete means for influence. Others advocated a tough policy to demonstrate to the Chinese leaders that their ambitions must be curbed. Senior minister Lee Kuan Yew of Singapore, who had always advocated a continued U.S. presence in the Pacific, expressed his hope that continued Japanese-U.S. understanding would help to balance China's immense potential power.

One great change in the Far East was clear, however: the old Maoist impulse to try to lead a world movement of Maoist Communist revolutions was gone forever. China had become a "normal" if somewhat threatening state. Equally important—a momentous event in modern history—was that China was on its way to becoming a Great Power, as it had not been before. It wanted to be treated as such, and its leaders' suspicion of the United States was that the latter was trying to block this ambition. When, in mid-1996, China engineered the rapprochement with Russia, when it insisted that it would exercise its prerogatives in Hong Kong after its takeover in 1997, when it demonstrated its determination that Taiwan would remain an integral part of China, and when it resisted interference with its arms sales, the message was that China must be treated as the Great Power it was now becoming.

North Korea

North Korea, one of the most heavily armed states in the world, was one of the last Communist countries, and its relations with South Korea in the 1990s were still strained. Relations became even more strained in late 1994, when a crisis arose over North Korean nuclear production facilities and issues of UN inspection. The crisis was defused when the United States agreed to help the North build civilian nuclear reactors, but there was still uncertainty over its political future, as it, too, tried to manage as an uneasy succession following the death of the long-lasting Kim Il Sung. Its economy appeared to be in shambles, and in 1996 it sought food aid from the world at large.

Pacific Basin Cooperation

Despite the numerous disputes in the Pacific, one development was evident: the United States, Japan, and other Pacific basin countries were bound in an increasingly complex web of trade and financial ties that had never existed before. These ties required a degree of consultation and mutual adjustment of policies that was difficult to achieve. Informal institutions developed, along with a leavening of more formal ones such as the Pacific Economic Cooperation Council and the Pacific Economic Basin Council, grouped in 1989 under an intergovernmental body, the Asia Pacific Economic Cooperation (APEC). APEC aimed to create, in the long run, a free trade area in the Pacific similar to the European Community and the North American Free Trade Area. The Association of South East Asian Nations (ASEAN) has provided a general forum for diplomatic discussion and resolving of some measure of security issues. By 1994, leaders of Asian states were beginning to lecture the West on the superiority of their forms of communitarian social organization over the excessive individualism of the West. But in one major way, "West" and "Far East" were in the process of becoming a single developed area.

Conclusion

With the Soviet Union gone, the United States appeared to be the sole superpower. The point raised many questions.

In the 1980s and the 1990s the United States showed that its capacity to impose its will in other parts of the world was severely limited. Only in the Gulf War against Iraq did it really manage, but there was good reason to think that this was an anomaly, as both the president and the Congress subsequently moved toward a less interventionist position. Russia and the United States might still be the only countries with a capacity to destroy world civilization, but it did them little good.

Presidents Bush and Clinton struggled to redefine the world role of what was still the country with the biggest single economy and the greatest capacity to project military power in distant places. Rearranging priorities was a difficult task, but to the military, at least, the shift from a primary focus on NATO to the possibility of global power projection through a "maritime strategy" seemed essential. Bill Clinton had run for president on a platform that stressed domestic reform: while having only limited success in achieving such reforms, he was also faced with foreign policy issues on which he had no clear focus. Balance-of-power considerations, issues of economic interdependence, and considerations of global issues and the global agenda were all mingled in a difficult tangle.

In the meantime, a resurgent and reactivated Western Europe moved in the direction of becoming an economic superpower—something the Japanese had already done—while some of its members raised the touchy issue of an independent military and foreign policy. If the war in former Yugoslavia was any test, however, Europe failed it miserably. It still had a long way to go. The late 1990s were another period of "Europessimism" in the face of intractable issues like unemployment. On the other hand, the European Union was enlarged by three new members—Austria, Finland, and Sweden—and Eastern European governments saw their association agreements as a step toward future membership, though the return to power of many former Communists in free elections in Lithuania, Poland, Hungary, Slovakia, Bulgaria, and Estonia did not augur well. Georgia and the Ukraine, both of which had looked to the West following the breakup of the USSR, were bogged down in local misery.

The rise of the Pacific basin prompted some analysts to argue that, whereas the Mediterranean had once been the center of international politics in the past, followed by the Atlantic, in the twenty-first century the Pacific would be the center. To other analysts, this theory seemed far-fetched. Japan certainly had created—peacefully—the Greater East Asia Co-Prosperity Sphere it had sought to create so brutally in the 1930s. (The fiftieth anniversary of the end of the war led to considerable soul-searching and even some apologies to other Asian countries on the part of Japanese leaders. Others focused on the dreadful damage done to Japan by American bombing, and refused to acknowledge any Japanese guilt.)

The end of the Cold War and the disappearance of Soviet military activism in the Pacific basin added to the weight of evidence that seemed to indicate a wide readiness to resolve conflicts peacefully through the web of new relationships. From Japan and Korea in the North to Malaysia and Indonesia in the south, the Pacific rim countries had broken out of the grouping called the Third World and joined the so-called First World. Even the Philippines seemed to be moving in the right direction. Only Indochina, still attempting to mend the ravages of thirty years of war, failed to adhere to the pattern, and even Vietnam gave promise of a brighter future. There were areas of potential conflict: a divided Korea, for example, was still an enigma.

The greatest puzzle in the area remained China. Its assertive military behavior when Taiwan turned to democracy only reinforced concern about what it would do when, finally, it achieved Great Power status in the Pacific.

Note

1. Eliot A. Cohen, "Tales of the Desert," *Foreign Affairs*, May/June 1994, p. 141.

Further Suggested Readings

Raymond Garthoff, *The Great Transition: American-Soviet Relations and the End of the Cold War* (Washington DC: Brookings Institution, 1994), surveys the Reagan/Bush/Gorbachev years. A good, brief introduction to developments in European affairs is Desmond Dinan, *Ever Closer Union? An Introduction to the European Community* (Boulder, CO: Lynne Rienner Publishers, 1994). Jonathan Dean, *Ending Europe's Wars: The Continuing Search for Peace and Security* (New York: Twentieth Century Fund, 1994), takes a broader view. Lawrence S. Kaplan looks at NATO in a time of transition in *NATO and the United States: The Enduring Alliance* (New York: Maxwell Macmillan International, 1994). Richard D. Leitch, Jr., et al., *Japan's Role in the Post-Cold War World* (Westport: Greenwood Press, 1995), is a thoughtful analysis, while Robert S. Ross (ed.), *East Asia in Transition: Toward a New Regional Order* (Armonk, NY: M.E. Sharpe, 1995), surveys relations in the area as a whole in a series of essays.

Part V

Three-Quarters of the World

10

The Periphery: G-77, Nonalignment, and North-South Dialogue

When the leaders of newly independent states first gathered at Bandung, Indonesia, in 1955, two-thirds of the world's three billion people lived in what became known as the Third World. By the year 2000, more than four-fifths of the world's six billion people will live in the countries that composed what was then called the "Third World." The centers of world politics and wealth—the United States and Canada; the European countries; Russia; Japan and other East Asian countries; and Australia and New Zealand—will at that point have only about 18 percent of the world's inhabitants, with another equal part living in China.

It was easy to lose sight of this underlying reality as most "Northerners" in the 1980s and 1990s paid attention to other matters: the dramatic breakup of the Soviet empire and the Soviet Union, upheaval in China, the new push for European integration, the rise of Japan as an economic superstate, and the rapid turnover of new administrations in the United States after the eight debt-ridden years of Reagan. The part of the world they lived in quite naturally dominated their interest. Insofar as the Third World was concerned—and the reality of any such grouping was rapidly fading—public attention turned occasionally to a dozen long-lasting, wearying, and seemingly insoluble military conflicts scattered through different regions; to occasional dramatic disasters shown on TV screens, such as the horrifying famines of the 1970s and the 1980s in Ethiopia, and of the 1990s in Somalia; to renewed massacres in the tiny territories of Rwanda and Burundi. Terrorism, as terrorists had learned from earlier First World terrorists, also captured media attention in the developed world. Although Western countries had their own home-grown terrorists, most terrorists now came out of Third World countries.

Some Third World leaders deplored the picture that terrorism as shown in the media tended to paint in the minds of the public it reached; but many such leaders were ready to excuse terrorism as the reaction of the oppressed. By the 1990s, terrorism had become the weapon of religious fanatics, most notably, but certainly not exclusively, of Islamic extremists.

In the 1980s, Third World debt made the headlines of the more serious newspapers, but in the 1990s the issue—though not all the reality—faded into obscurity.

In other words, people in the North—the developed, industrial countries—were vaguely aware of continued population growth, regional conflicts and civil wars, famines, terrorism, and debt. These, however, hardly exhaust the story of the Third World in the these decades. There was much more to it than that.

Most observers failed to realize that the Third World *as a whole* grew more rapidly both absolutely and in per capita terms during the 1960s and the 1970s than did the developed states. The World Bank's report for 1980 showed developing countries' growth rate to be three times that of the developed countries, where high energy and interest costs had helped to produce recession and inflation. This aggregate figure, however, masked vast differences between different Third World states: many, with a total population of at least a billion, remained mired in continued poverty and technical backwardness. The gap between these and wealthy states widened. In some of the states that grew rapidly, the benefits were limited to the few, and poverty remained the lot of the many. Nevertheless, in a World Bank listing of the world's fastest-growing states during those decades, the top forty-nine were all Third World countries; Norway was number fifty, the first developed country on the list. The extraordinary growth of some Third World countries demonstrated once again the possibility of borrowing and adapting the highest technological advances from older developed countries, and of leapfrogging over the stages of development the latter had gone through.

Most analyses of less developed country (LDC) aims were based on economistic interpretations, to the effect that the chief aim of their leaders was rapid economic development. As the Third World became differentiated into richer and poorer, or those growing rapidly and those not growing rapidly, it became more accurate to refer to that portion of it whose growth lagged by an older term, "less developed countries." Yet there remained, at the United Nations and elsewhere, organizations that represented the whole, differentiated Third World.

The strident, confrontational drive for the New International Economic Order (NIEO) came at this time of historically unprecedented Third World growth rates, and originated with wealthier Third World oil exporters

Map 17. **GNP per capita 1990**

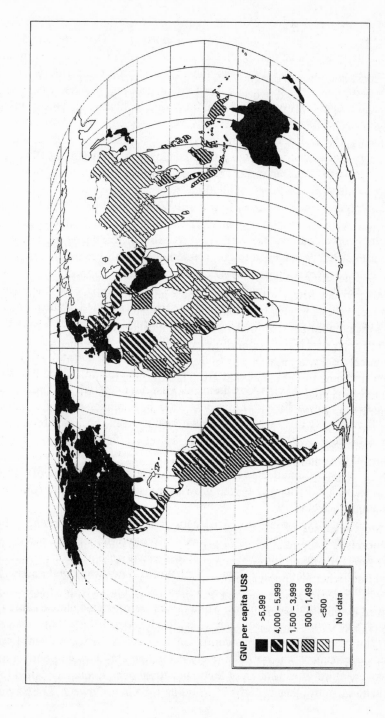

GNP per capita US$

■	>5,999
▨	4,000 – 5,999
▨	1,500 – 3,999
▨	500 – 1,499
▨	<500
□	No data

Source: Chris Dixon in Tim Unwin, ed., *Atlas of World Development* (Chichester, UK: John Wiley & Sons, 1994).

whose pricing policies would hurt mainly oil-importing LDCs. The first price rise of 1974 greatly increased oil-importing LDC indebtedness; the second increased the $26 billion LDC deficit of 1978 to $70 billion by the end of 1980. One conclusion was that the most prominent aspects of the NIEO really had little to do with the needs of many LDCs (see chapter 7). In fact, in many cases, rather than following policies that would favor economic development, many LDC governments seemed to follow policies designed primarily to keep them in power, or emphasized their conflicts with other states, or tried to spread their ideologies and religions. Revolutionary uprisings leading to repression and counterterrorism often occupied governments to the exclusion of all else.

Simple generalizations about the Third World therefore had little validity. There were too many differences. The major problem with G-77 at the United Nations and with the Non-Aligned Movement outside the UN was that these differences tended to get papered over, so that the common positions adopted often had little relevance to many of the members.

As a result, a new grouping came to be delimited in UN parlance—the "Fourth World"—the forty countries most seriously affected by the oil price rise. These were the poorest and weakest countries, often referred to as the "least developed countries," and most of them were in Africa.

The 1980s were different—a blighted decade for a majority of Third World states. Debt, low commodity prices, high interest rates, and the drying up of new capital flows took their toll. East Asian growth continued, but South Asian growth slowed. Latin debt brought retrenchment and decline, and Africa largely continued on its downward course. The 1990s brought a resumption of growth in many countries, but also a turning away of Western concern as a consequence of the end of Cold War competition. This situation was compounded both by the continued prevalence of Third World military conflict and by the growing sense that often little could be done about such conflict.

The extent of conflict should perhaps not have been surprising. The borders of new states—often established by Western imperialist powers— were often unclear; and tended to cut across ethnic groupings or to include different and hostile groups. Some Third World states were well endowed with usable or marketable resources, some not. Some were geographically located on important trade routes, while others were—as the phrase came to be in the UN context—"geographically disadvantaged." All these factors lay at the base of the numerous conflicts that occurred between them. Economic development was not, as already noted, the only foreign policy aim. Moreover, Third World states, or factions within them, frequently called for intervention from other countries, including the Great Powers. The Soviet

Union and the United States were often not responsible for the conflicts that tore at the fabric of smaller, weaker powers, but until the 1990s they were often involved. Nixon had articulated an American retreat from direct involvement in the early 1970s; in the 1980s Gorbachev did the same for the Soviet Union.

By the time Russian interest declined, however, Russian weapons were still widely available, and there were now many other sources of supply, including industrialized Third World countries. Rebels, ethnic or tribal groups or clans, guerrillas, and armies could find enormous numbers of lethal small arms at bargain prices. As a result, in some states in Africa, government sway extended no farther than the edges of the capital city, while the countryside was contested by armed bands with little clear political purpose but plunder. As armed conflict continued in war-torn Afghanistan, a new problem came to public attention: the presence there and in other parts of the world of millions of land mines, the legacy of past conflicts, ready to blow apart the unwary who stumbled upon them.

The Third World Organized

The Non-Aligned Movement

In 1961 Jawaharlal Nehru of India, Marshal Tito of Yugoslavia, and Gamal Abdel Nasser of Egypt presided over the first summit meeting of the Non-Aligned Movement in Belgrade, Yugoslavia. Nikita Khrushchev betrayed his contempt by setting off the monster fifty-megaton H-bomb at the time of the meeting (reportedly telling a Yugoslav diplomat to ask Tito, "Who, then, is more important—his Non-Aligned Movement or the Soviet Union?").

The silence in Belgrade about the Soviet moves set the tone for the future: the nonaligned countries would be circumspect in criticism of the Soviet Union and its allies, but harshly critical of the West. As the movement grew from the original twenty-five states that met at Belgrade to more than a hundred, it also tended to take off in different directions and to lose much of the unity of purpose and principle that had prevailed at its outset. Many of its members were, in fact, aligned with the Soviet Union. When the sixth summit was held at Havana in 1979, host Fidel Castro constantly referred to the Soviet Union as the Non-Aligned Movement's "natural ally," making somewhat ironic the movement's title. Imperialism was the enemy; by definition, there could be no Soviet imperialism, since imperialism was a consequence of capitalism.

Once the Soviet Union invaded Afghanistan, the latter's puppet government remained a member of the movement, and joined others in seeing that Russia was never mentioned by name when resolutions were passed in support of UN Undersecretary-General Perez de Cuellar's efforts at mediation.

More moderate members of the movement constantly worked behind the scenes to try to tone down the final communiques; since the economic sections always listed moves that ought to be taken by Western countries, it seemed counterproductive to attack these countries in the political sections. An Indian commentator on the New Delhi 1983 summit asked "whether nonalignment can claim any integrity if expedient appeasement of a handful of radical members demands ceaseless berating of the West." Significantly, the 1983 meeting had to be held in New Delhi instead of in Baghdad, Iraq, because of the Iran-Iraqi War: members who attacked the Great Powers or the West for their militarism were frequently at war with each other.

The ninth summit meeting, in 1989, back in Belgrade where the first was held almost three decades earlier, virtually marked the end of the movement: the easing of East-West tensions led to a declaration that the world had become a safer place. Its Yugoslav hosts, bent on increased and improved ties with the West, toned down radical rhetoric. Fidel Castro did not even attend. Much was made of the need for new economic initiatives: for many small, weak, poor countries, Third World unity still had strength as an ideal. It was here that apprehension surfaced about Western resources being used to support the transition taking place in the East, deflecting them from the South.

In the next five years, the whole context of the movement changed, as the Eastern bloc crumbled, the Soviet Union crumbled, and a leader of the movement—Yugoslavia—crumbled. Nonalignment became history. Dozens of Third World regional organizations continued in existence, but at the global level, the Group of 77, now with 130 members, remained the only global one.

North-South Dialogue

Starting at the end of the 1940s, a long North-South dialogue has taken place, leading to a number of measures to aid the South, but also to much frustration and disappointment. Early emphases on technology transfer gave way in the 1950s to a desire for increased capital flows—especially on concessional terms—and then in the 1960s to new and different trading arrangements from those maintained under the GATT regime: more provisions for commodity agreements, for special advantages for products from the South, for lowered barriers without a requirement for reciprocity, for a different negotiating method than that used in the GATT. The United Nations Conference on Trade and Development (UNCTAD) in Geneva, in 1964, marked the first concerted effort to rearrange trading relationships and to provide a new global framework to replace the Bretton Woods regime.

UNCTAD's limited success in changing the prevailing arrangements provided the background against which Algeria and a handful of other states were able to propagate the leading ideas of the New International Economic Order when the oil price rises of 1974 gave them both the opportunity and the need to do so if the Third World was to hold together. These included the absolute right to sovereignty over subsoil resources and the right to form export cartels—both measures from which the oil states benefited but which were of little use to other Third World countries. When these other countries sensed the limited utility of these rights, OPEC moved to use the "oil weapon" to pressure developed countries to agree to a conference to consider a number of pressing issues of concern to Third World traders. The Conference on International Economic Cooperation (CIEC) got under way in 1976, with limited results.

At Cancun, Mexico, in early 1981, LDCs got little but a lecture from Ronald Reagan on the benefits of the free market and a promise of global negotiations at the United Nations. (As mentioned earlier, many Third World countries had been growing at unprecedented rates during these years, regardless of the North-South negotiations and dialogue, while others had stagnated.)

Then, quite suddenly, the terms of the debate changed again. If, in "North-South dialogue" terms, the 1950s marked the growth of a consciousness of a "Third World," the 1960s were the UNCTAD decade and the 1970s the decade of NIEO confrontation, the 1980s became the decade of the global debt crisis, when it appeared that a large number of countries would be unable to service their debts (i.e., pay the ongoing interest), much less repay the capital on schedule.

The Debt Crisis

Debt was a global issue, a regional issue, and a country issue, differing at each level. Globally, the problem involved the possible collapse of the world's financial system if debt became unmanageable and repudiation the norm; globally, too, the reduction of Third World imports to accommodate to debt-servicing necessities meant a cut in exports from developed economies. The slowdown this produced in the developed countries reduced both their capacity and their will to continue aiding the Third World, which needed inflows of capital more than ever. At the regional level, difference existed between the causes and the consequences of East European debt,

African debt, and Latin American debt. At the country level, the performance of South Korea in rapidly reducing its debt in the late 1980s showed that, in an overall sense, debt per se was not the issue: if debt was incurred in the creation of productive facilities, it could be both serviced and repaid. In 1962 Korea and Ghana had the same low per capita income, about $490, and the same large percentage of people engaged in agriculture. Twenty years later, Korean per capita income was five times that of Ghana, and 90 percent of its exports were manufactured goods, against a figure of 2 percent for Ghana.

Nevertheless, global conditions and events were at the heart of the debt crisis and its ravages. The origins of the debt crisis lay in the increased debt incurred as a result of the first oil price rise of 1974. Loans were easy to obtain, interest rates were low, and oil income was there to be "recycled" by incautious private banks that received large deposits from oil exporters. In the early 1980s the bubble exploded. The second oil price increase brought increased oil import bills in both North and South, recession, and high interest rates used to combat inflation in the North. As a result, when it came time to roll over short-term debt, LDCs found they could get new loans only at much higher interest rates, making it much more difficult to service the loans: debt soared further. Banks became more cautious, finding themselves overextended to economies that now looked as though they might be unable to repay: the flow of funds began to dry up. Banks themselves faced possible collapse, and the world financial system was endangered, with all that this might imply for the collapse of world trade. The experience of the 1930s loomed large.

In August 1982 Mexico announced it would be unable to service its nearly $80 billion foreign debt. Brazil, Argentina, Venezuela, and others soon announced their own debt-servicing difficulties. Fears of possible debt repudiation spurred creditors and the International Monetary Fund to work together with debtors to manage the debt problem by "restructuring" old loans, finding new loans, and generally making it possible for debtors to keep interest payments on schedule. Debtors by and large wanted to avoid repudiating their debts, since such an action would immediately dry up any further flow of external funds. (Fidel Castro at one point championed debt repudiation on the part of poor countries, but his own government, anxious for continued foreign credit, avoided repudiation. The rhetoric and threat of repudiation was mainly a tactic to pressure creditors into easing terms.) As a condition for new loans, debtors were increasingly required to put their economic houses in order, to stop living beyond their means by reducing consumption of both imports and government services.

Map 18. **Foreign Debt as Percent of GNP**

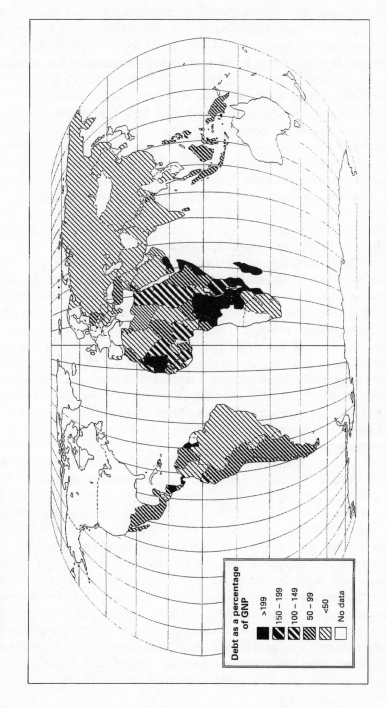

Debt as a percentage of GNP

- >199
- 150 – 199
- 100 – 149
- 50 – 99
- <50
- No data

Source: Alan Gilbert in Tim Unwin, ed., *Atlas of World Development* (Chichester, UK: John Wiley & Sons, 1994).

It was all called "structural readjustment," and tended to fall disproportionately on poorer classes, increasing misery and internal unrest. Moves toward democracy in Latin America—a feature of the 1980s—were therefore endangered by the debt issue, as new democratic governments imposed domestic austerity.

In 1989 the United States devised the Brady Plan for actual debt *reduction* as a replacement for its earlier Baker Plan that sought to encourage new loans. Already several European countries and Canada had forgiven some measure of African debt, and President Bush announced in July 1989 that he would cancel some $1 billion in official development loans of sub-Saharan African countries. Debt itself was being discounted by almost 60 percent on the world market. What the plan sought was to use one of several methods, by mutual agreement of debtors and creditors and with support of the IMF and World Bank, to find ways of reducing the debt and therefore easing both servicing and repayment.

There seemed little alternative. As the decade of the 1990s rolled around, general international agreement appeared to have emerged that the debt burden simply had to be lightened. Servicing and repayment in the 1980s meant, by one estimate, a net *outflow* of capital from the Third World to the developed countries compared to the previous decades' inflows.

Blame could be apportioned for the growth of the problem; Third World countries' elites certainly bore their share of the responsibility in terms of poor or simply self-serving policies. Those who had money in Latin America often invested it abroad. "Flight capital," as it was called, invested in the United States or Western Europe, represented a sum almost equal by some estimates to, or greater than, Latin American foreign debt. For example, domestic negative interest rates and an artificially strong currency had prompted wealthy Venezuelans to send $58 billion abroad, whereas the Venezuelan debt totaled $35 billion. It simply showed, Venezuelan President Carlos Andres Perez said, that domestic policies and domestic confidence in development were keys to growth as much as any international help might be.

The heterogeneous moves to deal with the debt crisis bore some fruit. In the 1990s most less developed countries resumed their growth of earlier decades, with the exceptions of too many in Africa, where population growth continued to outstrip economic growth, and a number of Middle East countries, where low oil prices brought considerable retrenchment. Debt ceased to grow relative to production. Most important, perhaps, was that the resumption of growth occurred despite continued slow growth in the developed countries. It meant that LDC economies had become less closely dependent upon those of the older countries.

Terrorism Captures the Media

Terrorism has a long and fruitful history. Widely prevalent at the turn of the century in Europe, it culminated in a terrorist act in the Balkans, in Sarajevo, on June 28, 1914—the act that sparked four years of a worldwide conflagration we now call World War I, in which whole generations died and empires fell. Some eighty years later, following two decades of renewed terrorism, on March 20, 1995, ten people in Tokyo died and thousands suffered when a religious sect inserted a small quantity of poison gas of a type developed during World War II in Nazi Germany into the Tokyo subway system. To some, the act was as important as the assassination of the Archduke Franz-Ferdinand of Austria-Hungary in 1914: it demonstrated to everyone the vulnerability of modern societies to such an act. Enormous quantities of this gas and many others as well as biological weapons existed in stockpiles around the world. With the demise of the Soviet Union, nuclear materials began to find their way onto the world market. It would be hard to prevent their use. In April 1995, just as a meeting was getting under way in New York on prolongation of the Nuclear Non-Proliferation Treaty, one report pointed out that nuclear deterrence could work in the case of nation-states, but not in the case of terrorists, who have no territory, no state, against which to threaten retaliation.

All through the decades of the 1970s, the 1980s, and the 1990s, terrorism grew as an international issue. Modern communications—satellite television transmission, the portable camcorder, audiocassettes, and videocassettes—gave it a new boost. It became easier than ever for a small group or a single person to force the attention of the world upon a planned yet random terrorist act, and to react to it. As a result of a few thousand terrorists, hundreds of millions of people behave differently, subjecting themselves to expensive scrutiny when they travel and taking other precautions. If new technologies made controls such as metal detectors possible, they also created a vast range of small, portable, cheap, sophisticated weapons. The effects of terrorism familiar to people in other countries were brought home to Americans when a Pan American Airways plane was blown up over Lockerbie, Scotland, in 1988 by a small plastic bomb, when the World Trade Center in New York was bombed in 1992, and when the Federal Building in Oklahoma City was bombed in 1995. Relatively few people have actually died at the hands of terrorists, compared to those who die in automobile accidents, of murder, at the hands of repressive governments, or in warfare. Yet terrorism has become a prime international issue, and the 1995 Tokyo incident alerted people to the possibility of losses on a much larger scale through terrorist action.

Terrorism exists throughout the world: there are Basque terrorists in Spain, and there are terrorists on both sides in Northern Ireland. Terrorists in Latin America have frequently provoked hideous counterterrorism by the states in which they operated. In the 1970s a well-financed terror network that was active throughout Western Europe kidnapped and assassinated prominent public figures; many of its members received training and financing from Eastern European countries, as well as tacit or sometimes open support from the Soviet Union. Fearing terrorism directed against itself or some of its clients, the Soviet Union eventually backed away from such support, and the indigenous networks in Italy, France, and Germany were largely broken up. In the meantime, terrorists emerged in North Africa and in the Middle East.

Since 1972 the United Nations has tried to deal with the issue, and the UN's difficulties in trying to define terrorism, establish its causes, and devise methods to deal with it have all revealed a basic cleavage within the organization, which was highlighted when a group of developed countries sought to secure condemnation of terrorism by the General Assembly in December 1985.

Those who sought condemnation and concerted international action saw terrorism as an unwarranted act of violence directed against innocent targets, outside the bounds of war and the laws of war, which represent civilization's attempt to lessen war's impact on civilians. Terrorists might cite injustice and repression, but would often themselves be worse perpetrators of both. Terrorism was a denial of legitimate politics, and itself prompted repressive counterterrorism. Analysts of terrorism argued that terrorists were often people who had found a home and a haven in the terrorist group such that, if its purposes were achieved, they would have to find another reason to pursue the terrorism that gave them a purpose in life and a home in the terrorist network.

Arguing against this position were, mainly, representatives of Third World states who hesitated to offer blanket condemnation. They saw terrorism as a political response of those too weak to cause essential social change unless they made the status quo uncomfortable or impossible to maintain for those in power. One person's terrorist was another's freedom fighter (and the frequent pictures on television showing the exultation of one group at the success of a bombing that tore apart the lives and bodies of innocent members of another group gave clear evidence of this).

In the 1980s it was also clear that a number of non-Western states, such as Libya, Syria, Iraq, Iran, and the Sudan, harbored terrorists or sponsored terrorism. Drugs and drug money became intertwined with terrorist activities. When the Soviet Union began to cooperate with Western antiterrorist forces, and as the Soviet empire crumbled, some of the bases from which terrorists had operated in Eastern Europe simply disappeared. Terrorism did not. The causes were varied, tactics changed, and negotiations and attempts at resolving conflicts might work in some cases and not in others. By the 1990s, fundamentalist religious groups had moved to the fore: the Algerian political situation and the peace process in the Middle East offered fertile ground. In April 1990 terrorist attacks threatened to derail Middle East peace talks. A more or less new factor entered the picture: with the promise of salvation given by an extremist religious group, suicide bombing was not only more likely but also far harder to deter.

Terrorism would continue to be a part of the world scene for any foreseeable future.

Conclusion

The notion of the "Third World" was born in the 1960s, codified at the UN and its organizations, and made concrete in the bloc system of voting and of filling places on governing boards of institutions such as UNCTAD. By the 1990s, it was essentially outmoded, as many Third World countries grew into the status of "developed" countries with an astonishing rapidity. In 1995 South Korea applied for membership in the OECD, that outgrowth of the Marshall Plan in Europe, representing mainly the developed countries. The word "South" came to replace "Third World" in much discourse, yet it, too, misrepresented reality as states in the South progressed. As a result, the older term "less developed country" was resurrected. One reality remained—that a number of countries in South Asia and Africa remained poor and that the conditions of the really poor would be dreadfully difficult to remedy. For this, social and political conditions and political conflicts were as responsible as geographical conditions and previous colonial status, but all were also conditioned by rapid population growth.

Terrorism became a scourge in many countries, and so did civil conflict. The nature of some of the prolonged military conflicts described in the next three chapters also underlined the growth of an alarming global arms trade, spurred on now not by Cold War or ideological conflict, but—as in a more distant past—by economic consideration. All through the period under review there were innumerable calls to stop it. The problem, in part, was that the number of sovereign states had increased threefold, their conflicts were real, and the leaders of each new state claimed the traditional foreign policy prerogatives of earlier sovereign states—which included having their own armed forces. Military rule was the case in many new countries, and the military were bound to find the arms they wanted through the numerous existing channels—if not from one country or supplier, then from another.

A progressive, peaceful, united Third World with its lessons for the older, imperialist states never developed as some of its founders had hoped it would. Some spokespersons still blamed the older powers, but most no longer did.

Further Suggested Readings

Steven R. David gives a good overview in *Choosing Sides: Alignment and Realignment in the Third World* (Baltimore: Johns Hopkins University Press, 1991) which was also cited in chapter 6. Nigel Harris, *The End of the Third World* (Harmondsworth, England: Penguin, 1986), discusses growing differentiation. Claire Sterling, *The Terror Network* (New York: Holt, Rinehart and Winston, 1981), is a fascinating early overview of the application of modern techniques to improving terrorist links and methods. A useful summary of official Western views and responses is given by Stanley Bedlington in *Combating International Terrorism: US-Allied Cooperation and Political Will* (Washington, DC: Atlantic Council, 1986). For conflicting views, see Charles W. Kegley Jr., *International Terrorism: Characteristics, Causes, Controls* (New York: St. Martin's Press, 1990). At the time the debt crisis broke, William Cline reviewed the implications in *International Debt and the Stability of the World Economy* (Washington, DC: Institute for International Economics, September 1983).

11

Asia and the Pacific

In the mid-1980s the Pacific basin countries entered a new era. At the end of World War II chaos, ruin and revolution were the norm and the future looked dark. Twenty-five years later, in the early 1970s, the long war in Indochina was only just winding down in Vietnam, but was about to take horrific dimensions in Cambodia; tension remained high between South Korea and North Korea; the Philippines under President Ferdinand Marcos were ripe for insurrection; Indonesia was still trying to withdraw from the confrontational stance taken by President Sukarno, who died in 1970; and Chinese leaders were struggling over the succession to Mao and over new policy directions, while expressing their bitter enmity for Brezhnev's Russia. The growth of Russian influence in Southeast Asia was evident to all as the Russians made increased use of their bases in Vietnam, and the Russian Pacific fleet had begun to undergo the rapid expansion necessary to maintain that influence.

The diplomatic constellation, however, underwent a startling shift in 1972 when Nixon flew to China. Chinese and Americans recognized a joint interest in providing a continued American counterweight to Russia in Asia despite the American withdrawal from Vietnam.

By the 1990s, the entire picture was different. Russia and China had mended their differences, and Russia had essentially ceased its effort to be a Pacific power, while China appeared ready to try to take its place, vigorously asserting what it considered to be its rights. In most of the region, economics seemed to take precedence over politics. Joining the arc of the four "Asian Tigers"—South Korea, Taiwan, Hong Kong, and Singapore— were Thailand, Malaysia, and to a lesser extent Indonesia, all of which were growing fast. Indonesia's sheer size and geographical position gave it an enormous potential. Wasted through Sukarno's mismanagement and foreign adventures earlier, the country's potential was now being realized under the sometimes harsh but generally canny authoritarian rule of President Suharto, who attracted substantial investments from Japan and Hong Kong.

Thailand, Malaysia, and Indonesia, along with Singapore and the Philippines, formed the Association of Southeast Asian States (ASEAN) in 1967, and were joined by tiny but oil-rich Brunei in 1984.* ASEAN contrasted strongly with the defunct Southeast Asia Treaty Organization (SEATO), which was formed under U.S. auspices at the time of French withdrawal from Indochina in 1954 and was closed down in the 1970s. SEATO reflected the Western concern with security in the area against "Sino-Soviet"-sponsored aggression and subversion. ASEAN, in contrast, clearly reveals the passing of these concerns as well as that of Sukarno's Indonesian ambitions for the area: its emphasis is economic and diplomatic, and no outside powers belong.

Even Vietnam appeared ready to move toward a more open polity and a more open economy, though Cambodia remained marked by the trauma of the Khmer Rouge period.

The main areas of conflict throughout the arc of East through Southeast Asia were those that concerned control over the resources of the many narrow seas and waterways.

In South Asia, India emerged as the prime regional power, far larger than a truncated Pakistan and a poverty-stricken Bangladesh. It faced enormous internal difficulties and centrifugal tendencies, and continued conflict within smaller neighbors mirrored some of those within India. The rulers of India were no longer the towering world figures a Nehru or an Indira Gandhi had been.

The Pacific Basin

Vietnam and Cambodia

The main focus of Asian political conflict in the last three decades of the century remained Indochina.

Many people expected that the withdrawal of the United States and the triumph of the Communists in Vietnam, Cambodia, and Laos might bring peace, reconstruction, and some economic prosperity to the area. It did not

---

*Brunei, with only 210,000 inhabitants, has about the twentieth highest per capita income in the world. It exports oil (produced by foreigners) and imports what it needs, leaving the retail trade to the Chinese. Its government seeks to find ways to keep its people busy. It is one of the best examples of the supreme global irony that resources belong to the sovereign state that encompasses them.

happen. A militant Marxist organization, the Khmer Rouge, headed by the mysterious Pol Pot—and originally supported by the Vietnamese—imposed an incredibly cruel, ideologically driven regime upon Cambodia, now renamed Kampuchea. Country and society were to be completely remade. The Khmer Rouge drove the population from the cities, executed thousands who appeared simply to be educated or otherwise unwelcome by the regime, and in the process a million—or two million—died horribly. The number will probably never be known. Refugees fled west into Thailand and east into Vietnam. In December 1978, the exasperated Vietnamese invaded Kampuchea, toppled the Pol Pot regime, and installed a government headed by former Khmer Rouge leaders. The Khmer Rouge and two smaller, non-Communist resistance groups proceeded to carry on guerrilla warfare against the 200,000 Vietnamese troops who provided support for the new government.

The Chinese, alienated by their erstwhile Vietnamese allies, and angered by the new Vietnam-Russian Treaty of Peace and Friendship and the influence it gave to Russia on their southern border, continued to support the Khmer Rouge, and helped rebuild and reequip its tattered forces on the Thai border. Most members of the international community also continued reluctant support for the Khmer Rouge coalition, including the ASEAN nations that saw in the Vietnamese invasion a resumption of old imperial designs by Vietnam against Cambodia, designs once checked by the French. In February 1979—three months after the Vietnamese takeover of Cambodia—the Chinese proceeded to invade northern Vietnam, where they faced unexpected resistance. On March 5, after laying waste several provincial capitals, they announced their withdrawal, on the basis that they had achieved all their objectives. Both sides appeared to have suffered heavy casualties, and both claimed victory. In the early 1980s, the border was never completely free of incident.

In the meantime, the Vietnamese were never able to secure control of the countryside in Kampuchea. By the late 1980s, they had suffered 25,000 dead and 55,000 wounded, and the Chinese-equipped Khmer Rouge still threatened the government. The Vietnamese, their own economy in shambles (and perhaps prodded by Gorbachev, anxious to mend fences with the Chinese), announced their decision to withdraw their troops by the end of 1990. Lengthy talks held in Jakarta, Indonesia, in early 1989, and then at an international conference in Paris in June, led to little agreement. Finally, with the support of ASEAN members, the United Nations was able to broker an agreement in Paris in October 1991. It set up a temporary coalition governing body under the leadership of Prince Sihanouk, representing all factions. A 20,000-man UN peacekeeping force would maintain a cease-fire, see to the disarming of most troops belonging to the different factions, prepare the repatriation of some of the hundreds of thousands of refugees in camps on the Thai border, and oversee free elections to be held in April–May 1993. It was something of a surprise that the elections were actually held. They brought into being a fragile coalition government in which the largest representation belonged to a pro-Sihanouk party. An equally fragile reconstruction process began, still opposed by Khmer Rouge guerrilla forces that government troops were unable to crush. Sihanouk approved the new constitution and was proclaimed king on September 24, 1993. The last UN forces vithdrew a year later. Under the circumstances it was no wonder that Cambodia, still not really pacified, remained one of the two poorest countries in Asia, along with Burma (now renamed Myanmar).

For Asia and Southeast Asia as a whole, the Cambodian conflict symbolized another issue: that of refugees. Within a few years after the Vietnamese peace agreement, 500,000 ethnic Chinese fled their homes and repression in Vietnam. Most of these received asylum in China, but hundreds of thousands of Indochinese fled to Thailand or took to boats to try to reach haven in other Southeast Asian countries. Those who survived their hazardous journeys, and the pirates who preyed on them in hostile waters, found refuge but only on a temporary basis; they must find permanent homes elsewhere. The United States, Australia, Canada, and France together took in a million. Thousands of others remained stranded in temporary camps. UN and UN-sponsored activity aimed at resettlement, but as the flow continued, the distinction between political refugees and those fleeing from bad economic conditions began to be accepted as the paramount consideration on who would be given asylum, with the result that thousands remained in a dreadful limbo.

As peace returned in the 1990s, the flow dwindled, and international attention turned to the millions of refugees elsewhere. In the 1990s, refugees became a major international problem in virtually all parts of the world, and the UN High Commissioner for Refugees became one of the most overtaxed global public servants.

Korea

The East Asian sphere—more and more growth-oriented, more and more entwined in the international economy—continued nevertheless to be marked by other tensions.

South Korea, for example, under a sometimes harsh military government marked by brutal infighting from 1971 until 1986, tripled its per capita income during the period. By the end of the 1980s, its export-driven economy began to loosen up internally, to allow a growth of imports and consumption. Political agitation led to the drafting of a liberal constitution acceptable to opposition parties, whose leaders were released from detention. The three opposition candidates split the vote in December 1987 elections, and General Roh Tae Woo was elected with 35 percent of the vote. North Korea, however, remained one of the most heavily militarized states in the world, one of the most rigid of Communist countries, and one whose economy produced a per capita income now about a sixth that of the South. Most South Koreans supported the government view that the continued American military presence was necessary for stability.

The 1990s brought reunification no closer, despite the startling example of Germany on the other side of the globe, but they did bring quite extraordinary changes: under President Kim Young Sam, who was inaugurated in February 1993, South Korea made unforeseen and audacious moves toward political and economic liberalization, including an opening of the economy to international influences. In North Korea, Kim Il Sung, president since 1948, finally died on July 8, 1994. His son Kim Jong Il, long groomed as his father's successor, gradually assumed most of the offices his father had held. In South Korea, Kim Young Sam reinforced ties with the' four states most important to Korea, visiting China, Japan, the United States, and Russia. South Korean trade with China increased rapidly, while Boris Yeltsin told the South Korean president that all the old Soviet treaties with North Korea were null and void.

But relations between the emerging Kim Jong Il and Kim Young Sam got off to a bad start when North Korea, which had withdrawn from the Nuclear Non-Proliferation Treaty and refused international inspection in 1993, heightened the tension in 1994 by withdrawing from the International Atomic Energy Agency. The United States reacted the most strongly, calling for sanctions in the UN Security Council. But the old North Korean president, Kim Il Sung, had been conciliatory when he met with former U.S. President Jimmy Carter, and the crisis was ultimately defused when the Clinton Administration negotiated an agreement with the Kim Jong Il regime in October 1994 for aid for civilian nuclear production in return for reinstated International Atomic Energy Agency inspection. In 1996 a different crisis appeared: blaming weather conditions, North Korea requested and received international food aid.

Reunification, in the meantime, seemed as far away as ever.

Taiwan and Hong Kong

Further to the south, the Taiwan issue remained a puzzling one for the future. Contact with the mainland increased, the old guard faded, and native

Taiwanese took over from exiled mainlanders as the majority in government. In the 1990s, political liberalization and democratic elections became the order of the day. Despite its uncertain position, Taiwan, with its population of only twenty million, entered the ranks of developed countries by the late 1980s. It could hardly merge with China except on terms of an autonomy that would probably be unacceptable to the mainland. China had pledged itself to peaceful reunification—but with no timetable. In 1978, when Jimmy Carter normalized relations with the People's Republic, Deng Xiaoping said that Taiwan's status "will inevitably be resolved—if not in ten years, then in 100; if not in 100 years, then in 1,000."

Fifteen years later, in April 1993, representatives from the two Chinas met in Hong Kong and established two "private" agencies to conduct discussions of important issues. Taiwan was now second only to Hong Kong in mainland investments, and was a large-scale investor throughout Southeast Asia. Although denied access to the APEC (Asian-Pacific Economic Council) meeting in Seattle in November 1993, in 1995 President Lee Teng-hui visited the Philippines, Thailand and Indonesia "informally." He met with officials at the highest levels of these governments. Finally he visited the United States, to attend an alumni reunion at Cornell, where he earned his Ph.D. The Chinese reacted strongly, scolding the Americans and insisting that there still could be only one China. In mid-1995 and again in 1996, they mounted military demonstrations to emphasize their stand. The United States reaffirmed its support for a single China, while demonstrating that it would not accept a solution by force. Yet an unstable (and in the long run probably impossible) two-Chinas reality had emerged: numerous countries—ten in Africa, most notably South Africa—had diplomatic relations with Taiwan, whose government sought their support through the provision of economic aid. What was clear was that China was determined to prevent Taiwan from achieving international status as a sovereign state.

China had other territorial issues, legacies of the colonial past, with which to contend.

After 1955, when Khrushchev relinquished the Russian naval base at Port Arthur to Mao, the only remaining foreign enclaves on the Chinese coast were British Hong Kong and Portuguese Macao. Hong Kong's population soared from 2.25 million in 1950 to well over 5 million in the mid-1980s, largely because of an influx of Chinese refugees from the mainland. Its per capita income rose to well above that of several European Community countries, and by 1994, it rose above that of the United Kingdom and Australia. Some of this prosperity derived from entrepôt trade between the mainland and other countries, but Hong Kong was also one vast factory and an enormously important financial center. The island itself and the town of

Kowloon on the tip of the New Territories Peninsula belonged to Britain, but the associated New Territories were on lease from China until 1997, and Hong Kong would not be able to exist without them. Hong Kong, on the other hand, was valuable to the People's Republic of China as it stood, producing two-fifths of all its foreign exchange.

As a result, Margaret Thatcher's England and Deng's China reached an agreement in 1985 to transfer Hong Kong to China in 1997, after which China would allow it a large degree of autonomy for fifty years. The people of Hong Kong were not happy with the arrangement, and considerable emigration took place in the next few years. When British Governor-General Chris Patten took it upon himself to institute a moderate degree of political liberalization in the early 1990s, the Chinese government again reacted sharply; prolonged discussions led to little result. The Chinese made it clear that no constitutional change made without their consent would have any validity after reunification. Yet the Hong Kong economy continued to grow.

The Philippines

The Philippines, independent since 1946, constituted another problem area. In 1965 the reformist Ferdinand Marcos was elected president. In 1972 he declared martial law in the face of renewed insurgencies on the part of Muslim Moros and Communist guerrillas, and in the next few years he consolidated a rule that turned brutal and corrupt. The United States, concerned both with blocking a Communist insurgency and possible political chaos, and with retaining its Subic Bay naval base and Clark airfield, continued supporting the Marcos regime; in June 1981, when Vice-President George Bush attended Marcos's inaugural to a new six-year term after an uncontested election, he told Marcos incautiously that Americans loved him for his commitment to democracy.

The internal political and economic situation deteriorated. Opposition grew, and in 1983 the main opposition leader, Benigno Aquino, was assassinated as he stepped off a plane bringing him home from exile. Widespread riots and demonstrations erupted. In a last desperate effort to save his regime, Marcos called for free elections in 1976. The obvious electoral fraud deprived Benigno Aquino's widow, Corazon Aquino, of her evident victory; this led to a relatively bloodless revolution that forced the dictator Marcos into exile in Hawaii, where he died in 1989. The new administration spent considerable effort trying to recapture some of the nation's wealth, which Marcos and his wife Imelda had misappropriated.

President Corazon Aquino, with no political or administrative experience, faced a deteriorating economy, a huge foreign debt, widespread internal insurrection, continued threats from Marcos loyalists who did not want to see their privileges disappear, and demands for agricultural reform. She received widespread support for closing the American bases, which symbolized continued dependence and were intensely resented by Filipinos, despite their economic advantages. For the American military, following the loss to the Russians of bases in Vietnam, these bases were of immense strategic importance to the Far Eastern defense perimeter.

This was not merely a matter for the Philippines and the United States. Singapore Prime Minister Lee Kuan Yew said only three things could disturb the optimistic course of Asian development: Japanese rearmament, protectionism in the United States, and an American withdrawal from the Philippines.

The strategic situation, however, was revolutionized by the changes in the Soviet Union and its eventual breakup. It was no longer so difficult for the American military to accept loss of the bases, and in 1991, following a legislative resolution demanding withdrawal, Corazon Aquino—who would have preferred a referendum in the face of the economic loss—agreed to a withdrawal by the end of 1992. Her freely elected successor, Fidel Ramos, worked hard at curbing the multiple domestic insurgencies and at bringing the Philippines into line with other rapidly growing Asian nations.

Australia and New Zealand

Following the end of the Vietnam War, Australia, partly in anticipation of American loss of the Philippine bases, embarked on a whole new defense strategy. Once protected by Britain, but then in World War II—when the Japanese were poised immediately to the north—protected only by the United States, the Australian government in the late 1980s moved toward greater self-reliance through a high-technology defense of the north and the northwest. With general easing of tensions in the area, Australia found itself more and more a part of Southeast Asia rather than a Western outpost in Asia. Its trade shifted to a more Asian orientation, and it abandoned a longstanding policy of whites-only immigration (and absorbed a large number of Vietnamese refugees). In addition, while maintaining defense ties to the United States, Australia took care to be able to fend for itself if a time of troubles resumed. Military cooperation agreements with Singapore and Malaysia led to joint exercises and patrols, and the Australian government strengthened cooperation with New Zealand. However, New Zealand suspended cooperation with the American military over the U.S. refusal to inform the New Zealand government about whether or not visiting American ships carried nuclear weapons.

Despite local tensions, for the first time in a century and a half, no threat of major power war hung over the Asian countries of the Pacific basin. There were still possibilities of conflict, including China's claims to Taiwan and areas of troubled relations in the South China Sea. Cambodia remained a distressed area with an uncertain future. Indonesia faced continued insurrectionary activity on the island of Timor, whose eastern half it had invaded and annexed when the Portuguese gave it up in 1975: the brutality with which the Indonesian army suppressed the left-leaning pro-independence forces caused large loss of life and boded ill for the future. There was friction, too, along the long border between the Indonesian western half of the island of New Guinea and the eastern half, known as Papua New Guinea, which had been independent since 1975. In Malaysia, as in other areas, ethnic tensions threatened domestic order and economic dynamism. All the ecological consequences of rapid industrialization and the growth of metropolitan areas needed to be met. Yet the area as a whole gave promise of a better future to most of its people.

South Asia

In reorganizing and modernizing its military forces, Australia was reacting in part to the declining capacity of the superpowers to successfully project their power in distant parts. In South Asia, the same factor led to the rise of India as a strong if unsteady regional power with no challenger in the area.

The Indian record was a mixed one. The second-largest nation in the world after China, it showed fairly steady per capita income growth through the decades of the 1970s and the 1980s, but continued population growth strained its capacities and most Indians remained poor in a way unimaginable to most Westerners. India nevertheless had become self-sufficient in grain and manufactured most of what it consumed: in the late 1980s industrial production was growing at an unprecedented 8 percent per annum. It had also, with the Philippines, become one of the two largest exporters of computer software in the world: the information and service explosion did not bypass all Third World countries.

India was now also the largest military power in the area. With the breakup of Pakistan and the emergence of Bangladesh in 1971 (see chapter 5), India had no challenger. Its 1.3 million men under arms constituted the third-largest army in the world, and its navy ranked only below the navies of the United States, Russia, Britain, France, and Japan. With two aircraft carriers, eighteen submarines (including its first nuclear-powered one), and a variety of destroyers and frigates, it was able to carry out what some people had come to call the South Asia Doctrine: Indira Gandhi had decreed that while India would not intervene in internal conflicts in the Indian Ocean area, it would not permit an outside power's intervention if judged to be against Indian interests. With one eye on China and the other on Pakistan, it demonstrated a nuclear capability with a single explosion in 1974. In 1989 it tested its first intermediate- and short-range ballistic missiles. No nuclear explosion has followed since the first one, and the Indian government has declared that it will not build nuclear weapons. But everyone knows the capability exists, fueling the Pakistan military's determination to try to build its own.

Twice in the 1980s India used military power in the Indian Ocean region—once unsuccessfully, once successfully.

In July 1987 the government of Rajiv Gandhi (who had succeeded his mother Indira Gandhi, assassinated in October 1984 by Sikh nationalists) sent several thousand Indian troops south to the island nation of Sri Lanka (formerly Ceylon), where a virtual state of civil war existed between the Sinhalese majority and the Tamil minority (strongly supported by Tamils in the south of India). The Indian peace force was to see to the disarming of the Tamil rebels and the withdrawal of the regular Sri Lankan army from the Tamil area in the north, where limited autonomy would be granted. It would thus demonstrate Indian regional power while calming events in the south of India. In any event, the move failed. The Indian troops found themselves fighting Tamils, and increased to a force of over 20,000 men, before being withdrawn in late 1989 at the request of the Sri Lankan government.

If anything, the peacekeeping effort worsened the situation. Tamils in India assassinated Rajiv Gandhi in 1991, and a wave of assassinations hit the Sri Lankan capital, Colombo, where both the president of Sri Lanka and his dissident opponent were killed in May 1993. His successor succeeded in calming political life on the island, though the Tamil rebellion continued in the north. (Strangely enough, all through the long-drawn-out rebellion, the Sri Lankan economy continued to grow at an average of 4 percent per year.)

In contrast to the failure in Sri Lanka, in November 1988 India mounted—and made much of—an efficient and professional military operation by paratroopers to crush a coup attempt against President Maumoon Abdul Gayoom of the Maldives Islands, 240 miles off the coast of India, being carried out by Tamil mercenaries from Sri Lanka.

Despite the heritage of nonviolence espoused by Mahatma Gandhi, the India of Indira Gandhi and of Rajiv Gandhi was willing to use force where its interests were concerned.

In 1985, leaders of Bangladesh, the Maldives, Sri Lanka, Pakistan, India, Bhutan, and Nepal met in Bangladesh to establish the South Asian Association for Regional Cooperation (SAARC). For smaller members, SAARC appeared to be a way to subject Indian influence to multilateral considerations: "India. . . ," said the then president of Sri Lanka, "larger than all the rest of us combined, can by deeds and words create the confidence among us so necessary to make a beginning." But Prime Minister Lee Kuan Yew of Singapore declared on a visit to Malaysia that China and India could be "potentially troublesome" for regional countries because of their capacity for power projection: "I am not saying they are troublesome, but if they want to be, there is very little we can do about it." In early 1989, India virtually blockaded the tiny mountain kingdom of Nepal on the basis that it had failed to renew transit and trade treaties with India, but in reality to indicate its displeasure at Nepal's purchase of weapons from China. Despite its own internal ethnic troubles—which had led to the assassination of the imperious Indira Gandhi—India towered over its neighbors.

Besides Sri Lanka, at least three of India's neighbors remained in bad shape through the decades of the 1980s and the 1990s: Burma, Bangladesh, and Pakistan.

Under military rule, Burma, a multiethnic state with a population of forty million, remained largely cut off from the rest of the world. The Burmese could feed themselves, but the rest of the economy was nurtured by the black market (estimated to total five times official external trade), and GNP per capita in the 1990s was among the lowest in Southeast Asia. (Pre–World War II Burma was the largest rice exporter in the world, and it also exported substantial quantities of petroleum, nonferrous metals, and teak. It had one of the highest standards of living in the area. Among its largest exports now are drugs.) In 1983 the country made rare headline news abroad when a South Korean government delegation touring Southeast Asia suffered a terrorist bombing attack. The attack was sponsored by North Korea and occurred during the delegation's stopoff in the capital city of Rangoon. Seventeen top government leaders were killed or injured, and President Chun Doo Hwan only just missed being killed.

In 1988 Burma again came to public attention when the military government was rocked by widespread student-led demonstrations in favor of democracy and liberalization. It responded with a combination of moves—a degree of economic liberalization, a promise of constitutional government, but a harsh crackdown on demonstrators, a purge of the universities, and martial law. Organized ethnic resistance groups were all outlawed. In pursuance of the promised constitutional reform, an election held in May 1990 produced a heavy majority in favor of an opposition party led by Aung San Suu Kyi. The result was immediate repression and the placing of Aung San Suu Kyi under house arrest. She received a Nobel Peace Prize in October 1991, and though she was liberated from house arrest in 1995, the greatly augmented military continued to rule, seeking to do what some other countries had done: maintain authoritarian military rule while allowing economic liberalization.

Bangladesh is one of the ten poorest countries in the world, with a population of 118 million—up from 70 million twenty years earlier—a very high birthrate, and one of the highest existing population densities. It managed to survive a series of governmental coups from 1975 to 1982. Devastating floods and cyclones occurred in 1988; instead of 20 to 30 percent of the country being flooded, as has occurred numerous times since independence, fully 60 percent of the country was under water. Contrary to expectations, and with considerable international aid, it managed to slowly improve the standard of living of its impoverished population, but its main international problem concerned the effect of the deforested foothills of the Himalayas to the north on the rivers that ran through and frequently flooded the country. A better future required difficult, important regional cooperation, but the rise of rival Islamic fundamentalisms following elections in 1991 and the influence of the Gulf War put cooperation with India into doubt.

Pakistan emerged from the war with India in 1971 a truncated nation of 100 million people—one-eighth the size of India (see chapter 5). Still one of the ten largest nations in the world and with a powerful army, it could no longer really vie with its much larger neighbor for influence in Asia. Nevertheless, throughout the 1970s, the 1980s, and the 1990s, it was suspected of trying to build a nuclear bomb to match the Indian one, drawing on support from Middle East Muslim states and from China, defying the United States, whose successive administrations tried to stop it under congressional mandates on nonproliferation. When the Soviet Union invaded Afghanistan in 1979, Carter funneled arms aid through Pakistan to the Afghan resistance. Reagan increased the flow, and when UN Undersecretary-General Diego Cordovez began secret talks with the Russians about future withdrawals, it was the Pakistani government that spoke for the Afghan resistance.

In the early years of independence, Pakistani and American interests coincided and a close relationship developed: Muslim Pakistan would have preferred support from other Muslim states but was willing to join Western alliances against possible Soviet encroachments when other Asian states were not—mainly because Pakistani leaders saw this as a means of securing support against India. The support failed to materialize during the 1965 war between Pakistan and India; by then, South Asia was an area of low priority for American foreign policy. As a result Pakistan turned to China for aid.

Temporarily, American and Pakistani interests coincided again in the early 1970s, when Pakistan served as a channel between the United States and China, and Kissinger "tilted" toward Pakistan in the 1971 war with

India when East Pakistan became Bangladesh. The Carter years, however, were ones of strain over the issue of nuclear weapons. Then the Afghanistan affair restored close ties, and Pakistan itself became one of the biggest recipients of American economic and military aid. When Pakistani President Mohammad Zia ul-Haq died in an unexplained air crash in 1982—most probably as a result of sabotage—American officials welcomed the return of democracy to Pakistan and the election of Benazir Bhutto, daughter of the former president. She faced enormous problems, not the least of which was that she was the first woman leader of a Muslim nation where the powerful military had ruled for years. Muslim clerics were riding the wave of fundamentalism, democratic parties were weak and divided, and democracy was not yet a habit. Ethnic divisions also had not yet been overcome. Steady economic growth across the decades did little to help. Ousted and then returned to power once more, Benazir Bhutto faced the long-term problems all Pakistani leaders faced: rampant corruption, conflict with India over Kashmir, competition over nuclear arms, and complicated relations with its neighbors to the north.

Whatever happened in Afghanistan was bound to influence politics within Pakistan and over border areas. No single government had emerged since the fall of the Najibullah regime, but in the mid-1990s a new, radical fundamentalist group, the Taliban, secured control of the capital city, Kabul (they still faced contesting groups elsewhere in the country). Issues of influence in Muslim lands within the former Soviet Union complicated matters even more.

Conclusion

North Korea remained a puzzle. The future of Taiwan and Hong Kong was uncertain, and China itself was something of an enigma: whether its economic liberalization would lead to continued growth, whether it could feed itself or would enter and disrupt world grain markets, and whether its political system could stabilize—all these were still open questions. China reinforced its harsh rule over Tibet, proceeded to modernize its armed forces, reinforced its territorial claims in the South China Seas, and reiterated its view that Taiwan was a part of China. It was accused of selling arms abroad to areas of open conflict. Yet it, like Russia, had become a "normal" state in the state system, not one determined to spread a universalist ideology. There were those who interpreted its seemingly aggressive stance as simply a consequence of continued Chinese fear of Russia, the United States, and a resurgent Japan.

Given the rapid internal growth of Pacific Basin countries, most people were optimistic about the future of the area. Projects for a free trade area were spurred by the enormous growth of economic integration that had taken place. Despite progress in resolving its internal conflicts, Cambodia continued to be a dark spot. The role of the United States in Pacific Basin affairs remained uncertain. However, the Pacific Basin, along with Europe, North America, and South America, was one of the areas where high technology was creating inextricable global ties that overlay the traditional state system. Over the space of twenty-five years, East Asian exports had risen thirtyfold. European and Asian leaders began to seek increased ties.

South Asia was another matter: the Indian giant had in many ways joined the emerging high-technology global system, but it remained politically unstable. Its secular basis was now challenged by Hindu fundamentalism, and large masses of its population still lived in extreme poverty. Poverty remained the primary issue for several of India's neighbors, too, though political conflict within Pakistan, Sri Lanka, and Bangladesh continued, and though Burma retained its closed, repressive system.

In South Asia, as elsewhere, the end of Russian-American competition had thrown the area back on its own resources.

Further Suggested Readings

In addition to earlier readings cited at the end of chapter 9, see Michael Mandelbaum (ed.), *The Strategic Quadrangle: Russia, China, Japan, and the United States in East Asia* (New York: Council on Foreign Relations Press, 1995). Ruth McVey (ed.), *Southeast Asian Capitalists* (Ithaca, NY: Cornell Southeast Asia Program, 1992), explores explanations for the growth of the NICs, and essays in Harold A. Gould and Sumit Ganguly, *The Hope and the Reality: US-Indian Relations from Roosevelt to Reagan* (Boulder, CO: Westview Press, 1992), provide a reliable overview.

12

The Middle East and the Persian Gulf

The Middle East remained one of the most troubled areas of the globe in the last three decades of the century. Old conflicts endured, new conflicts compounded old ones; and extremists hardened their positions, putting into jeopardy attempts by moderates to resolve matters through accommodation. Outside powers—in part because of their dependence on the region's oil—constantly renewed their attempts to try to find some solutions. For most of the period, "peace," "order," and "justice" seemed to be abstract concepts having little application to the area. In a country like Lebanon, children learned to shoot to kill early in life. In the Persian Gulf area, where most of the world's oil reserves lay, two destructive wars demonstrated that unstable governments had the potential to cause global trouble.

Yet in the midst of all this, in the mid-1990s, Yasir Arafat of the Palestine Liberation Organization (PLO) began talks about autonomy with the shaky Israeli Labour government. The PLO Charter was amended to accept the existence of the state of Israel, and the latter accepted the idea of a Palestinian state, toward which a series of intermediate steps were taken. Lebanon moved toward an unsteady peace. Extremists on all sides—fundamentalist and otherwise—tried hard to blot out this ray of light in a sea of darkness, but at least some measure of hope existed.

Israel and Palestine

The Effect of the 1973 War

Again and again, events in the relatively small area of Israel and the surrounding states had a decisive effect on the rest of the world. In 1973, having expelled the Russians, Egyptian President Anwar Sadat launched the Yom Kippur War against Israel, provoking a near-confrontation between Russia and the United States (see chapter 6). The war produced the OPEC-stimulated oil price rise that brought stagflation to Western economies and debt to the rest of the Third World, as well as the confrontational tactic of demand for the New International Economic Order (NIEO). It was also out of the Middle East in the early 1970s that terrorist tactics began to have their widespread effect on how people lived and traveled elsewhere.

Sadat's 1973 war brought wholesale changes to the Middle East itself. OPEC members followed Qaddafi's lead in nationalizing international oil companies' operations within their borders. The war brought to an end thirty years of Labour Party rule in Israel and the assumption of power by the right-wing Likud under the leadership of the ex-terrorist Menachem Begin. It also set Sadat upon a whole new course for Egypt that made the country a pariah in the Arab world for a decade and a half, rather than a leader: when American Secretary of State Henry Kissinger kept the Israelis from crushing the encircled Egyptian armies, brokered a cease-fire and began the "shuttle diplomacy" that brought disengagement in the Sinai and on the Golan Heights, Sadat concluded that the United States, not the Russians, could decisively influence the outcome of the Israeli-Arab conflict. In April 1974 Sadat ended reliance upon Russian weapon supplies, arguing that Russia had tried to use the relationship to unduly influence Egyptian policies. In 1976 he formally abrogated the treaty of friendship with the USSR. In October 1975 he became the first Egyptian president to visit the United States (where he became something of a media favorite). Resumption of diplomatic relations broken at the time of the 1967 war followed a month later.

In the meantime, on October 28, 1974, in Rabat, Morocco, twenty Arab nations called for the creation of an independent Palestine state on land liberated from Israeli occupation and declared that the Palestine Liberation Organization under the leadership of Yasir Arafat was the "sole legitimate representative of the Palestine people." Two weeks later Arafat—granted observer status at the United Nations by the Third World/socialist majority, a pistol holster visible sticking out of his pocket—addressed the UN General Assembly. The issues of a Palestine state and the status of the PLO were now at center stage, where they would remain in future years.

Egypt Makes Peace with Israel

Almost exactly three years later, President Anwar Sadat startled the world by accepting an invitation from Menachem Begin, newly named prime minister of Israel, to visit Israel and address the Knesset (the Israeli parliament). In his address to the Knesset, Sadat proposed peace between Egypt and Israel. On September 17, 1978, at President Jimmy Carter's retreat at

Camp David, Sadat and Begin reached an agreement creating the framework for a peace treaty that was signed six months later, in March 1979. It provided for the phased withdrawal of Israel from the Sinai, the establishment of normal relations that would include the right of passage for Israeli ships through the Suez Canal, and the beginning of negotiations over autonomy for the Palestinians in the occupied territories. Israel returned its precious captured oil resources to Egypt, which undertook to sell oil to Israel.

Other Arab nations and the PLO immediately denounced the pact, imposed an economic boycott of Egypt, and severed diplomatic ties with Cairo. Egyptian peace with Israel, they announced, had betrayed the Arab cause and had been achieved at the expense of the Palestinians. A year and a half later, the man who had regained all Egyptian territory by being willing to make peace with Israel was assassinated by Muslim extremists while he was reviewing a parade. He was succeeded by Vice-President Hosni Mubarak, who pledged to continue his policies.

Civil War in Lebanon

There would be no real peace in the area. In mid-1971 PLO units located in southern Lebanon mounted artillery, rocket, and guerrilla attacks across northern Israeli borders. In 1975 civil war broke out in Lebanon itself. For years a careful division of political power between Muslims and Christians in the government had permitted existence of a fragile political system in this diverse society. The presence of the Palestinian forces that had fled repression in Jordan and constituted virtually a state within a state broke the balance, and warfare between diverse factions ensued. One attempt after another to establish a cease-fire failed, as all government authority disappeared. In June 1976 the American ambassador was assassinated, and the first exodus of American civilians took place. In September a Syrian "Arab Deterrent Force" moved into Lebanon at the request of the Arab League. The Syrians dislodged Palestinian forces from near Beirut and moved into the city itself. They were welcomed with considerable caution, since the Lebanese had long suspected them of wanting to establish a "Greater Syria" at Lebanese expense. (Twenty years later the Syrians were still there.)

In 1978 fighting between Maronite Christian right-wing Phalangists and left-wing Muslims, in conjunction with PLO forces, led to a full-scale invasion in the south by the Israeli army, determined for once and for all to stop PLO raids and rocket fire across the border. A small UN peacekeeping force was created to permit Israeli withdrawal in June, but the Israelis allowed the Maronite Christian militia to establish a "Free Lebanon" border zone, into which neither the UN force nor any Lebanese central authority could penetrate. Israelis no longer trusted UN peacekeeping forces.

The security zone was not enough. Continuation of warfare between rival armed militias in Lebanon—where Beirut, once the "Paris of the Middle East," looked like a bombed-out city of World War II—provoked a second Israeli invasion in June 1982, in an attempt to force both the Palestinians and the Syrians to withdraw from Lebanon.

In this they only partially succeeded, despite a much deeper penetration. Within a week they had encircled Beirut and knocked the Soviet-equipped Syrian air force out of the skies. In August 1982, following intense and complicated American negotiations with innumerable parties, French, Italian, and American peacekeeping forces arrived to supervise the withdrawal of several thousand PLO guerrillas, evacuated to Syria and to other Arab states, and to keep the Israelis from destroying the capital. Plans to arrange a joint withdrawal of Israeli and Syrian forces came to nothing, as Syrian President Hafez al-Assad, bolstered by renewed Soviet support and anxious to maintain a precarious hegemony in Lebanon, refused to negotiate. In the meantime, the PLO set up a new headquarters in Tunisia, while Yasir Arafat, long in conflict with President Assad, was evicted first from Syria and then, in November, from the northern Lebanese port of Tripoli.

Fighting continued after withdrawal of the peace force. Then, while Israeli troops stood by in Beirut, Christian militia—in apparent retaliation for the assassination of Bashir Gemayel, a Christian, who was elected president of Lebanon on August 23 and killed ten days later—carried out a massacre of up to a thousand Palestinian men, women, and children in Sabra and Chatila refugee camps in Beirut. Although the Israeli government later conducted an investigation and punished those marked as having been derelict in preventing the massacre, the massacre indelibly stained the Israeli army. At Italian suggestion, the three-nation peace force returned, and President Ronald Reagan made an attempt to negotiate a wholesale settlement that would involve support for Christian President Amir Gemayel, who had replaced his brother. Gemayel agreed to a peace with Israel, but none of the half-dozen militia forces accepted the legitimacy of either Gemayel or his peace arrangement, and the horrific suicide truck-bombing of the U.S. Marine and the French headquarters led to withdrawal of the second peace force (see chapter 6).

By now the Lebanese situation had grown even more complicated, as the Ayatollah Khomeini's radical Iranian regime moved to extend its revolution to the one country that seemed promising—Lebanon. There Shiite Muslim extremists formed new militia that gained control of whole areas, began to clash with Syrian-backed groups, and eventually even clashed with Syrian troops. To Syrian discomfort, it was Iranian-backed Hezbollah extremists, suicidally willing to drive car bombs, who helped make the Israeli position in Lebanon untenable, driving the mighty Israeli army back south. Other Arabs took note. (Gemayel—fruitlessly, as it turned out—abrogated the peace agreement with the Israelis in an attempt to regain legitimacy.)

Fighting intensified in Lebanon in 1989, when Iraq, long occupied by its war with Iran and angered by Syrian support for Iran, began seriously to back a Christian faction that was opposed to Syrian and Iranian-supported Muslims. It seemed possible that, despite continuous efforts to recreate some government authority, Lebanon would stay divided into small, warring sectors. Iranian-backed extremists in Lebanon began to kidnap Americans and French in substantial numbers. Syrian President Assad was able to gain some leverage with the West by securing the release of a number of these. Israeli spokesmen were constrained to point out that Assad, more and more courted by Western statesmen, and viewed as something of a moderate, had used his troops to kill thousands of Muslim fundamentalists who had revolted in the Iraqi city of Hama in early 1982, and that Assad's army had proceeded to virtually level the town.

As the Iranian-backed groups gained strength, they refused further hostage releases. It was therefore to Iran that Reagan Administration figures turned in their ill-fated arms-for-hostages deal (see chapter 9). In late 1989, an Arab-sponsored attempt at settlement resulted in election of a new Lebanese president, but he was immediately assassinated.

Nevertheless, with Soviet support for Syria at an end by 1990, Saudi Arabia persuaded the Syrians to accept accords signed in the town of Ta'if, which the Saudis had negotiated and to which the various exhausted Lebanese factions had agreed. A precarious peace ensued, marked by occasional extremist assassinations. An unstable government was patched together, able to appeal for the foreign funds necessary for reconstruction. For now, the long civil war was over, but the border with Israel remained aflame.

Failed Peace Attempts in Palestine

In 1983 an attempt failed at settlement of the Palestine issue, based on the Reagan-sponsored concept of a Jordanian–West Bank federation as a framework for Palestinian self-determination. A renewed effort in 1985, again built around the idea of a Jordanian solution—now advanced by King Hussein—failed again in the face of the PLO's unwillingness to commit itself to the ultimate recognition of Israel and to abandonment of terrorism—and Israeli unwillingness to consider a Palestinian state under PLO auspices.

In fact, there was a revival of widespread terrorism by groups associated with the PLO in the latter half of 1985. In retaliation, Israeli planes flew all the way to Tunisia to bomb PLO headquarters in early October, and terrorists responded a week later by hijacking an Italian cruise ship, the *Achille Lauro*, and by attacking the Rome and Vienna airports. Presumably the terrorists were supported by Libya.

The Israelis, committed by the Camp David agreement to autonomy for the Palestinians, continued to refuse to have direct conversations with the PLO as representative of the Palestinians. The PLO, they argued, had been created by other Arab states; remained a terrorist organization, dedicated by its charter to the destruction of Israel; and could not be construed to represent the Arabs living in the West Bank and the Gaza Strip. The only solution was elections in the West Bank and Gaza, in which the PLO would not be allowed to terrorize the inhabitants, followed by an interim five-year period of autonomy while definitive solutions were worked out in the light of experience. An international conference, long suggested by other interested parties, such as the Soviet Union, would, Israelis argued, only allow these parties to fish in troubled waters. PLO offers to recognize Israel if it would recognize the PLO met with rejection.

In December 1987 a new element arose in the complex Middle East equation: Palestinians in the occupied areas of the West Bank and the Gaza Strip began a well-publicized and at its origin spontaneous uprising—the *intifada*—against the Israelis. The Israelis, used to occasional riots in the occupied territories, were determined to crush it within the few days they were sure it would take; but this time it was different. Night after night, world television showed well-armed Israeli soldiers taking action against stone-throwing Palestinians, and publicizing the casualties they inflicted. A year earlier, former Foreign Minister Abba Eban had declared that Israel must and could quit the territories before such a blowup occurred: the frustrations of years had built up to the point where they were bound to boil over. Now it was too late.

American Secretary of State George Shultz tried again to mediate, calling for an international conference that would bring about partial Israeli withdrawal and autonomy in the occupied territories for a period pending a permanent settlement. The formula ran up against the unhappy realities of several decades. Arabs insisted that UN Resolution 242 called for complete withdrawal, including withdrawal from the Arab section of Jerusalem, Israelis that it included partial, negotiated withdrawal—but that no withdrawal could take place until Arabs agreed to formal peace and recognition of Israel first. Sadat was willing to do this, but other Arab states or the PLO were unwilling. Nothing happened. Palestinians coped with the economic squeeze that Israel imposed, while the Israeli coalition government in Jerusalem equivocated, hoping that time would be on its side. Jerusalem's mayor Teddy Kolek (who had become an international figure through his attempt to show that, within a united Jerusalem, Arab and Jew could coexist peacefully and beneficially) now found his beloved city once again bitterly divided.

Two events now changed the situation. In a welter of considerable confusion—in Algiers, in Stockholm, and then in Geneva—the Palestine National Council and then PLO Chairman Arafat proclaimed the existence of a Palestinian state and "accepted the existence of Israel as a state in the region" while "renouncing all forms of terrorism, including individual, group and state terrorism." Within two hours, Secretary of State Schultz announced that the United States could now enter into a dialogue with the PLO. In the meantime, King Hussein of Jordan announced that he was cutting ties with the West Bank, which would now be on its own. In other words, the earlier, "Jordanian" solutions of federation, with Jordan and the West Bank as the real Palestine, were ruled out.

By 1989, the pressure on the Israelis to enter into negotiations for a Palestine state with the PLO had become very strong. Israel had hoped to reestablish diplomatic relations with the Soviet Union of Gorbachev, but Soviet Foreign Minister Eduard Shevardnadze announced in Cairo in February that diplomatic relations would not be resumed until Israel was willing to go into a conference with the PLO; President François Mitterrand of France upgraded the status of the PLO office in Paris and urged Israel to meet with PLO representatives; at the very moment Israeli President Chaim Herzog was attending Emperor Hirohito's funeral in Japan, the Japanese Foreign Ministry announced support for a conference including the PLO.

Israeli spokesmen tried to convince foreigners that the leopard had not changed its spots: the Palestine National Covenant of 1964 had still not been amended to remove its declaration that the existence of Israel was "null and void." Other PLO spokesmen than Arafat—his second in command, Abu Iyad, for example—continued to maintain that a Palestinian state in the occupied territories would be only a first step: "We shall liberate Palestine stage by stage . . . if the PLO succeeds in establishing a state in the West Bank and Gaza, it would not prevent the continuation of the struggle until the liberation of all of Palestine is achieved . . . ." Terrorist acts continued. Arafat himself approved of the killing of moderate Arabs who were ready to cooperate with Israeli authorities. Violence and counterviolence continued, despite Bush Administration efforts to broker a cessation of hostilities in Madrid in October of 1991, and in Washington in early 1992. (The Islamic Jihad organization destroyed the Israeli embassy in Argentina to demonstrate the extent of its reach, and Jews in that state found themselves the butt of increased anti-Semitism.) But Gorbachev's presence at the Madrid conference gave evidence of one changed factor in the equation: Soviet support for Arab hostility to the West and to Israel was beginning to fade out.

A Middle East Peace at Last?

With this, movement began in both the Israeli and the Palestinian camps. Labour, on a "land-for-peace" platform (i.e., that a Labour government would be willing to trade land in return for formal peace), defeated the Likud in Israeli elections, and Israel got long-delayed loan guarantees from the United States when the new government suspended distribution of land to settlers in the "occupied territories." In January 1993 the government quietly dropped a ban on Israeli contact with the PLO. In April, under Norwegian auspices, secret talks—out of the eye of the media—began between the Israeli government and the PLO in Oslo. On September 9, 1993, in front of the world, Prime Minister Itzhak Rabin of Israel and Yasir Arafat shook hands on the White House lawn in Washington, following the signing of an accord that put a peace process under way.

A letter from Arafat stated that "the Palestine Liberation Organization recognizes the right of the State of Israel to exist in peace and security," while Rabin declared, "The Government of Israel has decided to recognize the Palestine Liberation Organization as the representative of the Palestinian people." Moves got under way to transfer authority in the Gaza Strip and in the city of Jericho on the West Bank to the PLO, prior to further moves toward self-government.

The "peace process" would not be easy. Extremists on both sides opposed it as a betrayal of vital interests, and acts of terrorism multiplied, designed to thwart the peace agreement by showing it would produce only more terror. Labour's precarious hold on power in Israel was jeopardized, even as Rabin made allowances for Arafat's inability to curb terrorism by the growing opposition organization, Hamas. Both were trying hard. In October 1994 King Hussein of Jordan, two-thirds of whose subjects were Palestinian but who had not been informed of the secret Israeli-PLO negotiations, bowed to the inevitable and was able to do what his grandfather could not do forty-five years earlier: sign a peace treaty with Israel and stay alive. There were even signs that President Assad of Syria might move, depending on which way the wind seemed to blow.

The outcome, sadly, was made more doubtful in November 1995, when a fundamentalist Israeli student opposed to the peace process assassinated

Prime Minister Rabin. Grief there was, and Arafat, incredibly, visited the assassinated man's widow in Israel to condole with the family. The extent of jubilation in both Israeli and Arab circles showed how hard the road to lasting peace would be. Nevertheless—and despite resumed fighting on the Lebanese border—in April 1996 Arafat succeeded in having the PLO Charter amended to remove clauses calling for the replacement of Israel by a multinational Palestinian state. In response, Prime Minister Shimon Peres, who had replaced his longtime rival Rabin, announced that Israel would accept the existence of a Palestinian state.

Then, once again, to show that a peace of compromise was not inevitable, several Arab terrorist attacks in the heart of Israel led to a Likud victory in Israeli elections. A new, hard-line prime minister, Benjamin Netanyahu, promised the slim majority that had elected him that he would not make a peace that would jeopardize Israeli security. To the anger of Palestinians, he proceeded to allow expansion of Jewish settlements in the West Bank. Uncertainty returned in full.

The Unsettled Persian Gulf

Saddam Hussein's war against the Iran of Ayatollah Khomeini, as well as his invasion of Kuwait, which provoked the Gulf War of 1991, have already been described in chapter 9. Hussein's invasion of Kuwait provoked the enormous coalition that defeated his army in February 1991 and led to a curbing of Iraqi sovereignty, as the international community insisted on his dismantling of facilities for producing weapons of mass destruction. The most disturbing discoveries were that he was, in fact, much further advanced in chemical, bacterial, and nuclear weapons production than observers had thought. Defeat did not dislodge him from power in Iraq. His hegemonic aspirations, however, were at least temporarily thwarted, and the United States, against the wishes of its allies, maintained the UN embargo against Iraq until such time as Iraq exhibited "proper" international and domestic behavior. (The embargo was slightly relaxed for humanitarian reasons in mid-1996, when Saddam Hussein finally accepted international supervision of food distribution financed by limited oil sales.)

Yet the Persian Gulf area remained highly unstable in the mid-1990s. Saddam Hussein's Iraq was desperately seeking its way out of the embargo impasse, ready to rearm itself from willing French and Russian arms producers. Iran (still, as under the shah, the most potentially powerful regional state) undertook a considerable rearmament effort and worried observers by emplacing missiles on its Gulf Coast. Gulf Cooperation Council states felt the pinch of low oil prices; unrest exploded in

Map 19. **The Muslim World**

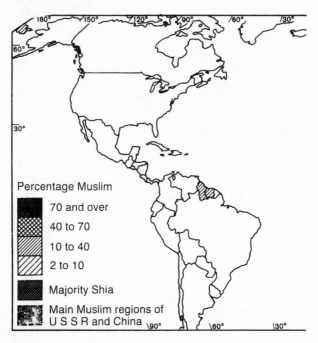

Bahrein. While the United States assumed a "dual containment" attitude vis-à-vis Iran and Iraq, it hardly looked like a policy. Moreover, while everyone involved had more or less acquiesced in leaving Saddam in place, preferring this to the possible breakup of Iraq with the chaos that might ensue, that breakup was still possible: it might, finally, mean a Kurdish state in the north. Establishment of such a state could embroil both Turkey and Iran, whose large Kurdish minorities would certainly want to break off to join it. A breakup might also mean a Shiite state in the south with a border on Saudi Arabia, a state in which Iranian influence would obviously be great.

Fundamentalist Unrest in the Muslim World

The 1979 revolution in Iran called attention to a growing phenomenon in the Muslim world, to which too many Westerners and Third World Westernized elites had paid little attention: the rise of Muslim fundamentalism. Islam has many houses, but some contemporary Muslims, in the face of their humiliation by the West and by the presence of Israel, were building a new one. Nasser, in his anger at the West, was a modernizing nationalist; Islamic fundamentalism was very different.* It was perhaps the depth of the revulsion to Western-style modernism that surprised Westerners the most.

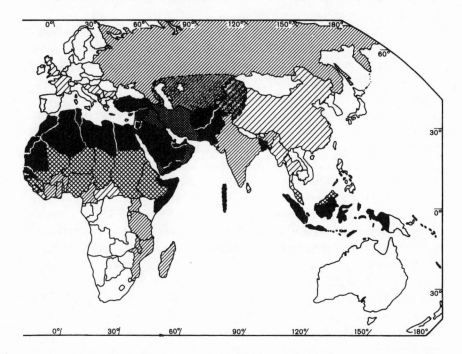

Source: Andrew Boyd, *Atlas of World Affairs* (London: Routledge, 1991).

To Muslim fundamentalists, liberal individualism in the West and its Marxist heresy meant materialism, luxury, lust, and pornography—the loss of soul. Western civilization was, as one writer put it, "aesthetically loathsome, ethically corrupt, and morally obtuse." Western influence should therefore be extirpated wherever it could be; Westernized elites should be destroyed; above all, Western-style education must be rooted out. Soviet influence, while inherently as bad as the Western, was always less pervasive, and therefore much less evil or dangerous.

Radical fundamentalists represented a minority among faithful Muslims. It was therefore a surprise when they won the struggle in Iran following the fall of the shah. There now arose a widening concern that the Ayatollah Ruhollah Khomeini might succeed in spreading Iranian-style radicalism to

---

*Islamic fundamentalism was not the only fundamentalist response to secular modernization and its discontents: Hindu fundamentalism grew in India, directing anger against the secular Indian state and heightening communal tensions. In addition, the extent of Christian fundamentalism in the United States, with its implicit and explicit rejection of separation between church and state, startled many people.

North Africa, the Arabian peninsula, Iraq, Pakistan, and Muslim areas of Russia, and even as far afield as Malaysia or Indonesia.

The Ayatollah ruptured ties with Israel, thereby removing one major barrier to Iranian influence in Arab countries. The view that the West was responsible for many of the ills and stresses within Arab societies certainly had a widespread appeal among certain classes, but the Iranian clerics over-estimated the centrality of their realm to the wider world of Islam.

The Shiite majority in Iraq did not rise up to overthrow their Sunni ruler, Saddam Hussein, despite all the incitement broadcast from Teheran. The tiny, oil-wealthy conservative Gulf states bound together in the Gulf Coop-erative Council appeared to be immune to the appeal of the Ayatollah. In November 1979, when Iranian-inspired extremists seized the Grand Mosque in Mecca, it took the Saudi government almost two weeks to cap-ture the last of them; the pilgrimage to Mecca in July 1987 (at a time of increasing Western naval presence in the Gulf) was the occasion for a clash between Iranian pilgrims and Saudi authorities, in which over 400 died. In far-off Tunisia the extremist Islamic Tendency Movement appeared to have been inspired by the Ayatollah, but the government resisted; in late 1987, shortly after decimating the leadership of the Movement, the aged Habib Bourguiba, in power since independence in 1956, was replaced by a more liberal-oriented General Ben Ali, rather than by anyone with a fundamental-ist orientation.

The possibility of fundamentalist appeal within the Russian sphere, much touted by Western observers, seems to have been exaggerated. On the other hand, as civil war continued in Afghanistan following Soviet withdrawal and the fall of Najibullah, several fundamentalist groups constituted the main contenders, and after the breakup of the Soviet Union, Iran reknit relations with Muslim successor states in the Commonwealth of Indepen-dent States (CIS), opening a number of new crossing points.

In Egypt there was more fertile ground: the army officers who assassi-nated Anwar Sadat in 1981 were radical fundamentalists. But Sadat's suc-cessor, Hosni Mubarak, consolidated his power, and was reaccepted into Arab ranks. Radicals remained on the political fringes (although in 1987 Mubarak broke off diplomatic relations with Iran after destroying an ex-tremist organization financed from there). In the 1990s radical funda-mentalists adopted a new tactic, attacks upon foreigners, designed to stop the lucrative tourist trade and weaken the government. In the ruins of the civil war of Lebanon, Iranian fundamentalism found a niche, inspiring and supporting fanatic groups like Hezbollah, the Party of God. At most—and unfortunately—such groups could sabotage moderates trying to achieve compromise. In Turkey, secular since the time of Ataturk, Muslim education was widened to check leftist tendencies in the 1960s and the 1970s, and to the considerable surprise of both Western circles ready to accept Turkey into European institutions and to Turkish governmental circles, a somewhat moderate fundamentalism gained ground rapidly. Following 1996 elections, the fundamentalist vote made it difficult to create a new government, but in July it was the leader of the fundamentalists who became prime minister.

In the early 1990s, following a time when the spread of radical Muslim fundamentalism appeared to have been checked, it reappeared in virulent form in numerous areas. Fundamentalism played a role among those who sought to derail the peace process in the Middle East, and as few benefits appeared to materialize for the inhabitants of the Gaza Strip and Jericho, it made substantial gains. In the Sudan, to the south of Egypt, fundamentalists who had received only 16 percent of the votes in 1986 elections seized power in 1989, backed by Iran. They sought to extend their sway to the countries surrounding Christian Ethiopia—Chad, Eritrea, and Kenya—and they supported fundamentalists in Egypt and in Saudi Arabia, Tunisia, and Algeria. Their resources, however, were slim. Nevertheless, Sudan was one country the United States named as a backer of terrorism, subject therefore to economic sanctions.

Algeria

Hundreds of miles to the west, in Algeria, a murderous Sunni extremism threatened to bring civil life to a virtual halt, and to spread to Muslims who now lived in large numbers in Western Europe. It was a fairly extraordinary development, for Algeria appeared to have been forged as a nation-state in the long war against France; until October 1988 it seemed to be one of the most stable of successor states to the French Union, governed from the time of independence by the National Liberation Front (FLN), the organization that had led the fight for independence and then realized a tight cooperation with the former colonial power. Exports of liquefied natural gas funded an extensive industrialization program, and much excess population had drained off into France, where two million Algerians and their offspring lived, maintaining close ties to Algeria itself. In the 1980s Algerian per capita income was four times that of neighboring Morocco, and the country enjoyed great prestige as a Third World leader. It was through Algeria that release of the American hostages in Iran was effected in 1981.

The stability proved deceptive: there had always been divisions within the FLN, population growth was enormous, the decline in oil income in the 1980s was disastrous, and the socialist economic structures created by the FLN were unwieldy. The Western crusade against Saddam Hussein stirred a

reaction. Democratic opposition to the FLN was divided, and fundamentalists of the Islamic Salvation Front (FIS) denounced the socialism of
the FLN, as well as corruption, secularism, and feminism. Riots in 1988 led
to the abolition of single-party government in 1989; to the flowering of
numerous democratic parties; and, in the first round of elections in January
1991, marked by only 50 percent participation, to the triumph of the FIS. To
keep the FIS from being voted into power, the army suppressed the second
round of elections and established military rule, bringing back into power
members of the FLN.

Since then, radical fundamentalists have resorted to an unprecedented
terror campaign of assassinations directed against intellectuals, journalists,
entertainers, writers, women in public life, and against the army. Since
1993, the campaign has also been directed against all foreigners, whose
governments by and large have warned them to leave. The government and
the army have resorted to bloody repression. If radical fundamentalists
attain power, another enormous flow of Algerians toward France will take
place.

In the meantime, all through Western Europe, the place of Muslims
within society has been brought into question, and Muslims suspected of
cooperating with the radicals in Algeria have been deported. In the United
States, radical Muslim fundamentalists set off an enormous explosion in the
World Trade Center in New York and planned numerous other bombings in
New York City, including the UN building, to protest America's role in the
Middle East. In the meantime, the European Union, long concerned about
demographic growth in North Africa and a resultant continued increase in
income differences between North Africa and Western Europe, began to
consider a partnership between the north and south coasts of the Mediterranean that harked back to a far older Mediterranean civilization. The EU
would now, however, have to consider the consequences of fundamentalism
for any such plans.

Arab Unity: The End of an Ideal

In the 1950s and the 1960s Egypt under Nasser was the center of the Arab
and Muslim world. Pride and honor were the hallmarks. Nasser had said to
the West, "may you choke on your own fury," when he had unilaterally
defied the strongest powers in the world to regain the Suez Canal and to
build the Aswan Dam; he had led an Arab world united in the one thing that
could unite it, the fight against Israel; he had become one of the most vital
leaders of a Third World organized to reclaim its heritage from the West.

Anwar Sadat tried to deal with Nasser's impossible legacy by abandoning the fight against Israel, reopening the Egyptian economy to the West, casting away the ambitious role of Arab and world leader. His successor Mubarak, seeking to deal with the continued weakness of the Egyptian economy, was even more cautious. One result was the shattering of even the idea of Arab unity, once personified by Nasser. Syria's Assad could not assume the mantle of Nasser, nor could Iraq's Hussein.

Qaddafi, in Libya, kept trying in the 1980s, but his base was too small and his views were too extreme. He signed pacts of union that led to nothing: with Egypt, Syria, and Chad in 1980, with Morocco in 1984. He backed opposition forces in Tunisia, Egypt, the Sudan, Somalia, and several West African states. A 1983 coup in Burkina Faso (formerly Upper Volta) installed a military regime that accepted Libyan subsidies. Qaddafi's agents, working out of diplomatic missions, carried out assassinations of dissidents who had fled Libya. Qaddafi subsidized and backed German, Irish, Palestinian, Basque, Corsican, and other terrorist groups. Claiming the Gulf of Sidra as international waters, he sent his fighters to tangle with American planes from aircraft carriers that sailed into the gulf to challenge his assertions. Libyan soldiers fought on behalf of the unspeakable Idi Amin Dada in Uganda and in Chad, where they tried to secure a northern strip that might provide uranium ore to be sent to Iraq and Pakistan for the "Muslim bomb." (A thousand French soldiers remain in Chad, presumably to deter further Libyan adventures.) The decline of Soviet bloc aid and the rise of a Muslim fundamentalism in disagreement with his political views appear to have kept him quiet in the 1990s.

In the circumstances, Arab unity remained a chimera.

Conclusion

While the grand ambitions of Nasser, Assad, Saddam Hussein, Khomeini, and Qaddafi have been blocked, the Middle East region together with North Africa remains a powder keg, its explosive power enhanced by the growth of the new force, radical fundamentalism. Enormously expensive wars were fought—inconclusively in the case of Iraq and Iran, conclusively so far as Iraqi control of Kuwait was concerned, and incredibly destructively so far as Lebanon and the city of Beirut were concerned. The Iran-Iraqi War saw both sides use poison gas; in 1988 Libya was accused of having built a very large chemical weapons plant and Syria of having nerve gas capability. Both Iran and Iraq used surface-to-surface missiles in their war, and Iraq used them against Israel in the Gulf War.

In April 1987, to try to cope with the missile race, the United States, the United Kingdom, France, West Germany, Italy, Canada, and Japan signed the Missile Technology Control Regime to restrict transfer of missile technologies. As long as major suppliers such as the Soviet Union, China, and Brazil were not parties to the agreement, its effect remained limited, and the breakup of the Soviet Empire freed enormous numbers of weapons to flow onto the international market. In March 1995, despite American protests, Russia agreed to build a nuclear reactor in Iran. Given political instability and extremism in the area, there was plenty of cause for worry.

The Arab-Israeli peace process gave some people hope, but it also raised the anger of others. Turkish politics were much concerned with whether Turkey was a part of Europe or a part of the Middle East; Egypt's capacity to grow fast enough to satisfy its growing population remained in doubt. Among other matters, no one in the rest of the world could forget that two-fifths of the world's known oil resources lay under the states of the Middle East—fully one-quarter under Saudi Arabia alone. The world price of oil had returned to pre-1973 levels. Westerners in their automobiles might rejoice, but Arabs fumed. There was always the question of whether political events would make a weakened OPEC a world player once again.

Suggested Further Readings

Michael Field, *Inside the Arab World* (Cambridge: Harvard University Press, 1995), is a serious and useful source, and so is A. Robert Springborg, *Politics in the Middle East* (New York: HarperCollins, 1994). On Turkey's dilemma, see Shireen T. Hunter, *Turkey at the Crossroads: Islamic Past or European Future* (Brussels: Centre for European Policy Studies, 1995). Geoffrey Kemp and Janice Gross Stein, (eds.), *Powder Keg in the Middle East: The Struggle for Gulf Security* (London: Rowman and Littlefield, 1995), is a collection of essays on a highly unstable and globally crucial region.

13

Africa and Latin America

To group Africa and Latin America in one chapter is not arbitrary: both continents have tended to play a lesser role in global politics.

Africa has nevertheless been a focus of international concern. As African countries became independent, the continent became briefly an area for Cold War struggle, complicated by the period of Chinese-Russian competition. The United States, early on, left African relations with the rest of the world largely to the Europeans, which meant mainly to France (though the United States and other European countries continued considerable economic aid). Nasser, in Egypt, flirted with becoming an African leader, but abandoned the attempt to concentrate on the Middle East. In the 1960s and the 1970s, domestic pressures in the United States pushed the government into punitive measures it was not eager to take with respect to mineral-rich southern Africa. The Nixon administration hoped to continue good relations with these governments; the corrupt and gradually collapsing polity of Zaire was retained by the United States as its chief client state in Africa.

The complications of African conflicts have engendered mostly despair, despite UN and Organization of African Unity (OAU) attempts to resolve some of them. The specter of famine has prompted international concern and action; the end of apartheid in South Africa brought celebration and cautious optimism. African diplomats and Africanists have tried to keep the area's problems alive in the hearts and minds of world leaders, but enduring and seemingly intractable conflicts within Africa have diminished the effect of the appeals.

Latin America has been less a matter of concern, although Fidel Castro has kept it in the public eye. In the post–World War II era, apart from the Castro/Russian attempt to influence affairs in the Caribbean and in South and Central America, Latin America's international relations have been largely between states within Latin America and with the United States, the "Colossus of the North." Only recently has the pattern begun to change somewhat, as Pacific and European connections have grown. Extension of the North American Free Trade Association (NAFTA), on the other hand, may reinforce the reality of "the Americas."

Africa: Darkness and Light

Darkness

In the 1980s and the 1990s, public attention focused on the drama of dismantlement of apartheid in South Africa; on the effect of this dismantlement on neighboring states, including Namibia and Mozambique; on continued civil war in Angola; on the withdrawal of Soviet-supported Cuban troops; on renewed, massive massacres in the tiny states of Rwanda and Burundi; and on "humanitarian intervention" in Somalia. These developments were all played out against a broader dark background: of falling incomes in the poorest states of the world; of decreased export earnings and growing debt; of drought and famine; of the spread of AIDS; and of continuing high rates of infant mortality.

In the area of infant mortality, part of the problem lay in the fact that the rates had actually declined sharply from even higher levels since World War II: African life expectancy at birth had soared from 30 in 1950 to 53 by 1980, collapsing into a short time a change that had taken hundreds of years in the West. As a result, African population growth rates were the highest in the world; Kenya held the record. By 1990, the demographic profile for the future was disheartening. Half of Africa's population was under sixteen years of age; its population of 500 million would double to a billion in a mere twenty-two years—a tenth the time it had taken the world at large to do the same thing. A continent that could feed itself in 1960 imported 25 percent of its food by the mid-1980s, at a cost in exports it simply couldn't afford. AIDS was widespread, in a broad swath across central Africa.

One result was that traditional modes of living were in many cases no longer sufficient, and an often wrenching change was now a necessity. But elites that benefited from having taken over the centralized administration from former colonial masters too often were able to milk an impoverished people to keep themselves and their bureaucrats and armies in control. Blame for the desperate situation could be placed upon former colonial masters, upon artificial boundaries created by imperialism, upon neocolonialism, upon capitalist-created dependency relationships, upon the unfair structure of the international economy, and upon the 1980s debt crisis. It was therefore up to the rest of the world to save Africa. There was some element of truth in any of these explanations and solutions.

Many observers argued, however, that indigenous factors—climate, topography, location, the nature of African societies, domestic politics and policies, and military conflicts, as well as the demographic factor—played a key role, although the oil price rises of 1974 and 1979 caused much of the debt and the resultant belt-tightening. There was bitter disagreement over the explanations of catastrophe: in 1988 the World Bank issued a report purporting to show that African countries relying upon state control of the economy had done the worst; the UN Economic Commission for Africa in Addis Ababa attacked this report, saying that it was unduly optimistic about market reforms. But the bank's follow-up report, issued in 1989, warned that unless agricultural productivity increased through the unleashing of individual energies (i.e., removing the deadening hand of bureaucracy) along with an increase in the flow of capital (which would happen only if governments interfered less), there might well be a "nightmare scenario." Many analysts agreed. In the meantime, the International Monetary Fund (IMF), in dealing with African debt, became a major player in African domestic politics, imposing "structural readjustment" on countries, without—critics charged—concern for the poorest classes who suffered the most. Even wholesale debt cancellation, however, would not resolve the problems the IMF was trying to deal with: restoring growth to stagnant economies with growing populations. Some Africans agreed: at the inaugural session of the Africa Leadership Forum in Nigeria in 1988, its organizer and former head of state, General Olusegun Obasanjo, declared that Africa had "marginalized itself." He contrasted African decay to the growth of Asian countries as poor as African states at the time of independence, as politically unstable, and no more historically self-confident. He blamed "human failure" and "our false political start."

Nevertheless, outside developments continued to play a role. The Ivory Coast represented a relative economic success story until the collapse of cocoa prices in the 1980s. The Ivory Coast had built its economy around commercial export, but the entry of Malaysia in force into the world cocoa market depressed prices drastically. In 1989 the coffee-exporting countries of East Africa faced a sharp drop in the price of the coffee they sold when the International Coffee Agreement collapsed in the face of increased world production and cut-rate sales to nonmembers. Far-away Brazil appeared to be selling as much as it could: African vulnerabilities to the actions and interests of other Third World states were once again apparent. Not until September 1993 was a new coffee producers' agreement negotiated, designed to restrict production and raise prices.

Nigeria, the most populous African state, demonstrated in a different way the extent to which African countries were subject to far-off events.

Rich in petroleum (concentrated in the area that would have become Biafra in 1967; see chapter 6), it participated almost disastrously in the oil boom of the 1970s. Per capita income rose by 50 percent, but the income went largely into government pockets and unsuitable projects, drawing agricultural workers into the cities and two million immigrants in from Ghana and other neighboring states. When oil prices collapsed in the mid-1980s, Nigeria found itself incurring an enormous debt for continued imports, its former agricultural self-sufficiency gone. Among other measures, the government responded by expelling the immigrants, who had to be reabsorbed in their own poverty-stricken countries. A chaotic political situation ensued, with one military coup succeeding another. A border conflict developed with the Cameroun, reflecting widespread internal disaffection. In 1995, when the military government that had prevented a civilian government from taking power hanged a number of well-known dissidents, international protest grew. (Significantly, the giant, multinational Shell Oil Company said that unless legal economic sanctions were voted, it would continue its operations in the area from which the dissidents had come, thus helping to keep the government in power.) The country many people had expected to become the industrial giant of Africa looked as though it might become bankrupt.

Hostilities East and West

Mismanagement clearly played a role. So, unhappily, did the many armed conflicts that continued to plague the continent. The difficulties the Organization of African Unity faced is exemplified by an incident in which so many heads of state stayed away from an OAU summit meeting in Libya that it could not muster a quorum—because Libya was mounting a large-scale intervention in Chad.

Many of those armed conflicts have already been cited: the civil war in Chad compounded by Libyan intervention; the bitter, lost war for Biafran independence in Nigeria that brought international support for both sides; the war in the former Belgian Congo (Zaire); the recurrent war in the Sudan; wars between Ethiopia and Somalia and between Ethiopia and Eritrea; the wars for independence in Portuguese Africa, Namibia, and Rhodesia (now Zimbabwe); the invasion of Uganda by Tanzania to oust Idi Amin Dada; and the massacres in Rwanda and Burundi, which were renewed in Burundi in August 1988, and in Rwanda in 1994. Millions have died in these wars, and the almost inestimable costs of war have come largely at the expense of possible development. At the OAU meeting in July 1986, President Yoweri Museveni of Uganda declared, "in twenty years almost 750,000 Ugandans perished at the hands of governments whose duty it was to protect them. Ugandans have a profound sense of betrayal in the face of the silence of most African governments as they were being massacred by tyrants." By 1989, however, gross domestic product in Uganda was reviving; half the Asians displaced in 1972 had regained their business; and Museveni had been able to provide a period of domestic peace and reconciliation that gave hope for the future, despite Islamic agitation from Khartoum and the presence of hundreds of thousands of refugees.

There were also innumerable coups and countercoups: ten of the fourteen states that formerly composed French West Africa and French Equatorial Africa suffered from such coups between 1960 and 1985, while only Senegal and the Ivory Coast retained relatively stable civilian governments. This, by itself, was not enough: Senegal per capita income stagnated through the decades (and Senegal had to absorb tens of thousands of black Senegalese in the late 1980s when they were expelled from Mauritania, where they held the most productive positions but for long years were subject to harassment).

The near-bankrupt Organization of African Unity continued to try to do what it could. Eight West African countries sent a 20,000-man peacekeeping force to Liberia following the outbreak of civil war in 1989, when President Samuel Doe was assassinated. An estimated 150,000 people died by the time the OAU was able to secure a peace between the three warring factions in 1993, and to begin disarming the estimated 60,000 armed militia men. The peace broke down, however, and by 1996 horrific warfare between the unruly factions resumed, with little prospect for an end to hostilities.

To the east, in the Horn of Africa, matters were little better, though again a few rays of light appeared. By the 1980s, the centrally managed Ethiopian economy under the regime of Mengistu Haile Mariam was in shambles. Corruption and mismanagement in the distribution of internationally supplied food shipments, and the blocking of shipments for political purposes, contributed to famine and the horrendous human rights record of the regime. In April 1988 President Mengistu ordered all foreign relief workers to leave the areas of insurrection in Eritrea and Tigre provinces and to turn over their supplies and equipment to the government, crippling the effort to care for the five to seven million estimated to be in danger of starvation.

Successive Ethiopian efforts to crush the Eritrean and Tigre rebel movements all failed. Soviet and Cuban support began to disappear in the late 1980s. The 25,000 Cuban troops melted away, and in May 1991 the Mengistu government fell, to be replaced by a coalition. One result was that an impoverished and war-torn Eritrea achieved its independence after thirty years of intermittent armed conflict.

Somalia, to the south and east of Ethiopia, was where the UN and the

United States undertook their much-heralded humanitarian intervention (recounted in chapter 9), whose results were highly mixed. Somalia demonstrated the dilemmas facing countries and organizations devoted to development aid. Italy, the United States, the World Bank, the IMF, and the African Development Bank all provided agricultural aid during the time of the Siyaad Barre regime. Some critics argued that such aid helped to prop up the horrendous regime and should be contingent on an end to gross human rights violations, but others argued that aid should go to people who might otherwise starve, regardless of the regime. After an intervention took place to see that aid went to those who needed it, Americans saw jubilant Somalis on television dragging a dead American helicopter pilot through the streets, and many asked why the United States should be helping.

Immediately to the west and north of Ethiopia, Sudan is the largest—and one of the most miserable—of African countries. There the brutal Sixteen Years' War, or Long War, dragged on from 1956 until 1972, pitting dominant Arab Muslim north against black Christian and animist south. The Emperor Haile Selassie and the World Council of Churches secured an end to the fighting in 1972 and a seemingly successful integration of north and south that lasted for a decade, until broken again by revolt against the government's application of Islamic law throughout the country in September 1983. The southern rebels, this time known as the Sudan People's Liberation Army, were now backed by the Ethiopian government of Mengistu.

Successive changes of regime in Khartoum (the capital of Sudan) and the fall of Mengistu in Ethiopia brought little relief. In 1989, following three years of rule by an ineffective elected government, Sunni Islamic fundamentalists, who had long worked at penetrating governmental institutions, seized power. They had, as noted earlier, broader aims of spreading their religion to neighboring countries; to do this, they needed to reconquer the south and its richer agricultural lands. In their brutal attempt to capture these lands, an estimated 3.5 million people have been displaced, and hundreds of thousands have died. Sudan was named by the United States as a state sponsoring terrorism, its membership in the International Monetary Fund was suspended, and it was condemned by the UN Commission on Human Rights. With the country impoverished by the cost of the war in the south, the rulers of Sudan face the south's demand for independence, which was articulated at a conference between all parties held in Washington in 1993. The failure of the most important offensive in the winter of 1993–94, combined with penury and war weariness in the north, may lead to partition. It would mean wholesale defeat of the universalist fundamentalists in control in Khartoum.

The Maghreb

In the 1980s, in the northwest, across a thousand miles of desert, the region known as the Maghreb (Tunisia, Algeria, and Morocco) appeared to be on its way to resolving many of its problems and moving toward close ties with a united Europe. For one thing, the longstanding battle between Morocco and the Algerian-backed Polisario National Front over the area formerly known as the Spanish Sahara, abandoned by Spain in 1976, appeared to wind down in the 1990s. The OAU at one point favored admitting the Polisario as the Saharan Arab Democratic Republic, by a vote of 26 to 24, but a threat of withdrawal by Morocco prevented it, and support later dwindled. UN peacekeeping forces were introduced to oversee a referendum, which still had not been held as of this writing. In the meantime, Moroccan King Hassan moved toward a constitutional monarchy, free elections, better observance of human rights, and an association agreement with the European Union. When Itzhak Rabin and Yasir Arafat signed their peace accord in Washington in 1995, Rabin and Foreign Secretary Shimon Peres stopped off in Rabat, the capital of Morocco, on their way home, symbolizing the Moroccan interest in the Middle East peace process and the king's growing international role.

Despite the ongoing guerrilla warfare in the Western Sahara, in 1988 Algeria and Morocco reestablished diplomatic relations, which had been broken in 1976. The act appeared to symbolize a new realism in the Maghreb, and the influence of European dynamism, as well as the entry of Spain and Portugal into the Common Market: the two countries had been important markets for the Maghreb. The Moroccan economy, hampered by debt and a very high birthrate, began to react positively to a program of liberalization set in motion in the late 1980s. Tunisia removed the word "Socialist" from the name of its ruling party, opened the doors of its jails to release political prisoners, and began a program of privatization, while improving its relations with Libya, Egypt, and the United States all at once. A new government in Algeria also began to tackle the problems of the economy. By the 1990s, the Maghreb leaders appeared determined to share in the benefits of European integration rather than to be shut out. In late 1995 Morocco and Tunisia signed new cooperation accords with the European Union.

What was the hope of the 1990s, however, became the despair of 1996: the Algerian fundamentalists' response to suppression of elections in 1991, recounted in chapter 12, meant there was little possibility of a united Maghreb associated with the EU, and stimulated anti-Arab feeling throughout Europe.

Light: Southern Africa and the End of Apartheid

At the opposite end of the continent, however, cautious elation emerged as apartheid—the legally imposed separation of black, white, and colored—disappeared in South Africa.

The fight against apartheid in South Africa was intimately linked to continued warfare in Namibia, Angola, and Mozambique, countries to the immediate north of South Africa. In the 1980s, while warfare continued to decimate the region, the Reagan Administration was ultimately able to negotiate a settlement between Angola, Namibia, and South Africa that resulted in independence for Namibia and the withdrawal of Cuban troops from Angola. It was a package in line with UN resolutions, and with something in it for everyone: the withdrawing Cubans were able to claim that they had pressured South Africa into granting independence to Namibia, while the Russians who had supported the Cuban troops cut their costs and improved relations with the United States. The contending parties in Angola both gained: the governing Popular Movement for the Liberation of Angola (MPLA), despite loss of Cuban support, gained from withdrawal of South Africa from Namibia, across which aid had flown to the opposition National Movement for the Total Independence of Angola (UNITA). UNITA gained from the withdrawal of Cuban troops: the MPLA would now have to negotiate with UNITA rather than trying to crush it.

Cuban troops began their withdrawal in 1989. (Castro once boasted that 400,000 Cuban troops had received combat training over the years in Angola.) In June 1989, a gathering of African leaders persuaded the MPLA and UNITA to sign a cease-fire and to prepare for some form of Angolan coalition government. UN-supervised elections took place in Namibia, where a fragile peace was established. In 1993 South Africa turned over a deep-water port to the Namibians.

Unfortunately, while UN-supervised Angolan elections took place in September 1992 and the victorious MPLA formed a government, UNITA returned to the bush to carry out what became an even more murderous civil war. Famine, pauperization, and corruption were the inevitable outcome. Only in 1995 did it appear that the exhausted UNITA forces might lay down their arms.

Mozambique, to the northeast of South Africa, had also followed a downward but somewhat different course since independence from Portugal in 1975: drought, administrative incapacity, political disaffection, and South African—supported rebellion on the part of the Mozambique National Resistance (RENAMO) all helped give Mozambique the distinction of being the poorest state in the world. With agriculture as virtually its only source of income, by the late 1980s it nevertheless relied upon international food aid for more than half of its consumption. Hundreds of thousands of refugees huddled in camps after their villages were destroyed, and an estimated 600,000 to 700,000 persons died. Only the beginnings of change within South Africa in the early 1990s weakened RENAMO. The government of Mozambique dropped many of its disastrous statist policies, and with heavy international pressure RENAMO joined in elections in 1995. For the first time in a decade there appeared a glimmer of light.

In the meantime, and key to the developments in Angola and Mozambique, the unthinkable happened in South Africa.

For years the UN General Assembly had passed resolutions condemning South Africa—for its racial policies, its continued illegal occupation of Namibia, and its attacks upon black South African rebel bases in neighboring countries—and had called for economic sanctions. While growing black consciousness and resistance played, perhaps, the crucial role, the limited sanctions movement also began to have some effect in the 1980s: economic growth fell below population growth, investor confidence declined, the country could no longer attract necessary new foreign capital, capital flight developed, and South Africa had to borrow heavily to maintain imports. South African currency depreciated, inflation grew, and increasing black unemployment fed growing unrest.

In previous years the government had followed a policy of trying to create "independent" black homelands—the "Bantustans"—into which it could move unemployed blacks. The ultimate result would be a federal patchwork of black and white regions (in which, however, blacks would have to provide much of the labor for the white regions). Other countries refused to recognize the Bantustans as independent, and most black leaders argued that the only solution for South Africa was a one-person/one-vote system for the area as a whole: segregated residential areas and voting lists would have to go. In 1989 South Africa was now relieved of the burden of Namibia, after seventy-five years and the new government of Prime Minister Frederick W. de Klerk began making cautious moves toward total change. It increased its contacts with opposition leaders and activists, freed leaders of the outlawed African National Congress (ANC), and allowed mass demonstrations and marches by antiapartheid campaigners. It desegregated all public facilities.

Then, dramatically, de Klerk released Nelson Mandela, the African National Congress leader who had been in jail since 1962. After meeting with Mandela—but reassuring the Parliament that change would only be made by consensus—de Klerk lifted the emergency decrees it had been operating under for so many years. Mandela made a triumphant tour of Western

Europe and the United States. De Klerk, following him a few months later, promised President Bush and the U.S. Congress that he would install a one-person/one-vote system, and would free the last political prisoners.

With this, on July 10, 1991, President Bush lifted the economic sanctions against South Africa. Within three years, elections were open to all races. Extremist opposition on the right had to be neutralized; so did the leaders of the Bantustans created under previous policies, who did not want to lose their governing powers. (When the leaders of Bophuthatswana and Ciskei were overthrown, it became obvious that both these and the two other Bantustans—Transkei and Venda—would have to give in.) Despite widespread violence the elections of April 26–29, 1994, led to an ANC victory. Nelson Mandela, the long-imprisoned black leader, became president. He continued the policy of power sharing by naming one ANC vice-president and Frederick W. de Klerk as his second vice-president. All this constituted a remarkable performance on the parts of both Mandela and de Klerk. They now faced the vast job of economic and social integration following the years of apartheid and the decade of economic decline. The play was far from over.

Latin America: Development, Democracy, and Drugs

Development

In the 1960s and the 1970s, most Latin American and Caribbean countries underwent fundamental economic and social changes that would force analysts to recast many of their views of Latin American underdevelopment.

As noted earlier, enormous population growth persisted in many areas, and urbanization continued almost unchecked. By 1995, three-quarters of the population lived in urban centers; ten cities with populations of a million in 1960 will give way to forty-eight such cities by 2000, of which ten will have populations of over five million. Mexico City and Sao Paulo became the largest urban agglomerations in the world. Life expectancy at birth grew from fifty-one years at the time of World War II to sixty-four years; educational expenditures and enrollments soared; rates of literacy increased substantially; and greatly increased numbers of university-educated technologically oriented elites competed with traditional landholding, church, and military elites. In Colombia, where women had no right to vote until 1957, 50 percent of university students were women by the 1980s. Per capita income throughout Latin America doubled between 1960 and 1980, while there was an extraordinary increase in industrial exports. Internally, to avoid traditional state controls on economic activity, an enormous parallel unofficial economy developed in many countries (often falsifying official statistics that indicated lower levels of economic activity than actually existed).

Markets for Latin exports diversified: West Germany, France, Spain, and Japan joined the United States as major purchasers. Canada indicated its interest in Latin America by finally joining the Organization of American States (OAS). For a while, in the Brezhnev era and then in the Gorbachev era, the possibility of increased relations with the socialist bloc seemed an attractive possibility. Most Latin governments reestablished relations with the Soviet Union in the 1960s and the 1970s. Argentina and Brazil took advantage of the new situation to sell large quantities of grain to the Soviets when President Jimmy Carter embargoed grain sales in retaliation for the invasion of Afghanistan in late 1979. But sales to the Soviet Union never grew to more than 1 percent of total exports, and the collapse of the Soviet system ended the attempt to cultivate important economic relations with Russia. Nevertheless, by the 1990s, most Latin American economies were much more involved in the world economy than previously—as, unfortunately, the debt issue of the 1980s and the drug issue both showed.

The debt crisis (already discussed; see chapter 10) reversed growth trends for a period of years in the 1980s, provoking austerity policies with unhappy consequences for much of the population, and also provoking numerous internal conflicts. Yet, in contrast to the 1970s, the 1980s were by and large the era of restoration of fragile democracy. Border issues still existed, born of nineteenth-century wars, but most were being resolved peacefully. Some, like that of Venezuela's claim to large parts of Guyana or Bolivia's claim to Chilean lands that cut it off from the sea, lay dormant. In 1984 a conflict between Argentina and Chile over islands to the south was finally settled peacefully in favor of Chile. Only occasional border skirmishes made headlines, such as the one between Peru and Ecuador in early 1995. The brief war between Argentina and the British over the Malvinas, or the Falkland Islands, as the British called them, in 1982 (see chapter 9) had the serendipitous result of toppling the brutal military regime in Argentina, producing a return to civilian, democratic rule. The economic results, during the rest of the dismal decade of the 1980s, were not so happy, but in the 1990s a remarkable if fragile recovery began to restore optimism.

The debt problem was, ostensibly, resolved through various reduction schemes and through discounted sales of liabilities. Latin countries by and large resumed growth in the 1990s, with many resorting by necessity to harsh, structural, market-oriented reforms, and with a few, like Venezuela, falling further behind. The benefits of growth were still not widely shared.

Map 20. **South America**

As the dream of Marxist revolution faded, and most guerrilla movements with it (with the signal exception of the murderous "Shining Path" movement in Peru, which persisted despite capture of its leader in December 1992), countries looked again to possible regional solutions to the problems of continued growth: Venezuela, Mexico, and Colombia signed a free trade agreement in 1994, which is due to come into effect over a ten-year period, overlapping the earlier Andean Pact. Further to the south, Argentina, Brazil, Uruguay, and Paraguay created "Mercosur," a giant customs union inaugurated on January 1, 1995. In December its members signed an agreement with the European Union to work toward a free trade agreement: already one-fourth of Mercosur trade was with the EU. The Pacific beckoned also: Asian countries were doing what many Latins thought their own countries ought to be able to do, and many wanted to share in the process. (South Korea's ability to grow itself out of its debt was taken by many as an indication that culture, not dependency, lay at the heart of the issue of development.) The Peruvians elected a president of Japanese extraction, Alberto Fujimoro, hoping he might attract Japanese investment. By the mid-1990s, Latin American trade with the major Asian trading states was second only to that with the United States, outstripping trade with Europe, and South Korea became a major investor throughout Latin America. One new regional solution loomed large: the North American Free Trade Association (NAFTA).

The North American Free Trade Association

The United States and Canada signed a free trade agreement in 1989, and Mexico joined in 1994, creating NAFTA. NAFTA assembled countries with far more differences than those composing the European Union. Mexico might be as urbanized as the other two, but its official per capita income was one-eighth that of its two partners. In addition, its indigenous population was far greater—and the signing of NAFTA took place just at a time of reassertion of their identity by such groups all through the Americas (coincident with the five-hundredth anniversary of Columbus's first landing). Negotiations were arduous, and the Mexican government, anxious to sign an agreement that would give Mexico the standing of a developed country, agreed to a number of provisions favoring American agriculture and investments in Mexican petroleum. Opposition in the United States mounted, on the grounds that industry would move south to a lower-wage area with, as environmentalists noted, lower environmental standards. American jobs—perhaps very many jobs—would be lost. To obtain ratification, President Clinton had to renegotiate certain clauses of the treaty that would ensure job security and respect for environmental norms. The treaty came into force on January 1, 1994, and South American countries like Chile and Venezuela began to knock at the door. Proponents of an American free trade area to face off the European Union or the Pacific rim began to make their voices heard.

The bubble burst in late 1994. The Mexican government was fearful of taking action to correct a growing balance-of-payments deficit financed by short-term bonds before presidential elections in the fall. Assassination of a presidential candidate (in which the brother of President Carlos Salinas was later implicated, and which made Salinas himself lose the possibility of becoming head of the new World Trade Organization, or WTO) provoked further pessimism. A run on the peso ensued; as the short-term bonds came due, the government was forced into a massive austerity program, and the United States came to the rescue of the currency, pumping billions of dollars into support of the currency through an international rescue effort. The further result was capital flight not only from Mexico but from other Latin countries. The collapse of the peso was followed by a sharp drop in the dollar, as dollars flooded the market and the decrease in exports to Mexico from the United States increased the U.S. payments deficit. The global effect on other currencies was equally spectacular: the three strong currencies—the Japanese yen, the German mark, and the Swiss franc—soared.

What had started in North America as an optimistic response to resumption of Latin growth and the classing of Mexico and other Latin countries among the newly industrializing countries (NICs) of Asia resulted in gloomy pessimism and international financial turmoil. The enormous flows of capital made possible by the computer and communications revolution inspired comments about the need for further strengthening of international institutions and their controls, as well as other comments on the need to find ways to isolate states and their economies from international fluctuations over which they had no control.

Nevertheless, Latin recovery from the new crisis began in mid-1995. A few months earlier, in Miami, Florida, representatives from both North America and South America had affirmed their will to create a free trade zone stretching from Alaska to Tierra del Fuego, and Brazil approached the Andean Pact nations with a view to signing a South American Free Trade Agreement that might negotiate with NAFTA on a more even basis.

In the meantime, as earlier chapters have indicated, the collapse of the Soviet Union, its cessation of aid to Cuba, and the resulting isolation of the island state, all redounded to a lessening of the guerrilla activities that had so long fostered repressive military governments throughout Latin America, and had encouraged American intervention. As the year 2000 approached, despite numerous problems—in particular, that of an increasing gap in incomes between rich and poor—Latin America as a whole looked as though it might, finally, begin to attain the growth and success its countries had sought for so long.

The Caribbean

The Clinton Administration pioneered a new style of U.S. intervention in Haiti in 1994.

American hegemony was secured in the Caribbean when the United States drove Spain from Cuba in 1898, completed the Panama Canal in 1914, and bought the Virgin Islands from Denmark in 1917. Some of the smaller Caribbean islands have remained French overseas departments; some have remained Dutch or British; and a dozen that once constituted the West Indian Federation, broken up in 1962, opted for independence from Britain. A number formed the Organization of Eastern Caribbean States, and it was this group that called for the American invasion of neighboring Grenada in 1982. Among the larger islands, Jamaica toyed with a Marxist, democratic-socialist, pro-Castro orientation under Prime Minister Michael Manley between 1972 and 1980. A fear of otherwise dire consequences prodded the Reagan Administration into launching the Caribbean Basin Initiative (CBI) to stimulate trade; to provide investment incentives; and to renew aid to a region hard hit by the high interest rates, debt, and fall in commodity prices of the early 1980s. The initiative had some success in countering the negative trends. Puerto Rico, in the meantime, continued in its uncertain "commonwealth" status with the United States, facing continual international challenge as to the validity of its self-governing status.

The Cuban revolution of 1959 brought a Soviet presence into the area. As the Soviet empire crumbled, however, Soviet naval power was withdrawn and Russian aid tapered off. Castro himself railed at Gorbachev's glasnost, perestroika, and "new thinking." Castro was forced to institute a drastic austerity program, and to allow an opening of the economy to private enterprise. He also suggested that he would be willing to negotiate compensation for some of what had been nationalized in the early years, as well as to allow more emigration. Trade with other Latin states rose from 7 percent of overall Cuban trade to 47 percent, as trade with the former socialist bloc dropped off, and the Latin states in the Organization of American Unity called for a lifting of the embargo on Cuba.

Debate within the United States centered on whether an opening and an accommodation would lead to a soft landing for the Cuban polity, or whether continuation of a hard line would lead, finally, to Castro's over-

338 THREE-QUARTERS OF THE WORLD

throw. (In the meantime, the resilient "Maximum Leader" received a re-
sounding reception at the Copenhagen world conference on social affairs in
March 1995, and was an honored guest in Paris, at the home of French
President François Mitterrand, whose wife told the public that Castro represented the summum of what socialism could accomplish.) Then, in mid-
1996, the Cubans shot down two small, civilian, Miami-based planes
belonging to anti-Castro forces, which were deliberately violating Cuban air
space. The American Congress rapidly passed a bill tightening sanctions on
Cuba, extending them to foreign firms that dealt in any property that might
have been expropriated from Americans earlier. (It also passed a bill pun-
ishing foreign firms that dealt with countries presumably supporting international terrorism—Libya, Syria, and Iran.) Both bills were condemned by
foreign governments as violations of their sovereignty, which might be
punished by trade sanctions against the United States. It was hard to argue
the legality of the American laws.

Haiti

Reagan's Caribbean Basin Initiative might well have helped some Caribbean islands, but it did little for impoverished Haiti, and it was events in
Haiti upon which international attention focused in the 1990s.

Upheaval followed the flight of the last of the Duvalier dictators in
1986. In 1990 a liberation theologian, Father Jean-Bertrand Aristide, was
elected president. He was overthrown by a military coup in September
1991, which was supported by the few wealthy Haitian families and by
narcotics dealers. Under UN auspices, halfhearted pressures were brought
to bear against the military government. The Clinton Administration, embarrassed by turning back Haitian refugees after condemning the Bush Administration for doing so, sought and seemingly obtained a negotiated
solution in June 1993, after a tough embargo was put into place.* The
mighty United States was then publicly humiliated on October 11, when a
ship bearing an advance landing party of 200 lightly armed U.S. marines,
sent to supervise the peaceful turnover of power in Haiti, was told to turn
tail in the face of a group of thugs assembled by the military government at
the disembarkation point. Again the ruling class resorted to armed repres-

---

*Like previous administrations, the Clinton administration made a distinction be-
tween refugees from political persecution, to which it would grant asylum, and refugees
fleeing poor economic conditions, which it could not accept. Though this distinction is
often unclear, it is more and more globally accepted by developed countries, as floods of
refugees attempt to cross their borders.

sion and assassination of opponents. A new flood of refugees, joined now by a new outflow of Cubans, finally led President Clinton to act with resolve, preparing an open military intervention of which virtually every government approved. Following UN Security Council unanimity about reestablishment of sanctions in October 1993, and a total embargo in May 1994, the council then authorized the use by the United States of "all means necessary" to overthrow the military. Only a last-minute personal mission by former President Jimmy Carter and former Chief of Staff Colin Powell secured the departure of the military, averting the planned invasion. On October 15, 1994, Jean-Bertrand Aristide, the first man to be popularly elected president of Haiti since the slave revolt secured Haitian independence two centuries earlier, returned to the capital, Port-au-Prince. His task of forging "national reconciliation" and building "a modern and prosperous nation" would not be an easy one, and he faltered badly. But in April 1996, for the first time, elections resulted in a peaceful turnover of power to a new government that might do better.

Nevertheless, turmoil in the Caribbean now represented local conflict. The old balance-of-power considerations that had prompted the Monroe doctrine and American hegemony were gone with the last possible foreign challenge, that of the Soviet Union. The newest challenge was in a different form: drugs.

Drugs

In the last decades of the century, one export from the Caribbean basin and South America increased enormously: the area emerged as the world's single largest source of cocaine and marijuana, and one of the largest sources of heroin. The highlands of Peru alone produced perhaps 65 percent of the world's coca, Colombia refined 80 percent of the cocaine reaching the United States, and Bolivian authorities estimated that illegal drug exports were greater in value than those of legal exports from the country. Panama, Cuba, and Mexico were all important transit points. Money-laundering operations of the billions of dollars involved in drug-traffic produced private and public corruption everywhere.

What had once been merely an unsavory trade, of interest mainly to police forces, roiled the waters of international politics as the U.S. government intensified its "war on drugs" and sought cooperation from battered governments to its south. In Colombia thousands of officials from top to bottom in the executive, the legislative, and the judicial branches of government lost their lives in what became a de facto civil war threatening decades of democracy. Manuel Noriega's government in Panama was toppled as a result of drug involvement, and U.S. relations with Mexico and other governments were frequently strained by the activities of zealous U.S. agencies.

Latins concerned about the drug trade blamed the United States for much: it was U.S. demand that had made whole segments of their societies and their economies dependent upon the trade, that had corrupted their governments and police forces, and had produced a criminal element that was almost a second government in some areas, as powerful as the first. Unilateral and bilateral U.S. efforts were inadequate: at the United Nations, Latin governments argued that without a concerted international effort, including a reduction of arms flows to drug lords, restriction of imports by drug consumers, and control of money laundering, Latin states could do little.

Some Latin states were ready to cooperate with U.S. efforts to stem the trade if the United States was ready to bear a part of the cost; the Bush Administration was more forthcoming than the Reagan Administration had been. Cooperation to restrict money laundering began to develop, but only a few Latin leaders were ready to admit the presence of U.S. armed forces to help in interdiction efforts.

One thing seemed certain: millions of peasants now lived on the drug culture, and until a substitute means of survival could be more widely adopted, they would continue to do so. Economic growth would help, but other measures were essential.

Conclusion

Africa and Latin America presented decidedly mixed but very different pictures as the end of the decade approached. The enormous and hopeful steps taken in South Africa and nearby states might yet falter if blacks did not begin to sense some economic benefits in the end of apartheid; in other areas, some wars had come to a halt, but others ground on. Africa had produced the phenomenon of territorial states without sovereign governments, although representatives from states like Liberia and Somalia still sat in their UN seats. A measure of aid from developed countries still flowed to Africa; arms sales—by far the largest percentage of which had come from the Soviet Union in the past—had declined sharply. But aid had leveled off as the developed dealt with their own domestic problems, and enough arms existed to continue to supply ethnic and tribal-based and other contestants. In the early 1980s, foreign intervention mainly supported armed conflict; by the 1990s, it occurred in the form of mediation and peacekeeping. The misadventure in Somalia—and the fact that the last peacekeepers to leave were from Pakistan and Bangladesh—revealed that Western nations had become reluctant to place their men in danger. Horrific developments in Rwanda brought foreign aid; but some aid agencies withdrew as refugee camps were reorganized by the very thugs who had organized massacres in Rwanda in the first place, and no one was willing to send troops to take over the camps. In the Maghreb, no one knew how to deal with the virtual civil war that was decimating the educated elites of Algeria.

Hope was in short supply in much of Africa.

There was more of it in Latin America where, finally, energies seemed to begin to be harnessed to genuine development, but where debt still hung heavily overhead, and where the flourishing drug trade with the United States created so much corruption. The 1995 peso crisis in Mexico, coincident with a peasant uprising in the south, indicated the fragility of developmental strategies; recovery from it indicated that international cooperation was now much more a matter of course. Brazil, which should have been showing great progress, was mired in scandal, unemployment, and maldistribution of wealth that might well yet provoke military intervention; the rest of the southern cone appeared to be doing better, and Brazilian participation in the regional Mercosur pact gave promise for the future. Results were mixed elsewhere.

The lack of international sponsorship of guerrilla movements meant, at least, less government repression and less open conflict.

Suggested Further Readings

Sebastian Edwards, *Crisis and Reform in Latin America: From Despair to Hope* (New York: Oxford University Press, 1995), is, as the title indicates, optimistic. Timothy Ashby traces the now-departed presence of the Soviet Union from the Caribbean in *The Bear in the Backyard: Moscow's Caribbean Strategy* (Lexington, MA: Lexington Books, 1987), while developing multilateralism can be seen in Barbara Stalling and Gabriel Azekely, *Japan, the United States, and Latin America: Toward a Trilateral Relationship in the Western Hemisphere* (Baltimore: Johns Hopkins University Press, 1993). David L. Lindauer and Michael Roemer (eds.) provide the basis for the interesting Asian-African comparisons referred to in *Asia and Africa: Legacies and Opportunities in Development* (San Francisco: ICS Press, 1994), while Raymond W. Copson, *Africa's Wars and Prospects for Peace* (Armonk, NY: M.E. Sharpe, 1994), reviews the tragic conflicts that have riven the continent. But see also Alister Sparks, *Tomorrow Is Another Country: The Inside Story of South Africa's Negotiated Revolution* (New York: Hill and Wang, 1995).

Conclusion

World War II began more than half a century ago. No one at that time could imagine the changes that have since overtaken the global system. Adolf Hitler deliberately launched his war to create the Thousand Year Reich in conjunction with fascist Italy and Imperial Japan and in short-term alliance with Stalin's Russia. Both Hilter and the Japanese achieved unlooked-for short-term success, but the fuhrer died in his Berlin bunker in 1945, with Germany in ruins around him, while the Japanese empire collapsed in the ashes of Hiroshima and Nagasaki. These losses meant that the battered Soviet Union became dominant in the heart of the Eurasian continent, while the undamaged United States, with its economy intact and its prestige enormous, dominated much of the rim lands of the Eurasian continent. Between the two giants lay vast areas of destruction and chaos. Ruined Western European countries clung to their imperial holdings as one of their few assets in a world their people hoped might be a better one. One thing was certain, though hard to assimilate: Europe was no longer the center of the world political system it had dominated for three centuries.

Hope and idealism were embodied in the new UN system, designed to maintain a just, peaceful, and prosperous world. Instead, a harsh bipolar world soon emerged, while the central UN concept of collective security became a dead letter. Under Stalin's iron leadership, the USSR, the rearmament of which began in 1946, established a tightly controlled socialist bloc, much against the wishes of most of the people in the so-called people's republics that composed it. The United States set out on a new path, helping to reconstruct Western Europe. Reluctantly, Western Europeans also persuaded the United States to maintain military forces in Europe to counter the Soviet presence. NATO in the West and the Warsaw Pact in the East were the result, with a divided, reconstructed Germany in the middle. In the Far East, success of the Communists in China, along with the North Korean attack on South Korea, entailed more American security commitments and launched the world upon a new arms race. Only recent opening of Soviet archives has shown how ready Stalin was to risk World War III at the time. Even the foresighted American effort to reconstruct a liberal world trading system under international direction became largely confined to the Western states.

Bipolarism did not last long. In the 1950s, following the new American commitments, an unlooked-for surge of European reconstruction developed at the same time that the European empires broke up, to be succeeded by a hundred new states. These, in conjunction with existing Latin American states and with the support of the socialist bloc, proceeded to take over the United Nations as an agent for change of the previously Western-dominated international system. In the meantime, subsequent to the death of Stalin in 1953, an ebullient Khrushchev brought the first winds of change to the Soviet Union and created a temporary détente with the United States, which, however, was slow to react to the changes.

In competition with Mao's China, Khrushchev could not resist vaunting the military and economic superiority of the Soviet Union, and he steered it into a new path of cooperation with forces of revolution in what became known as the "Third World." John F. Kennedy, leading a United States that seemed at the peak of its postwar power, sought to counter Khrushchev. In so doing, he led the United States into the quagmire of the Vietnam War. The height of their confrontation, the Cuban missile crisis, stimulated Khrushchev and his successors into a military buildup that made Brezhnev's Soviet Union for the first time a global rather than a continental power. In the early 1970s Nixon responded to defeat in Vietnam and to Russian global assertiveness by engineering an extraordinary rapprochement with Communist China and by seeking to cut other, too loosely defined, American security commitments, concentrating on Europe and Japan and the support of regional powers. Mao's China, once closely aligned with the Soviet Union, sought in the rapprochement with the United States a balance to the threat its leaders saw in their erstwhile ally, Russia. A major realignment in world politics had taken place.

The 1960s and the 1970s also brought the Third World to the forefront of world politics, its leaders arguing that the bipolar East-West confrontation had been replaced in global politics by North-South affairs. For the first time in the history of the global system, poor states coexisted side by side with much wealthier states. Organized in the Non-Aligned Movement and the Group of 77 at·the United Nations, Third World countries sought to persuade and coerce the developed states into a series of concessions that would presumably redress an unjust balance in the distribution of wealth. While the North responded with aid programs and other concessions, its leaders refused to accept that the North was responsible for the conditions in the South or that the wealth of the North came from exploitation of the South. It was not a question of "distribution" of wealth, but of creation of wealth through modernization processes. Confrontation grew strident in the 1970s, when one group of Third World countries, united in OPEC, forced an oil price rise that contributed both to First World "stagflation" and to crippling, non-OPEC Third World indebtedness.

In the meantime, a number of Third World countries grew at unprecedented rates, some industrialized rapidly, and some outpaced supposedly developed countries. Others, most notably in South Asia and Africa, remained mired in poverty. Under the circumstances, Third World unity disintegrated. It was marred, too, by a number of long-lasting and seemingly intractable conflicts between various Third World countries, into which other powers were occasionally drawn. An early tendency on the part of the Soviet Union and the United States to see these conflicts in East-West balance-of-power terms abated somewhat, although Brezhnev's 1970s globalism rekindled the view.

The 1980s appeared to change everything, once again bringing wholesale realignments in global politics. Until this time, and despite the decline of bipolarism, the two "superpowers" bestrode the world like giants: they were unlike other states in that each had an almost infinite destructive capacity at its command, in that they were the two largest economies in the world (and were relatively isolated from worldwide economic disturbances), and in that each had an ideology that it considered to have ultimate universal appeal.

But, by the 1980s, the nuclear weapons—to the building of which these two superstates had diverted enormous economic resources—appeared to have no use except for "deterrence"; transforming the incredible destructiveness of the weapons into political influence had proved impossible. The superpowers' capacity to project conventional power also appeared to be greatly limited after the U.S. failure in Vietnam and the Soviet failure in Afghanistan. America's economy faltered, and the United States rapidly became the world's largest debtor, while becoming more entangled in the more and more interdependent global economy. The Soviet economy simply collapsed, and the worldwide appeal of Marxism-Leninism as the inevitable, progressive future disappeared, along with Marxist-Leninist regimes in Eastern Europe.

By the 1990s, the Eastern bloc—one of the two poles of bipolarism—was gone. What was more startling, in 1991 the Soviet Union itself disappeared, to be replaced by a loose grouping of successor states—the Commonwealth of Independent States (CIS), which were often at odds with one another—with the unstable Russian Federation at the center. The Soviet

Union was, in a remarkable historical process, the last of the great multinational empires held together by force to go. In short order, the United States and Russia began to dismantle their nuclear stockpiles. The total number of tactical and strategic nuclear warheads in the American arsenal declined from 25,000 in 1986 to 9,000 in 1996, while the number in the Russian arsenal declined from 45,000 in 1986 to 11,000 in 1996. Most people felt there were still far too many.

The Western bloc had more viability, since it was built upon democratic legitimacy, common interests, and economic success. Yet a part of its raison d'être had been the existence of the Eastern bloc. While cutting American forces in Europe by two-thirds, American spokesmen continued to insist that the United States would not abandon Europe. But Europe itself was no longer the Europe to whose defense America had come in the 1940s, and relations were now much more those of equals, in which the United States asked for as much as it gave.

The resurgence of Europe was certainly one of the most remarkable developments of these decades—along with the rise of Japan as an economic superpower with the third most powerful armed forces in the world. Much could be made of the Pacific rim, where the newly industrialized countries (NICs) and a growing number of Southeast Asian countries increased their trade and investment between and within one another. Transpacific trade outdistanced transatlantic trade. Chinese transformation promised further change.

Yet the Pacific economies were not yet quite a rival for the European economies, and as the European Union of 1992 gradually came into being and accepted new members, Europe—despite record post–World War II unemployment—became the largest and most productive single area in the world.

Europe faced uncertainty over relations with the newly liberated Eastern European states, several of which were knocking at the door, and over developments within what had been the Soviet Union. Initial reaction was to speed the creation of the European Union of 1992 and to establish some form of partnership with Eastern Europe and the CIS through a variety of loose institutions. The euphoria engendered by the democratic revolutions of 1989 in the East was quickly dashed, however, and the return of ex-Communists to power through electoral processes in several showed that no one knew quite how to make the transition from a moribund socialism to a working market system.

Over the space of five years, however, many made remarkable progress. The Czech Republic, Hungary, Poland, and Slovenia could look westward with some confidence. Important moves toward both democracy and a working market economy took place in many of the successor states to the Soviet Union, including the Russian Federation, but some problems remained intractable, and the rise and influence of nationalists led to some horrific consequences in countries like the Ukraine and Georgia, both of which had sought a westward orientation, and in the central Asian states, where both Turkey and fundamentalist Iran developed a new interest. The Russian decision to use force against one of its own breakaway constituent republics, Chechnya, and to do so brutally, put in doubt the future of reform and democracy in Russia, and brought into question the viability of the Russian Federation itself, with its many differing peoples conquered in earlier centuries.

For a brief period following the breakup of the Soviet Union, there had been optimistic expectations on the part of Russians of the rewards of a Russian partnership with the West, and a measure of self-denial in foreign policy. Now traditional Russian goals and interests were being reasserted—both within the old Soviet Union and by Russia's warning the West that it still considered Eastern Europe to be an area of vital interest to Russia.

The conflict brought by the breakup of Yugoslavia was as horrific as the Russian assault on Chechnya. For five years, Europe, NATO, and the United Nations all failed to find ways to resolve the armed conflict between Serbs and Muslim Bosnians that displaced hundreds of thousands and brought a new flood of refugees in Europe. Only late in 1995 did active American intervention appear to bring a possible halt to the conflict; many intractable problems remained to plague the area.

Western Europe failed to act in the former Yugoslavia, in part because it had its own set of problems. Not the least of these—though less dramatic than the Soviet problems of unification and of relations with the East—was how it would cope with the increasing flow of legal and illegal immigrants from the upheavals of North Africa. The United States faced a similar intractable problem with respect to Central America and the Caribbean, where increasing populations had simply begun to spill over established borders.

These problems highlighted the background to the political trends: continued demographic increase beyond any earlier projections, primarily in the poorest of Third World countries. The 1970s had seen the growth of some consciousness that only global policies could cope with what were becoming global problems—in the intertwined realms of energy depletion, potential resource scarcity, environmental effects of increasing population with increased industrialization and pollution, and as yet unforeseen technological developments. Much had been done to cope with these problems, but much more remained to be done.

One optimistic school of thought put its faith in the growth of science and technology: modernization in the West had produced the explosion in productivity that brought longer, healthier life to the mass of the population. If it produced increased population, it also brought a subsequent transition to decreased population growth. Modernization had spread to the rest of the world, where already its benefits were widely felt. The global economy produced new problems, but these too would be resolved with policies that drew upon even newer technologies adapted to the changing global situation. The glass, in other words, was half full. Doomsayers twenty years earlier who stressed that it was half empty had been proved wrong. The trend toward democratization seen in the 1980s would also—as philosopher Immanuel Kant had predicted 200 years earlier—bring increased peaceful relations.

In early 1990 writer Vaclav Havel, recently released from a jail in Communist Czechoslovakia and now, amazingly, president of a democratic Czechoslovakia (soon to break up), spoke to the Congress of the United States, assuring its members that the surest guarantee of peace between East and West would be—not a balance of power or of terror, as had existed for forty years—but the spread of democratic institutions in the East. Democracy in the Soviet Union would mean that, in the long run, there could be no more Afghanistans, no more Czech and Hungarian invasions, no more Cuban missile crises. Gorbachev had seen this in abandoning the Communist protective zone in Eastern Europe; writers in the Soviet Union now admitted that NATO did not really constitute a military threat to the Soviet Union, simply because of the democratic institutions of the NATO states. "Realists" who had seen in geopolitical determinism the reason for inevitable conflict between the United States and the Soviet Union were wrong; ideology, now fading from the scene, had been a major cause. The trading state was replacing the warrior state.

Havel's optimism had to be tempered by later events—the rise of an ominous right and a reborn Communist party in Russia, the threats to democratic development throughout the CIS, and especially the possible consequences of the Russian military action in Chechnya in 1995. Moreover, while the 1980s had seen a surge of democratization in many Third World countries, especially in Latin America but also in North Africa and southern Africa with the end of apartheid, the rise of fundamentalist extremism with its resort to terrorism along with continued communal and ethnic conflict cast a pall.

The 1980s had also been a bad decade economically for many Third World states, but the overall trend had been upward over the decades, and in most Third World states, growth resumed in the 1990s. Finally, many

Figure 3. **Changing Patterns of World Military Spending**

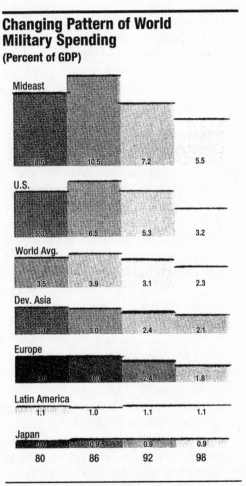

Changing Pattern of World Military Spending
(Percent of GDP)

	80	86	92	98
Mideast	8.5	10.5	7.2	5.5
U.S.	5.3	6.5	5.3	3.2
World Avg.	3.5	3.9	3.1	2.3
Dev. Asia	3.1	3.0	2.4	2.1
Europe	3.0	3.0	2.4	1.8
Latin America	1.1	1.0	1.1	1.1
Japan	0.8	0.9	0.9	0.9

SOURCE: IMF, World Economic Outlook, October 1993.

Source: IMF, *World Economic Outlook*, October 1993.

hoped that revitalized international institutions would produce the necessary global policies to cope with global problems: increased support for such policies could well come as the Cold War faded and acceptance of the need for such policies grew. A new series of conferences on global issues took place under UN auspices: at Rio de Janeiro on the environment in 1992; at Vienna on human rights in 1993; at Cairo on population issues in 1994; and at Copenhagen in 1995, where 180 states and 130 heads of state or governments met to map out a global plan on social development that aimed at reduction of world poverty, creation of jobs, and an attack upon social exclusion. Looking back at the last fifty years, some writers saw not so much a "cold war" as a "long peace" in which no major states had gone to war against each other, and which the decline of ideological confrontation now made more certain.

There were other, far less optimistic interpretations. Some analysts saw in the record of these fifty years a growing crisis not so far being met: the increase in population, the spread of modernization, and the growing interdependence of states had not been matched by increasing international political integration with a consequent capacity to devise and implement global policies. The state itself was often too weak in the face of surging internal demands, conflict was too pervasive, the fate of the "commons"—clean air and water, the temperature and composition of the atmosphere itself, the resources of productive land necessary to feed the people—was uncertain. Too many of the innumerable conferences and calls for action constituted mere window dressing, a triumph of words over action, as states opted to be "free riders" in the hope that others would pay the costs of action. Earlier doomsayers were wrong in most of their predictions, and technology continued to provide new possibilities, but the globe continued to be a finite system supporting more and more people whose impact upon its fragile ecosystem was recognized by some, but not by many. Optimists might point out that food production increases had outstripped population growth, but hunger and malnutrition remained the fate of hundreds of millions. In addition, the problems of nuclear proliferation and of the spread of other weapons of mass destruction had hardly been solved.

The 1970s was the first decade in which global issues led to calls for global action. As chapter 7 indicated, these calls to action were often sidetracked by political conflict. In the 1990s, growing global consensus about new critical issues such as atmospheric warming and ozone layer depletion led to plans for global action adopted at the innumerable international conferences. Again, political conflicts would continue to intervene. Upheaval in the Eastern bloc had led to revelations that socialist countries had an even worse record in matters of pollution than capitalist countries. To grapple

Map 21. Warfare Since 1945

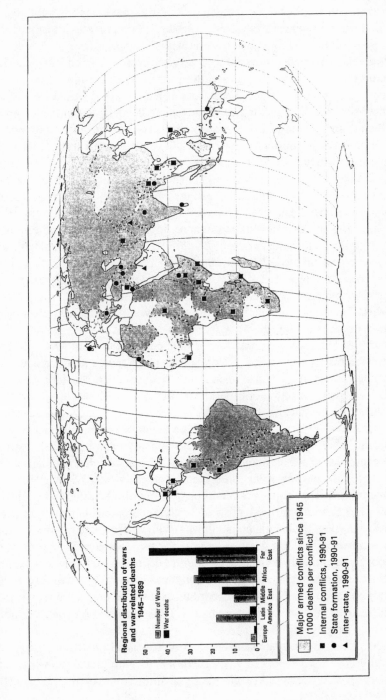

Regional distribution of wars
and war-related deaths
1945–1989

▦ Number of Wars
■ War deaths

50
40
30
20
10
0

Europe | Latin | Middle | Africa | Far
America | East | | East

▦ Major armed conflicts since 1945
(1000 deaths per conflict)

■ Internal conflicts, 1990-91
● State formation, 1990-91
▲ Inter-state, 1990-91

Source: Steve Wyn Williams in Tim Unwin, ed., *Atlas of World Development.* (Chichester, UK: John Wiley & Sons, 1994).

with pollution would be enormously costly at a time when the new, tentative democratic regimes were trying to establish political legitimacy partly through providing their people with productive economies.

Pessimists pointed out that the emerging shape of European security structures was still very vague, and the possibility of renewed conflict remained. The future orientation of Russia and its associates remained in doubt. There was little ideological fervor in the People's Republic of China, but the regime maintained its renewed repression and became more assertive about what it considered its rights—several of them in conflict with what other countries considered their own.

In the rest of the world, political conflict remained the order of the day for too many countries. In South Asia, the Middle East, the horn of eastern Africa, and Central America, much remained to be settled. How to resurrect economies in an African continent whose population would double in less than a quarter of a century remained a chilling puzzle. Revolt and demands for democracy directed at long-established single-party regimes boiled up throughout the continent. It could only be hoped that new regimes might do better than old ones; Western countries conditioned their aid programs on reforms. Ominously, the number of countries with no effective government whatever continued to grow.

Whether the glass was half full or half empty, the Cold War that had dominated global politics for so long was dead. Democratic liberalism with its emphasis on individual human rights had come to the fore in many places where it was for long derided. That, in itself, was a remarkable conclusion to the fifty years following World War II. States were far more interdependent than ever before, their sovereignty and independence to a greater or lesser degree much diminished. When the Group of 7 industrialized countries held their annual summit in 1995, it was devoted entirely to issues of management of the "information superhighway." However weak formal international structures might be, a web of global, interlinked, high-technology institutions was growing, making possible global industries, global factories, global financial flows—with consequences for the state and for international politics that were as yet far from clear. The growth of regional integration in some areas vied with disintegration in others. Resurgent nationalism, ethnic assertiveness, and intolerant religious fundamentalism all presaged more conflict. The globe as a whole had come a long way from the balance-of-power system that still characterized international politics at the start of World War II.

The global organizations that had grown in such great numbers since World War II were supposedly designed to cope with global problems, and they were often supported by growing global interest groups. Yet they still depended on the support of supposedly sovereign, independent states catering primarily to internal demands. Could they really cope with the issues of the twenty-first century?

The horrors, fifty years after World War II, of Somalia, Rwanda, and Burundi, of Chechnya and Bosnia, of Sudan and of numerous lesser conflicts, testified that the world still needed—and lacked—a capacity to deal with immediate, localized issues as well as the long-run global ones. There was a chilling contrast with the time at the end of World War II when the UN system was created in hopes that cooperation of major powers and representation of smaller countries could produce a brighter global future, when the Holocaust produced the cry "Never again!"

The challenges of the global future are enormous.

Selected Bibliography

This is, of necessity, a highly selective bibliography. It consists mainly of nontechnical and relatively general works in English. These can, in turn, lead the reader to other, more specialized sources and thus more deeply into events summarized in this book. With isolated exceptions, textbooks are not included. Numerous works listed here are outdated from the point of view of history or policy recommendation, but serve as sources for how events and developments were viewed at the time the books were written.

Readers should be aware of a number of ongoing general references highly useful to any person interested in international affairs. The reader can use the *New York Times* and its helpful index, or the excellent *Keesing's Record of World Events* (formerly *Keesing's Contemporary Archives*), which summarizes current reporting from dozens of sources organized according to particular issues. A vast number of yearbooks or handbooks exist for both global affairs and for particular geographic areas. Among the globally oriented are *The International Yearbook and Statesman's Who's Who* and the monumental *Europa World Yearbook*, both published in Britain but available in American libraries, and the French *L'État du Monde*. All of these give current information on all the countries of the globe. The Institute for Strategic Studies publishes *The Military Balance* for each year, covering all areas of the world, and the Stockholm International Peace Research Institute (SIPRI) publishes the invaluable *SIPRI Yearbook*, with articles on global and regional conflicts and security issues, on arms developments, and on arms control and disarmament. It is complemented by Ruth Leger Sivard's annual *World Military and Social Expenditures*. The *Yearbook of International Organizations*, published in Germany, is equally important, and so is the *Yearbook of the United Nations*, published with a delay of five years. See also the *Human Rights Watch World Reports*. There are too many regional yearbooks to list here: several exist for each area of the world.

Among the most useful American periodicals are *Current History*, with each issue devoted to a region; the authoritative and generally establishment-oriented *Foreign Affairs*; *Foreign Policy*; *International Affairs*; *International Organization*; *International Security*: *Orbis*; *World Politics*; and the Foreign Policy Association's *Headline* series, with each number devoted to a particular issue.

A number of institutes provide series of papers or reports on current issues. Among the best of these are those of the Atlantic Council, the Council on Foreign Relations, the Center for Strategic and International Studies, the Tri-Lateral Commission, and the Institute for International Economics.

Generally not listed here, but enlightening, fascinating, and often essential, are memoirs of and books by participants, such as those of U.S. presidents—Truman, Eisenhower, Johnson, and Nixon—and of other leaders, including Byrnes, Kissinger, Gromyko, Eden, Macmillan, Nehru, Nasser, and de Gaulle.

General Works

Aron, Raymond, *The Century of Total War*. Garden City, NY: Doubleday, 1954.
David, Steven R., *Third World Coups d'État and International Security*. Baltimore: Johns Hopkins University Press, 1987.
———, *Choosing Sides: Alignment and Realignment in the Third World*. Baltimore: Johns Hopkins University Press, 1991.
Emerson, Rupert, *From Empire to Nation*. Cambridge: Harvard University Press, 1960.
Gaddis, John Lewis, *The Long Peace: Inquiries into the History of the Cold War*. New York: Oxford University Press, 1987.
Harris, Nigel, *The End of the Third World*. Harmondsworth, England: Penguin, 1986.
Herz, John, *International Politics in the Atomic Age*. New York: Columbia University Press, 1952.
Hyland, William G., *The Cold War*. New York: Random House, 1990.
Nelson, Keith L., *The Making of Détente: Soviet-American Relations in the Shadow of Vietnam*. Baltimore: Johns Hopkins University Press, 1995.
Rodman, Peter W., *More Precious than Peace: The Cold War and the Struggle for the Third World*. New York: Charles Scribner's Sons, 1994.

International Organizations

Boyd, Andrew, *United Nations: Piety, Myth and Truth*. Baltimore: Penguin, 1962.
Claude, Inis, *Swords into Plowshares*. (4th ed.). New York: Random House, 1971.
Gardner, Richard N., *In Pursuit of World Order*. New York: Praeger, 1966.
Gordon, Wendell, *The United Nations at the Crossroads of Reform*. Armonk, NY: M.E. Sharpe, 1995.
Kay, David. *The New Nations in the United Nations*. New York: Columbia University Press, 1970.

Kratochwil, Friedrich, and Mansfield, Edward D. (eds.), *International Organization: A Reader*. New York: Harper Collins, 1994.

Nicholas, Herbert, *The United Nations as a Political Institution* (3d ed.). New York: Oxford University Press, 1967.

Taylor, Paul, *International Organizations in the Modern World: The Regional and the Global Process*. New York: St. Martin's Press, 1993.

Urquhart, Brian, *Hammarskjold: The Diplomacy of Crisis*. New York: Knopf, 1972.

World War II and Its Aftermath

Feis, Herbert, *Churchill, Roosevelt, Stalin: The War They Waged and the Peace They Sought*. Princeton: Princeton University Press, 1957.

————, *From Trust to Terror: The Onset of the Cold War, 1945–1950*. New York: Norton, 1970.

Gaddis, John Lewis, *The United States and the Origins of the Cold War*. New York: Columbia University Press, 1972.

Kennan, George F., "The Sources of Soviet Conduct," *Foreign Affairs* vol. 25, no. 4 (July 1947), pp. 566–82.

Maddox, Robert James, *Weapons for Victory: The Hiroshima Decision Fifty Years Later*. Columbia: University of Missouri Press, 1995.

Mastny, Vojtech, *Russia's Road to the Cold War: Diplomacy, Warfare, and the Politics of Communism*. New York: Columbia University Press, 1979.

Paterson, Thomas G., *On Every Front: The Making of the Cold War*. New York: Norton, 1979.

Perlmutter, Amos, *FDR and Stalin*. Columbia: University of Missouri Press, 1993.

Thomas, Hugh, *Armed Truce: the Beginnings of the Cold War*, London: Hamish Hamilton, 1986.

Wheeler-Bennett, John, and Nicholls, Anthony, *The Semblance of Peace: The Political Settlement After the Second World War*. New York: St. Martin's Press, 1972.

Yergin, Daniel, *Shattered Peace: The Origins of the Cold War and the National Security State*. Boston: Houghton Mifflin, 1977.

Military and Security Affairs

Beres, Louis Rene (ed.), *Security or Armageddon: Israel's Nuclear Strategy*. Lexington, MA: DC Heath, 1986.

Brennan, Donald G. (ed.), *Arms Control, Disarmament, and National Security*. New York: Braziller, 1961.

Brodie, Bernard (ed.), *The Absolute Weapon*. New York: Harcourt, 1946.

Bundy, McGeorge, *Danger and Survival: Choices About the Bomb in the First Fifty Years*. New York: Random House, 1988.

Freedman, Lawrence, *The Evolution of Nuclear Strategy*. New York: St. Martin's Press, 1981.

Herken, Gregg, *The Winning Weapon: The Atomic Bomb in the Cold War, 1945–1950*. New York: Knopf, 1980.

Holloway, David, *The Soviet Union and the Arms Race*. New Haven: Yale University Press, 1983.

Kegley, Charles W., Jr., *International Terrorism: Characteristics, Causes, Controls*, New York: St. Martin's Press, 1990.

Lewis, John Wilson, and Litai, Xue, *China Builds the Bomb*. Stanford, CA: Stanford University Press, 1988.

Miller, Steven E., and Van Evera, Stephen (eds.), *The Star Wars Controversy*. Princeton: Princeton University Press, 1986.

Newhouse, John, *Cold Dawn: The Story of SALT*. New York: Holt, Rinehart and Winston, 1973.

Paret, Peter, and Shy, John W., *Guerrillas in the 1960's*. New York: Praeger, 1962.

Reiss, Mitchell, *Without the Bomb: The Politics of Nuclear Nonproliferation*. New York: Columbia University Press, 1988.

Rhodes, Richard, *The Making of the Atomic Bomb*. New York: Simon and Schuster, 1986.

———, *Dark Sun: The Making of the Hydrogen Bomb*. New York: Simon and Schuster, 1995.

Sterling, Claire, *The Terror Network*. New York: Holt, Rinehart and Winston, 1981.

Talbott, Strobe, *Endgame*. New York: Knopf, 1979.

———, *Deadly Gambits*. New York: Knopf, 1984.

Weissman, Steve, and Krosney, Herbert, *The Islamic Bomb*. New York: Times Books, 1981.

Wieviorka, Michel, *The Making of Terrorism*. Chicago: University of Chicago Press, 1993.

Economic, Social, and Environmental Affairs

Baehr, Peter R., *The Role of Human Rights in Foreign Policy*. New York: St. Martin's Press, 1994.

Bailey, Ronald (ed.), *The True State of the Planet*. New York: The Free Press, 1995.

Cline, William, *International Debt and the Stability of the World Economy*. Washington, DC: Institute for International Economics, September 1983.

Easterbrook, Gregg, *A Moment on the Earth: The Coming Age of Environmental Optimism*. New York: Viking, 1995.

Ferry, Luc, *The New Ecological Order*. Chicago: University of Chicago Press, 1995.

Gardner, Richard, *Sterling-Dollar Diplomacy: The Origins and the Prospects of Our International Economic Order*. New York: McGraw-Hill, 1969.

Gordenker, Leon, *Refugees in International Politics*. New York: Columbia University Press, 1987.

Kegley, Charles W., Jr., and Wittkopf, Eugene R. (eds.), *The Global Agenda: Issues and Perspectives* (4th ed.). New York: McGraw-Hill, 1995.

Keohane, Robert O., *After Hegemony: Cooperation and Discord in the World Political Economy*. Princeton: Princeton University Press, 1984.

Keohane, Robert O., and Nye, Joseph S., Jr., *Power and Interdependence: World Politics in Transition*. Boston: Little, Brown, 1989.

Krasner, Stephen, *Structural Conflict: The Third World Against Global Liberalism*. Berkeley: University of California Press, 1985.

Kirshner, Orin (ed.), *The Bretton Woods–GATT System*. Armonk, NY: M.E. Sharpe, 1995.

Rosecrance, Richard, *The Rise of the Trading State: Commerce and Conquest in the Modern World*. New York: Basic Books, 1986.

Soroos, Marvin, *Beyond Sovereignty: The Challenge of Global Policy*. Columbia: University of South Carolina Press, 1986.

Spruyt, Hendrik, *The Sovereign State and its Competitors*. Princeton: Princeton University Press, 1994.

Teitebaum, Michael S., and Weiner, Myron, *Threatened Peoples, Threatened Borders*. New York: Norton, 1995.

Tinbergen, Jan, et al., *Reshaping the International Order: A Report to the Club of Rome*. New York: Dutton, 1976.

Vernon, Raymond, *Sovereignty at Bay: The Multinational Spread of U.S. Enterprises*. New York: Basic Books, 1971.

The United States

Acheson, Dean, *Present at the Creation*. New York: Norton, 1969.

Borg, Dorothy, and Heinrichs, Waldo (eds.), *Uncertain Years: Chinese-American Relations, 1947–1950*. New York: Columbia University Press, 1980.

Brands, H.W., *The Devil We Knew*. New York: Oxford University Press, 1993.

Brown, Seyom, *The Faces of Power: Constancy and Change in United States Foreign Policy from Truman to Johnson*. New York: Columbia University Press, 1968.

Burnham, James, *Containment or Liberation: An Inquiry into the Aims of U.S. Foreign Policy*. New York: Day, 1953.

Hoffman, Stanley, *Gulliver's Troubles, or the Setting of American Foreign Policy*. New York: McGraw-Hill, 1968.

Isaacson, Walter, and Thomas, Evan, *The Wise Men: Six Friends and the World They Made*. New York: Simon and Schuster, 1987.

Johnson, Robert H., *Improbable Dangers: U.S. Conceptions of Threat in the Cold War and After*. New York: St. Martin's Press, 1994.

Jones, Joseph, *The Fifteen Weeks*. New York: Viking Press, 1955.

Kennan, George, *American Diplomacy, 1900–1950*. Chicago: University of Chicago Press, 1951.

Lippman, Walter, *The Cold War: A Study in United States Foreign Policy*. New York: Harper's, 1947.

Maddox, Robert James, *The New Left and the Origins of the Cold War*. Princeton: Princeton University Press, 1973.

McNamara, Robert S., *In Retrospect: the Tragedy and Lessons of Vietnam*. New York: Times Books, 1995.

Mahoney, Roland D., *J.F.K: Ordeal in Africa*. New York: Oxford University Press, 1983.

Nathan, James A. (ed.), *The Cuban Missile Crisis Revisited*. New York: St. Martin's Press, 1992.

Olson, James S., *The Vietnam War: Handbook of the Literature and Research*. Westport, CT: Greenwood Press, 1993.

Packenham, Robert A., *Liberal America and the Third World*. Princeton: Princeton University Press, 1973.

Spanier, John W., *American Foreign Policy Since World War II* (13th ed.), Washington, DC: Congressional Quarterly Press, 1995.

Thompson, Robert Smith, *The Missiles of October: The Declassified Story of John F. Kennedy and the Cuban Missile Crisis*. New York: Simon and Schuster, 1992.

Thornton, Richard C., *The Nixon-Kissinger Years: Reshaping American Foreign Policy*. New York: Paragon House, 1989.

Tucker, Robert W., *Nation or Empire?* Baltimore: Johns Hopkins University Press, 1968.

Williams, William A., *The Tragedy of American Diplomacy*. Cleveland: World, 1959.

The USSR, Successor States, and Eastern Europe

Andrew, Christopher, and Gordiesvsky, Oleg, *KGB: The Inside Story*. New York: HarperCollins, 1990.

Aspaturian, Vernon, *Process and Power in Soviet Foreign Policy*. Boston: Little, Brown, 1971.

Bialer, Seweryn, *The Soviet Paradox: External Expansion, Internal Decline*. New York: Knopf, 1986.

Carnegie Endowment, *Nuclear Successor States of the Soviet Union, No. 2*. Washington, DC: Carnegie Endowment, 1994.

D'Encausse, Hélène Carrère, *The End of the Soviet Empire*. New York: Basic Books, 1993.

Djilas, Milovan, *Conversations with Stalin*. New York: Harcourt, Brace and World, 1962.

Dobrynin, Anatoliy, *In Confidence: Moscow's Ambassador to America's Six Cold War Presidents*. New York: Times Books, 1995.

Garthoff, Raymond L., *Soviet Military Policy: A Historical Analysis*. New York: Praeger, 1966.

Glantz, David M., *The Military Strategy of the Soviet Union: A History*. Portland, OR: Frank Cass, 1993.

Goldenberg, Suzanne, *Pride of Small Nations: The Caucasus and Post-Soviet Disorder*. Atlantic Highlands, NJ: Zed Books, 1994.

Grishchenko, Anatoly et al., *Danger—NATO*. Moscow: Progress Publishers, 1985.

Holloway, David, *Stalin and the Bomb: The Soviet Union and Atomic Energy, 1939–1956*. New Haven: Yale University Press, 1994.

Khazanov, Anatoly, *After the USSR: Ethnicity, Nationalism, and Politics in the CIS*. Madison: University of Wisconsin Press, 1995.

Korbel, Josef, *The Communist Subversion of Czechoslovakia, 1939–1948: The Failure of Coexistence*. Princeton: Princeton University Press, 1959.

Laqueur, Walter Z., and Labedz, Leopold, *Polycentrism: The New Factor in International Politics*. New York: Praeger, 1962.

Lieven, Anatol, *The Baltic Revolution: Estonia, Latvia, Lithuania and the Path to Independence*. New Haven: Yale University Press, 1993.

Seton-Watson, Hugh, *The East European Revolution*. New York: Praeger, 1954.

Shulman, Marshall D., *Stalin's Foreign Policy Reappraised*. New York: Atheneum, 1969.

Talbott, Strobe (trans. and ed.), *Khrushchev Remembers*. Boston: Little, Brown and Company, 1970.

Taubman, William, *Stalin's American Policy*. New York: Norton, 1982.

Ulam, Adam B., *Titoism and the Cominform*. Cambridge: Harvard University Press, 1952.

———, *The Rivals: America and Russia Since World War II*. New York: Viking, 1975.

———, *Dangerous Relations: The Soviet Union in World Politics. 1970–1982*. New York: Oxford University Press, 1983.

West, Richard, *Tito and the Rise and Fall of Yugoslavia*. New York: Carroll and Graf, 1995.

Woodward, Susan L., *Balkan Tragedy: Chaos and Dissolution After the Cold War*. Washington, DC: Brookings, 1996.

Zinner, Paul E., *Revolution in Hungary*. New York: Columbia University Press, 1962.

Europe, Western European Countries, the European Union, and the Atlantic Alliance

Beaufre, André, *NATO and Europe*. New York: Knopf, 1967.
Benoit, Emile, *Europe at Sixes and Sevens*. New York: Columbia University Press, 1961.
Calleo, David, *The Atlantic Fantasy*. Baltimore: Johns Hopkins University Press, 1970.
Davison, W. Phillips, *The Berlin Blockade: A Study in Cold War Politics*. Princeton: Princeton University Press, 1958.
Dean, Jonathan, *Ending Europe's Wars: The Continuing Search for Peace and Security*. New York: Twentieth Century Fund, 1994.
Dinan, Desmond, *Ever Closer Union? An Introduction to the European Community*. Boulder, CO: Lynne Rienner Publishers, 1994.
De Porte, Alexander, *Europe Between the Superpowers* (2d ed.). New Haven: Yale University Press, 1986.
Duchene, François, *Jean Monnet: The First Statesman of Interdependence*. New York: Norton, 1994.
Grosser, Alfred, *French Foreign Policy Under De Gaulle*. Boston: Little, Brown, 1967.
———, *The Western Alliance: European-American Relations Since 1945*. New York: Vintage Books, 1982.
Henning, C. Randall, et al., *Reviving the European Union*. Washington, DC: Institute for International Economics, 1994.
Hogan, Michael, *The Marshall Plan: America, Britain, and the Reconstruction of Western Europe, 1947–1952*. New York: Cambridge University Press, 1987.
Holborn, Hajo, *The Political Collapse of Europe*. New York: Knopf, 1951.
Iatrides, John O., *Revolt in Athens: The Greek Communist "Second Round" 1944–1945*. Princeton: Princeton University Press, 1972.
Louis, William Roger, and Bull, Hedley (eds.), *The Special Relationship: Anglo-American Relations since 1945*. New York: Oxford University Press, 1986.
Mayne, Richard, *The Recovery of Europe: From Devastation to Unity*. London: Weidenfeld and Nicolson, 1970.
Merkl, Peter, *The Origins of the West German Republic*. New York: Oxford University Press, 1963.
———, *German Unification in the European Context*. University Park: Pennsylvania State University Press, 1993.
Ward, Barbara, *The West at Bay*. New York: Norton, 1948.
Winand, Pascaline, *Eisenhower, Kennedy, and the United States of Europe*. New York: St. Martin's Press, 1993.
Woodhouse, C.M., *The Struggle for Greece, 1941–1949*. London: Hart-Davis, MacGibbon, 1976.
Young, John W., *Britain and European Unity, 1945–1992*. Basingstoke, England: Macmillan, 1993.
Zelikow, Philip, and Rice, Condoleezza, *Germany Unified and Europe Transformed: A Study in Statecraft*. Cambridge: Harvard University Press, 1995.

Asia and Asian Countries

Banuazizi, Ali, and Weiner, Myron, *The New Geopolitics of Central Asia and Borderlands*. Bloomington: Indiana University Press, 1995.

Barnett, A. Doak, *A New U.S. Policy Toward China.* Washington, DC: Brookings, 1971.

Drifte, Reinhard, *Japan's Foreign Policy.* London: Royal Institute of International Affairs, 1990.

Eberstadt, Nicholas, *Korea Approaches Reunification.* Armonk, NY: M.E. Sharpe, 1995.

Fall, Bernard, *Street Without Joy: Indochina at War, 1946–1954.* Harrisburg, PA: Stackpole, 1961.

Feis, Herbert, *The China Tangle.* Princeton, NJ: Princeton University Press, 1953.

Fifield, Russell H., *The Diplomacy of Southeast Asia, 1945–1958.* New York: Harper, 1958.

Goncharov, Sergei, Lewis, John W., and Xue Litai, *Uncertain Partners: Stalin, Mao, and the Korean War.* Stanford, CA: Stanford University Press, 1994.

Gould, Harold A., and Ganguly, Sumit, *The Hope and the Reality: US-Indian Relations from Roosevelt to Reagan.* Boulder, CO: Westview Press, 1992.

Hammer, Ellen J., *The Struggle for Indochina, 1940–1955.* Stanford, CA: Stanford University Press, 1966.

Higgins, Trumbull, *Korea and the Fall of MacArthur: A Précis in Limited War, 1950–1953.* New York: Putnam, 1962.

Leitch, Richard D., Jr., et al., *Japan's Role in the Post–Cold War World.* Westport, CT: Greenwood Press, 1995.

Mandelbaum, Michael (ed.), *The Strategic Quadrangle: Russia, China, Japan, and the United States in East Asia.* New York: Council on Foreign Relations Press, 1995.

McVey, Ruth (ed.), *Southeast Asian Capitalists.* Ithaca, NY: Cornell Southeast Asia Program, 1992.

Moraes, Frank, *Revolt in Tibet.* New York: Macmillan, 1960.

Pye, Lucian, *Guerrilla Communism in Malaya.* Princeton: Princeton University Press, 1956.

Robinson, Thomas W., and Shambaugh, David (eds.), *Chinese Foreign Policy: Theory and Practice.* New York: Oxford University Press, 1994.

Rosinger, Lawrence K., et al., *The State of Asia: A Contemporary Survey.* New York: Knopf, 1951.

Ross, Robert S. (ed.), *East Asia in Transition: Toward a New Regional Order.* Armonk, NY: M.E. Sharpe, 1995.

Simon, Sheldon, *The Broken Triangle: Peking, Djakarta, and the PKI.* Baltimore: Johns Hopkins University Press, 1968.

Swaine, Michael D., *China: Domestic Change and Foreign Policy.* Santa Monica: RAND, 1995.

The Middle East

Bill, James A., *The Eagle and the Lion: The Tragedy of American-Iranian Relations.* New Haven: Yale University Press, 1988.

Bill, James A., and Louis, William R. (eds.), *Mussadiq, Iranian Nationalism and Oil.* Austin: University of Texas Press, 1988.

Cordesman, Anthony H., *Iran and Iraq: The Threat from the Northern Gulf.* Boulder, CO: Westview Press, 1994.

Cremeans, Charles D., *The Arabs and the World: Nasser's Arab Nationalist Policy.* New York: Praeger, 1963.

Field, Michael, *Inside the Arab World.* Cambridge: Harvard University Press, 1995.

Hunter, Shireen T., *Turkey at the Crossroads: Islamic Past or European Future.* Brussels: Centre for European Policy Studies, 1995.

Kemp, Geoffrey, and Stein, Janice Gross (eds.), *Powder Keg in the Middle East: The Struggle for Gulf Security*. London: Rowman and Littlefield, 1995.

Neff, Donald, *Warriors at Suez: Eisenhower Takes America into the Middle East*. New York: Simon and Schuster, 1981.

Peretz, Don, *The Middle East Today* (5th ed.) New York: Praeger, 1988.

———, *Palestinians, Refugees, and the Middle East Peace Process*. Washington, DC: U.S. Institute for Peace, 1993.

Salem, Paul, *Bitter Harvest: Ideology and Politics in the Arab World*. Syracuse, NY: Syracuse University Press, 1994.

Springborg, A. Robert, *Politics in the Middle East*. New York: HarperCollins, 1994.

Africa and African Countries

Andereggen, Anton, *France's Relationship with Subsaharan Africa*. Westport, CT: Praeger, 1994.

Chaliand, Gerard, *The Struggle for Africa: Conflict of the Great Powers*. New York: St. Martin's Press, 1982.

Clough, Michael, *Free at Last? U.S. Policy Toward Africa and the End of the Cold War*. New York: Council on Foreign Relations Press, 1992.

Copson, Raymond W., *Africa's Wars and Prospects for Peace*. Armonk, NY: M.E. Sharpe, 1994.

Crabb, Cecil V. Jr., *The Elephants and the Grass: A Study of Non-Alignment*. New York: Praeger, 1965.

Hodgkin, Thomas, *Nationalism in Colonial Africa*. London: Muller, 1956.

Lindauer, David L., and Roemer, Michael (eds.), *Asia and Africa: Legacies and Opportunities in Development*. San Francisco: ICS Press, 1994.

Ojo, Olusola, *Africa and Israel: Relations in Perspective*. Boulder, CO: Westview Press, 1988.

Meredith, Martin, *In the Name of Apartheid: South Africa in the Postwar Period*. New York: Harper and Row, 1988.

Nkrumah, Kwame, *Africa Must Unite*. New York: Praeger, 1963.

Sparks, Allister, *Tomorrow Is Another Country: The Inside Story of South Africa's Negotiated Revolution*. New York: Hill and Wang, 1995.

Whitaker, Jennifer Seymour, *How Can Africa Survive?* New York: Council on Foreign Relations Press, 1989.

Young, Crawford, *The African Colonial State in Comparative Perspective*. New Haven: Yale University Press, 1995.

Zartman, I. William, *Collapsed States; The Disintegration and Restoration of Legitimate Authority*. Boulder, CO: Lynne Rienner, 1995.

The Americas

Ashby, Timothy, *The Bear in the Backyard: Moscow's Caribbean Strategy*. Lexington, MA: Lexington Books, 1987.

Ball, M. Margaret, *The OAS in Transition*. Durham, NC: Duke University Press, 1969.

Coatsworth, John H., *Central America and the United States: The Clients and the Colossus*. New York: Twayne Publishers, 1994.

Edwards, Sebastian, *Crisis and Reform in Latin America: From Despair to Hope*. New York: Oxford University Press, 1995.

Fenwick, Charles G., *The Organization of American States: The Inter-American Regional System*. Washington, DC: Kaufmann, 1963.

Gil, Federico, *Latin American-United States Relations*. New York: Harcourt Brace Jovanovich, 1971.

Harrison, Lawrence, *Underedevelopment Is a State of Mind: The Latin American Case*. Washington, DC: University Press of America, 1985.

Hufbauer, Gary Clyde, and Schott, Jeffrey J., *Western Hemisphere Economic Integration*. Washington, DC: Institute for International Economics, 1994.

Martz, John D. (ed.), *United States Policy in Latin America: A Decade of Crisis and Challenge*. Lincoln: University of Nebraska Press, 1995.

———— (ed.), *Cuba: After the Cold War*. Pittsburgh: University of Pittsburgh Press, 1993.

Mesa-Largo, Carmelo (ed.), *Cuba in the World*. Pittsburgh: University of Pittsburgh Press, 1979.

Stallings, Barbara, and Azekely, Gabriel, *Japan, the United States, and Latin America: Toward a Trilateral Relationship in the Western Hemisphere*. Baltimore: Johns Hopkins University Press, 1993.

Szulc, Tad, *Fidel: A Critical Portrait*. New York: William Morrow, 1986.

Whitaker, Arthur P., *The Western Hemisphere Idea: Its Rise and Decline*. Ithaca, NY: Cornell University Press, 1954.

The Post–Cold War World

Castaneda, Jorge, *Utopia Unarmed: The Latin American Left After the Cold War*. New York: Knopf, 1993.

Cleveland, Harlan, *Birth of a New World: An Open Moment for International Leadership*. San Francisco: Jossey-Bass, 1993.

Garthoff, Raymond L., *The Great Transition: American-Soviet Relations and the End of the Cold War*. Washington, DC: Brookings, 1994.

Huntington, Samuel P., *The Clash of Civilizations and the Remaking of World Order*. New York: Simon and Schuster, 1996.

Juergensmayer, Mark, *The New Cold War? Religious Nationalism Confronts the Secular State*. Berkeley: University of California Press, 1993.

Kegley, Charles W., Jr., and Raymond, Gregory, *A Multipolar Peace? Great Power Politics in the Twenty-First Century*. New York: St. Martin's Press, 1994.

Lebow, Richard Ned, and Stein, Janice Gross, *We All Lost the Cold War*. Princeton: Princeton University Press, 1994.

Snow, Donald M., *Distant Thunder: Third World Conflict and the New International Order*. New York: St. Martin's Press, 1993.

————, *The Shape of the Future: The Post–Cold War World*, 2d. ed. Armonk, NY: M.E. Sharpe, 1995.

Index

About the Author

Charles L. Robertson is Emeritus Professor of Government at Smith College. He received his B.S. and M.A. from Northwestern University and his Ph.D. from Princeton. In addition to teaching at Smith College, Professor Robertson has taught at the University of Massachusetts and at Amherst College and served as an Associate Dean for International Studies, Smith College. He has published two previous short histories of the postwar world (1966, 1975), as well as *The International Herald Tribune: The First Hundred Years* (New York: Columbia University Press, 1987).